PERSONAL CONSTRUCT THERAPY CASEBOOK

Robert A. Neimeyer, Ph.D., serves on the faculty of the Center for Applied Psychological Research in the Department of Psychology at Memphis State University, Memphis, Tennessee. His acquaintance with personal construct theory dates from his undergraduate years at the University of Florida, after which he earned his Ph.D. in Clinical Psychology at the University of Nebraska. His publications include his book on *The Development of Personal Construct Psychology* (1985) and, with Franz Epting, an edited volume entitled *Personal Meanings of Death: Applications of Personal Construct Theory to Clinical Practice* (1984). The author of over 60 articles and book chapters, he is currently conducting research on depression, cognitive approaches to therapy, and the development and breakdown of close relationships. Dr. Neimeyer serves on the editorial boards of a number of journals, including the *Journal of Consulting and Clinical Psychology* and the *Journal of Cognitive Psychotherapy*.

Greg J. Neimeyer, Ph.D., is Associate Professor in the Department of Psychology at the University of Florida in Gainesville, Florida. Dr. Neimeyer earned his Master's and Ph.D. degrees in Counseling Psychology at the University of Notre Dame after completing his undergraduate degree in psychology at the University of Florida. He has been an active contributor to personal construct psychology over the past 10 years, with more than 50 publications in the areas of interpersonal, marital, and cross-cultural relationships. He is a member of the American Psychological Association and the American Association of Counseling and Development and serves as Research Editor for the *Journal of Counseling and Development*. His current interests include the integration of personal construct psychology with other orientations to therapy and interpersonal influence.

In addition, the Neimeyers served as co-organizers of the Seventh International Congress on Personal Construct Psychology, and they currently serve as co-editors of the *International Journal of Personal Construct Psychology*.

PERSONAL CONSTRUCT THERAPY CASEBOOK

Robert A. Neimeyer, Ph.D.
Greg J. Neimeyer, Ph.D.
Editors

SPRINGER PUBLISHING COMPANY
New York

Copyright © 1987 by Springer Publishing Company, Inc.

Springer Publishing Company, Inc.
536 Broadway
New York, NY 10012

87 88 89 90 91 / 5 4 3 2 1

Library of Congress Cataloging-in-Publication Data

Personal construct therapy casebook.

  Includes bibliographies.
  Includes index.
  1. Personal construct therapy—Case studies.
I. Neimeyer, Robert A., 1954–   . II. Neimeyer,
Greg J. [DNLM: 1. Personality. 2. Psychological
Theory. 3. Psychotherapy—methods. WM 420 P4665]
RC489.P46P47 1987   616.89'14   87-4601
ISBN 0-8261-5530-8

Printed in the United States of America

To Don,
who lived the spirit of the theory

Contents

III.   MARITAL AND FAMILY THERAPY

IV.   GROUP THERAPY

V.   SPECIAL APPLICATIONS

Contributors

Pamela C. Alexander
Department of Psychology
Memphis State University
Memphis, Tennessee, USA

Eric J. Button
Department of Psychiatry
Royal South Hants Hospital
Southampton, England

Larry Cochran
Department of Counseling Psychology
University of British Columbia
Vancouver, B.C., Canada

Gavin Dunnett
Redcliffe Centre for Community
  Psychiatry
Wellingborough, Northants, England

Franz R. Epting
Department of Psychology
University of Florida
Gainesville, Florida, USA

Victoria M. Follette
Department of Psychology
Memphis State University
Memphis, Tennessee, USA

Fay Fransella
Centre for Personal Construct
  Psychology
London, England

Vincent Kenny
Senior Clinical Psychologist
Garden Hill House
Department of Psychiatry
University College-Dublin
Dublin, Ireland

Larry M. Leitner
Department of Psychology
Miami University
Oxford, Ohio, USA

Sue Llewelyn
Department of Psychology
University of Nottingham
Nottingham, England

Dorothy E. McDonald
Saint Catherine's Center for Children
Albany, New York, USA

James C. Mancuso
Department of Psychology
State University of New York–Albany
Albany, New York, USA

Andres Nazario, Jr.
Gainesville Family Institute
Gainesville, Florida, USA

Harry G. Procter
Psychology Department
Tone Vale Hospital
Fitzwarren, Taunton
Somerset, England

Stephen Soldz
Boston Center for Modern
  Psychoanalytic Studies
Brookline, Massachusetts, USA

David A. Winter
Principal Clinical Psychologist
Barnet Health Authority
Napsbury Hospital
Herts, England

Linda L. Viney
Department of Psychology
University of Wollongong
Wollongong, New South Wales
Australia

Preface

When George A. Kelly published the *Psychology of Personal Constructs* in 1955 he envisioned that his theory would hold special promise in the psychotherapeutic arena. Despite these expectations, the theory has found its main applications in the study of personality and psychopathology, leaving its specific relevance for psychotherapy relatively unexplored. In fact, of the over 1,000 publications utilizing personal construct concepts and methods, less than 10% represent theoretical or predominantly clinical discussions of the therapeutic process (Neimeyer, 1985).

In recent years, however, there have been signs of renewed interest in construct theory's potential contributions to clinical practice. For example, Epting (1984) has summarized Kelly's original formulations concerning psychotherapy, and Landfield and Leitner (1980) have included a number of clinically pertinent chapters in their edited volume on psychotherapy and personality. In a more empirical vein, Button (1985) has collected a useful set of research reviews on various disorders, and Beail (1985) has published a volume examining the application of repertory grid technique to clinical as well as educational topics. In fact, a number of volumes on personal construct theory that have appeared since 1980 have contained chapters on selected clinical issues (e.g., Adams-Webber & Mancuso, 1983; Epting & Landfield, 1985; Epting & Neimeyer, 1984), indicating a general rekindling of interest in this long-neglected aspect of Kelly's pioneering work.

Our aim in this book is to further this trend by presenting for the first time a volume devoted exclusively to case studies of personal construct therapy. *Personal Construct Therapy Casebook* was designed to fill a void in the existing literature by illustrating the creative applications of the theory to actual clinical cases in a way that would be informative to a broad range of students, scholars, and helping professionals. In particular, chapters interweave construct theory conceptualizations of case material with discussions of specific interventions and illustrate the therapeutic process with transcripts of actual therapy dialogues. Several also show a concern for outcome evaluation by citing suitable grid and other psychometric data that document the extent of personal change in the cases described.

A second distinguishing feature of this volume is its emphasis on an integration of a Kellian approach with other constructivist psychotherapies. While all of the contributions draw upon fundamental features of the basic theory as discussed in the introductory chapters, they also illustrate the considerable diversity of contemporary personal construct therapy. Thus, in addition to providing fresh discussions of traditional procedures, several chapters also explore original interventions in individual, marital, family, and group contexts.

The completion of this volume is owed not only to the visible efforts of each of our contributors, but also to the invisible labors of our informal "editorial board." Thanks are due to April Metzler and Ken Rice for their careful and constructive review of each of the chapters. Special thanks are due to Kathleen Bagley, whose buoyant enthusiasm and indefatigable efforts have helped sustain us through the more mundane aspects of manuscript preparation and revision. We hope that the results of our collective efforts will stimulate continued innovation in the practice of personal construct therapy.

Robert A. Neimeyer   Greg J. Neimeyer
Memphis, Tennessee   Gainesville, Florida

REFERENCES

Adams-Webber, J.R., & Mancuso, J. (Eds.). (1983). *Applications of personal construct theory.* Toronto: Academic.

Beail, N. (Ed.). (1985). *Repertory grid technique and personal constructs.* London: Croom Helm.

Button, E. (Ed.). (1985). *Personal construct theory and mental health.* London: Croom Helm.

Epting, F.R. (1984). *Personal construct counseling and psychotherapy.* New York: Wiley.

Epting, F.R., & Landfield, A.W. (Eds.). (1985). *Anticipating personal construct theory.* Lincoln: University of Nebraska Press.

Epting, F.R., & Neimeyer, R.A. (Eds.). (1984). *Personal meanings of death: Applications of personal construct theory to clinical practice.* New York: Hemisphere/McGraw Hill.

Kelly, G.A. (1955). *The psychology of personal constructs.* New York: Norton.

Landfield, A.W., & Leitner, L.M. (Eds.). (1980). *Personal construct psychology.* New York: Wiley.

Neimeyer, R.A. (1985). *The development of personal construct psychology.* Lincoln: University of Nebraska Press.

I
Introduction

1

An Orientation to Personal Construct Therapy

Robert A. Neimeyer

> Psychotherapeutic goals have to be understood as part of the psychologists' functional involvement with a theoretical position in which his working assumptions about the nature of mankind, and of his client, have been made to stand out as clearly as possible.
>
> —GEORGE A. KELLY, 1967/1980, p. 26

Given the unusually systematic presentation of Kelly's (1955) massive magnum opus, it would be easy to conclude that personal psychology was the product of armchair theorizing. In fact, nothing could be farther from the truth: Kelly's formal theory represented his attempt to distill and organize the lessons he had learned during 20 years of intensive and creative practice as a diagnostician, therapist, and consultant (c.f., R. Neimeyer, 1985a; Zelhart & Jackson, 1983). In the preface to his major theoretical statement, Kelly (1955) noted that the work actually had started out years before as a handbook of clinical procedures, providing detailed guidelines for every aspect of psychological practice from history taking and diagnosis to psychotherapy and vocational guidance.[1] But as Kelly (1955) reported, "time after time, the writing bogged down in a morass of tedious little maxims. It was no good—this business of trying to tell the reader merely *how* to deal with clinical problems; the *why* kept insistently raising its puzzling head" (p. ix). Kelly backed off and started writing about the *why*, and the

[1]The original 1936 version of this handbook has recently been edited and published by Jackson, Zelhart, and Markley; see Kelly (1985).

result was a uniquely relevant clinical theory that continues to inspire innovations in therapeutic practice over 30 years later.

This chapter reflects Kelly's assumption that there is nothing as practical as a good theory and, conversely, nothing as theoretical as good practice. In the pages that follow, I will present some of the basic theoretical scaffolding that supports each of the later chapters in the book, presenting in re-organized form those tenets of construct theory that Kelly identified formally as the fundamental postulate and its eleven corollaries. Each of these, in my view, can be read at two levels. On the one hand, each theoretical proposition fleshes out a constructivist view of what it is to be human; it clarifies those processes and structures that characterize our functioning as individuals and groups. On the other hand, each tenet of the theory also carries at least one embedded prescription for the practicing therapist. Thus, Kelly's basic theory can be viewed as a structure for surveying the field of clinical psychology, which is built on certain foundational assumptions about the nature of persons and which offers a unique perspective on the domain of psychotherapy.

In keeping with my aim of presenting construct theory as an orienting framework for clinical practice, I will focus on its utility as an integrative approach to therapy. Discussions of specific techniques and strategies of treatment are presented in the next chapter (G. Neimeyer, this volume), as well as in other published books and articles (e.g., Bannister, 1975; Epting, 1984; Kelly, 1955; R. Neimeyer, 1986).

THE ANTICIPATORY POSTURE

Kelly's most fundamental assumption about the nature of human beings was that they were essentially interpretive, always in the process of attributing meaning to their ongoing experience. In a construct theory view individuals are like incipient scientists (Tschudi, 1983) who attempt to devise hypotheses that render events understandable and, to some degree, predictable. Thus, unlike theorists who view human behavior as determined by either past traumas or present reinforcement contingencies, construct theorists consider peoples' behavior as ways of testing their beliefs about the future, given the limits imposed by their current understandings. Kelly (1955) regarded this posture of anticipation as the very cornerstone of his theory and so established it as his fundamental postulate: "A person's processes are psychologically channelized by the way in which he anticipates events" (p. 46). Kelly's personal scientist model, with its implication that all persons seek to understand, predict, and control the course of their lives, has since been adopted by many schools of cognitive therapy (Beck, Rush, Shaw,

& Emery, 1979; Ellis, 1979; Guidano & Liotti, 1983; c.f. R. Neimeyer, 1985b).

From the standpoint of the therapist, this fundamental postulate implies an equally fundamental question: *What crucial prediction is the client testing with his or her behavior?* That is, if we assume that the client—like more formally accredited members of the scientific establishment—is actively interpreting, hypothesizing, and theorizing on the basis of her experience, then even "disturbed" behavior can be seen as an experiment (Kelly, 1970) designed to test important implications of the client's personal theory. Stated differently, symptoms have significance (R. Neimeyer, in press); they represent urgent but often muddled questions about what can be expected of oneself and other people. For example, the sharp escalation of client demands on a therapist's time through an endless series of "crisis" calls, walk-ins, and prolonged therapy hours may represent a behavioral test of a deeply held prediction: "even my therapist will reject me in the end." This enacted hypothesis may in turn be part of a larger self-theory that stresses one's essential unlovability. By attempting to grasp the anticipatory meaning of a client's behavior, we as therapists are better able to help clients recognize when their predictions border on self-fulfilling prophesies. Subsequent therapy can then take the form of collaborating with the client in clearly articulating and fairly testing those personal constructions that are most bound up with his current distress. The corollaries of personal construct theory offer further guidance to the therapist in playing this collaborative role. For the sake of clarity, I have grouped these eleven propositions into three sets, those concerned with the construing process, with the structure of knowing, and with the social embeddedness of our construing efforts.

THE CONSTRUING PROCESS

The Search for Regularity

Construct theory's emphasis on our anticipatory posture presupposes that the human organism possesses certain basic dispositions or tendencies. Chief among these is our "set" to perceive regularly recurring patterns in the world around us, a disposition that is "logically *a priori* to all observational experience" (Popper, 1963, p. 48). Kelly (1955) acknowledged this feature of our construing activity in his construction corollary: the proposition that "a person anticipates events by construing their replications" (p. 50). Confronted with the complexity of the universe, a person "attunes his ear to recurrent themes" in order to punctuate the unending flow of experience. "Like a musician, he must phrase his experience in order to make sense of it.

The phrases are distinguished events . . . Within these limited segments, which are based on recurrent themes, man begins to discover the bases for likenesses and differences" (Kelly, 1955, p. 52).

In the clinical context, it is often useful for the therapist to ask, *"How does the client phrase or punctuate events, and what are the major themes he sees in them?"* For example, it may be instructive to ask a client to consider the major stages of his life and to write "chapter titles" for each of them.[2] Tasks of this kind can be helpful, not because they provide an accurate account of inexorable events in the past that have molded the client's current life but because they suggest the turning points that he sees in his biography and the personal meanings that he attributes to them. As Bannister (1975) has suggested, successful therapy often entails reconstruing one's past and discerning in it new themes that point toward a more hopeful future. As an illustration, a client may come to reconstrue her parents' failings as the human limitations of individuals who were themselves struggling with a difficult world, rather than as an intentional neglect targeted at her personally. This reinterpretation might then generate fresh approaches to interacting with her parents, which could be tested by behaving toward them differently.

The Quest for Validation

If the world stood still for the construing person, then it might be enough simply to develop a coherent set of conceptual boxes into which things and events could be placed. But as Kelly realized, the universe changes along a temporal dimension, and "the successive revelation of events invites the person to place new constructions upon them whenever something unexpected happens. Otherwise one's anticipations would become less and less realistic" (Kelly, 1955). Kelly recognized this progressive, evolutionary quality of our construing in his experience corollary: the axiom that "a person's construction system varies as he successively construes the replications of events" (Kelly, 1955, p. 72).

The relationship between anticipation and change in one's construct system can be clarified by a consideration of the *experience cycle* depicted in Figure 1.1. Any given behavioral sequence can be seen as anchored in the sometimes explicit but often implicit expectations of one or more persons. For example, a male client entered an intake session with me with the tacit *anticipation* that I would become extremely uncomfortable with him once I discovered that he was gay. He was clearly *invested* in this prediction, as

[2]A clinical application of a related technique, the Biographical Construct Repertory Test (BioRep), is illustrated in R. Neimeyer (1985b). For a more rigorous experimental application of such methods, see G. Neimeyer, Rice, and Berzonsky (1986).

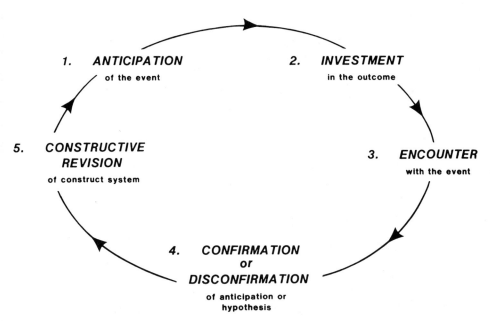

FIGURE 1.1. The experience cycle. (Reprinted with the permission of Academic Press from R. A. Neimeyer, 1985b.)

evidenced in his apparent nervousness and hesitation in broaching the topic with me in the opening minutes of the session. But upon *encountering* my reaction—a reassurance delivered in a comfortable tone of voice—he experienced a gentle *disconfirmation* of his initial prediction. This led him to *revise* his construction of me as a therapist and paved the way for us to examine in a less inhibited way the relationship disturbances that had prompted him to seek therapy. The succession of experience is based on an overlapping series of such cycles, some as immediate as the above illustration and others as long-range as those that involve expectations about the outcomes of a particular career choice. In fact, the experience cycle is so basic to construct theory that the inability to successfully revise one's construing when it is disconfirmed can be considered the hallmark of psychological disturbance. As Kelly (1955) notes, "we may define a disorder as any personal construction that is used repeatedly in spite of consistent invalidation" (p. 831).

This discussion implies an important orienting question for the psychotherapist: "*At what stage of the experience cycle has the client become 'stuck,' so that constructive revision of her system has become impossible?*" In general, it appears that the earlier in a given experience cycle an individual is arrested, the more serious his or her degree of disturbance (see R. Neimeyer, 1985b, for details). Thus, clients diagnosed as adjustment reactions may have progressed through the cycle to the point of recognizing the disconfirmation of their previous construing but may need assistance in making sense of and behaving adaptively toward the invalidating event. At the other extreme, the thought disordered schizophrenic may find it impossible to organize any coherent predictions regarding social experience at all (Bannister, 1960). By considering the point at which the client has become interrupted in the cycle of prediction, investment, encounter, validation, and constructive revision, the therapist can assess what steps are required to restore the client's psychological movement.

The Elaborative Attitude

Like prototypic scientists, individuals are engaged not only in testing isolated hypotheses about their experiences but also in building ever more satisfactory overall theories that integrate and interpret their observations. The structure of these personal theories will be addressed below. But at this point it is important to note that any given behavioral experiment conducted by a person plays a role in her overall research program (c.f., Lakatos, 1970); it helps elaborate the system of meaning through which she lives.

As Kelly pointed out, this elaboration can take two forms. In accordance with the choice corollary (Kelly, 1955), "a person chooses for himself that alternative . . . through which he anticipates the greater possibility for extension and definition of his system." (p. 64). When the person chooses to *extend* his system, he opts for adventure over security by "living on the frontiers of experience rather than within cosily settled conventions"(Mair, 1977, p. 268). By ranging widely over the field of possible experiences, the extending individual tries "to become vaguely aware of more and more things on the misty horizon" (Kelly, 1955, p. 67). On the other hand, persons sometimes choose to *define* their systems by making them explicit and clear-cut, accepting the inevitable sacrifice of comprehensiveness that this entails. The potential conflict between these two extremes is often observed in individuals struggling with difficult career decisions. Should they pursue further specialized training in their current line of work (definition of their existing system) or face the uncertainty of pursuing a new career path altogether (extension)? Ultimately, the individual in this situation will make what she regards as an *elaborative choice* that optimizes the anticipatory potential of her system.

From a clinical vantage point, the choice corollary challenges the therapist to ask the question, "*How can the client's present behavior be understood as an informed choice, in light of the alternatives that he himself envisions?*" Construed in this way, the client's choices can then be closely examined for their problematic implications, rather than dismissed as either irrational or predetermined by his learning history, genetics, or family dynamics. Do his choices overly constrict his field of vision or confront him with so many new issues as to be bewildering? By encouraging the client to tack back and forth between these two extremes, the therapist can help promote a more balanced evolution of the client's system for living.

The Limits of Change

Although personal construct theory highlights the capacity of personal systems of meaning to change across time, this change typically takes the form of systematic evolution rather than random variation. Stated differently, *the processes of change are themselves patterned*; construct systems evolve to encompass new experiences, but only within the constraints imposed by one's current constructions. Kelly (1955) addressed this principle in his modulation corollary: "The variation in a person's construction system is limited by the permeability of [its superordinate] constructs" (p. 77). This implies that our constructs for interpreting reality are functionally stratified, with some being more superordinate or more central to our outlook than others (a concept that will be discussed more fully below). Kelly formulated the modulation corollary to describe how these very central constructs modulate or regulate the changes that our systems can accommodate. Like the formal research programs of science, our personal belief systems are built around a "metaphysical hard core" of basic assumptions (Lakatos, 1970), so that changes that are incompatible with these core beliefs tend to be resisted.

For the practicing psychotherapist, the most important implication of this viewpoint is that it provides a useful reinterpretation of the phenomenon of *resistance*. Rather than representing a kind of obstinacy or irrational inflexibility, a client's ambivalence or difficulty in changing fundamental aspects of her outlook or behavior may be seen as essentially adaptive, at least from her point of view. As Mahoney (1985) notes, "resistance processes are often most apparent when significant meaning structures are being challenged . . . There is a sensed survival value in protecting and perpetuating old reality constructions, especially those which have been central to our experience" (p. 32). For example, it is a common observation in social skills training that many passive clients fail to develop more assertiveness not because they do not "know how" but because to do so would be at odds with their core beliefs about what constitutes "moral" social behavior (D. A. Winter, *this volume*). Thus, a useful orienting question for the therapist is, *"Are there superordinate constructs in the client's system that are too rigid or impermeable to permit change?"* Once recognized, these constricting beliefs can be modified indirectly through the use of fixed role therapy and other enactment techniques (R. Neimeyer, 1986).

THE STRUCTURE OF KNOWING

Meaning and Contrast

Implicit in the above discussion of the construing process is the assumption that individuals devise personal theories as frameworks for interpreting their ongoing experience. But if it is to be maximally useful, the personal science metaphor should also detail the structural properties of these theories: What is the basic unit of meaning used to classify and order experience? How are the particular beliefs or hypotheses of the person organized to form a system? To provide an approach to such questions, construct theory offers a structural model of knowing, which will be outlined in this section.

In his dichotomy corollary, Kelly (1955) assumed that "a person's construction system is composed of a finite number of dichotomous constructs " (p. 59). Thus, at its most molecular level, our construing involves the use of *bipolar* dimensions of meaning to differentiate and relate various aspects of our experience. It is obvious that one's construction of "masculinity" makes sense only by contrast to "femininity," "success" in contrast to "failure," and so on. But at a personal level, the implicit contrasts that constrain our perception and behavior are typically more subtle and idiosyncratic. Consider the refusal of a parent to stop "punishing" her unruly daughter, a refusal that is understandable in light of her seeing this as the only alternative to "letting her get away with things." From this perspective, every assertion implies an unstated negation. For example, a husband's comment to the co-therapists in a marital therapy session on how refreshing it is to have sophisticated discussions with people who are his "equal" may carry the veiled implications that his less communicative wife is both naive and beneath him. Thus the practicing therapist should consider the questions: *"What is the client not saying? What are the implied alternatives, as the client sees them?"* Attending to both poles of the client's fundamental constructs helps the therapist appreciate the personal meanings that the client attributes to people and events and can suggest the need to revise those constructs that limit, rather than promote, the client's adaptation to life.

Implication and Identity

As Sarason (1979) points out, a common failing of cognitive clinical theories is that they treat cognitions as individualized "thought units" or "self-statements," thereby missing the way in which cognitions interact to form integrated networks of meaning. Kelly (1955) was aware of these complex, systemic features of our personal theories and drafted the organization corollary to acknowledge them: "Each person characteristically evolves . . . a construction system embracing ordinal relationships between constructs" (p. 56). In other words, some constructs are *superordinate* to others; they are implicatively linked to more perhiperal or *subordinate* constructs that typically are more concrete and specific. An example of this hierarchical relationship among constructs was provided by Katherine, a client whose interpersonal difficulties I have detailed elsewhere (R. Neimeyer, 1985b). Katherine noted that her friends frequently criticized her for being "businesslike" with them, but added that this more formal and aloof demeanor was far preferable in her mind to being "emotional." Sensing that Katherine's choice of the businesslike role was determined by more superordinate but unarticulated constructs pertaining to her identity, I decided to explore her network of core role constructs using the laddering technique (c.f., Bannister & Mair, 1968). By asking her *why* she preferred to be businesslike rather than emotional, I learned that she regarded it as the "mature approach to life," which contrasted with "being unstable." Repeating this cycle of questioning, I discovered that this approach carried further superordinate implications for her "being in control" and, ultimately, for "survival" itself. From this systemic perspective, the meaning of any particular construction (e.g., of oneself as businesslike in this illustration) is largely determined by the linkages it has with other constructs in one's system.

Clinically, this suggests that it is often crucial to ask, *"What are the implications of this behavior for the client's central identity constructs, and vice versa?"* Failure to attend to this question can result in serious therapeutic errors. An example occurred in a marital therapy I recently supervised, in which the well-meaning co-therapists allied with the working wife's need to contribute to the family's finances. As they begin to formulate an apparently straightforward homework assignment in which the couple would collaborate in paying routine bills, the husband interrupted, "If I need her money, I'll ask for it!" Although the surprised therapists mollified him and continued the session, he refused to return. In retrospect, we realized that the concrete behavior change the therapists were requesting carried powerful and *threatening* implications (Kelly, 1955) for the husband's core identity as sole breadwinner and head of the household. Had the superordinate implications of sharing monthly bills been explored in advance, an unfortunate disruption in therapy might have been averted. Of course, one's most fundamental constructs are often tacit and hard to explicate, since they typically represent ways of schematizing self–other relationships that were acquired quite early in life (Guidano & Liotti, 1983; R. Neimeyer, 1981). From this perspective, the articulation and modification of these central preverbal identity constructs may be a major goal of therapy, as illustrated in transcripts of Kelly's own clinical practice (R. Neimeyer, 1980).

Structural Multiplism

A superficial reading of the personal scientist metaphor may lead one "to expect any true construct system to be logic-tight and wholly internally consistent" (Kelly, 1955, p. 85). Yet as Kelly recognized, the personal theories we devise to encompass reality are typically far less coherent and well-ordered than the idealized conceptual frameworks we attribute to professional scientists. Instead, as the fragmentation corollary states, "a person may successively employ a variety of construction systems which are inferentially incompatible with each other" (Kelly, 1955, p. 83). In other words, individuals operate with a multiplicity of construct subsystems, which may or may not be well integrated at superordinate levels. For example, a person may employ one relatively distinct subsystem of constructs to construe relationships in her work environment, which may be quite different from those used to schematize the relationships that comprise her social life. At a finer level of analysis, she may devise still others that organize her anticipations and regulate her behavior in a variety of specialized tasks or particular social situations. If her superordinate identity constructs are sufficiently comprehensive and permeable, she may negotiate the movement from one system to the next with no personal sense of inconsistency, even if her personality seems to change appreciably across situations in the eyes of other people. For instance, she may construe all of her "situated identities" (G. Neimeyer & R. Neimeyer, 1985; Schlenker, 1985) as modulated by a core role that emphasizes "living intensely" or "getting to know people on their own terms." However, all of us occasionally experience a sense of fragmentation among our subsystems, as when we behave inconsistently with a friend or experience a conflict between two incompatable but equally compelling courses of behavior. Such experiences may be an inevitable concomitant of what Mahoney (1985) terms the "decentralized distribution of knowledge and the emergence of control from an endless internal coalition and competition among interdependent systems of systems" (p. 19).

Given the pervasiveness of internal conflict in psychotherapy, it is useful to ask oneself the orienting question, *"What are my client's radical inconsistencies, and how can they be bridged?"* At its dramatic extreme, clinically significant fragmentation may take the form of a multiple personality, whose sudden transitions from one pattern of behavior to another can be seen as "a desperate experimentation with different social role alternatives" (Landfield, 1982, p. 216). Treatment of such a case is illustrated by L. M. Leitner *(this volume)*. More typically, the fragmentation encountered in therapy may stem from the client's attempt to grapple with behavior that may not fit his or her prevailing identity constructions. For example, I am currently supervising the therapy of Todd, a young man whose overarching view of himself focused on his being socially inept and powerless to determine the direction of his own life. Yet, as therapy progressed into its third month, it was clear to both his therapist and me that he had made striking progress at a behavioral level. In a two-week period, for instance, he organized his housemates to help him eject a disruptive fellow renter, provided tangible and emotional support to a relative in distress, reaffirmed several lapsed friendships, and successfully founded a campus organization. Yet a review of these accomplishments did nothing to alter Todd's self-construing; he considered them all as isolated fragments of behavior, each of which he dismissed as trivial or lucky occurrences. However, Todd's therapist gently persisted in encouraging him to integrate the meaning of these events, with responses like, "These are just steps, but what do they symbolize?" and "What do these things say about who Todd is?" After one such question, Todd's self-deprecating laughter fell away, and he quietly replied that his actions showed that he could be "a motivator, someone who could inspire people and get things done." Movingly, he went on to say very tentatively, "It seems like bragging . . . it's so *new* . . . but I seem to be coming out of my shell . . . It feels so right." He fell silent for a moment and then concluded by noting tearfully that he suddenly felt "flooded with all the proud things I've done in my life." In personal construct terms, the recovery of these proud memories could be attributed to his having glimpsed, for the first time, the outlines of a new identity structure that gave his previously fragmented behaviors a fresh, comprehensive meaning.

Boundaries of the Known

Psychotherapy, like science, presses us forward to the boundaries of human knowledge. Just as progressive science requires theorists to revise their assumptions to interpret experimental anomalies (Lakatos, 1970), successful therapy confronts the client with the limits of her construing. In his range corollary, Kelly (1955) recognized that "a construct is convenient for the anticipation of a finite range of events only" (p. 68). This was a way of acknowledging that no construction, whatever its scientific credentials or personal relevance, could be an apt interpreter of all experiences we encounter. With each new step in our epistemic or individual evolution, "something, which before we thought was all settled, begins to look questionable. It is not that each new fact displaces an old one, but that gradually, almost imperceptibly as our ventures progress, a darkening shadow of doubt begins to spread over the coastline behind us" (Kelly, 1977, p. 7).

Clinically, this shadow of doubt is experienced as *anxiety*, defined as "the recognition that the events with which one is confronted lie outside the range of convenience of one's construct system" (Kelly, 1955, p. 495). Simply stated, anxiety arises when we are "caught with our constructs down," when we confront events that we are unable to anticipate or control. Frequently, clients may constrict their options in an attempt to minimize the anxiety that would attend moving into poorly structured areas. For example, the reluctance of a woman to leave a long-standing but dysfunctional marriage may stem not only from the threat this could pose to her existing core role structure (G. Neimeyer & Gold-Hall, 1987) but also from the anxiety engendered by considering an unfamiliar and largely unpredictable life alone. Construed in this way, anxiety is not so much a pathological emotion to be controlled as a harbinger of change in one's construct system. Therapeutically, it is important to ask, *"What are the current boundaries of my client's construing, and what important experiences lie beyond them?"* The therapist then can help the client elaborate her construing of the anxiety-provoking area, either by extending old constructs to interpret it or by creating new ones. In either case, such exploration pushes back the frontier of the client's personal world and in so doing increases her range of movement.

SELF IN SOCIAL CONTEXT

Individuality and Uniqueness

If one had to catch the essence of construct theory in a phrase, it might be described as a psychology of personal meanings. With his statement in the individuality corollary that "persons differ from one another in their construction of events," Kelly (1955, p. 55) made clear his commitment to the primacy of the personal. From this viewpoint, the crucial differences between two people have less to do with the disparate events they have encountered than with the unique constructions they place upon these events. The importance of this idiographic perspective is nowhere more evident than in psychotherapy, where the therapist should persistently ask herself the question, *"What are the private meanings of the client's words?"* The value of this was illustrated in the recent case of Walt, a middle-aged businessman who consulted me with marital difficulties and increasing conflict over an extramarital affair he had initiated. In our first session, he described himself as "easy-going," a comment I at first took to be a simple description of his sociability and relaxed attitude toward life. But a subsequent repertory grid analysis (see G. J. Neimeyer, Chapter 2, *this volume*) disclosed that for Walt, being "easy-going" contrasted with acting "emotional" and represented the construct on which he perceived his wife and himself to be most sharply polarized. Moreover, grid results indicated that this dimension was among the most superordinate in his system. Being "easy-going" implied being "sensitive," "understanding," and "childlike inside," all of which were highly valued core role constructs. Without an appreciation of the subtle personal meanings of Walt's apparently casual self-characterization, I might have missed some of the crucial issues provoking his mid-life crisis.

The Social Construction of Reality

Construct theory's emphasis on the idiographic aspects of construing should not be taken as an endorsement of philosophical solipsism, the position that each individual is encapsulated in a private universe that makes no contact with that of other people. In the usual case, substantial overlap in our construing with that of others is ensured by our common membership in a family, subcultural, or cultural group. In part, this is because our personal constructs often have a social origin (Procter & Parry, 1978); our construct systems are constrained by the ideologies of the social systems in which we live. But individuals also contribute to the social realities constituted by the groups to which they belong, a phenomenon that is particularly evident at the dyadic and small group level. For example, in cultivating friendships, interactants attempt to establish their psychological similarity with potential partners, defined by Kelly's (1955) commonality corollary as the similarity in their basic "construction of experience" (p. 90). As empirical research suggests, dyadic partners who succeed in validating and extending one another's views of reality tend to form enduring close relationships, whereas those whose personal epistemologies conflict do not (Duck, 1977; 1979; G. Neimeyer & R. Neimeyer, 1985). Evidence from larger social systems such as families (Procter, 1981; Reiss, 1981) and even whole societies (Berger & Luckmann, 1966) points toward a similar conclusion: groups evolve so as to articulate and maintain a common view of social reality in general and their own identity in particular.

In marital and family therapy, the clinician often confronts groups of individuals whose collaboration in constructing a common reality has broke down or become dysfunctional. This prompts the orienting questions: "*Is the family construct system of my clients too tight to permit change or too loose to allow members some ability to predict one another's behavior? Does it represent a view of the family's reality that was once appropriate, but is now being outgrown?*" An example of the latter was provided by John and Bess, a couple of their early thirties who consulted me about increasing marital tension and impending divorce. I soon learned that their behavior in therapy mirrored their interaction at home; time after time Bess would insistently question John about "why he didn't love her anymore," and John would angrily withdraw, unable to formulate an answer that would satisfy her. A careful relationship history provided a partial answer to Bess's questions. When they had begun dating in high school, Bess had seemed like a kind of savior to John. The clear and compelling construction of life deriving from her fundamentalist religious convictions offered a sharp alternative to John's own "semidelinquent" lifestyle, forged in his chaotic family of origin. Adopting Bess's views as the framework for their relationship proved viable for a number of years, until John started feeling confined and stunted by the implications this held for their day to day life and their identity as a couple. Seen in this developmental perspective, their difficulty in forging a new relational construct system had precipitated their request for help. While the processes that impair mutuality differ from case to case, research has documented that dissatisfied as opposed to satisfied couples are characertized by generally lower levels of commonality in the content and application of their relational constructs (G. Neimeyer & Hudson, 1985). The deleterious effects of ambiguous and rigidly polarized family construct systems are illustrated in several chapters in this book (e.g., P. C. Alexander & V. M. Follette, *this volume*; V. Kenny, *this volume*; H. G. Procter, *this volume*).

The Risk of Relationship

Perhaps none of the corollaries of construct theory has more direct relevance for therapy than the sociality corollary, which asserts that "to the extent that one person construes the construction processes of another, he may play a role in a social process involving the other person" (Kelly, 1955, p. 95). Obviously, there are many social relationships we enact with others that require us to construe only very limited segments of their outlooks, as is the case in the highly "scripted" social behavior described by Goffman (1959). Even in some cases of psychotherapy, a limited attempt to subsume or "indwell" the client's construct system may be adequate to promote change, if all that is required is a small scale technical change within the client's existing system. But in therapies that attempt more fundamental personality change, the therapist must often ask the questions: *"Have I adequately gained access to the client's core role, his 'deepest understanding of being maintained as a social being' (Kelly, 1955, p. 502)? To what extent do I reveal my own core identity to the client, as a means of helping him elaborate his interpersonal constructions?"* Rarely is such access gained by the therapist—or permitted by the client—in a casual or direct way, since this opens the client to the threat of therapeutic invalidation of identity structures or the experience of "terror," as Leitner (1985) has aptly described it. Especially in more deeply disturbed clients, whose lives may be patterned around a global retreat from this intimate type of role relationship (Leitner, 1985), therapy can be delicate and protracted. Successful intervention in such cases will require the therapist to attend carefully to the client's emotions as clues to limitations in his interpersonal construing (Soldz, 1986) and, ultimately, to gently invalidate the dysfunctional transference expectations of the client (R. Neimeyer, 1986). Discussions of such therapies are provided by L. M. Leitner (*this volume*) and S. Soldz (*this volume*).

CONCLUSION

In the present chapter, I have tried to enunciate a few of the tenets of personal construct theory—a theory that has guided and informed my clinical practice for the past 10 years. This book stems from the conviction that construct theory offers a bold, integrative, and immensely practical framework for psychotherapy, the potential utility of which is only beginning to be explored. But it would be misleading to assume that the theory determines one's therapeutic interventions in a unilinear way—as a reading of the diverse contributions to this volume will quickly attest. Instead, theory and practice interplay with one another in a dialectical fashion: theory provides a coordinating framework for one's strategies and techniques, and intensive case studies provide a major creative heuristic (McGuire, 1983) for generating further revisions and extensions of theory. It is my hope that the case studies collected here will contribute to this ongoing process, ultimately enhancing our capacity as therapists to assist individuals engaged in the courageous process of personal reconstruction.

REFERENCES

Bannister, D. (1960). Conceptual structure in thought–disordered schizophrenics. *Journal of Mental Science, 108,* 1230–1249.

Bannister, D. (1975). Personal construct theory psychotherapy. In D. Bannister (Ed.), *Issues and approaches in the psychological therapies.* New York: Wiley.

Bannister, D., & Mair, J. M. M. (1968). *The evaluation of personal constructs.* New York: Academic.

Beck, A. T., Rush, J., Shaw, B., & Emery, G. (1979). *Cognitive therapy of depression.* New York: Guilford.

Berger, P.L., & Luckmann, T. (1966). *The social construction of reality.* New York: Doubleday.

Duck, S.W. (1977). Inquiry, hypothesis, and the quest for validation. In S.W. Duck (Ed.), *Theory and practice in interpersonal attraction.* London: Academic.

Duck, S.W. (1979). The personal and the interpersonal in construct theory. In P. Stringer & D. Bannister (Eds.), *Constructs of sociality and individuality.* London: Academic.

Ellis, A.(1979). Rational-emotive therapy. In A. Ellis & J.M. Whiteley (Eds.), *Theoretical and empirical foundations of rational emotive therapy.* Monterey, CA: Brooks/ Cole.

Epting, F.R. (1984). *Personal construct counseling and psychotherapy.* New York: Wiley.

Goffman, E. (1959). *The presentation of self in everyday life.* Garden City, NY: Doubleday.

Guidano, V.F., & Liotti, G. (1983). *Cognitive processes and emotional disorders.* New York: Guilford.

Kelly, G.A. (1955). *The psychology of personal constructs.* New York: Norton.

Kelly, G.A. (1967/1980). A psychology of the optimal man. In A.W. Landfield & L.M. Leitner (Eds.), *Personal construct psychology: Psychotherapy and personality.* New York: Wiley.

Kelly, G.A. (1970). Behavior is an experiment. In D. Bannister (Ed.), *Perspectives in personal construct theory.* London: Academic.

Kelly, G.A. (1977). The psychology of the unknown. In D. Bannister (Ed.), *New perspectives in personal construct theory.* London: Academic.

Kelly, G.A. (1985). The handbook of clinic practice (1936 veresion). *Fort Hays Studies, Third series (Science), 6* (entire issue).

Lakatos, I. (1970). Falsification and the methodology of scientific research programmes. In I. Lakatos & A. Musgrave (Eds.), *Criticism and the growth of knowledge.* Cambridge: Cambridge University Press.

Landfield, A.W. (1982). The construction of fragmentation and unity. In J.C. Mancuso & J.R. Adams-Webber (Eds.), *The construing person.* New York: Praeger.

Leitner, L.M. (1985). The terrors of cognition. In D. Bannister (Ed.), *Issues and approaches in personal construct theory.* London: Academic.

Mahoney, M. J. (1985). Psychotherapy and human change processes. In M. J. Mahoney & A. Freeman (Eds.), *Cognition and psychotherapy.* New York: Plenum.

Mair, M. (1977). Metaphors for living. In A.W. Landfield (Ed.), *The Nebraska symposium on motivation.* Lincoln: University of Nebraska Press.

McGuire, W. J. (1983). A contextualist theory of knowledge. In L. Berkowitz (Ed.), *Advances in experimental social psychology (Vol. 16).* New York: Academic.

Neimeyer, G. J., & Gold-Hall, A. (1987). Personal identity in distorted marital relationships. In F. Fransella & L. Thomas (Eds.), Experimenting with personal construct psychology. London: Routledge and Keegan Paul.

Neimeyer, G. J., & Hudson, J. (1985). Couples' constructs: Personal systems in marital satisfaction. In D. Bannister (Ed.), *Issues and approaches in personal construct theory.* London: Academic.

Neimeyer, G.J., & Neimeyer, R.A. (1985). Relational trajectories: A personal construct contribution. *Journal of Social and Personal Relationships, 2,* 325–349.

Neimeyer, R.A. (1980). George Kelly as therapist: A review of his tapes. In A. W. Landfield & L. M. Leitner (Eds.), *Personal construct psychology: Psychotherapy and personality.* New York: Wiley.

Neimeyer, R.A. (1981). The structure and meaningfulness of tacit construing. In H. Bonarius, R. Holland, & S. Rosenberg (Eds.), *Personal construct psychology: Recent advances in theory and practice.* London: Macmillan.

Neimeyer, R.A. (1985a). *The development of personal construct psychology.* Lincoln: University of Nebraska Press.

Neimeyer, R.A. (1985b). Personal constructs in clinical practice. In P. C. Kendall (Ed.), *Advances in cognitive-behavioral research and therapy (Vol. 4),* New York: Academic.

Neimeyer, R.A. (1986). Personal construct therapy. In W. Dryden & W. Golden (Eds.), *Cognitive-behavioral approaches to psychotherapy.* London: Harper & Row.

Neimeyer, R.A. (in press). Symptom and significance: The origin of questions in the clinical context. *Questioning Exchange.*

Popper. K.R. (1963). *Conjectures and refutations.* London: Routledge.

Procter, H. (1981). Family construct psychology. In S. Walrond-Skinner (Ed.), *Developments in family therapy.* London: Routledge.

Procter, H., & Parry, G. (1978). Constraint and freedom: The social origin of personal constructs. In F. Fransella (Ed.), *Personal construct psychology 1977.* London: Academic.

Reiss, D. (1981). *The family's construction of reality.* Cambridge, MA: Harvard University Press.

Sarason, J. (1979). Three lacunaue of cognitive therapy. *Cognitive Therapy and Research, 3,* 223–235.

Schlenker, B. (Ed.)(1985). *The self and social life.* New York: McGraw-Hill.

Soldz, S. (1986). Construing of others in therapy. *Journal of Contemporary Psychotherapy, 16,* 52–61.

Tschudi, F. (1983). Constructs are hypotheses. In J. R. Adams-Webber & J. Mancuso (Eds.), *Applications of personal construct theory.* New York: Academic.

Zelhart, P., & Jackson, T. T. (1983). George A. Kelly, 1931–1943: Environmental influences on a developing theorist.In J. R. Adams-Webber & J. Mancuso (Eds.), *Applications of personal construct theory.* New York: Academic.

2

Personal Construct Assessment, Strategy, and Technique

Greg J. Neimeyer

> There is no particular kind of psychotherapeutic relationship—no particular kind of feelings—no particular kind of interaction that is itself a psychotherapeutic panacea, nor is there any particular set of techniques that are the techniques of choice for the personal construct theorist. The relationships between therapist and client and the techniques they employ may be as varied as the whole human repertory of relationships and techniques. It is the orchestration of techniques and the utilization of relationships in the ongoing process of living and profiting from experience that makes psychotherapy a contribution to human life.
> —GEORGE A. KELLY, *1969a, p. 223*

In emphasizing the technical eclecticism of his approach, Kelly underscored the fundamental flexibility of personal construct therapy. Both this eclecticism and the theoretically consistent context in which it operates have been discussed elsewhere (Epting, 1984; Karst, 1980; R. Neimeyer, 1985, 1986). This chapter is aimed at addressing the primary objectives of personal construct therapy and discussing some of its distinctive contributions to assessment, conceptualization, and intervention. It is designed to convey an overview of the therapeutic venture from the vantage point of a personal construct therapist. My hope is that the perspective is sufficiently lofty to provide a reasonable panorama of the approach but also sufficiently grounded to reveal the details essential to understanding its pragmatics. Wherever possible I have tried to illustrate concepts with clinical material and to reference more detailed, related discussions (in *this volume* and elsewhere) in order to highlight the theory's concrete therapeutic implications.

THERAPEUTIC OBJECTIVE: WHEN MEANS AND ENDS ARE ONE IN THE SAME

Kelly's (1969a) description of therapy as "an experimental process in which constructions are devised or delineated and then tested out" (p. 220) suggests his commitment to viewing therapy as an adventure in inquiry. Psychological maladjustment is viewed as bad science in the sense that it reflects restricted processes of construction that thwart the development of productive personal inquiry. Thus, "disordered" individuals find themselves confined by the limits of their construct systems, unable to effect genuinely elaborative choices by virtue of self-imposed boundaries. Because "a person's behavior must take place within the limited dimensions of his personal construct system" (Kelly, 1969b, p. 84), liabilities in the system restrict the range of alternatives, and therapy is aimed at helping clients to develop the means to expand the horizon of their available options. Thus, therapy is aimed at helping individuals to better understand how they have run aground in their processes of living and at helping them to develop the means to set themselves afloat again. The therapeutic end is developing the means: the means to dislodge themselves from unproductive patterns by experimenting with constructive alternatives.

This objective contrasts with the goals of therapies designed primarily to remediate "response deficits" or to alter "faulty cognitions" (see D.A. Winter, *this volume*). For construct therapists behavior is viewed as an experimental instrument, as a means of inquiry, rather than as an end in itself. Therefore, therapy does not concentrate on discrete dysfunctional behaviors, eradicating these trouble spots in a person's life as if applying some sort of therapeutic spot remover to the soiled aspects of the behavioral repertoire. Rather, as with object-relations therapies (e.g., Wachtel, 1977; Wile, 1981) it addresses the range of presenting concerns with the understanding that they likely converge on relatively few superordinate features of the system, reflecting a prism of apparently discrete colors that emanate from a more limited number of light sources. In this exploratory venture clients anticipate and experiment with their constructions in a way that the underlying system of beliefs is affected, not the behavior only. This is the task that Kelly assigned to therapy, "not to produce behavior, but rather to enable the client, as well as the therapist, to utilize behavior for asking important questions. In fact, the task of psychotherapy is to get the human process going again so that life may go on and on from where psychotherapy left off" (Kelly, 1969a, p. 223).

THERAPEUTIC ATTITUDE AND RELATIONSHIP

Just as Kelly recognized that "there is no one psychotherapeutic technique," he also noted that "there is no one kind of interpersonal compatibility between psychotherapist and client" (Kelly, 1969a, p. 221). Instead, he suggested that the therapist create a spontaneous and natural working relationship with the client. As with other therapies an effort is made to develop a sense of collaborative empiricism, with the therapist serving as a consultant to the principal investigator—the client. This constrasts both with the exhortational approach of some cognitive-behavioral approaches and with the reflective orientation of some humanistic therapies. As Kelly (1969b) noted:

> Instead of assuming, on the one hand, that the therapist is obliged to bring the client's thinking into line, or, on the other, that the client will mysteriously bring his own thinking into line given the proper setting, we can take the stand that the client and therapist are conjoining in an exploratory venture. The therapist assumes neither the position of judge nor that of sympathetic bystander. He is sincere about this; he is willing to learn along with his client. He is the client's fellow researcher who seeks first to understand, then to examine, and finally to assist the client in subjecting alternatives to experimental test and revision (p. 82).

The cornerstone of this relationship is the therapist's *credulous approach* to the client's concerns. The credulous approach alerts the clinician to the fact that the client's presentation "possesses and intrinsic truth which the clinician should not ignore" and therefore he or she "never discards information given by the client merely because it does not conform to what appear to be the facts!" (Kelly, 1955, p. 322).

This approach conveys to the client a sense of *acceptance,* which Kelly (1955) regarded as "the readiness to utilize the client's modes of approach—his system of axes, his reference points, his way of approaching problems" (p. 587). These understandings are then subsumed within the larger system of professional constructions that the clinician uses to guide the process of therapy. From this perspective, the hidden rationality (Wile, 1981) of the client's apparently irrational and self-defeating behavior emerges, paving the way for genuine *reassurance* of the client's shaky structures. Reassurance operates as a "temporary way of reducing anxiety" (Kelly, 1955, p. 650) by shoring up the client's defenses in cases where impending change might seriously jeopardize the integrity of the system. Kelly's concern with gradual and measured progress toward substantial therapeutic gains underlines his fundamental respect for the dignity of the person and his concern for the long-range implications of therapy. This distinguishes personal construct therapy from some of its cognitive-behavioral offspring in terms of process and outcome (c.f. R. Neimeyer, 1986). As Kelly (1955) noted:

> If the task of therapy were always to disrupt the use of faulty constructs as soon as possible, one might say that reassurance should never be used. However, the task of therapy is to prepare the client for achieving long range goals, and not simply to perform surgery on his misconceptions (p. 652).

This preparation beings with the development of a collaborative alliance between the therapist and client and continues through the processes of assessment and intervention.

ASSESSMENT

Kelly (1969c) described constructs as "the axes of reference man contrives to put his psychological space in order and to plot his varying courses of action" (p. 36). Assessment is aimed at articulating these courses of action so that their opportunities, as well as limitations, are more clearly apparent. Within the personal construct literature the most commonly reported method of assessment is the Role Construct Repertory Test (reptest).

The basic features of the reptest can be illustrated by the case example of Joan, a 53-year-old woman who sought treatment after 29 years of physical abuse by her husband. A reptest was administered to her in a structured interview format as part of a larger study of spouse abuse (G. Neimeyer & Gold-Hall, 1987). The administration consisted of three stages. Because we were interested in understanding Joan's intimate role relations, including her relationship with her husband, the first step involved generating a suitable list of close relationships. These figures are called elements, and they appear at the top of the reptest in Figure 2.1. In each case, Joan was asked to personalize the list by filling in the name of the person who best fit each description, though these names have been deleted in the figure.

The second stage of the reptest involved eliciting her constructs. This was done by writing the names of each of the 12 elements on separate 3 × 5 index cards and presenting them to her three at a time. This triadic-sort method is the original method for construct elicitation, although dyadic, monadic, and opposite techniques are contemporary variants (Epting, Suchman, & Nickerson, 1971). In this case, she was first asked to consider her husband, her father, and a former lover and to "think of any important way in which two of them might be alike in some way, but different from the other." In response, she identified her husband and father as similar in that they "make me feel inferior," whereas the former lover "made me feel

DESCRIPTION			Husband	Father	Mother	Best friend	Person who rejected you	A child or someone who depends on you	A person you dislike	Former lover	Happiest person you know	Person who makes you feel uncomfortable	Yourself in an ideal marriage	Yourself in your current marriage
	POSITIVE	NEGATIVE	1.	2.	3.	4.	5.	6.	7.	8.	9.	10.	11.	12.
1.	Makes me feel important	Makes me feel inferior	-3	-2	-2	+2	-1	+5	+2	+1	-2	+2	+6	-3
2.	Feel protected	Feel used	-4	+2	-2	+1	-2	-2	+1	-1	+1	-2	+6	-3
3.	Feel loved	Feel unloved	-3	-2	+3	+1	-2	+4	+2	+1	+2	+2	+6	-3
4.	Can be myself	Have to put on a front	-1	-3	-2	-1	-2	-3	-1	-1	+2	+2	+6	-3
5.	Accepted for what I am	Unaccepted	-3	-3	+2	+2	-2	+3	+2	-2	-1	+2	+6	-2
6.	Honest	Puts on a show	-5	-4	+2	-1	-2	-2	-2	+1	+2	-3	+6	-3
7.	Care about person	Hate person	-2	+1	+2	+2	+2	+3	+1	+1	+1	-2	+6	+3
8.	Trust	Don't trust	-1	-1	-2	+2	-2	+5	-1	-1	-1	+3	+6	-3
9.	Responsible	Irresponsible	-2	+2	+2	+1	-2	-3	-2	-1	+2	+1	+6	+3
10.	Straightforward	Conniving	+1	-2	-2	-1	-2	+2	-2	-2	-2	-3	+6	+1
11.	Feel for person	Uncaring	+1	+3	-1	+2	+2	-2	+1	+1	+2	+1	+6	+3
12.	Makes me feel mature	Makes me feel childish	-1	-2	+2	+2	-2	+1	+2	+2	-2	+2	+6	-3

Scale: +6 +5 +4 +3 +2 +1 0 -1 -2 -3 -4 -5 -6

FIGURE 2.1. Joan's reptest.

important." This construct (makes me feel inferior vs. makes me feel important) was entered in the grid according to the pole of the construct she viewed as most positive. The procedure was then repeated, this time considering the three different elements in the second row of the grid. Here she identified her "husband" and a "person who rejected her" as being similar in that she "feels used" by both of them, in contrast to feeling more "protected" by her best friend. This construct was then entered in the second row of the grid and the process repeated until all twelve constructs were elicited. These twelve constructs were viewed as a sample of the means by which Joan construes her close relationships, the dimensions along which she moves in relation to important people in her life.

The third and final step involved asking her to apply her constructs to each of the elements by using a 13-point rating scale [e.g., (feel used) -6, -5, -4, -3, -2, -1, 0, 1, 2, 3, 4, 5, 6 (feel protected)]. This matrix of ratings can be subjected to a wide variety of analyses, ranging from simple descriptive summaries, to principle components analyses. Some of these are discussed below.

Among the richest sources of data is the content of the constructs themselves. In Joan's case, it is clear that her system of interpersonal constructions is dominated by her feelings for others, many of them quite powerful. The negative poles of her constructs convey a potent pathos in her descriptions of feeling inferior, used, unloved, unaccepted, etc. These dimensions can be grouped according to various postcoding categories in order to identify underlying themes in the system. In our study of abused women (G. Neimeyer & Gold-Hall, 1987), for example, we postcoded constructs according to selected categories of Landfield's (1971) system for content analysis. Results indicated abused women's constructs reflected generally higher levels of forcefulness (e.g., "dominating, aggressive, intolerant") and lower levels of social interaction (e.g., "outgoing, friendly, tender") than the systems of women in more satisifed and stable relationships. Other systems of content analysis have been tailored to such diverse areas of investigation as communication (Applegate, 1983; Delia, Kline, & Burleson, 1979), interpersonal acquaintance (Duck, 1973), death threat (R. Neimeyer, Fontana, & Gold, 1984), and cognitive anxiety (Viney & Westbrook, 1976). Applications of postcoding schemes are also included in the chapter by L. L. Viney in this volume.

Beyond content analyses, Joan's matrix of numerical ratings can also be studied. At the most basic, descriptive level it is interesting to note her predominantly negative perceptions of her husband (83% negative) and her father (67% negative), as well as her ambivalence toward such figures as her mother (50% negative) and even her best friend (25% negative). In stark contrast to these is her apparently idealized version of herself once extricated from her relationship (100% positive).

An analogous reading across her constructs suggests that she has few people with whom she feels important (42%), protected (33%), or loved (42%) and fewer still that she feels she can be herself with (25%) or who she perceives as being straightforward with her (25%). Despite this, she has evident sources of support, in part drawing from the positive aspects of her relationships with her mother, best friend, and a child who depends on her.

Other aspects of Joan's construct system can be gleaned from generating a matrix of correlations among her constructs (see Table 2.1). From this table a better understanding of the linkages among her constructs is possible. For example, for Joan, feeling important is significantly related to feeling loved ($r = 0.73$), accepted ($r = 0.83$), trusting ($r = 0.89$), and mature ($r = 0.79$) but relatively independent from her level of "feeling for the person" ($r = 0.07$) or their perceived level of "responsibility" ($r = 0.10$).

One way to sketch a rough outline of the structure of her system is to identify those relatively superordinate constructs that correlate most highly with all the other constructs in the system. Correlations cannot be added together directly, but they can if they are first squared (to remove the sign) and multiplied by 100 (to remove the decimal). The result is a "relationship score" (Fransella & Bannister, 1977) for each construct that reflects how much variance in the overall construct system is accounted for by that one construct. Constructs that account for greater variance might be more superordinate, since, by definition, they carry greater implications for the overall system. In Joan's case for instance, being "accepted for what I am vs. feeling unaccepted" was her most highly intercorrelated construct, followed closely by feeling "loved vs. unloved," "mature vs. childish," and "important vs. inferior." Among other things, this alerts the clinician to the centrality of feeling accepted for Joan and the likelihood that changes in these feelings would carry major implications for her feeling loved, important, protected, etc.

FURTHER ASSESSMENT

These simple analyses can be augmented by more sophisticated methods for interrogating the grid data. For example, Higginbotham and Bannister (1983) provide a computer program that allows a pictorial graph of all the constructs in relation to the two most important, but independent, dimensions (for clinical examples, see Fransella & Bannister, 1977; G. Neimeyer & R. Neimeyer, 1981). Thomas and Shaw (1976) provide programs for illustrating the linkages among constructs using tree diagrams, and Slater's (1976) programs provide principle component analyses of reptest data.

Table 2.1. Joan's construct correlations

Constructs	1	2	3	4	5	6	7	8	9	10	11	12
1. Feel important vs. inferior												
2. Feel protected vs. used	0.52											
3. Feel loved vs. unloved	0.73*	0.60*										
4. Can be myself vs. put up a front	0.48	0.63*	0.50									
5. Accept me for what I am vs. unaccepted	0.83*	0.51	0.83*	0.56								
6. Honest vs. puts on a show	0.44	0.64*	0.81*	0.67*	0.60*							
7. Care about person vs. hate person	0.46	0.58*	0.61*	0.21	0.52	0.66*						
8. Trust vs. don't trust	0.90*	0.47	0.63*	0.56	0.78*	0.36	0.35					
9. Responsible vs. irresponsible	0.10	0.69*	0.31	0.58*	0.40	0.57	0.49	0.14				
10. Straight forward vs. conniving	0.49	0.38	0.44	0.42	0.48	0.39	0.66*	0.59*	0.34			
11. Feel for person vs. uncaring	0.07	0.67*	−0.03	0.57	0.06	0.34	0.41	0.19	0.72	0.43*		
12. Feel mature vs. childish	0.80*	0.53	0.76*	0.61*	0.85*	0.63*	0.35	0.70*	0.34	0.40	0.12	

*Significant at 0.05 level.

27

Additional clinical illustrations are provided in recent volumes by Beail (1985) and Thomas and Harri-Augstein (1985).

In addition to these numerically oriented approaches to assessment, construct therapists employ other diverse methods for assessment ranging from interview methodologies (Leitner, 1985; G. Neimeyer & Hudson, 1985), self-characertizations (Fransella, 1981), and enactments (Kelly, 1955) to nonverbal forms of construct elicitation (R. Neimeyer, 1981). Each of these is aimed at articulating the implications of the interpretive system that joins the client to the world. The objectives of assessment follow from Kelly's (1955) realization that, "Like the scientist who must first explore the implications of his theoretical system before he can design a meaningful experiment, the client often needs to explore the implications of his construing system before he plans venturesome activity for himself" (Kelly, 1955, p. 1124).

STRATEGIES FOR CHANGE

Kelly's (1955) insistence that psychotherapeutic techniques "run the gamut of man's devices for coming to grips with reality" (p. 23) underscores not only the theory's technical eclecticism but also its emphasis on the underlying continuity between the experience of psychotherapy and the experience of life itself. As a result, "the techniques employed [in psychotherapy] are the techniques for living . . . Hence one may find a personal construct psychotherapist employing a huge variety of procedures—not helter-skelter, but always as part of a plan for helping himself and his client get on with the job of human exploration and checking out the appropriateness of the constructions they have devised for placing on the world around them" (Kelly, 1955, p. 222).

It is significant in this regard that Kelly's (1955) discussion of the methods for producing psychotherapeutic movement (pp. 1088-1140) is directly preceded by the discussion of one major diagnostic reference axis: loosening vs. tightening. Loosened construing is characterized by constructs that lead to varying predictions, whereas tightened construing leads to more fixed or certain predictions. At one extreme is the radical uncertainty of thought-process disorder (c.f., Bannister, 1963) and at the other is the rigid certainty of obsessive construing (c.f., Rigdon & Epting, 1983). Kelly envisioned therapy as enhancing the fluidity of construing, as facilitating movement along the tight–loose dimension. He regarded the alteration between loosening and tightening as "an important feature of deep therapy. New constructs are formed by loosening up old ones and tightening up the tentative formulations which begin to take shape in the resulting disarray" (Kelly, 1955, p. 484). In marital therapy, for example, spouses sometimes have fairly tight systems for construing the nature of their relationship. The beliefs that men and women are differentially emotional or differentially sexual, for instance, carry restrictive implications for the expression of intimacy in a relationship. In this case, therapy might be aimed at "loosening and broadening each spouse's schemata, that is, the implicit matrix of assumptions, expectations, and requirements of intimate interpersonal contact" (Gurman, 1981, p. 433). More specific discussion of the techniques of change are provided in Kelly's (1969a) synoptic account of eight therapeutic strategies.

Slot change, which constitutes the client's reversal along an existing dimension, represents the first and most superficial therapeutic change. It is regarded as a cosmetic alteration because the contruct system itself remains unchanged; the person is simply asked to enact the opposite side of an existing construct. The danger inherent in slot change is not only its impermanence (since the person is likely to switch back to the preferred pole at the first opportunity) but also the hazard of not fully appreciating the nature of the contrasting pole prior to encouraging the slot movement. For example, Joe was a quiet, unassuming individual who sought help for assertiveness training and stress management. In encouraging him to "be more expressive" his therapist had little idea of the uncontrolled torrent of explosive rage he was encouraging Joe to exercise. Later discussion clarified that Joe's unassuming self-presentation and lack of assertiveness was related to what he viewed as a "controlled" posture. Its opposite, "being uncontrolled," was an equally dysfunctional and understandably avoided alternative. Joe's immediate return to his earlier posture, somewhat guilty over his loss of control, highlights the transient nature of "slot rattling." Kelly (1955) dubbed this superficial movement, which is "produced by sliding the client back and forth in his construct slots," (p. 938) as *contrast reconstruction* to distinguish it from more significant forms of change in the context, organization, or content of the system.

A second strategy involves encouraging the client to *select another construct* from the existing repertoire and apply it to the relevant issue(s). For example, Steve came to the university counseling center with issues of "dating anxiety." Instead of directly asking women out for a date, he "hedged his bets" by hinting at his interests in hopes that they would respond to his heavily veiled intentions. When they did not, he construed this as "an indication that they don't like me," and he impulsively withdrew from interacting with them. Kelly viewed impulsiveness as foreshortened circumspection — truncated consideration of alternative constructions. The task was to prolong Steve's circumspection, and this was accomplished by asking him to "brainstorm for as many different ways as possible" of interpreting the women's behavior. Among the other constructions available to him was the possibility that they had not fully gathered his intent, and this made it possible to test out this rival hypothesis in subsequent social situations.

A third approach is to "*make more explicit those preverbal constructs* by which all of us order our lives to a considerable degree" (Kelly, 1969a, p. 231). Kelly (1955) likened this process to "handling a live fish in the dark; not only does it wiggle but it is slippery and hard to see." Nonetheless, the articulation of these dimensions throws the light of day on these elusive constructions, tightening them sufficiently to subject them to subsequent experimentation. It is not necessary that preverbal constructions be verbalized in order to be tested (c.f., R. Neimeyer, 1981), only that they be symbolized by means that render them available to experimentation and reconstruction.

An example of this followed from my work with Karen who came to therapy with the concern that she was a psychopath. I had never known a psychopath to be concerned over being psychopathic, and I reflected this to Karen in hopes of invalidating her construction. It turned out that she thought she was psychopathic because she felt unable to establish intimate relationships with anyone, reporting a sense of panic whenever "someone gets too close." We talked around this elusive sense of panic for a couple of sessions and then began to articulate it behaviorally by taking special note of the contexts in which she experienced it. It became evident that it was especially prominent in her relationships with men, particularly when these interactions carried implications for sexuality, however remote. In a sort of "backward elaboration" (Kelly, 1955, pp. 951–952), I asked her if she could identify any previous times in her life when she felt similarly. Only in childhood, following an ambiguous but uncomfortable advance by one of her uncles, could Karen find a parallel. This was a powerful emotional connection, and, for the first time, Karen could see the link between this early sexual intrusion and her current difficulty with intimacy 15 years later. The benefit of this insight was not so much in its accompanying catharsis, as in its articulation of a preverbal dimension. It helped Karen to locate in personal space the coordinates of her panicky feeling in a way that opened it up to further interventions.

Among these interventions was a fourth major tactic: *testing a construction for its predictive validity*. This involved helping Karen formulate clear predictions from her sense of panic and then to gradually test those formulations in controlled interpersonal experiments. Among the implications of this panic was a perceived loss of control where Karen feared that she would be unable to prevent or guard against unwanted sexual advances by men in dating situations. We began to test the validity of this construction by having her initiate contact with interesting men while circumscribing the interactions to public places or gatherings with groups of friends. Gradually she began to differentiate a variety of methods she could use to modulate the intimacy of her interactions. As she differentiated alternative means of control, the importance of the original dimension (retain control–lose control) gradually receded and eventually fell prey to an alternative reconstruction. As Karen later expressed it, "It's not so much that you have to stay in control of things, it's more that you need to let your feelings be known."

A fifth approach to reconstruction involves *testing the system for internal consistency.* This amounts to building bridges between various subsystems of constructs in a way that promotes personal integration. One means to promote this integration is through controlled elaboration, which amounts to "a reorganization of the hierarchical system of one's constructs, but not an essential revision of the constructs themselves" (Kelly, 1955, p. 938).

An example of this approach is clear in the case of David, who sought a counselor's advice in preparing his application for graduate studies. He was particularly anxious about the apparent discontinuity between his previous work as a successful electronics salesman and his aspiration to become a clinical psychologist. To help him bridge what he perceived to be an enormous gulf between these two aspects of himself, the counselor encouraged David to consider whether his sales work ever required him to "connect with people quickly, to create a positive relationship, to try to understand their needs, or to influence them covertly or overtly." This hit a responsive chord with David, who regarded himself as particularly adept interpersonally. But he had never really considered the importance of these characteristics to psychology, let alone the applicability of other familiar functions such as his experience in group decision-making, management presentations, or performance evaluation. In this way, the counselor helped David to "bring his constructs into line with his system as a whole" by working "on the internal consistency of his system rather than attempting to make outright replacements of constructs" (Kelly, 1955, p. 938).

Altering the range of convenience of a construct represents the sixth mode of intervention. In this strategy, the therapist encourages the client to apply the construct to a wider or to a narrower range of events. Increasing the range of convenience of a construct can sometimes be accomplished by importing constructs into anxiety-provoking areas from better structured domains. For example, Jim sought a counselor's help regarding his relationship with his wife. As a professional musician he traveled a good bit and consequently had little time at home, just enough time to "crash for a few days before hitting the road again." His wife's growing dissatisfaction with him struck him as "incessant whining," and he sought help to better understand what was suddenly going wrong in their relationship.

Jim was understood as experiencing a disrupted relationship (R. Neimeyer & G. Neimeyer, 1985) where accustomed levels of support and attention have been neglected. Efforts to encourage his attention to the relationship, without blaming him, were provided metaphorically, by asking him to view a relationship like a musical instrument. Like a chord, a relationship sounds "off" if any of its component parts is "out of tune." Just as you would never wait to break a string before you retune your instrument, small adjustments can be made regularly in order to prevent the instrument from sounding off key. In this way Jim was encouraged to view his marriage, like his music, as an ongoing process (Duck & Sants, 1983) that required continuous adjustment and work in order to keep it in harmony. This view was facilitated in this case by extending the range of convenience of his "musical constructs" to an interpersonal domain.

Just as extending the range of convenience of a construct may at times be useful, so can *reducing* the range of events to which it is applied. Kelly (1955, pp. 1074–1075) discussed methods of binding constructs as means to restrict their ranges of convenience. In binding, the therapist sharply delimits the people, places, or times to which the construct may be usefully applied, reducing the dimension to impermeability (for further examples, see chapters by G. Neimeyer and by Winter, *this volume*). For example, Karen, who had experienced a traumatic sexual advance by an uncle when she was a child, was enouraged to think that "feeling 'panicky' and 'out of control' were very understandable, even *useful*, ways for a child to deal with that particular experience. Now, however, they are not as useful as they once were. Now you need new ways to deal with the situation." By embalming the dimension in the past the therapist preserves the integrity of Karen's existing structures while simultaneously freeing her to cope with her contemporary conflicts differently. As with this type of time binding, the therapist could encourage other forms of symbol binding as well; perhaps by suggesting that "that was a useful way of understanding that particular person (person binding) in that one unusual circumstance (situation binding) but there are other ways to understand different people in different circumstances."

A seventh therapeutic maneuver aims at *altering the meaning of a construct*. Kelly's (1969a) description of this as "rotating the references axes" corresponds closely to the concept of "reframing" in the systemic literatures. The intent is to embed a construct within a new context, or background, from which it derives new meaning. So, for example, Mark and Denise were encouraged to consider their son Allen's disruptive behavior at school "as a barometer of your household tension," rather than what the school counselor described as a series of "unprovoked acting out behaviors." Over the course of only a few sessions, Denise and Mark began to see a patterned relationship between their own strident exchanges at home and Allen's behavior at school. This enabled them to reconstrue the meaning of his behavior and to intervene accordingly, in this case by redirecting the focus of their attention from him to themselves.

An eighth and final therapeutic approach is designed to *erect new construct dimensions*. Kelly (1955) described these efforts at construct revision as "the most difficult to achieve and the most likely to produce basic changes in the way a man construes his world" (p. 945). Kelly (1955) discusses a variety of conditions that are favorable and unfavorable to the formation of new constructions. Many of the chapters in this volume incorporate these conditions into treatment plans aimed at revising dysfunctional constructions. Basic to these ventures is the formation of test-tube sized experiments that can be conducted initially within the controlled and supportive confines of the therapeutic laboratory. Often clients are invited to retain their own way of viewing things while simultaneously entertaining the possibility of alternative viewpoints. The client is asked "to suppose for a minute that you are in your boss's shoes," or "to see if we can sketch an understanding of what might have happened if . . . ." Because construct theory allows that two inferentially incompatible viewpoints can be retained simultaneously (c.f., fragmentation corollary, Kelly, 1955, pp. 83–90), constructive revision does not have to be preceded by assaulting existing structures. In fact, Kelly was particularly critical of a therapeutic siege mentality, recognizing instead that "there is something in stating a new outlook in the form of a hypothesis that leaves the person . . . intact and whole" (1969d, p. 156) and still free to explore constructive alternatives.

Efforts to develop new constructs frequently incorporate this "as if" stance, since it temporarily circumvents the threat associated with significant change in the system. Instead, the client is asked to try on a series of different masks for a while with the realization that "masks have a way of sticking to our faces when worn too long" (Kelly, 1969d, p. 158). In this way, the therapist invites the client to attempt alternatives without first sacrificing the security of existing structures.

This invitation is carried out through the medium of *enactment:* brief role-playing techniques between the client and the therapist that are conducted spontaneously in the therapy room. Kelly's (1955) discussion of enactment makes it clear that "the therapist should take an experimental point of view toward the enactments used" (p. 1166), since they are designed to foster the client's process of discovery, rather than the therapist's need to demonstrate. Because "the purpose of enactment is to give the client a chance to experiment, not to indoctrinate him" (Kelly, 1955, p. 1165), the client is encouraged to enact parts that will ultimately be rejected as well as those that may be incorporated into subsequent revisions (for a detailed discussion of fixed role enactment see F. R. Epting & A. Nazario, *this volume*). As the client experiments with new outlooks, he/she interprets familiar events in unfamiliar ways, gradually forging new axes of reference against which the events of the world are reconstrued. This type of change is so fundamental to the objectives of personal construct theory that Kelly (1955) considered replacing the word therapy with *reconstruction* as a description of his efforts and might have done so, "if", as he observed, "it had not been such a mouth-filling word" (Kelly, 1955, p. 187).

SUMMARY

We hope that these introductory chapters have conveyed something of the orientation and flavor of personal construct therapy. It is a therapy in which the efforts of client and therapist are viewed as a joint research enterprise. The whole therapeutic approach is experimental, built on the model of clients as personal scientists whose inquiring ventures have somehow gone awry. The therapist's efforts are aimed at helping the client to design and implement controlled experiments and to incorporate their evidence into an evolving understanding of the world around them. The therapy room is the laboratory in which the therapist germinates constructive change by marshalling "all of the techniques for doing this that man has yet devised" (Kelly, 1969a, p. 221).

The chapters that follow illustrate these processes of constructive revision. They represent studies of the psychotherapeutic process, a process that Kelly (1969d) characterized as "imaginative inquiry into how an immobilized person can utilize his own capacity for experimental behavior to answer important questions that seem now only to confront him with inexorable conclusions" (Kelly, 1969d, p. 143).

REFERENCES

Applegate, J. L. (1983). Construct system development, strategic complexity, and impression formation in persuasive communication. In J. Adams-Webber & J. C. Mancuso (Eds.), *Applications of personal construct theory* (pp. 187–205). Toronto: Academic.

Bannister, D. (1963). The genesis of schizophrenic thought disorder: A serial invalidation hypothesis. *British Journal of Psychiatry, 109,* 680–687.

Beail, N. (1985). *Repertory grid technique and personal constructs: Applications in clinical and educational settings.* Cambridge, MA: Brookline Books.

Delia, J. G., Kline, S. L., & Burleson, B. R. (1979). The development of persuasive communication strategies in kindergarteners through twelfth-graders. *Communication Monographs, 46,* 241–256.

Duck, S. W. (1973). *Personal relationships and personal constructs: A study of friendship formation.* London: Wiley.

Duck, S. W., & Sants, H. (1983). On the origin of the specious: Are personal relationships really interpersonal states? *Journal of Social and Clinical Psychology, 1,* 27–41.

Epting, F. R. (1984). *Personal construct counseling and psychotherapy.* New York: Wiley.

Epting, F., Suchman, D. I., & Nickeson, R. J. (1971). An evaluation of elicitation procedures for personal constructs. *British Journal of Psychology, 62,* 513–517.

Fransella, F. (1981). Nature babbling to herself: The self-characterization as a therapeutic tool. In H. Bonarius, R. Holland, & S. Rosenberg (Eds.), *Personal construct psychology: Recent advances in theory and practice* (pp. 219–230). London: Macmillan Publishers.

Fransella, F., & Bannister, D. (1977). *A manual for repertory grid technique.* New York: Academic.

Gurman, A. S. (1981). Integrative marital therapy. In S. Budman (Ed.), *Forms of brief therapy* (pp. 415–457). New York: Guilford.

Higginbotham, P. G., & Bannister, D. (1983). *The GAB program for the analysis of repertory grid data* (2nd ed.). (Available from D. Bannister, High Royds Hospital, Menston, Ilkley, West Yorkshire, England).

Karst, T. O. (1980). The relationship between personal construct theory and psychotherapeutic techniques. In A. W. Landfield & L. M. Leitner (Eds.), *Personal construct psychology: Psychotherapy and personality* (pp. 166–184). New York: Wiley.

Kelly, G. A. (1955). *The psychology of personal constructs (Vols. 1 and 2).* New York: W. W. Norton.

Kelly, G. A. (1969a). The psychotherapeutic relationship. In B. Maher (Ed.), *Clinical psychology and personality: The selected papers of George Kelly* (pp. 216–223). New York: Wiley.

Kelly, G. A. (1969b). Man's construction of his alternatives. In B. Maher (Ed.), *Clinical psychology and personality: The selected papers of George Kelly* (pp. 66–93). New York: Wiley.

Kelly, G. A. (1969c). Ontological acceleration. In B. Maher (Ed.), *Clinical psychology and personality: The selected papers of George Kelly* (pp. 7–45). New York: Wiley.

Kelly, G. A. (1969d). The language of hypothesis: Man's psychological instrument. In B. Maher (Ed.), *Clinical psychology and personality: The selected papers of George Kelly* (pp. 147–162). New York: Wiley.

Landfield, A. W. (1971). *Personal construct systems in psychotherapy.* Chicago: Rand McNally & Company.

Leitner, L. (1985). The terrors of cognition. In D. Bannister (Ed.), *Issues and approaches in personal construct psychology* (pp. 83–103). London: Academic Press.

Neimeyer, G. J., & Gold-Hall, A. (1987). Personal identity in disordered marital relationships. In F. Fransella & L. Thomas (Eds.), *Experimenting with personal construct psychology.* London: Routledge and Kegan Paul.

Neimeyer, G. J., & Hudson, J. E. (1985). Couple's constructs: Personal systems in marital satisfaction. In D. Bannister (Ed.), *Issues and approaches in personal construct theory.* (pp. 127–141). London: Wiley.

Neimeyer, G. J., & Neimeyer, R. A. (1981). Personal construct perspectives on cognitive assessment. In T. Merluzzi, C. Glass, & M. Genest (Eds.), *Cognitive assessment* (pp. 188–232). New York: Guilford Press.

Neimeyer, R. A. (1981). The structure and meaningfulness of tacit construing. In H. Bonarius, R. Holland, & S. Rosenberg (Eds.), *Personal construct psychology: Recent advances in theory and practice* (pp. 105–113). London: Academic.

Neimeyer, R. A. (1985). Personal constructs in clinical practice. In P. C. Kendall (Ed.), *Advances in cognitive-behavioral research and therapy* (Vol. IV) (pp. 275–339). New York: Academic.

Neimeyer, R. A. (1986). Personal construct therapy. In W. Dryden & W. Golden (Eds.), *Cognitive behavioral approaches to psychotherapy* (pp. 224–260). London: Harper & Row.

Neimeyer, R. A., Fontana, D. J., & Gold, K. (1984). A manual for content analysis of death constructs. In F. R. Epting & R. A. Neimeyer (Eds.), *Personal meanings of death: Applications of personal construct theory to clinical practice* (pp. 213–241). New York: Hemisphere.

Neimeyer, R. A., & Neimeyer, G. J. (1985). Disturbed relationships: A personal construct view. In E. Button (Ed.), *Personal construct theory and mental health: Theory, research, and practice* (pp. 195–223). Beckenham, England: Croom Helm.

Rigdon, M. A., & Epting, F. R. (1983). A personal construct perspective on an obsessive client. In J. Adams-Webber & J. Mancuso (Eds.), *Applications of personal construct psychology* (pp. 249–263). Toronto: Academic Press.

Slater, P. (1976). *The measurement of intrapersonal space by grid technique (Vols. 1 and 2)*. Chichester: Wiley.

Thomas, L. F., & Harri-Augstein, S. (1985). *Self-organised learning*. London: Routledge & Kegan Paul.

Thomas, L. F., & Shaw, M. C. G. (1976). *FOCUS manual*. Center for the Study of Human Learning, Brunel University, England.

Viney, L. L., & Westbrook, M. T. (1976). Cognitive anxiety: A method of content analysis for verbal samples. *Journal of Personality Assessment, 40,* 140–150.

Wachtel, P. L. (1977). An interpersonal alternative. In *Psychoanalysis and behavior therapy: Toward an integration* (pp. 41–63). New York: Basic.

Wile, D. B. (1981). *Couple's therapy: A nontraditional approach*. New York: Wiley.

II
Individual
Therapy

3
Crisis of the Self: The Terror of Personal Evolution

Larry M. Leitner

Personal construct psychotherapy (Kelly, 1955) has been construed in many ways (e.g., Epting, 1984; Karst, 1980; Landfield, 1980b; Leitner, 1980, 1982; Neimeyer, 1980). These differing interpretations no doubt would have pleased Kelly whose fundamental philosophy was "constructive alternativism." One elaboration of personal construct therapy centers upon the client's struggles with the terrors of deep interpersonal understanding, or ROLE relating (Leitner, 1985). In this chapter, I will examine the utility of such a conceptualization by presenting a summary of the therapy of a young man (Mike). Before discussing the case, however, I will briefly review the linkage of ROLE relationships and terror.

ROLE RELATIONSHIPS AND TERROR

The nature of ROLE relationships can be seen in Kelly's (1955) sociality corollary: "To the extent that one person construes the construction process of another, he may play a role in a social process involving the other person" (p. 95). Leitner (1985) argues that construing the construction process of another is a potentially terrifying proposition. Essentially, one's construction processes are governed by core ROLE constructs. These core constructs *"govern a person's maintenance processes—that is, those by which he maintains his identity and existence"* (Kelly, 1955, p. 482, emphasis in original). Thus, in a ROLE relationship, we risk our most important constructs as we struggle to understand one another in most fundamental ways. If this venture turns out badly, what is most central to us has been invalidated. In a ROLE relationship, then, we risk experiencing a combination of threat, fear, anxiety, hostility, and guilt, which can be termed terror (Leitner, 1985).

If ROLE relationships are too terrifying, we may retreat from them. If there is massive avoidance of ROLE relationships, we are left experiencing life "without an important aspect of the human condition—deep interpersonal relating" (Leitner, 1985, p. 88). Such an avoidance can be seen as pathological in two ways. First, it seriously limits the potential of the person. In addition, persons respond to this retreat by experiencing emptiness, meaninglessness, and guilt. Psychotherapy, therefore, involves struggling with the client around the terrors associated with ROLE relating.

Similar conceptualizations of psychopathology and psychotherapy have been offered by other clinical theoreticians. For example, Guntrip (1969) describes such avoidance from an object-relations perspective. Similarly, Yalom (1980), taking an existential perspective, views isolation as an ultimate concern. With this as background, let us turn to a discussion of Mike.

PRESENTING COMPLAINTS

Mike was 28 years old when treatment began. He was seen for a total of 107 sessions spanning 28 months. On intake, he complained of "depression" and "being unable to make decisions." These problems had been occurring for "at least 10 years." However, upon closer questioning, it became apparent that these complaints were among many which he faced.

Depression

Mike was quite depressed at intake and reported feelings of hopelessness and despair. He had daily "crying spells" and constantly felt "tired and apathetic." His school and work performance suffered badly from his needing to "withdraw from the world" every 6 weeks. During these periods, Mike would stay in bed for several days and avoid contact with others. At these times, he was quite suicidal. Indeed, he had attempted suicide by drug overdose twice within the 4 years prior to initiating therapy. He was determined to die before reaching the age of 30.

Indecisiveness

Mike's inability to make decisions could be seen in many aspects of his life. Since he was unable to decide on career or educational objectives, he drifted from job to job and college major to college major. He constantly questioned and qualified any statement he made about himself. Further, he reported often "staring into the closet for 45 minutes trying to decide what clothes to wear." The indecisiveness also was manifested in his initiating therapy. Mike cancelled our first appointment three times as he struggled with the decision to enter therapy. Obviously, the risk of committing himself to therapy was going to be a major issue for him.

Sexual Confusion

Mike was actively struggling with questions of sexual identity. At intake, he could not decide if he was "straight, gay, or bisexual." He was involved in a sexual relationship with a woman (Joan) for the first time in his life. He also reported having several homosexual relationships since he was 13 years old. This had resulted in many oppressive experiences in his small-town high school.

Impulse Control

Mike also had serious issues with impulse control. He had a long history of polydrug abuse. Further, he described instances in which he had acted in an impulsive and hostile manner when he felt someone had wronged him. For example, when a woman took a parking space by cutting in front of him, Mike flattened her tires. He described scratching the paint of a car which took two parking spaces and "forced me to park further from the store." He also put sulfur in the heating system of the car of someone who angered him.

Identity Confusion

Mike described experiencing himself as seven different individuals. Six of these seven personalities were female. He was afraid that an eighth personality might exist as he had experienced "blank periods" (intervals of time which he could not recall). These periods, which dated to the age of five or six, were increasing in frequency of late.

Mary Grace, one of the seven personalities, was described as a "lady in all things." She was "quiet and soft spoken" and would make a "perfect wife and mother." Judy was "very self-centered and talented." She "likes attention but doesn't like all that goes with it." Kate, on the other hand, was a "queen" with noble carriage and posture. She comes out "when there is a need for great dignity and courage." Marilyn had "no self-esteem." Consequently, she needed "constant reassurance" and liked "to be taken care of." Vi was the "efficient one." She worked hard and did not like any "nonsense" on the job. However, she wished she could be more like "one of the girls."

Mary, the contrast to Mary Grace, was the personality who dealt with therapy at many crucial junctures. She was "very seldom a lady in anything she did." She was "very free" where men are concerned and was "very bored with the sexual and social standards of the middle class." She was also quite envious of the other personalities. All in all, she was a "hostile, seductive bitch." Finally, Alexander, the only male personality, was *"very"* attractive to women." He was aware of this and often used it to manipulate women to his advantage.

PERSONAL CONSTRUCT CONCEPTUALIZATION

ROLE Relationships

Obviously, such problems affected Mike's abilities to develop intimate ROLE relationships (Leitner, 1985). However, Mike's constructions of others also showed a systematic withdrawal from interpersonal contact. According to Mike, others were to be used before they used him. The other person was not valued and understood as a unique, evolving self. When someone would begin to care for him, Mike tried to destroy the relationship. For example, Mike described one experience where he agreed to meet a man at a bar. While there, he allowed himself to be seduced by a stranger while the caring man watched helplessly, severely damaging the developing relationship.

In this context, one way of construing each of his symptoms involves looking at their role in Mike's avoiding the terror of ROLE relationships. For example, fragmenting the self into several personalities minimizes the impact of invalidation. First, such complexity is difficult to understand. If others could not understand Mike, they would be less able to invalidate his core constructs. Further, if different aspects of the self are kept in different personalities, Mike can choose to reveal only limited aspects of himself in relationships. As a result, core structures involving the other personalities could avoid invalidation in that particular relationship.

Mike's other symptoms also can be construed as protecting him from the devastating implications of core ROLE construct invalidation as they have the effect of preventing Mike from risking the extended commitment needed in ROLE relationships. Depression saps the energy to make such a commitment. Indecisiveness allows him to ruminate incessantly without "taking the plunge." Impulsiveness scares others away or leads Mike to flee the relationship suddenly. However, as with most individuals seeking therapy, Mike viewed the symptoms as devastating experiences to be eliminated at the earliest possible moment. Helping Mike construe his symptoms as inventions made to protect himself from potential devastation would be an important therapeutic goal.

Construct System Diagnosis

The precipitating event for Mike's seeking therapy was the threat he experienced in his sexual relationship with Joan. This can be seen in one of Mike's core ROLE constructs: "self as male–self as female," obviously a construct of sexual and personal identity. Until the relationship with Joan, Mike had been trying to identify himself as "female." Interestingly, Mike's six female personalities experienced his sexual encounters with men as heterosexual, not homosexual.

In this context, "self as male–self as female" must be understood in the context of two other constructs: "good self–bad self" and "good other–bad other." Being female was equated with power, control, and others being attracted to him. Mike believed that every male was in Mary's power and that, in any interpersonal duel, he would "win," making the other person weak and dependent on him. Being a male (Alexander) also implied making others weak and dependent on him. In both scenarios, Mike is powerful while the other is pathetic. Obviously, either construction prevents invalidation of Mike's self-worth.

These points become clearer if Mike's relationship with his parents is considered. His father had a serious drinking problem dating from Mike's early childhood. When drunk, his father physically assaulted his mother and the children. Once, when his mother was being beaten, Mike hit his father with a baseball bat. His father lost consciousness for several minutes. Subsequently, Mike has experienced recurring fears of having caused his father permanent brain damage. When drunk, his father now tells Mike how much he loves him.

His mother's interactions with Mike involved the use of guilt. His mother described how much suffering she experienced and the amount of work she performed because of Mike. She stated that she wanted a divorce because of his father's violence but that she could not do so "for the kids' sake." His mother was too depressed about the marriage to give emotionally to her children. In spite of that, she stated that she would sacrifice everything for them.

Thus, Mike's construction of these relationships led him to feel a contradiction between positive constructions of self and other. If his parents are "good parents" (which they must be since they love and sacrifice for their children), he is a "bad self" (for causing them physical and mental pain). Mike would have to believe that his parents "deserved" their pain for him to construe himself as "good." Hence, "good self" implied "bad parents."

Since events with his parents were Mike's first experiences with the "good self–bad self" construct in relationship to "good other–bad other," it is understandable why he experienced others who threaten him with closeness as "bad," "weak," and "pathetic." As a result, others were treated with contempt. This particularly became the case in regard to sex. When Mike became sexually involved with someone, the other person was no longer a person; he was a "trick." The construct of "friend-trick" was a central one for Mike. "Friends" were totally asexual; "tricks" were sexual.

Therefore, as long as Mary or Alexander could seduce anyone they desire, anyone threatening Mike with closeness was reexperienced as a "trick." By using sexuality as a retreat from ROLE relationships, Mike continued to construe the self as "good" by construing the other as "bad." As long as he or she can be seduced, the other cannot threaten him. However, with age, Mike believed he would become less attractive and, therefore, less able to use sex to protect himself from terror. Hence, Mike was determined to kill himself before growing old.

Thus, both "self as male" and "self as female" offered Mike equal opportunities and dilemmas. He used both poles as a protection against experiencing himself as a "bad self." However, he experienced profound loneliness and emptiness due to inadequate and incomplete ROLE relationships. Obviously, resolving this issue would be linked to the "good self-bad other" experience.

Since relationships with parents often form the bases of other ROLE relationships, one can understand why Mike had structured his relationships with others in the ways described above. Mike's seven personalities also make sense. Each personality can handle part of a relationship without risking devastation by the implications of total ROLE relating. Thus, the terror is not experienced totally by any one personality; it is spread over several. In other words, the forming of the seven personalities is consistent with Kelly's (1955) principle of the elaborative choice. The system is preserved, albeit tenuously.

Repertory Grid Data

Early in therapy, Mike completed a repertory grid (repgrid) involving the 15 roles utilized by Landfield (1971). Constructs were generated by having Mike describe an important characteristic of each person on the list followed by an opposite to that characteristic. Mike's confusion and disorganization were quite evident on the grid. For example, his FIC score (a measure of construct differentiation ranging from 2 to 30) was 25. FIC scores greater than 20 are linked to a confused and chaotic experience of the world (Landfield & Epting, 1986). His NEWORD score (an indirect measure of the ability to organize complexity in hierarchy) was 33.2; this is a standard deviation below the mean of 39.8 for this measure (Curtin & Leitner, 1983). Thus, Mike's ability to integrate his high degree of differentiation is limited.

As might be expected with such confusion, there is little meaning in

Mike's life. The extremity score, a measure of subjective meaningfulness derived from rating scale polarization on the grid, can range from 0 (low meaningfulness) to 1,350 (extreme meaningfulness). Mike's score of 460 is almost three standard deviations below what is typically seen (Curtin & Leitner, 1983). He could not apply constructs to individuals on the grid an extraordinary 47% of the time. Further, the meaningfulness of the construction of any individual on the grid can vary from 0 to 90. Only two of the 15 persons construed by Mike had scores greater than 40. Such results highlight Mike's difficulty in understanding others in a meaningful manner. The sole meaningful figures in Mike's life seemed to be the seven personalities. In this context, the meaningfulness of these seven personalities ranged from a low of 45 (Judy) to a high of 89 (Kate and Mary). This led me to hypothesize that Mike used these personalities to prevent the total collapse of a meaningful construct system; at least these seven "persons" could be meaningfully understood.

TREATMENT

Based upon this assessment, it seemed critical for Mike to resolve the massive potential invalidations associated with ROLE relatedness. He had an empty, meaningless existence rather than a life filled with personally construed meanings. It seemed clear that my task involved helping Mike to reconstrue the relationship between sex and intimacy in ways that would allow him the freedom to risk the terror of ROLE relating. Before this reconstruction could be accomplished, some resolution of the "self as male–self as female" and "gay self–straight self" constructs had to occur. (My hope was that Mike would arrive at a construction of himself as male but without the implications that maleness had before therapy.) However, Mike would not risk these constructs until the "good self–bad other" dilemma was resolved.

Once Mike could risk ROLE relating, the seven personalities could be abandoned as they would no longer be useful. Of course, Mike's terror of ROLE relating would manifest itself repeatedly in his relationship with me. These terrors would present both great difficulties as well as opportunities. If handled appropriately, they would allow for the "here and now" testing of core constructions in a living relationship. By struggling through the terror with him, opportunities for reconstruction would emerge.

Initial Phase

The initial phase of the therapy was used to accomplish several goals. I was extremely concerned about setting ground rules for the therapy that would allow both of us to feel free to be creative in thinking about his life. With this in mind, I wanted to reduce time pressures, pressures to act on ideas prematurely, and destructive feelings of guilt. These pressures hinder the weaving from loose to tight construing necessary in the creativity cycle. To set the stage for this, I told Mike:

Therapy is a bit different than other relationships you may have. My view of therapy is that it is a place to come and think about your life more deeply than you may have ever thought about it before. Most of the time in the real world, we are too busy going from day to day to stop and just *think* about who we are and what we are about. Within these four walls, you are safe to think and feel anything without there being *any* requirement to do anything about it. As a matter of fact, you do not have to tell anyone anything about what we discuss here. What we will do is talk about your feelings about the issues and people in your life. We will try to understand how you have come to live your life as you have as well as how you want your life to go from here. Such exploration takes time. It is important that you give us the time we need to think things through carefully. As we do this, I may very well become a part of your life and you may have feelings about me. If so, we can talk about these just as we can talk about your feelings about other people.

(This last part opened the way for the critical exploration of the therapy relationship.)

I continued to support this position throughout the therapy. For example, our 10th session was concerned with how he and Joan were using no contraceptive devices. Mike hoped she would get pregnant so that, if the relationship ended, they could fight over the baby. Mike spoke of how he might kill her if they were to fight.

Clinical Vignette 1

LARRY: Tell me about these thoughts.

MIKE: It would be romantic to kill your lover during a fight over the baby. Then I could spend my life in jail for having killed for my child. How romantic.

LARRY: So a part of you thinks it would be romantic to kill her in a fight over the baby. I wonder what role romanticism has played in your life.

MIKE: I've always been a romantic. I wish I had been born a Southern Belle in the early 1800s.

LARRY: Have there been any romantic experiences in your life?

MIKE: Are you kidding? We've talked about my folks.

LARRY: What would your life have been like if you had not been romantic?

MIKE: I couldn't have made it. The romanticism gave me my only escape. I would have died.

LARRY: So you became a romantic in order to survive the situation with your parents.

MIKE: That's right.

LARRY: That implies that, on some level, you don't want to die. Rather, you want to love and be loved. Tell me about those desires.

This excerpt demonstrates my implementation of the therapy ground rules. I refused to do anything other than explore and understand his experience of the fantasies about Joan. I did not urge Mike to change his behavior concerning contraceptives nor did I attempt to extract reassurance that he would not kill her. Rather, I dealt with the latter point as I would any fantasy or feeling. Premature concern over unwanted pregnancies or fantasies of killing his lover could communicate to Mike that I felt aspects of his experiences were so frightening that they would force me to deviate from my therapeutic stance. If these experiences were so frightening to me, how could he be expected to deal with them?

Mike validated my stance by elaborating beyond the fantasy into the role romanticism played for him in his life. His adoption of a romantic lifestyle to stay alive at all costs gave me a powerful experiential argument against his determination to commit suicide in the near future. I then used this to open a discussion of the costs of romanticism. In particular, Mike kept this core romantic ROLE divorced from his relationships with people. While he did not have to experience others crushing it, he also prevented others from seeing and validating these core experiences. I commented that it would be interesting to see him struggling with more openly showing the vulnerable romantic part of him with me. (This once again is my inviting him to explore and understand the implications of his life.)

This vignette also illustrates Mike's goals for the initial phase of therapy. Essentially, he had to determine whether it was safe to discuss the devastating experiences of his life. Through his actions, Mike was asking, "Is this person strong enough to respect my struggle with these issues or will he hide from my by giving me answers, advice, medication, etc.?" Until he knew that I was not going to retreat from understanding his experiences, he was not going to discuss openly the profound terrors of his life.

In response to my stance in clinical vignette 1, Mary (one of the personalities described earlier) was present at our next session.

Clinical Vignette 2

LARRY: (after learning that Mary was in the session): So, tell me about yourself.

MIKE: (Mary): I am a slut and proud of it. The others hate me for it but who gives a fuck.

LARRY: What makes you proud of being a slut?

MIKE: Everyone is a slut, only some people don't know it. That gives me power over them. I know it. No man can resist me. Their desire for me allows me to crush the fuckers.

LARRY: So, tell me, why is having power over and crushing the fuckers so important?

MIKE: Listen, in this world it is use or be used . . . Crush or be crushed. If you don't understand that you're a pathetic fool.

LARRY: (noting the construct of crush or be crushed–a pathetic fool): So you crush others before they can crush you.

MIKE: That's right.

LARRY: So, while they think you are a "bitch," you really protect them by crushing other people before they crush y'all. What made you decide to come out now?

MIKE: You're lying to them. You're telling them to hope when there is no hope. You're making them want to trust. The fucking fools.

LARRY: I'm curious. How am I doing that?

MIKE: By how you interact with them.

LARRY: My sitting back and understanding makes them want to hope and trust. Since you are their protector, you must have some interesting feelings about me.

MIKE: I am going to find a way to get you just like I've gotten everyone else. Everyone has their soft underbelly and can be had.

LARRY: It sounds like I threaten you right now. Tell me about that.

MIKE: No way. You aren't gonna trick me like the others.

LARRY: Trick you?

MIKE: Yeah. Get me to talk so that I might hope.

LARRY: Hmmm. So, if you would talk, you would hope also. It sounds like you also have stong needs to be understood and cared for. The only way you can control them is to crush. Otherwise, *your feelings,* not theirs, may lead to pain.

MIKE: (Cries.)

LARRY: What's it like to be so misunderstood? To want others to care and yet not be able to let them?

These two vignettes illustrate my approach to the initial phase of psychotherapy—exploring and understanding Mike's constructions of his experiences. In addition to the themes covered in the vignettes, Mike was quite ambivalent about the therapy process. I responded to his ambivalence by trying to explore and understand it in the same manner as I explored other material. I had predicted his ambivalence in the initial session due to his complaints of indecisiveness. On intake, I stated that it would be interesting to see how his indecisiveness "played itself out" in terms of deciding about therapy. By predicting his experience, I attempted to communicate to Mike that part of his construct system was understandable. I hoped this communication would reduce the terror associated with self-exploration.

Intimacy

By session 15, Mike was ready to struggle more actively with the issue of intimacy in the therapy relationship. This struggle manifested itself in Mary and Mary Grace's dueling over who would talk to me. Mary was determined to distrust me as I would destroy them in ways other people had never been able to. When I commented that this only seemed possible if Mary herself was beginning to trust me, Mike became most upset. It was true that she was trusting. She felt like a fool. Trusting someone meant being trapped by the commitment and exposing yourself to being crushed. (Note the dilemma between the terror of invalidation in a ROLE relationship and the need for such a relationship.) We spent many sessions exploring the ways in which commitment is entrapping as well as the traps one gets into when there is no commitment. This culminated when Mike stated that he had to choose between caring for others as people (ROLE relating) with the risk of being "crushed to the core" (terror) and "having loneliness and emptiness eat away at my soul like a cancer" (Leitner, 1985, p. 93).

The Core

The focus of therapy shifted at this point. Mike began to deal with the two central constructs described earlier (self as male–self as female and self as gay–self as straight). I viewed this as implicit validation of our work to this point. Since these constructs could not be explored until the "good self–bad other; good other–bad self" dilemma had been resolved, I construed this shift as Mike's telling me that both of us could be "good." With this as background, he was willing to explore core ROLE constructs in therapy. In other words, he was willing to risk potentially devastating invalidation in this relationship.

Mike shared his struggle in two ways. First, he described his confusion over whether he was "really" a man or a woman trapped in a man's body. In addition, he described his pain over others (particularly his parents) not accepting his sexual preference. These sessions alternated between periods of great confusion (for both of us) and tremendous pain. At times, the pain would be so severe that he expressed fantasies of terminating therapy. These fantasies differed from earlier ones in that they were clearly tied to the pain Mike was feeling between sessions. Further, Mike recognized that these wishes reflected his desire to retreat from openly sharing his experiences in the ROLE relationship of psychotherapy. Finally, Mike always concluded that the pain, though "unbearable" at times, was preferable to "the empty excuse for an existence" he led while ignoring these issues.

Clincial Vignette 3

MIKE: I'm not in a good mood today.

LARRY: You're not in a good mood? Tell me about it.

MIKE: "Tell me about it." There you go again.

LARRY: (Silence.)

MIKE: I can't stop thinking about these issues. They are with me all the time. They permeate my existence.

LARRY: So tell me what happens when these issues are so powerful.

MIKE: I leave the sessions all upset. I cry all the time. This makes me decide that I'm never coming back again. What's strange is that, after three or four days I'm ready to come back.

LARRY: How do you understand that?

MIKE: I think these sessions have made me realize how hurt, angry, and lonely I am. (Voice cracks.) I'm afraid I'll just hurt forever.

LARRY: Yeah. I know.

MIKE: I need to let others see me. But people have never liked me. They find out about me, then cuss me, yell at me, or beat me up. They call me names.

LARRY: (after getting Mike to elaborate on some of the specific situations): So our visits are causing you to look at some pretty awful things that have happened to you when you've gotten close to people. What makes you decide to come back?

MIKE: (Beginning to cry.) Understanding these things is my *only hope* to change. I know that.

This vignette illustrates how far Mike had come at this point in the therapy. I can be significantly less active than earlier as Mike is working productively. His willingness to elaborate these issues with little prompting from me is a sign he has become less threatened by the therapy process (i.e., we can both be "good"). While none of Mike's *specific* complaints had been resolved (e.g., self as male–self as female), he was willing to risk ROLE relating with me. Once this risk was taken, resolution of the specific issues could occur. It remained to be seen, though, what form the resolution would take.

Male–Female

Mike began exploring the self as male–self as female construct in great detail. In particular, he actively began to elaborate how he would think, feel, and act toward others if he was a woman as well as how they would interact with him. We also explored how he would think, feel, and act toward others if he decided he was a man. Being a man was strange to him as it implied that he was homosexual. In contrast, construing himself as a woman made him "feel free."

Exploration of this issue involved Mike's considering the implications of the construct "having a sex change operation–staying a biological male." An operation was appealing as it would mean "freedom" to be the woman he always felt he was. However, if his request for an operation was denied, his "biological self" and his "psychological self" always would be incompatible. This would be "total hopelessness" for Mike. Thus, considering an operation led to risking the construct of "freedom–total hopelessness." On the other hand, "staying a biological male" was appealing in that he could "always have hope for the future" (i.e., he could be evaluated for surgery at some later point). However, not trying for an operation made him "feel like a hypocrite."

After many sessions, Mike concluded that the potential freedom of a sex change operation was worth the risk of "total hopelessness." Thus, he decided to risk testing the core construct of "self as male–self as female" in the public arena. He was stating, "I define myself as female. Let's see what happens." At this point, he contacted a clinic that evaluated and performed sex change operations.

I would like to make a few points about this phase of psychotherapy. First, my initial hope for the "self as male–self as female" construct involved Mike's defining himself as "male" but reducing constellatory implications associated with being male. Thus, Mike's potential solution differed from my "ideal" one. At the same time, I viewed Mike's decision as healthy. He was willing to risk testing his construct system publicly, knowing invalidation would be devastating. His willingness to assume responsibility for dealing with that invalidation showed courage (Leitner, 1983). (Note the greater concern with issues around the *process* of construing rather than the specific *content* of the constructs.) Finally, as detailed above, Mike's testing of the construct self as male–self as female was tied to the security of our ROLE relationship.

Mike's placement of himself on the female side of this construct was validated when, after a thorough medical, psychological, and historical examination, the professionals decided that a sex change operation was in order. This agency began a two year program with Mike that would culminate in the sex change operation. The agency's decision led us to consider the self as male–self as female construct in a different context—represented by his parents.

Mike was very concerned about his parents reactions to his decision. This led us into issues of how much he wanted his parents' approval, support, and love. Mike was enraged at their not giving him the love he desired. McCoy (1977) has defined anger as the "awareness of invalidation of constructs leading to hostility" (p. 121). Within personal construct theory, hostility is refusing to reconstrue events in order to protect the system from overwhelming invalidation. The constructs being invalidated are too important to give up. It was important, therefore, to understand what constructs were being threatened in relationship to his parents.

It appeared that Mike's placement of himself on the "good self" pole of the "good self–bad self" construct was being threatened. He lived at home in order to "take care of" his folks while his brother and sister had moved away. He provided most of the money for family needs. He ran errands for them. He allowed his mother to use his charge cards on which he paid the bill. He genuinely loved them and had done much to show them his love. However, they viewed him as "weird" and "sick," because he was either gay or going to have a sex change operation. His brother and sister (who were seen as "normal") had been through countless divorces, breakups, and job terminations. He wondered why they got approval while he did not.

This illustrates that rage (and, by implication, hostility) is not always negative. Rather, one must look at the constructs the anger is trying to protect. In this case, the rage was tied to testing his construction of self-worth. Rather than being an irrational or dangerous emotion to be eradicated or controlled, anger can be construed as an indication of therapeutic growth. My response to the experience of anger was to explore the implications of this experience for Mike's relationships with his family.

Clinical Vignette 4

LARRY: What's it like for you in this sort of relationship?

MIKE: Very stressful. It takes all of my financial and emotional energy.

LARRY: So, tell me, how did you get yourself in such a situation?

MIKE: Somebody has to take care of them. I mean they are old and sick.

LARRY: So you feel an *obligation* to take care of them. How did this obligation get put on you?

MIKE: Well, you know my brother and sister. They don't do nothin' for them.

LARRY: What would it be like if you were less involved in doing things for them?

MIKE: My parents couldn't make it. It's that simple.

LARRY: They sound as dependent on you as you on them.

MIKE: You know . . . that's right.

LARRY: I wonder why you three have structured your relationships such that dependency is so sticky?

As clinical vignette 4 illustrates, Mike began to explore his parents dependency on him. My final question was the basis for productive work in subsequent sessions. Mike talked to his parents about their "stifling" interdependency. He began to view his willingness to let them be so dependent on him as a way of permitting them to avoid the responsibility of solving their difficulties. Mike then decided that it was in everyone's best interest to become less dependent on one another. (During this period, I was afraid Mike might slot-rattle and forever stop relating to his parents. Since I viewed this as antitherapeutic, I worked hard to help him see the advantages *and* disadvantages of dependency. The construing of dependency in more complex ways lessens the likelihood of slot-rattling.) Mike paid off the charges, had his mother's name removed from his charge cards, and moved to a house in the same neighborhood as his parents. He wanted to have some independence yet still be available should they need him.

As Mike reconstrued his parents, he began to test the possibility of linking "good self" to "good other" in different contexts. Based upon his struggling with ROLE relationships both in and out of therapy, Mike decided to risk caring for another person. Mike began a relationship with a man in which sex was not used as a retreat. Rather, he was determined to know more about him as a person. At about the same time, he took a job in a social service agency so that he could "help people." In other words, he was willing to invest in others and risk the terror of invalidation of core constructs.

TERMINATION

Mike felt like he was ready to consider ending therapy because of improvements in the major issues which had led to his seeking therapy. Clinically, he was less depressed and isolated. He had several friends who seemed to be genuinely interested in his welfare. He enjoyed his job and was respected by his peers. He was more able to make decisions and was willing to live with the consequences of those decisions. The issues of sexual confusion and emotional closeness were clearer to him. Finally, he no longer experienced himself as fragmented into seven personalities. Rather, he had sorted through the terror that led to the fragmentation and experienced himself as more integrated.

I agreed with Mike that termination seemed appropriate. We set a date for termination 3 months from that point. Since Mike was significantly invested in our ROLE relationship, I wanted him to have sufficient time to work through the pain of leaving therapy. Thus, termination from therapy became the focus of our final sessions. In our final session, Mike said, "There are two things that stand out about our visits. First, I'm not always responsible. Second, you can bitch as long as you want but eventually you gotta *do* something." This statement shows that Mike's construction of issues of responsibility had grown substantially.

POST-THERAPY REPERTORY GRID

At the conclusion of therapy, Mike completed another repgrid. The mathe-
matical analysis of the grid was consistent with the clinical changes described
earlier. His FIC score (25 on the first grid) had declined to 14 while his
NEWORD score (33.2 on the first grid) had risen to 41.5. These scores
suggest that the profound confusion and disorganization seen on the first
grid had been replaced by a complex, yet integrating structure. Similarly,
people were seen as more meaningful in his world, although his extremity
score (579) was almost two standard deviations below what is typically found
(Curtin & Leitner, 1983). Finally, his percentage of "not apply" ratings had
decreased from 47% to just 10%. This latter result showed Mike's increased
ability to use his constructs in understanding other people.

It can be recalled that the seven personalities were construed meaningfully by Mike at the beginning of therapy. All seven personalities showed a
decrease in meaningfulness on the final repgrid. Mary, for example, had a
decrease in meaningfulness of 41 points (89 to 48). Similarly, Violet had a
meaningfulness score of 11, Alexander 13, and Judy 0. Kate, the other
extremely meaningful pretherapy personality, declined from 89 to 45. In
other words, Mike felt less "need" to fragment himself into various
"personalities."

SOME INTEGRATING THOUGHTS

I have presented a summary of a complicated psychotherapy case. The focus
has been more on what was actually said and done in therapy as opposed to
a discussion of theoretical or technical issues. However, some discussion of
the underlying technical principles appears to be in order.

First, my approach throughout the therapy focused on the establishment
of a ROLE relationship with the client: I attempted to construe his
construing process. My view of his construing as a process was my greatest
ally in therapy. Mike explored his ways of retreating from ROLE relationships in therapy. As we dealt with these issues, I did not get involved in
telling him he was doing it wrong. Rather, by exploring and understanding,
I provided an environment in which constructs potentially could be
clarified, tested, modified, or abandoned. However, it was Mike's process of
construing and reconstruing that led to profound growth. Having faith in
the process of growth within the client is a prerequisite of psychotherapeutic
success.

Since the person construes and reconstrues based upon his/her experiences, the therapist does not provide new constructs for the client.

Rather, therapy is exploring the person's life in order to give the client experiences to reconstrue in his or her own way. Thus, I did not "integrate" a "multiple personality." I explored a person's life in order to understand why he fragmented himself. It was Mike's decision to risk the potential terror of ROLE relating over the emptiness of a life without deep interpersonal understandings. In other words, my responsibility was to provide him with therapeutic experiences. Mike's responsibility was to construe and reconstrue those experiences.

Further, my preconceived notions of what constructs Mike should end up employing were not used to force Mike into living life my way. Once again, I focused more on Mike's handling of the process of construing and reconstruing his ROLE relationships in making clinical judgments about therapeutic growth. I feel that more content-oriented approaches may solve the immediate problems but can damage the person in the long-run. In this context, it should be noted that constructs of process may not be verbalized. Rather, one must pay careful attention to more implicit indications of change. Often the major validations or invalidations of one's therapeutic work occur on this implicit level. Further, if the implicit messages are invalidating the therapeutic work, I reconstrue the client. In other words, I assume I am wrong—not that the client is resisting.

A final technical principle concerns the therapist's comfort with intense emotions. Kelly (1955, p. 666) stated that emotion is to the therapist as blood is to the surgeon. In order to be helpful with severely disturbed persons, the therapist must be comfortable with intense and often negative affect. There were many instances in the therapy when Mike's emotions were quite intense. Rather than being blown away by his emotions, I continued exploring and understanding Mike's experiences. In so doing, the process of therapy helped Mike to experience greater freedom in approaching ROLE relationships, as emotions could be seen as something other than literal truths about who he was as a person (Landfield, 1980a; Leitner, 1982). Ultimately, I believe the goal of personal construct psychotherapy is increasing personal freedom.

REFERENCES

Curtin, T., & Leitner, L. M. (1983, July). *Organization of the construction of self.* Presented at the Fifth International Congress on Personal Construct Psychology, Boston.

Epting, F. R. (1984). *Personal construct counseling and psychotherapy.* London: Wiley.

Guntrip, H. (1969). *Schizoid phenomena, object relations, and the self.* New York: International Universities Press.

Karst, T. O. (1980). The relationship between personal construct theory and psychotherapeutic techniques. In A. W. Landfield & L. M. Leitner (Eds.),

Personal construct psychology: Psychotherapy and personality (pp. 166-184). New York: Wiley Interscience.

Kelly, G. A. (1955). *The psychology of personal constructs.* New York: Norton.

Landfield, A. W. (1971). *Personal construct systems in psychotherapy.* Chicago: Rand McNally.

Landfield, A. W. (1980a). The person as perspectivist, literalist, and chaotic fragmentalist. In A. W. Landfield & L. M. Leitner (Eds.), *Personal construct psychology: Psychotherapy and personality* (pp. 289-320). New York: Wiley Interscience.

Landfield, A. W. (1980b). Personal construct psychotherapy: A personal construction. In A. W. Landfield & L. M. Leitner (Eds.), *Personal construct psychology: Psychotherapy and personality* (pp. 122-140). New York: Wiley Interscience.

Landfield, A. W., & Epting, F. R. (1986). *Personal construct psychology: Clinical and personality assessment.* New York: Human Sciences Press.

Leitner, L. M. (1980). Personal construct therapy of a severely disturbed woman: The case of Sue. In A. W. Landfield & L. M. Leitner (Eds.), *Personal construct psychology: Psychotherapy and personality* (pp. 102-121). New York: Wiley Interscience.

Leitner, L. M. (1982). Literalism, perspectivism, chaotic fragmentalism and psychotherapy techniques. *British Journal of Medical Psychology, 55,* 307-317.

Leitner, L. M. (1983, July). *Sociality and optimal functioning.* Presented at the Fifth International Congress on Personal Construct Psychology, Boston.

Leitner, L. M. (1985). The terrors of cognition: On the experiential validity of personal construct theory. In D. Bannister (Ed.), *Issues and approaches in personal construct theory* (pp. 83-103). London: Academic.

McCoy, M. M. (1977). A reconstruction of emotion. In D. Bannister (Ed.), *New perspectives in personal construct theory* (pp. 93-124). London: Academic.

Neimeyer, R. A. (1980). George Kelly as therapist: A review of his tapes. In A. W. Landfield & L. M. Leitner (Eds.), *Personal construct psychology: Psychotherapy and personality* (pp. 74-101). New York: Wiley.

Yalom, I. (1980). *Existential psychotherapy.* New York: Basic Books.

4

Core Role Reconstruction in Personal Construct Therapy

Robert A. Neimeyer

It is typically the case that people seek professional therapy only when their efforts at surmounting a life problem have failed, that is, when "self-change" (Mahoney, 1979) has already been attempted but has proven unsuccessful. In spite of the diversity of presenting problems associated with such impasses, these situations share a common feature: the person is unable to envision fresh paths of action that would lead to problem resolution. In personal construct terms, this might be understood as a breakdown in constructive alternativism: the sense that all workable means of approaching the problem have been exhausted and that one is indeed the victim of one's biography, hemmed in by circumstances beyone one's control.

Although it is undeniable that factors in our social and physical environment frequently contribute to these impasses (e.g., lack of satisfying work opportunities, failure of relatives to cooperate with our change attempts), it is equally true that obstacles to change often originate within ourselves. Perhaps the most fundamental of these obstacles arises when those changes necessary to resolve the problem are somehow precluded by our very sense of who we are. Clinically, difficulties of this sort may be reflected in a client's guilt after having engaged in what (to the therapist) was a new, adaptive behavior. Even more often, it may take the form of resistance to the therapist's directives to change, on the grounds that "I just couldn't be like that" or "That just wouldn't be me." Common to all of these predicaments is the vague sense that one's *identity* is bound up with one's *problem,* so that changes in the latter necessitate changes in the former.

In trying to clarify difficulties of this kind, Kelly (1955) introduced the concept of *core role structure.* In contrast to our colloquial use of the term "role" to designate a simple set of behaviors appropriate to a given situation, Kelly used it to refer to "one's deepest understanding of being maintained as a social being" (1955, p. 502). Thus,

> Our constructions of our roles are not altogether superficial affairs—masks to be put on and taken off for the sake of social appearances only. Our constructions of our relationships to the thinking and expectancies of certain other people reach down deeply into our vital processes. Through our constructions of our roles we sustain even the most autonomic life functions (Kelly, 1955, p. 909).

In order to understand how our identities can become problematic and at the same time resist change, it is useful to recognize the multifaceted nature of the self as conceptualized within personal construct theory (Bannister, 1983; G. Neimeyer & R. Neimeyer, 1985). Rather than representing a solitary psychological entity or object, our sense of self is mapped within a complex network of interrelated role constructs, each of which helps us situate one aspect of our identity in relation to other people. For example, in various interpersonal contexts I might describe myself as "competitive" as opposed to "uninvolved," "listening to others" as opposed to "tuning them out," and "playful" as opposed to "overly serious." These subordinate constructions might in turn be tightly or loosely organized under more comprehensive superordinate constructs related to "living intensely vs. just existing," or "caring vs. not caring."

Problems arise when the individual confronts situations in which neither behavioral alternative represented by a salient construct is viable (as when one applies "competitive vs. uninvolved" in an intimate relationship instead of on the racquetball court). These difficulties are further compounded when necessary changes along a subordinate dimension (e.g., learning to "tune out" as opposed to "listen to" a chronically complaining acquaintance) imply fundamental changes in one's identity on superordinate core constructs (e.g., from being "caring" to "uncaring"). In the first case, one's responses may be ineffective because they are construed in inadequate or inappropriate terms; in the second, they may be inhibited altogether because they are seen as incompatible with one's most basic values. In both cases, regaining psychological movement toward problem resolution may require a delicate elaboration or realignment in one's core role structure. This task of *core role reconstruction* can be one of the central aims of personal construct therapy and will be illustrated by the case study of Tally presented below.

BACKGROUND INFORMATION

Tally S. was a 48-year-old black woman who sought help from a university sponsored psychological services center for a variety of personal and relational problems. She had been raised, along with an older sister and brother, by a devoutly religious mother and a forceful, but emotionally distant father in a small town in the southern United States. Tally had married early and had one son by her husband, Lawrence, before divorcing him for his verbally abusive behavior and excessive drinking. For the past 16 years she had raised her son, Randy, as a single parent, and at age 24 he continued to live at home, which in Tally's eyes was a sign of his immaturity.

Tally had never been especially healthy, and her several physical problems, including partial vision loss, controlled epilepsy, and possible malignancies in her breasts, had combined to force her retirement from teaching some years before. As a deeply religious woman, Tally explained during intake that she was able to deal with her illnesses because "the Lord has removed my anxiety about them." But despite its functioning as a major resource, her religion also complicated her life. In particular, it contributed to her feeling uncomfortably "different" from others, a condition that was underscored by her experience of "mystical" precognitive dreams and visions that few others could understand. In fact, she admitted that even her friendships tended to "go sour," in spite of her apparent social poise and general likability. Tally summed up her problems with the observation that she didn't "fit into the world," even though she remained very active in the church community.

Tally's most acute relational problems centered around her son, Randy, who had a long history of drug use, vandalism, and petty theft. Recently, this behavior had led to his serving time and his subsequent placement on probation. Upon his release from jail, Randy had moved back into Tally's home and worked in a series of unskilled jobs, which he would quit impulsively. At home as well as at work, this arrangement had gone badly, with Randy failing to follow through on promises to cooperate with household chores and become more self-sufficient. Tally was at a loss as to how to manage the situation, agreeing with her sister Fay's description of her as "too easy, weak, and tenderhearted" for her own good.

SLOT CHANGE

Tally opened our second session with a barrage of complaints about Randy's cursing, tantrums, and noncompliance with household chores, likening him to "the beast of Revelation" for his contemptuous disregard for Christian values. This alerted me to the operation of the sort of rigidly dichotomized

family construct system discussed by Procter (1981), in which Tally enacted
the role of "saint" and her son the reciprocal role of "sinner." In an effort to
help her transcend this dysfunctional means of construing their relationship, I asked Tally to try to explain Randy's behavior from his own
standpoint, an attempt that met with limited success. Having failed at this
cognitive intervention, I then resorted to a more behavioral one, on the
assumption that "sometimes it is more feasible to produce readjustments by
attacking the symptoms than by going directly after the faulty structures"
(Kelly, 1955, pp. 995–996). Since Randy had refused to accompany her to
therapy, Tally and I collaborated on a straightforward behavioral contract
for her to initiate with her son—his performing mutually agreed upon
chores in return for certain privileges and spending money. Interestingly, in
light of her religious background, she spontaneously referred to this as
forming a "covenant" with Randy, terminology I also adopted in later
references to the assignment.

In the third session, Tally noted that her covenant with Randy had
"worked for a fleeting moment" before he reverted to his procrastination
and noncompliance. Reenacting their discussion of the pact, it seemed as if
Tally had approached the task in a calm, self-assured manner, disarming
Randy to the point that they had a candid talk about his use of street drugs
since his youth. But in subsequent days he failed to follow the program they
had outlined and was angered by his mother's refusal to give him money
anyway. We then explored the "act" they went into in response:

TALLY (T): That's that spoiled act. So he, he started talking ugly. Oh, I don't know
what all he said. Anyway, I reacted. First, I got my hand on the waste can.
And then I be chasing him through the house to hit him. And he got out of
my way, so I didn't get him.

BOB (B): Wait a minute! This is a real change of pace here! At first you guys are, seem
to be getting along pretty well. He's not too threatened by (the convenant),
a little surprised by your questions about drugs, but he answers them. And
now suddenly, you're chasing him through the house with a trash can.

T: Yeah, because he was standing there talking ugly to me, cause I wouldn't
give him five bucks.

With a little prompting, Tally described the content of her son's "ugly
talk"—which she had heard many times before (e.g., "You make me sick! I
hate you! I hate everybody in the world!"). I then suggested that Randy's
"hateful" shouting and Tally's "getting riled up" could be construed as a
well-rehearsed script that each of them read off in response to the other's
cues and described two ways of breaking the pattern: to "set the stage" for a
different kind of play (as she had tried with the covenant) and to refuse to
enact her part in the "tragedy." Smiling, Tally then told me about a very
different resolution that she arrived at in the aftermath of their altercation:

she contacted Randy's parole officer to arrange halfway house placement. Alert to the possibility that this was simply an extrapolation of her "raging" at him, I asked her about how she informed him of the plan:

B: And how did he react to that?

T: He's hurt. He didn't say anything. He's very quiet. And see when I take a certain tone of voice, he knows it's final. And all through the conversation when I was talking, I used the same tone of voice.

B: Is it this tone of voice?

T: I think it is. It's kind of resigned, very positive.

B: Yeah.

T: And no turning back . . . I think I was too soft now that I look back.

I began to conceptualize Tally's abrupt movement from being meek and long-suffering with her son to being enraged and threatening as a superficial *slot change* along her well-worn "weak vs. strong" role construct. In contrast, I envisioned her germinal use of a deliberate but positive tone of voice as an element representing one pole of a new and more adaptive integrating construct, one superordinate to the sharply dichotomized "strong vs. weak" dimension.

B: Do you know, what strikes me is that you've got there really three different gears that you're operating in with relation to him. And two of them seem almost like opposites to me. On the one hand you have this angry mad woman who chases him with the trash can. On the other hand, you've got this equally unrealistic, very giving mother, who will forgive anything, always give him another chance, bend over backwards for him, etc., etc., etc. And then, quite different from both of those, is this Tally who speaks with this assured tone of voice, kind of resigned but pretty positive, and who says, "Enough is enough. This is the way it's going to be." And it seems that it's only in that third gear that you don't get pulled into something. You don't get suckered in and you don't get enraged. Does that make sense?

T: Yes, that makes sense.

Tally then described how she had given Randy several chances to make good on their convenant, and how she felt he had just "pushed her around." I used this description to flesh out the contrast pole of her emerging superordinate construct concerning being assured and "in control" as opposed to "manipulated" by someone else.

B: I guess the thing that strikes me about this is that when you're operating in either of these two modes, chasing him around the house with a trash can or giving him chance after chance, in both of those cases you're being manipulated by him. He's the one who's pulling the strings and you're the one who's dancing.

T: And he knows that. He knows he is. He's just manipulated me his whole life.

B: But on the other hand, when you come across with this self-assured, self-confident approach, you know, it's clear you're in control of your actions. You know he isn't pulling the strings.

T: Right.

B: That sounds like where you need to be more often; that you'd be less frustrated if you could deal with him out of that position.

T: Well, I'm going to try, because I know it doesn't pay to handle him in those other ways. I probably am just as much responsible for his behavior, because I shouldn't have done it through the years.

INITIAL REPGRID TESTING

In session four, I decided to focus more closely on the network of role constructs that undergirded her problematic interactions with other people. This entailed the administration of a Repertory Grid (repgrid) to help Tally articulate her constructions of several important figures in her life. The results of this technique were especially valuable in suggesting later therapeutic goals and so will be discussed more below.

The grid I administered to Tally took the form of a structured interview, in which I provided her sets of three index cards, on which I had printed the names of various significant others (e.g., parents, sister, ex-husband, son, friends, self, and therapist) who she had mentioned in our earlier interviews. After placing each sort in front of her, I asked her to "tell me some important way in which two of the figures are alike and different from the third," and recorded her answer (e.g., "My Grandma and sister are sincerely religious, whereas my father had no real religious experience") as a bipolar construct on a separate form. This procedure was repeated with different triads of elements until Tally had provided ten construct dimensions. Following this construct elicitation step, she was asked to rate each of the figures on thirteen point (-6 through 0 to $+6$) Likert type scales anchored by the two construct poles. Tally's responses to this task are summarized in Figure 4.1, where the numbers beneath each figure represent Tally's rating of that person on the corresponding construct pole on that line. Thus, she rated her mother as very religious (-5 on construct 1) and fairly outspoken (-4 on construct 2). A more detailed explanation of this form of "rating grid" has been provided by G. Neimeyer and R. Neimeyer (1981), and background reading on grid construction and analysis can be found in several sources (Beail, 1985; Button, 1985; Fransella & Bannister, 1977; Shaw, 1981; Slater, 1976; Thomas & Harri-Augstein, 1985).

Tally's pattern of ratings of figures on constructs was then analyzed using Landfield's (1983) Reptest Scoring Program, one of several computerized grid analysis packages now available. The results of this scoring yielded several provocative hypotheses concerning the framework she used for

RESPONSE SHEET

Column 1 (−6 to −1)	Mother (1)	Father (2)	Tally (3)	Therapist (4)	Son (5)	Grandmother (6)	Friend (7)	Ex-husband (8)	Prayer group (9)	Sister (10)	Column 2 (+1 to +6)
1 sincerely religious	−5	(+1)	−5	+1	+1	(−6)	−4	+6	−5	(−6)	no real religious experience 1
2 outspoken	(−4)	−5	(+5)	+2	−4	(−2)	−5	−6	+2	−5	timid, hesitant 2
3 cruel, pushy	+4	−2	+6	+4	(−5)	+5	+3	(−6)	(+5)	+5	kind, concerned 3
4 loving	(−5)	−2	−4	(−2)	+2	−5	−4	+5	+6	(−5)	unaffectionate 4
5 hard	+4	(−3)	+5	(+4)	−3	+5	(−5)	−6	+5	+4	kind 5
6 lot of problems	−1	+3	(−6)	−3	(−5)	−2	(−5)	+5	−4	−4	free of concerns 6
7 selfish	−1	+2	+3	(+3)	−5	(+5)	+5	−5	(+4)	+6	unselfish 7
8 reliable	(−5)	−6	−6	−1	(+5)	−4	−4	−5	−5	−6	let you down 8
9 stingy, mean	+4	+2	+3	+3	−5	+5	(+5)	(−6)	+4	(+6)	give 9
10 strong	−5	−6	(+5)	+3	−4	−5	−5	(−6)	(−3)	−5	weak 10

(Values in parentheses are circled in the original grid.)

FIGURE 4.1. Results of initial Repgrid testing with Tally S.

63

perceiving the social world and the way she construed specific others within it. For example, the construct "strong vs. weak," which was implicit in much of her earlier discussion of her relationship to Randy, emerged on the grid and generated the most polarized or extreme ratings of any construct, a pattern suggesting that it functioned as an intensely meaningful dimension for her (Bonarius, 1971). Nonetheless, it appeared to be relatively independent of other constructs, as reflected in its low intercorrelations with them. Stated differently, construing a person as "very strong" did not necessarily imply for Tally that they were "selfish," "cruel," and so on (for methodological details, see Landfield, 1977). Taken together, these results suggested that although "strong vs. weak" was a very salient dimension for her, the fact that it was not implicatively bound up with many of the constructs in her system signalled that she might be freer to reconstrue herself along this construct than along other dimensions (e.g., "stingy and mean vs. giving") that occupied more interrelated positions within her construct system. These and other structural scores derived from Tally's initial repgrid appear in the first column of Table 4.1.

Implied linkages among particular constructs were also of interest. The most striking of these concerned her construction of her superordinate construct of religiosity. In performing her ratings, Tally used the constructs of "being religious" and "having problems" virtually synonymously: figures seen as religious were also construed as beset with difficulties, while people

TABLE 4.1. Structural changes in Tally's construct system over the course of therapy

Measure	Repgrid testing session		
	Initial	Mid-therapy	Post-therapy
Tightness/looseness (FIC$_c$)	2	4	2
Number of implications of specific constructs[a]			
Religious	4	2	3
Problems	4	4	7
Hard	4	3	—
Giving/caring	7	—[d]	7
Self-identification[b]	3	0	6
Meaningfullness[c]			
Self	48	40	39
Therapist	26	44	38
Son	39	41	25

[a]Number of constructs with which a given construct is significantly correlated.
[b]Number of other figures to whom the self is seen as similar.
[c]Extremity of ratings of each figure across entire set of constructs.
[d]Construct did not reemerge at later assessment point.

with "no real religious experience" were seen as "free of concerns." This suggested to me the sort of "snag" discussed by Ryle (1982): Tally might be blocked from overcoming many of her problems in therapy, because to do so would be at odds with her valued core role of being a sincerely religious person. When I later brought up this possible connection in discussing the grid results with her, she stated emphatically her belief that "the devil gets to God's people and gives them a hard time!" Conversely, she contended that "people who don't care about the Lord seem to prosper." This conception was obviously validated repeatedly in sermons she heard on "the trials of the faithful." Nevertheless, this suggested the need to help Tally "rotate the reference axes" concerning this construction so that she could maintain her spiritual identity without its automatically implying a deeply problematic existence.

A similar kind of analysis was performed for the figures on the grid, indicating which particular persons were seen as similar to which others. This disclosed that Tally identified herself with her sister and her prayer group, as well as me as her therapist. I, in turn, was contrasted with the ungiving male figures in her life—her son and ex-husband. However, these findings were clarified when the extremity of her ratings of various figures was considered. On the one hand, she had a very clear-cut (perhaps too clear-cut) view of her own identity in terms of her role constructs but saw me as the most ambiguous or least meaningful of the elements she rated (see Table 4.1). Given the importance of establishing a deep-going "role re-lationship" in psychotherapy (Leitner, 1985; R. Neimeyer, 1986), I hypo-thesized that this latter finding would change as therapy progressed and I became an increasingly meaningful figure to her.

Finally, the Landfield program yields a Functionally Independent Construction (FIC) score, representing the total number of independent construct clusters in the individual's system. This analysis indicated that Tally's system was "tightly" organized, with all of her constructs except "strong vs. weak" and "outspoken vs. timid" constellated into one major cluster (see Table 4.1). This suggested that therapeutic change for Tally would require a general "loosening" of her role construct system, so that "facts, long taken as self-evident" could be released "from their rigid conceptual moorings" (Kelly, 1955, p. 1031). In operational terms, I suspected that experimentation with new constructs and revision of older ones would produce some differentiation in her existing structure so that a later assessment of her system would show it to be less cohesive than her current one.

EXPERIMENTING WITH A NEW ROLE

The results of the grid testing suggested that one overarching goal of therapy would be to help Tally modify her construction of herself as a weak person, while retaining her identity as someone who was giving and religious. A representative intervention along these lines occurred in the following session, after Tally discovered that halfway house placement for Randy would not be feasible because no vacancies were available. Following the circumspection-Pre-emption-Control (C-P-C) cycle, we generated alternative plans and evaluated their implications. The best of these seemed to be sending him to live with his father in town, who had in recent years overcome his drinking problem, remarried, and begun acting like a caring, if stern, father to his new children. But Tally balked at contacting Lawrence, who she feared would be inconvenienced by such an arrangement. This led us to role-play how she might make such a phone call if she were "a strong but sensitive person" who could "stick by her guns" but still "pay attention to his reaction." She subsequently was able to carry out such a phone call as a between-session behavioral experiment in relating differently to Lawrence and managing her son's problems more effectively at the same time. The experiment was successful, Randy went to live with his father, and Tally began to generalize her newfound strength to relationships beyond that with her son.

The inevitable set-backs that happened as she tried to consolidate this new identity were reconstrued in more hopeful ways. An example occurred in the sixth session, when Tally recounted an episode in which she had "loaned" her son $3 instead of the $10 he had asked for. Her sister Fay had reacted by accusing her of gullibility, thereby validating Tally's construction of herself as weak and manipulable. I attempted to help her reconstrue the event in terms of her more valued "giving vs. stingy" construct:

B: Well, you're soft-hearted, I guess. It seems you're always willing to do for somebody or give to someone. But that has its advantages as well as its disadvantages.

T: It usually works against me because people take advantage of that. And through the years Randy has done that.

B: But as you talk about this, Tally, it doesn't sound like it's an "either-or" kind of thing. It's not that you're either a Rock of Gibralter or a weak puppet being pulled on your strings. It sounds like in this case, for example, you were "pretty strong." You gave him a limited amount of money and delivered that along with the message that "This is it. I'm not a money tree you can pull handfuls of bucks off of. There's a limit." And that's a middle ground that makes sense to me.

T: That's not bad. But I did tell him, I said "Now when you come back to get your clothes, be sure you have your own money." So that *is* better. I'm not as down on myself as I could be.

DISRUPTED RELATIONSHIPS

With Randy's father sharing responsibility for his son for the first time in years, therapy was able to enter a new phase. Thus, by the eighth session we had begun to shift the focus somewhat to other, subtler relational problems she experienced with people. In doing this, I attempted to help her refine the constructions by which she interpreted such problems by asking "Is this person difficult in the same way that Randy is difficult or in a different way?" In response, she began to construe different varieties of problematic relationships: some people she dealt with were "argumentative and critical," while others were "too shy," and so on. One group of people that she was particularly ambivalent about, for example, was her bridge club, a group of women she had known for years before she deepened her religious commitment. Despite her fondness for several of them as friends, Tally had become increasingly uncomfortable in their presence. As she explained:

T: I guess we were once friends. But when I came out from among them, from playing a lot of bridge, I kind of classify them now more as associates. They're totally different people. Very strong, very into the sociable role. That's kind of why I pulled away from them. I don't fit in a social role anymore. I don't like the stuff they do. They want me to come and play bridge with them on Friday night, and I told them I couldn't come. I told them a story.

In personal construct terms, Tally's relation to her bridge associates represented a form of *disrupted relationship* (R. Neimeyer & G. Neimeyer, 1985) in which Tally chose to elaborate her system along different lines than other members of the group so that the consensual validation she originally experienced with them for her outlook was not sustained. Specifically, a central part of her core role—her religiosity—was threatened by what she perceived as their "worldliness," their tendency to engage in social drinking, dress "vainly," and tell racy jokes at their parties. Tally had reacted by pulling away, thereby increasing her sense of "not fitting in with people." When she did attend an annual club event, she announced in the next session that "I got depressed afterwards, and I don't know why." I conceptualized this in terms of Kelly's (1955, p. 502) definition of *guilt*, "the awareness of dislodgement from one's core role structure." This led me to ask if Tally felt that in going, she had "deviated from her own standards for herself." She replied that she had and, in so doing, had betrayed both herself and her God. She then began to discuss her deep desire to be a nun in a contemplative order and agreed with my suggestion that doing so "would provide a kind of validation, a setting that would allow her to be what she wanted."

At this point in our discussion I asked Tally if she saw any connection between two themes that had come out of our talks together—"being under her own control vs. being controlled by others," and "being worldly vs. religious." Without hesitation, she replied that in her religious life, she was under her own control, whereas "in the world" she responded tensely to the expectations of others. I then inquired about possible "exceptions to this rule," in an effort to rotate these dimensions so that she could begin to use them independently. She thought for a moment and then cited watching basketball games as a pleasurable but worldly activity where she felt no pressure to accommodate to others' expectations. With my encouragement, she also described in great detail one particularly conflictual relationship in her churchwork, in which she felt another woman was constantly trying to control her and others. As with earlier interventions, attempts like this were targeted at reducing the constellatory implications of her "religious vs. worldly" construct so that it could become a less dichotomous means of schematizing her experience and regulating her actions (c.f., Dunnett, 1985).

In the following weeks, Tally began to spontaneously elaborate her "religious vs. worldly" construct. For example, during a week-long trip to a church convention, she alone took time out to visit the World's Fair, a decision that surprised some of the stodgier members of her congregation. Upon returning to therapy, she laughingly remarked, "I guess I'm not as serious as I thought!" We used this as evidence for a new construction of her "real me:" someone who could be both "serious and fun." When I asked her how she saw herself in terms of being worldly vs. religious, she described herself as an "ambivert," still religiously committed, but able to enjoy the world as well. Shortly thereafter, she also evidenced her "new strength" by taking a leadership role in coordinating church committees that were organizing a revival.

THE THERAPEUTIC RELATIONSHIP

A second feature of this mid-phase of therapy was an intensive discussion of the therapy relationship. In mentioning previous sources of support she had experienced, Tally brought up her working with a "spiritual director" appointed through her church. I took this as an opportunity to examine more directly her construction of me as a secular therapist, in order to determine possible linkages she perceived between her construction of religiosity and caregiving.

B: How would having a spiritual director differ from having a therapist?

T: Umm, if they didn't tell you what their title was, you wouldn't know the difference I don't think. Once you know who they are, then its the name, really. You feel that the psychologist knows more about it, you know, and can come at it from a psychological standpoint, where the other would come strictly out of the spiritual part. . . . Cause if I had known she wasn't a psychologist, I don't think I would have known the difference.

B: It's interesting, because what you seem to be saying is that if you were just to look at their behavior, you might not notice that there was any difference between a spiritual director and a therapist. But once you know what the title is, you sort of create a different role relationship with them.

T: Right, right. Like if they had told me you were a spiritual director, I wouldn't have had the same attitude towards you that I have knowing you're a psychologist.

B: Yeah. That's fascinating! How would it differ?

T: Well, I would think that you came out of the Bible, had spiritual discernment, and that you really didn't know any more about the mind than I do. But they told me you were a psychologist, so immediately I put you up there where "he knows the mind" and "she can really help me." I think its a credibility thing.

B: Yeah. Well, this is an important thing for me, cause I need to decide whether I'm going to wear a white collar or a tie next week! (Client laughs.)

Alerted by her implication that only the spiritual director "could really help her," I was concerned that there might be important issues that we had neglected because of my lay status.

B: (After pause) I wonder what we would be talking about if I were a spiritual director instead of a therapist?

T: (After long pause) Demons! (Laughs.) Demons and persecution. And coincidences.

B: Coincidences?

T: Coincidences. And Randy and Lawrence, probably, but maybe from a more spiritual angle, you know, as to why has all this happened to me. God is so powerful, and yet he permits all this to happen to the people I love. Things like that.

B: Are these really the questions you'd like to have answered here?

T: Yeah . . . I talked to her a little bit about these things, but I didn't go very long.

B: You know, if I were to summarize the kinds of things that you would talk about with her, at least I guess part of that would concern the *meaning* of the problems you have now, seeing some kind of purpose in the suffering that these important people in your life are going through, and your own sense of persecution, having to bear these burdens. . . . Are the things that we talk about in here relevant to these questions?

T: The things we talk about in here are very relevant to me. I really, you know, have gotten some help in here. It may not be discussed in the same way that I would with a spiritual director, but it has helped me a lot. . . . Talking it out with you and having someone to throw the questions out, to make your comments. . . . Then I can ponder these things when I get home, and I can think them over. Somehow it—I can't explain it—but somehow or another it helps me. It really helps me.

Tally's increasingly detailed construction of me as a "worldy" therapist was significant, not so much because she saw me as a source of help, but primarily because our relationship provided a crucial testing ground for a new and less rigid construction of being religious.

MIDTHERAPY REPGRID TESTING

The extent of Tally's reconstruing of the social world was reflected in her responses to a second repgrid, which was administered in our fourteenth session. In order to tap her new understandings of herself and on-going relationships, I readministered the original figure-sorts to her but permitted her to reconstrue their similarities and differences in whatever way she currently felt appropriate. Several clinically interesting changes were evident. Her fundamental "strong vs. weak" construct was reformulated as "hard and unyielding versus merciful and concerned," with the latter pole having less pejorative connotations. Even more provocative was the emergence of an altogether new construct, "hard in a benevolent way vs. hard in an unloving way," which permitted her to differentiate between different types of strength, a discrimination that was previously foreign to her system. The most meaningful construct on the grid was "Christocentric vs. not concerned about God," indicating the continuing importance of religiosity in her world view. But the construct now functioned in a much less constellatory fashion, being associated only with "being merciful" and "listening to problems" (see Table 4.1). Just as significantly, being religious no longer automatically implied experiencing great personal difficulties, and indeed the "problem" construct on her first grid ("having a lot of problems") had been replaced by one suggesting an active, caregiving role ("listening to problems"). Thus, the grid analysis registered changes on two of the most significant constructs in Tally's system.

Specific figures also were rated differently than in the previous testing. Dramatic changes occurred in her construing of me as therapist, for example. Not only did I move from being perceived as the least to the most meaningful figure on the grid, but I also was seen as very similar to her prayer group, suggesting some breakdown in her earlier dichotomization of religious and secular sources of support. Tally also changed her perception of her own relationship to other persons rated on the grid. No longer did she contrast herself diametrically to Randy and Lawrence, as she had on her first grid, but neither did she see herself positively identified with others. This latter finding implied that the work of core role reconstruction was only half completed: while she no longer validated her self-image by contrasting herself with contemptuous others (R. Neimeyer & G. Neimeyer, 1985), she had not yet perceived the extensive similarities with others that would help validate her in her new role. Finally, as hypothesized, Tally's FIC score doubled from the first to the second testing, reflecting appreciable "loosening" in her social cognitive structure. Together, these findings implied that ameliorating her continuing sense of isolation and helping her retighten her construing represented remaining therapeutic goals.

CONSOLIDATING A NEW ROLE

The end phase of therapy with Tally focused more deeply on broader relational problems while attempting to consolidate gains made in enacting a more self-assured role with others. For instance, in our 16th session, Tally mentioned that she was "still having problems getting along with worldly people." When I asked what about worldly people made them difficult to relate to, Tally replied that they were "always trying to change her." Asking for an example, I discovered that Tally was referring again to her bridge club and to her anticipations of an upcoming tournament in which she had agreed to play. Instead of trying to persuade her that her fears were irrational, I encouraged her to formulate her anticipations as "hypotheses to test out by going." We then discussed exactly what sorts of behaviors on the part of the club members she would interpret as attempts to change her and what behaviors would be incompatible with her prediction. The session following the event she reported that she had "changed her ideas" about the group: not only had they given her a warm reception, but they actually started the meeting with a brief prayer. She acknowledged that there were differences between their values but concluded that "Whatever distance there was between us, I put it there." Although she later decided to reduce her involvement in the club's bridge parties, because they were no longer "her truth," she preserved her relationships with many of its members by seeking them out in other social contexts.

In our nineteenth session, I raised the issue of termination. Tally admitted that she was "scared of going it alone," but felt increasingly able to do so. We then spent much of the session discussing changes in her image of herself that had taken place over therapy. For example, she described a recent incident in which she felt she was "stepping out of character" in refusing someone's unreasonable request without guilt. I formulated this as an explicit choice point: "Will you change your behavior to go back to your old character, or change your character to accommodate your new behavior?" Tally replied that she liked the new behavior but feared that others did not. Questioning this global conclusion, I learned that while Randy and a few others preferred her as the timid person she once was, many others "affirmed" her for the obvious changes she had made.

A temporary set-back occurred the following week, when Randy's father unexpectedly dropped him off at Tally's house, because he could no longer tolerate his son's "laziness." At first, Tally "raged at him and cursed him out" for failing at his father's and then lapsed into resigned helplessness at ever resolving the problems with him. As a means of putting in perspective the "regressive alteration of her self-concept" that this represented (c.f., Horowitz and Zilberg, 1983), we made use of *controlled elaboration* (Kelly,

1955, p. 886). This entailed a careful discussion of two yet unintegrated parts of her—"the mother in me who holds back from making him move out" and the "new me who says go ahead and do it." This led to a consideration of whether it was kinder in the long run to foster his continued dependence upon her or to force him to function more autonomously. A step toward recovery of her nascent "hard but benevolent" self was taken when she later firmly confronted Randy about his insulting her without resorting to responding in kind. I construed this as evidence that she again had found "that new third option to extreme strength and extreme weakness:" she was not limited to responding with either "Old Testament vengeance" or "complete passivity." The following week she spontaneously set a deadline for his making arrangements to move into his own quarters.

FINAL REPGRID TESTING

In our last scheduled session, our 22nd, I administered the repgrid a third and final time to assess reconstruction that had taken place since mid-therapy. A new construct, "unyielding vs. compromising," emerged but was a much less salient and evaluative dimension than her original "strong vs. weak" construction. Interestingly, "giving vs. determined to have one's own way" reemerged and again assumed the superordinate, central position in her system that it had had on her initial grid. "Religious vs. not religious" was retained on the grid, recovering some of the positive but none of the negative implications with which it had once been associated. In addition, Tally had begun to construe herself as a highly interrelated figure on the grid, being identified with most of the positively construed people in her life (see Table 4.1). Even Randy had been reconstrued in a more positive light: he was seen as displaying many of the qualities exemplified by the therapist (understanding, concern, love) but to a more limited degree. Finally, at a more abstract structural level, Tally's construct system showed a sharp reduction in her FIC score, indicating a "retightening" of her construing after the loosening that had been produced by mid-therapy. In effect, her therapy could be conceptualized as one large-scale *Creativity Cycle* in which her initially tight but dysfunctional system was first loosened, revised and expanded, and then reintegrated along more adaptive lines.

Tally herself summarized the results of the "self-analysis" she had engaged in during the therapy:

> I realize now that I was trying to make Randy what I wanted him to be. I've tried to put my values on him, but he doesn't like mine, and I don't like his. I may as well let Randy be Randy, and Tally be Tally. . . .
>
> If this crisis hadn't happened, I might have let these things go along for a long time. Now I see things differently. My outlook has changed. I'm still not *well:*

I'm still nervous, but I know that some of that is physical. I can say to Randy, "You've got to carry your own crosses, suffer through the problems you create yourself." I don't know what's going on in Randy, but I do know what's going on in here (pointing to her chest). I have a right to love God, other people and myself. If I want to give this freedom to myself, I need to give it to him. . . .

I feel like I'm ready to face the real world some. I know it won't happen overnight, but I'm ready to start giving up my *ideal* world. I can pray, convert my prayers into actions, and work on it. I'm not idealizing the process of regaining my mental health. And those coincidences in my life—like having Randy treat me like Lawrence did—I thought they were caused by demons, and they might be. But I'd like to have another way of looking at them. I want to be able to see things from many sides.

CONCLUSION

In summary, I had conducted therapy with Tally using a credulous approach, accepting her mystical and psychic experiences as loose forms of construing having meaning for her, rather than rejecting them as merely psychotic or irrational. I frequently operated within her own system of language and values, minimizing the use of technical vocabulary in our interactions. This permitted us to articulate—through our own interactions and through the medium of the repgrid—some of the problematic core role structures by which she had previously organized her interactions with others and that prevented her from solving her own interpersonal problems. Making extensive use of casual enactment and controlled elaboration, we were able gradually to flesh out alternative constructions and test their application to her own emerging identity, to me as her therapist, and to the figures in her day-to-day life. In particular, we were able to restructure two of the major constructs having problematic consequences for her system: reducing the preemptive implications of "religious vs. nonreligious" and superordinating "strong vs. weak." In its broad outlines this movement represented a Creativity Cycle that loosened the preemptive hold of Tally's "idealized" construing and fostered the development of more "realistic" and flexible constructs for channelizing both her social experience and her own identity.

Tally's quest illustrates the essential nature of human life as envisioned by Kelly (1967/1980):

Psychotherapeutic movement can be said to get under way when a man starts questioning for himself what his immediate objectives may be and is thus led to initiate actions that challenge whatever previous notions he may have had as to what his limitations were. . . . He sets out to be what he is not.

The long-range objective of the psychotherapeutic effort is an extension of
this first step. It, as well as that of any other worthwhile human undertaking, is
not to conform oneself to society, lay or ordained; or to nature, whatever the
latest version of that happens to be. The objective is for man . . . to keep moving
toward what he is not—surmounting obstacles as best he can—and to keep on
doing [this] as long as he has anything to invest. To render and utilize technical
aid in this ontological venture is the special transaction we call "psychotherapy"
(p. 20).

REFERENCES

Bannister, D. (1983). Self in personal construct theory. In J. Adams-Webber & J.
    Mancuso (Eds.), *Applications of personal construct theory* (pp. 379-386). New York:
    Academic.
Beail, N. (1985). *Repertory grid technique and personal constructs.* London: Croom
    Helm.
Bonarius, J. (1971). *Personal construct theory and extreme response style.* Amsterdam: Swets
    and Zeitlinger.
Button, E. (Ed.) (1985). *Personal construct theory and mental health.* London: Croom
    Helm.
Dunnett, G. (1985). Construing control in theory and therapy. In D. Bannister (Ed.),
    Issues and approaches in personal construct theory (pp. 37-46). London: Academic.
Fransella, F., & Bannister, D. (1977). *A manual for repertory grid technique.* London:
    Academic.
Horowitz, M. J., & Zilberg, N. (1983). Regressive alterations of the self-concept.
    American Journal of Psychiatry, 140, 284-289.
Kelly, G. A. (1955). *The psychology of personal constructs.* New York: Norton.
Kelly, G. A. (1967/1980). A psychology of the optimal man. In A.W. Landfield & L.
    M. Leitner (Eds.), *Personal construct theory: Psychotherapy and personality.* New
    York: Wiley.
Landfield, A. W. (1977). Interpretive man: The enlarged self-image. In A. W. Land-
    field (Ed.), *Nebraska Symposium on Motivation.* Lincoln: University of Nebraska
    Press.
Landfield, A. W. (1983). *Reptest scoring program.* Unpublished manuscript, University
    of Nebraska.
Leitner, L. M. (1985). The terrors of cognition. In D. Bannister (Ed.), *Issues and
    approaches in personal construct theory.* London: Academic, 83-104.
Mahoney, M. J. (1979). *Self-change.* New York: Norton.
Neimeyer, G. J., & Neimeyer, R. A. (1981). Personal construct perspectives on cogni-
    tive assessment. In T. Merluzzi, C. Glass, & M. Genest (Eds.), *Cognitive assessment*
    (pp. 188-232). New York: Guilford.
Neimeyer, G. J., & Neimeyer, R. A. (1985). Relational trajectories: A personal con-
    struct contribution. *Journal of Social and Personal Relationships, 2,* 325-348.
Neimeyer, R. A. (1986). Personal construct therapy. In W. Dryden & W. L. Golden
    (Eds.), *Cognitive behavioral approaches to psychotherapy* (pp. 224-260). London: Har-
    per & Row.

Neimeyer, R. A., & Neimeyer, G. J. (1985). Disturbed relationships: A personal construct view. In E. Button (Ed.), *Personal construct theory and mental health* (pp. 195-223). London: Croom Helm.

Procter, H. (1981). Family construct psychology. In S. Walrond-Skinner (Ed.), *Developments in family therapy* (pp. 350-366). London: Routledge.

Ryle, A. (1982). *Psychotherapy: A cognitive integration of theory and practice.* New York: Academic.

Shaw, M. (Ed.) (1981). *Recent advances in personal construct technology.* New York: Academic.

Slater, P. (1976). *Explorations of intrapersonal space.* New York: Wiley.

Thomas, L., & Harri-Augstein, S. (1985). *Self-organized learning.* London: Routledge.

5
The Flight from Relationship: Personal Construct Reflections on Psychoanalytic Therapy

Stephen Soldz

Psychotherapy is a difficult undertaking. The therapist faces the task of listening to a client's verbal ramblings, deciding what the client "really" means by her or his statements, and formulating appropriate interventions. Clinical theories are used by the therapist as an aid to the process of making sense of the client's utterances. Furthermore, such theories prescribe therapeutic interventions to deal with various clinical situations.

Kelly (1955), through his psychology of personal constructs (PCP), tried to develop a general scientific theory that would elucidate the processes whereby individual persons make sense of the world. Unlike many other approaches, such as phenomenology, Kelly's theory contains an elaborate set of constructs that can be used to conceptualize an individual's personal construct system. In addition, Kelly's theory contains at least the rudiments of a theory of how and why people change their constructs.

Despite the fact that PCP was originally devised largely as a theory of clinical practice, the greatest strengths of PCP so far have been in the realms of theory and research. There have been only a few attempts to derive a therapeutic technique from the theory (e.g., Epting, 1984; Fransella, 1972; Leitner, 1980; R. Neimeyer, 1986). Thus, personal construct psychologists who wish to benefit from the efforts of previous clinicians are likely to dip into work from other traditions.

The dominant theories among clinicians engaged in verbal therapy have been psychoanalysis and variants of humanism such as Rogers' client-centered approach. Of these, psychoanalytic theory has provided the most broad-based framework for understanding clients' psychological functioning. Psychoanalytic approaches have been popular especially among therapists engaged in long-term treatment aimed at bringing about personality change. Perhaps because of this dominance, the psychoanalytic tradition reflects the clinical knowledge gained by numerous therapists over several generations.

My own clinical work has been influenced by both the personal construct and psychoanalytic traditions. Both PCP and psychoanalysis place a strong emphasis on understanding the client's unique way of relating to and making sense of the world. PCP provides a coherent theoretical structure that is especially helpful in elucidating the structural aspects of the client's meaning-making processes. Psychoanalysis contributes access to a rich clinical tradition built up over decades by hundreds of therapists. Among the most important themes in this clinical tradition are an emphasis on the role of childhood experience in the creation of adult personality and on the central role people's experience of others plays in psychic life.

The psychoanalytic tradition, interpreted broadly, also provides a variety of technical approaches for dealing with difficult therapeutic situations. I have been influenced especially by the Modern Psychoanalytic school that developed out of the work of Spotnitz (1976, 1985; Spotnitz & Meadow, 1976). While space precludes even the briefest summary of this approach, I will present a few modern analytic concepts that will be referred to in the case discussion that follows. I will then discuss material from two therapy sessions that illustrate the use of these concepts in guiding therapeutic interventions. Simultaneously, the clinical material will be conceptualized from the perspective of PCP to demonstrate my integration of psychoanalytic and personal construct concepts.

PSYCHOANALYTIC CONCEPTS

Resistance is a central modern psychoanalytic construct. However, the concept should not be understood as the pejorative accusation of client misconduct that has typified some psychoanalytic writing and that Kelly (1955) appropriately rejected. Spotnitz (1985) broadened the idea "to cover whatever obstacles to personality growth become manifest in the treatment relationship" (pp. 23–24). Resolving resistances becomes the central task of the modern analytic therapist. Spotnitz proposed a hierarchical classification of resistances such that those lower in the hierarchy should be dealt with before higher ones. The lowest level of resistance, which is prominent in the clinical material discussed in this chapter, is treatment-destructive resistance, namely, "any mode of behavior, that, carried far enough, would break off the treatment" (Spotnitz, 1985, p. 171). For example, tendencies to be late, to miss appointments, or to refuse to talk are treatment-destructive resistances that, in this approach, are dealt with before other resistances, such as resistances to cooperative functioning.

In the early stages of a therapy, the modern analytic clinician intervenes minimally while paying special attention to the client's *contact functioning* (Spotnitz, 1985), that is, to the client's overt or covert attempts to elicit a verbal response from the therapist. Cuing therapeutic interventions to the client's contact functioning can allow the client to regulate how much personal interaction he or she can tolerate. In PCP terms, following the client's contact functioning protects him/her from premature invalidation of essential core constructs. Furthermore, study by the therapist of the client's contact functioning can provide much valuable information about the nature of the client's personal relationships and what kind of relationship the client anticipates engaging in during the therapy process.

Modern psychoanalysis is in agreement with Kelly (1955) that understanding and insight are not necessarily instrumental in bringing about therapeutic change. Both approaches advocate the therapist's adopting various roles in order to elucidate and change a client's habitual ways of dealing with the world. Spotnitz (1985) proposed a set of techniques which involve the therapist's adopting a certain role in regard to the client. These techniques, collectively known as *joining,* have in common that "the therapist agrees with the patient's words or his conscious or unconscious attitudes" (p. 264). The therapist communicates that "I am a person like (a part of) you," which reduces the threat of invalidation the client experiences, allowing a resistance to be overcome and new material to evolve. As a simple example, if a client says she doesn't feel like talking, the therapist can join this feeling by informing the client that she doesn't have to talk if she doesn't want to. This intervention often spontaneously produces much material on the meaning of silence for the client. From a PCP perspective, such interventions temporarily validate a portion of the client's construct system, which encourages him/her to elaborate further and conduct experiments with these modes of construing. Thus, paradoxically, support and validation of certain constructs allows their modification.

The last modern analytic concept to be discussed is that of the *object-oriented question,* which is a question about something or someone outside of the client. While such questions can take many forms, the most characteristic object-oriented question is about the personality and behavior of the therapist. For example, if the client describes feeling bored, the therapist might ask "What am I doing to bore you?" Or, if the client says the therapist is angry, the therapist could respond "Why am I angry?" Such questions serve many functions, among which are to protect clients from premature invalidation of their constructs and to help clients elaborate their constructs for construing other people (Soldz, 1986).

The rest of the paper will illustrate how the modern analytic and personal construct theories have informed my clinical work with one client. The client chosen is one I have seen for the last four years as part of my training at the Boston Center for Modern Psychoanalytic Studies. As is common with modern analytic cases, she has been seen once weekly, using the analytic couch.

THE CLIENT

Ms. K. was a 31-year-old woman who started seeing me 4 years ago. At that time she was in art school, studying advertising design. She had considered herself to be a painter since adolescence but had recently decided to return to school in order to develop a profession that would provide her with income.

Several years ago Ms. K had been in therapy for two distinct eight-month periods with the same therapist. In her current efforts to find a therapist, she had twice begun to see someone, agreed to a therapeutic contract, got into a conflict about the contract, and decided the therapist was not right for her.

When a client has had several previous attempts at therapy, I usually speculate (to myself) that her difficulties are likely to be predominantly characterological in nature. Psychoanalytically, this means that the person's intrapsychic conflicts pervade her personality and have become rooted in characteristic ways of relating to the world. In PCP terms, this implies that the person is likely to have major difficulties in construal of herself and others. Realistic fine discriminations between people will not be made by her. Either a few constructs will be applied to all people indiscriminately, or she will fail to perceive similarities among others, leading to conceptual confusion. That is, her construct system will most likely not be properly differentiated and integrated (Crockett, 1982; Landfield, 1977). Consequently, her social constructs will be invalidated frequently, but she will not be able to spontaneously reconstrue people in more useful ways. As a result, social interaction will lead to a predominance of "negative" emotions, such as anxiety, fear, and guilt. (For PCP definitions of these emotions, see Kelly, 1955; McCoy, 1977.) Since she doesn't construe people in ways that usefully guide her interactions with them, she will try to force people to behave in ways that she can predict. That is, as described by personal construct theorists (Kelly, 1955, 1969a; Soldz, 1983), hostility is likely to play a prominent role in her interactions with others.

Because characterological problems pervade the entire personality and have developed over the client's entire life, they take a long time to change. Therapy of characterological difficulties can thus be expected to be an extended procedure requiring, at a minimum, several years to complete. Shorter therapeutic approaches frequently can produce relief of the immediate presenting symptoms of such clients but are unlikely to affect significantly the underlying characterological issues.

If my speculations are correct, the client's interpersonal difficulties should become manifest in the relationship between client and therapist. In the case of Ms. K., I speculated, on the basis of her treatment history, that she had had a history of relatively transient relations with others and that closeness would lead to a desire to flee the relationship. If this pattern were to change, it was to be expected that we would go through many cycles of engagement and detachment, with a predominance of treatment-destructive resistances during a good portion of the therapy.

During her first session Ms. K. provided further evidence of her pattern of engagement followed by the creation of distance. She raised the issue of whether I would answer her questions. When this was explored she said that when a question wasn't answered, she felt like she didn't exist—an extreme form of distancing. She indicated the attractions and fears of isolation while talking of a winter when she lived alone in England. There were long silences (construed by me as a form of withdrawal) in the session. She made contact with me by asking me to ask her questions, but when I asked her what kind of questions, she was silent. Hostility was evident when she described analysis as like 20 questions—that is, the mold for the relationship was already formed, and I was told what role I was to play.

Material from two sessions during the third year of her therapy will be presented in the remainder of the chapter. The material is based upon notes taken during the sessions. At points my notes were virtually verbatim; at other points, they were more condensed. What is presented here is a close reconstruction from my notes of the sessions. At points, a phrase actually represents a condensation of an extended portion of the session, but the sequence of ideas and interventions is faithfully preserved. Due to my more extensive notes, the second session presented is much closer to the actual dialogue.

The discussion of the case presented here represents, of course, a small fraction of the thoughts that I have had about this client during the time I have seen her. I have chosen to concentrate on a couple of themes that illustrate, I hope, the value both of modern analytic interventions and of PCP's theoretical concepts in clinical work. If space allowed, many additional comments could be made about the sessions presented.

"TELL ME WHAT TO DO!"

Session 110

(We rescheduled a future session.)

CLIENT (C): (Sigh.) Too much to schedule. I'm not excited about work. I'm dragging my heels to see if anyone notices. It gets too disciplined. . . . I love reading archeological history, where you have to make up what it was like. At work, however, all I have to do is draw ads for florescent light bulbs. How creative can you be with that?

THERAPIST (T): Would you like help with this issue?

C: Yeah.

T: What kind of help?

C: I fear and I want you to tell me to be disciplined. I fear being scolded and I don't want to be told the answer. But, if the right way to do it, or your way, isn't me, then I don't want to. You could tell me to get a new job.

T: Should I?

C: In a couple of months. (She described how her new job would involve leaving Boston and her boyfriend, John. She then discussed her difficulties doing her work.)

T: What you're doing wrong is you're not figuring out what they want and giving it to them.

C: Yeah.

T: Why not?

C: I don't look at the others' work carefully enough to know what the bosses want. I'm lazy and unmotivated. I sit around all day and read the newspaper. Actually I'm angry about having to redo an ad over and over. Maybe boredom is really anger. Why should I write if I can't please them? I'm afraid of doing work in case it's not what they want. To do the work and have them change the ad is discouraging. I should do more talking to other people in the field, but it's hard for me. I need someone to tell me what to do but not the central office.

My first intervention during this session, asking "Would you like help with this issue?" introduced myself into her discourse and was an indirect way of inquiring about why she's telling me this material. Is she just complaining, or does she hope that I will help her? In response, she presented her dilemma: she wanted someone, me, to tell her what to do, but she didn't want to be obligated to follow the advice. She perceived herself as undisciplined and inadequate and expected that others would agree with her. But if others did agree, she would feel scolded and would assert herself by criticizing (whether aloud or not would depend on the circumstances) the criticisms.

After having indicated that any advice I could have given her would have been rejected, she tried to set me up by telling me I could tell her to get another job and then rejected that suggestion. My object-oriented question here, "Should I?," was a further exploration of the role that I, as a representative of others in her life, was expected to play. It was also a way of avoiding the set-up of giving advice that would be rejected. As a result, she indicated that the advice she sought would lead to rejecting the important people in her life, her boyfriend and, understood by both of us, myself. That is, escape was as much escape from the entanglements of relationships as it was from a difficult work situation.

I then engaged in a bit of acting from within the relationship. I told her that "What you're doing wrong is you're not figuring out what they want and giving it to them." This intervention served several purposes. It was likely to be experienced as a criticism, leading her to demonstrate in the session her typical manner of responding to criticisms. It constituted a joining of her feeling that she was doing something wrong. If the joining was an accurate representation of her self construal at the moment, it likely would have helped her feel understood by me, leading to more self-revealing material (Meadow, 1974). By externalizing her own self-criticism, I gave her an opportunity to respond toward me as she usually responded to her own self-critical tendencies. In addition, the intervention was designed to explore how her rebellious tendencies interfered with her accomplishing the goals that she set for herself by finding out why she didn't do what would please her superiors. The goal was not to get her to behave better but to explore how her ways of construing interpersonal situations led to repetitive behavior contrary to what she overtly desired. Finally, the intervention was a gratification of her wish for a strong parental figure who would tell her what to do. It indicated that I was not afraid of those wishes, while allowing me to examine how she responded to advice. In other words, the intervention was a form of experiment (Kelly, 1955) on my part, designed both to allow her to talk about and become aware of other aspects of herself and to increase my knowledge of her construct system through a study of her response. That is it would lead to a deepening of my role relationship with her (Kelly, 1955; Soldz, 1986).

Ms. K.'s immediate response to this intervention was to attack herself: she described herself as lazy and unmotivated. As Kelly (1969b) once pointed out, terms like "lazy" are typically used to describe behaviors that do not match what the describer desires. Ms. K.'s description of herself as lazy was an assertion that she was misbehaving, not an explanation. It expressed her sense that something was wrong with her, that she was defective or bad in some way. However, it also expressed an identification with how she imagined others were construing her behavior or would have construed it if they had known her well enough.

Two of her superordinate constructs appeared to be involved in her construal of herself as "lazy" and "unmotivated." These can be loosely described as "passive acceptance vs. active engagement" and "self is responsible vs. others are responsible." This construal of hers involved her placing herself at the "passive acceptance" pole of the first construct and at the "self is responsible" pole of the second. However, these self-construals provided no room for her to elaborate her construct system. Kelly's (1955) choice corollary suggests that "a person chooses for himself that alternative in a dichotomized construct through which he anticipates the greater possibility of extension and definition of his system" (p. 64). In Ms. K.'s case, she had boxed herself into a corner. "Laziness" was not an articulated construct for her, and, like the behavior it described, it was a statement of her being stuck, not a stopping-off point for further development of her construct system.

Two factors, however, encouraged her to experiment with other construals of her situation. One was the process of verbalizing her largely preverbal constructs, called "word binding" by Kelly (1955), which allowed her greater maneuverability in examining her construction processes. Describing herself as "lazy" made evident to her that this construal allowed for little elaboration. The other factor encouraging her to try alternative construals was my intervention that emphasized that she could have behaved differently and had chosen not to do so, that is, that she was not simply a passive victim of fate but an active contributor to it. The intervention thus also represented an implicit statement that I thought that she was ready to try some new construals. Timing was an important factor here, and an account of my previous sessions with Ms. K. would be necessary in order to clarify why I chose this intervention at this time.

In any case, after construing herself as "lazy" and "unmotivated," Ms. K. conducted an experiment in construal: "Actually, I'm angry about having to rewrite pieces over and over. Maybe boredom is really anger. Why write if I can't please them." She thus placed herself on the opposite pole of her "passive acceptance vs. active engagement" construct. She was now construed as an active creator of her fate. She was angry and spiteful and hence refused to do what was required for successful performance of her job. Meanwhile, the "self is responsible vs. others are responsible" dimension became less relevant. It seemed that both shared responsibility. She was responsible for her angry, spiteful behavior, while her employers were responsible for not providing her with the support that she desired. Glimpses can be seen here of a new construct that she appeared to be in the process of creating. While its content is not clear from the session, it can be speculated that the new construct resembles "situations that are good for me vs. situations in which I don't function well." If this supposition is correct, one would expect further elaborations of this construct in future sessions. Her later decision to seek another job can, perhaps, be viewed as confirmation of this hypothesis.

"YOU'RE NOT SUITABLE!"

I indicated in the discussion of the initial session that Ms. K. tended to engage in a relationship and then withdraw. She had entered therapy as a lonely, isolated woman who remained emotionally bound to her mother, who had died 15 years previously, and with her sister who had competed with her for the mother's attention. The few contemporaries who peopled her life were of importance to her only in terms of their usefulness for her. For example, she contacted a former graduate school advisor whenever she needed professional advice. She had had a history of relatively unsatisfying relationships with men. Typically, she used these relationships to support her construal of men as people unaware of the wishes of others or of social norms for behavior, who use women only to satisfy themselves. When she met a man, she quickly forced him into this mold. Thus, she found a construction engineer to be unsuitable because he didn't clean his fingernails except when reminded by Ms. K. It became clear that every man she met was destined to disappoint her, leading to rejection by her. That is, her attitude toward men was one of hostility: all men were to be forced into the strait-jacket already prepared for them, resulting in her rejection of them.

It was inevitable that this dynamic would play itself out in her relationship with me. Most intensive verbal psychotherapy involves the creation of a strong emotionally significant relationship between client and therapist in which the client's habitual patterns of relating are recreated in the relationship with the therapist. That is, a transference is developed, and much of the therapeutic work involves changing the client's patterns of construing others by having her experiment with different patterns of relating to the therapist. "It is safe to say that the therapist enacts a series of carefully chosen parts and seeks to have the client develop adequate role relationships to the figures portrayed" (Kelly, 1955, p. 664; R. Neimeyer, 1986).

It is especially important that negative patterns of relating be brought into the therapeutic relationship, despite the personal difficulties that it might create for the therapist. "Sometimes the therapist feels the client is acting in an unfriendly manner. . . . (T)he behavior of the client may indicate that he now sees the therapeutic situation as one in which the 'negative' construct can safely be brought to light. The therapist has been successful in producing a laboratory situation which enables the client to invoke such a construct. . . . The client does not merely talk about the construct in terms of some polite superordinate construction; he actually perceives in terms of the construct and he acts out its implications. Indeed, he may not be able to haul it into the laboratory in any other way, for its word handles may be loose. The symbolization may be expressable only in terms of verbal acts and not in terms of name words (Kelly, 1955, p. 665)."

In Ms. K.'s case, it was hardly surprising that a good portion of her therapy revolved around her expressing her dissatisfactions with me and her desiring to leave. When this pattern erupted, as it did frequently, I had a number of goals in mind:

1. Making the pattern clear to her and helping her develop a desire to change it.
2. Clarifying exactly how her hostile pushing others into the molds she had prepared for them was accomplished.
3. Finding out what frustrations, or invalidated predictions, led her to want to end relationships.
4. Helping her to develop the capacity to maintain a relationship despite the inevitable frustrations that would develop.
5. Have her develop new constructs for social construing so that she could find greater satisfactions in relationships. These constructs should involve the creation of role relationships, that is, of relationships in which her interest is on the other person's ways of construing the world, rather than simply the other's behavior.

Session 148

C: I really don't feel like talking about anything. I'm tired from moving. The alcoholic family underneath the new apartment fight all the time. This made me sad but doesn't detract from the new apartment.

T: Should I go along with your not talking or encourage you to talk?

C: We should talk about my leaving therapy. I feel like I'm coming out of habit.

T: You don't like that thought?

C: Obviously I'm not getting what I need. It would be okay if I thought that I was going to come to places along the way. But I'm not feeling that. (We then engaged in a fairly intellectual discussion of the nature of therapy.)

C: You're not saying anything new. I've been telling you I ought to be talking about my difficulties in doing my art. I don't want to talk about my art, I want to do it. . . . You don't understand what creativity means. You don't understand the process, how a person uses their personality, no matter what condition it may be in.

T: Do you have any understanding of why I'm that way?

C: You don't have that many clients who are artists. You don't write. Academic writing is different. You haven't demonstrated any understanding.

T: How could I demonstrate it?

C: You'd ask better questions. You'd pick up sooner on problems. You've chosen to be a therapist, which isn't the same thing as choosing to be an artist.

T: How would it be different for you if I was an artist?

C: You'd be a different kind of therapist. You'd say different things. I haven't heard a lot of creativity.

T: What are you feeling now?

C: That it's hard to get through to you. Frustration. Some anger.

T: What happens when you feel frustration?

C: I don't feel like talking.

T: Why that response rather than trying harder?

C: Why try harder when you're not getting what you need in the first place? You've already made up your mind that I should talk about things with you.

T: Should I have been more insistent about your talking about these difficulties earlier?

C: Yes!

T: Have I missed my chance?

C: I don't know if you had a chance in the first place. I've used you for certain things, and it's time to move on.

T: Why is it time to move on rather than time to change the relationship?

C: That's a partisan remark. I don't feel that there's a capacity for change.

T: I'm irremediably flawed?

C: You're not suitable! What do you think you should have done?

T: Not take "no" for an answer when you say you don't want to talk about something. . . . You've been keeping your hand on your forehead. Do you feel a need for protection?

C: That's not it. It's hard fighting with you.

T: What makes it hard?

C: You're not very direct. Also, you hold your position.

T: How does a fight usually end?

C: What fight?

T: Any fight.

C: In the family, people separated and went to bed. Other fights end with admissions. Others with people leaving. Others with people being shot. Others with people saying it's okay—people deciding on something, or deciding just to be angry and saying "See you next week."

T: What's your preferred way to end fights?

C: With admissions and agreed settlements. Admit right and wrong and give in a little bit on your position. (She put her arm down from behind her head.) (Silence.)

T: Having any new thoughts?

C: Oh, I'm thinking of my new job. I start Monday at Central Graphics Design. The guy offered me a salary and then knocked it down in a letter today. They're letting me go on vacation the first two weeks in January, so I won't be here. I was thinking about the boss.

T: What were the thoughts?

C: I'm not going to bring it up with him, but I'll be cautious.

T: He didn't tell you why he lowered the salary?

C: No.

T: Are you mad at him?

C: No, disappointed that he wasn't who he was reported to be. He's also a heavy drinker, by report.

T: Are you anticipating any difficulties?

C: I don't know. The work's similar to my last job.

This session illustrates several aspects of Ms. K.'s negative feelings about me and the therapy and displays some of the techniques I used to deal with this issue. Her statement that she didn't feel like talking appeared to be an attempt to get a response from me; it was an instance of her contact functioning. I thus decided to intervene at that point, rather than let her talk as I would have done had I not perceived a desire for contact on her part. Like everyone in her life, I disappointed and frustrated her, leading to a desire on her part to flee the relationship. This desire is evident both in her expressed wish to leave therapy, a treatment-destructive resistance, and in her feelings at particular moments within the session. As she expressed it, when she feels frustrated "I don't feel like talking. . . . Why try harder when you're not getting what you need in the first place." That is, frustration led her to place herself at the "passive acceptance" pole of her "passive acceptance vs. active engagement" construct.

I explored Ms. K.'s resistance through asking a series of object-oriented questions about the role that I played and was expected to play in our relationship. As a result, Ms. K. went on to indicate a dawning awareness of her contribution to the dilemma the two of us were in: "I don't know if you had a chance in the first place. I've used you for certain things, and it's time to move on." However, Ms. K. was not yet ready to openly commit herself to an attempt to improve the relationship. Instead, she symbolically communicated her attitude in her discussion of her feelings toward her new boss, indicating that he was disappointing to her, and she would neither seek to change the situation nor leave. She would still accept the job but be cautious with him. This attitude was an improvement for her in that it indicated a weakening of her need to flee frustrating situations, but it left room for further improvement before she could commit herself to certain relationships and fight to get through the difficulties that would inevitably arise.

Further information about what was at stake for her in leaving was revealed in the following session when she indicated that leaving without my permission would have induced a sense of guilt in her. According to Kelly (1955) "perception of one's apparent dislodgement from his core role struc-

ture constitutes the experience of guilt" (p. 502). Ms. K.'s core role structure
contained constructs representing herself as a "good" person who does the
right thing and is a competent woman who plays an active role in shaping
her fate. Had she left therapy prematurely, she would have been forced to
construe herself on the opposite poles of these constructs, leading to a self-
perception as a bad, passive failure at shaping her fate. Previously she would
have chosen this alternative; this choice was what had led to the sense of
isolation and depression with which she had presented at the beginning
of therapy.

In the year that has elapsed since session 148, Ms. K. has remained in
therapy and has made substantial progress in committing herself to relationships. This change has become apparent largely through changes in her
behavior toward me. Her expressions of desires to leave therapy have decreased in frequency. She appears often to perceive therapy as a haven from
the stresses of her life, and I am perceived, at times, as a supportive presence
who can be counted on to help her accomplish what she wants. For example,
she has expressed wishes to have various of her friends come in and see me,
as if doing so would magically resolve the difficulties in relating with them
that plague her life. Bringing these people in to see me is also an alternative
to the desire to leave problematic relationships, which predominated earlier
in therapy.

As her treatment-destructive resistance has gradually resolved, the intense preverbal wishes and fears that are evoked in her by relationships have
come to the fore. As indicated, these constructs are presently manifest
largely in her behavior and are not yet verbalizable by her. It appears likely
that I am currently construed with the preverbal constructs that she
developed early in life in order to construe the loving, supportive aspects of
her mother. It is to be expected that fears of separation and even annihila-
tion were also developed in her early interactions with her undependable
alcoholic mother and that these constructs will eventually be applied to me
at those times when I am perceived as rejecting her as her mother did. The
next phase of therapy will probably focus on her verbalizing and conducting
experiments with these preverbal modes of construing, lessening their effect
on her life as the ever-present chaotic alternative that looms whenever her
more adult ways of functioning are unsuccessful. Integrating this split-off
construct subsystem with her more readily accessible constructs should free
her of her fixation on past models of relationships, allowing her to adopt a
more experimental, forward-looking approach to other people.

REFERENCES

Crockett, W. H. (1982). The organization of construct systems: The organization corollary. In J. C. Mancuso & J. R. Adams-Webber (Eds.), *The construing person* (pp.
62–96). New York: Praeger.

Epting, F. (1984). *Personal construct counseling and psychotherapy*. New York: Wiley.

Fransella, F. (1972). *Personal change and reconstruction: Research on the treatment of stuttering*. New York: Academic.

Kelly, G. A. (1955). *The psychology of personal constructs*. New York: Norton.

Kelly, G. A. (1969a). Hostility. In B. Maher (Ed.), *Clinical psychology and personality: The selected papers of George Kelly* (pp. 267-280). New York: Wiley.

Kelly, G. A. (1969b). Man's construction of his alternatives. In B. Maher (Ed.), *Clinical psychology and personality: The selected papers of George Kelly* (pp. 66-93). New York: Wiley.

Landfield, A. W. (1977). Interpretive man: The enlarged self-image. In A. W. Landfield (Ed.), *Nebraska symposium on motivation, 1976: Personal construct psychology* (pp. 127-177). Lincoln: University of Nebraska Press.

Leitner, L. M. (1980). Personal construct treatment of a severely disturbed woman: The case of Sue. In A. W. Landfield & L. M. Leitner (Eds.), *Personal construct psychology: Personality and psychotherapy* (pp. 102-121). New York: Wiley.

McCoy, M. M. (1977). A reconstruction of emotion. In D. Bannister (Ed.), *New perspectives in personal construct theory* (pp. 93-124). London: Academic.

Meadow, P. W. (1974). Research method for investigating the effectiveness of psychoanalytic technique. *Psychoanalytic Review, 61,* 79–94.

Neimeyer, R. A. (1986). Personal construct therapy. In W. Dryden & W. L. Golden (Eds.), *Cognitive behavioral approaches to psychotherapy* (pp. 224-260). London: Harper & Row.

Soldz, S. (1983, July). *Hostility and the severely disturbed personality: Clinical considerations.* Paper presented at the Fifth International Congress on Personal Construct Psychology, Boston, MA.

Soldz, S. (1986). Construing of others in psychotherapy: Personal construct perspectives. *Journal of Contemporary Psychotherapy, 16,* 52-61.

Spotnitz, H. (1976). *Psychotherapy of preoedipal conditions: Schizophrenia and severe character disorders.* New York: Jason Aronson.

Spotnitz, H. (1985). *Modern psychoanalysis of the schizophrenic patient: Theory of the technique.* (2nd ed.). New York: Human Sciences Press.

Spotnitz, H., & Meadow, P. W. (1976). *Treatment of the narcissistic neuroses.* New York: Manhatten Center for Advanced Psychoanalytic Studies.

6

Psychotherapy in a Case of Physical Illness: "I Have a Choice"

Linda L. Viney

Alice M. was referred to our team of consultant personal construct psychologists in a country hospital in Australia. She had been hospitalized a week earlier after a myocardial infarction. Until that time she had been working in a small family grocery business on a full-time basis. At 48 years old, she had recently seen her two adult sons leave home for jobs in the army, and her 18-year-old daughter was likely to do so soon. She was referred by her physician for treatment of anxiety and depression. The nursing staff, when asked about her, also mentioned these problems and added that they found her to be a "difficult" patient. When the therapist first saw Alice, she was tense and fearful. She showed considerable anxiety and depression, as well as a predominantly passive expression of anger. Much of this anger proved to be associated with feelings of helplessness generated by frustrations she was experiencing.

In this account of psychotherapy in a case of physical illness, the personal construct model of psychological reactions to illness underlying the psychotherapy will be described; then, some of the psychotherapeutic techniques used with Alice will be examined. Finally, the outcomes of these interventions for the patient will be evaluated.

ALICE'S PSYCHOLOGICAL REACTIONS TO HER ILLNESS

The main factors in this personal conduct model of psychological reactions to physical illness will become apparent as Alice's reactions to her heart attack are described.

ALICE: I am still so shocked that it's happened. I always thought it would be Greg [her husband] and not me who had the heart attack. I suppose I was a bit tired the day before, and I still can't do much. Nothing like this has ever happened to me. I've always been the healthy one. And I can't seem to find out what is going on now I'm in hospital. The nurses get sick of me asking them, and they won't tell me anything. I'm still trying to work out when and how things happen in hospitals. And I feel so depressed. I just feel sad for no reason, really.

Alice was trying, like all patients, to make sense of what was happening to her (Viney, 1983a). Since most of her experiences of her myocardial infarction and hospitalization were new to her, she was having difficulty doing so. Her construct system was not functioning effectively, making it difficult for her to act effectively. Her old constructs were not sufficiently permeable to be applied to these new experiences (Kelly, 1955). Other constructs (for example "I've always been the healthy one") were too tight, that is, too limited to their predictions.

ALICE: I lie here, especially at night, and worry about whether I'm going to have another attack, and, if I do, how bad it will be and will I survive it? I don't want to die yet. I'm too young. When I feel like this I can't enjoy anything. I don't suppose I'll work in the shop again. I used to enjoy that, meeting the people and all that. Now, I'm just not up to it. Poor Greg! He's going to have a pretty useless lump on his hands. I can't make any plans. We were going to do a trip around Australia with a caravan but now . . . I can't even seem to go to sleep when I want to. When they wake me up for medication I toss and turn for hours.

Alice, because her construct system was not enabling her to interpret and anticipate effectively, was experiencing distress (Viney, 1985a). She was anxious for this reason and also because the threat of her own eventual death had been made immediately real to her. She was depressed. She was also expressing much helplessness in her mourning of her lost abilities to travel at will and to control her own body. All of these psychological reactions are common in physically ill patients (Viney & Westbrook, 1981, 1982a). One of the striking omissions from Alice's comments during the early stages of her psychotherapy was any direct expression of anger, which must have been generating the frustrations she was experiencing. The closest she came to such an expression in her statement above was the reference to the nurses waking her when she had difficulty sleeping. The reports of the nurses that she was "difficult" also indicated that she was expressing this anger only indirectly and not directly, a poor prognostic sign for her later rehabilitation (Viney & Westbrook, 1982b).

The other main aspect of the personal construct model of psychological reactions to illness, which has yet to be considered here, is the social isolation brought about by both the illness itself and consequent hospitalization.

Alice was used to being the pivotal figure in her family, not only at home but at their business as well. But when she had her myocardial infarction, her family tended at first to withdraw from her.

ALICE: Greg and the boys have hardly come to see me at all. Jenny comes, and it's good to see her. But I feel she should be at home studying. Greg, especially, seems to shut me out of things now. I ask him how things are at home or at the shop, and he says: "Fine! Don't worry!" Of course I worry. I'd feel a lot better if they'd let me in on things. I feel left out.

Alice's family were probably trying to show their concern for her. Yet their clumsy attempts were making her feel more and more isolated. Their reactions to her illness, like those of Alice herself, are very common (Viney, 1983b; Wortman & Dunkel-Schetter, 1979).

ALICE'S PSYCHOTHERAPY

After an initial assessment by another psychologist, Alice had only four three-quarter hour sessions of brief bedside psychotherapy with her psychotherapist. These sessions were based on a crisis intervention model (Viney, Clarke, Bunn, & Teoh, 1985). The aims of this intervention were to help her deal more effectively with her illness-generated stress in the short term and, in the long term, to help her use her crisis to develop better ways to minimize future failure and maximize resolution of other crises in the future (Viney, Clarke, Bunn, & Benjamin, 1985a). During this brief psychotherapy her therapist showed Alice that she and her construct system were accepted and understood (Landfield, 1980). This was accomplished through the attentive listening of the therapist, coupled with periodic validating summaries of the constructs she had heard. Her therapist also expressed a reality-based hope for the future, in statements such as "It may take a while for you to get back on your feet, but I know you can" (Viney, Clarke, Bunn, & Benjamin, 1985b). The therapist also helped Alice to identify her own strengths by questions like: "How did you cope with other similarly difficult periods of your life?" Alice was also encouraged to express distressed feelings about her illness and hospitalization. A trusting therapeutic relationship developed between client and therapist, so that psychotherapeutic experiments could be made (Bannister, 1975; Viney, 1981). Finally, whenever possible, Alice was encouraged to be self-reliant in order to avoid prolonged dependency on the therapist (Small, 1979). For example, what she could now achieve for herself, she was encouraged to do.

The specific aims of the brief psychotherapy with Alice were to lower her anxiety, resolve her depression, reduce her feelings of helplessness, and encourage more direct expression of her anger resulting immediately from the crisis induced by her myocardial infarction and subsequent hospitalization. It was also intended that, through working therapeutically with her during this period of crisis, long-term gains in the levels of her anxiety, depression, helplessness, and expression of her anger would be achieved. Two other more positive aspects of her experience were also considered. Perceptions of herself as competent were to be encouraged, together with positive emotions such as happiness and enjoyment. A personal construct approach to psychotherapy with these aims has been described in *Images of Illness* (Viney, 1983b). The techniques employed come from a wider range of theoretical orientations than personal construct theory. The personal construct view that psychotherapy provides the client with the opportunity for personal experimentation makes the use of such techniques possible.

Some further comments on the personal construct view of psychotherapy as experimenting with experience may now be helpful. In such psychotherapy, the constructs and choices of the client are the focus of both therapist and client. The client is provided with a series of new, experimental experiences that start close to her established construct system but then move further away from it. The range of her construct system and her choices are expanded in this way. Therapist and client work as co-researchers, creating hypotheses about the client and her world and testing them.

Alice's anxiety was dealt with by her therapist in two main ways. The threat of death, which has been explored by personal construct psychologists (Epting & Neimeyer, 1984), was one of her main concerns, but it was difficult at first for her to talk about it. Her therapist found herself needing to give permission to allow Alice to pursue this concern. It should be remembered that this therapy was conducted in a hospital ward in which the staff did not encourage "gloomy" thoughts and feelings. The psychoanalytic technique of catharsis was used (Fine, 1979). In personal construct terms, catharsis has a loosening effect on a construct system that is functioning too tightly. Alice was only dimly aware of the threat of imminent changes to the most central parts of her construct system. This was the threat posed by the possibility of her own death occurring sooner than she had expected. She was also excluding other events that were anxiety-arousing, like the thought of leaving her family to cope without her. When she was first seen by her therapist, Alice's ways of handling her anger were noticeably tightening. She did not directly seek validation from others for her now useless constructs but expressed her anger passively. How this was dealt with will be described later in the case study. For now, it is sufficient to point to Alice's initial need for the loosening provided by catharsis, before she could go on to work on her distressing feelings and the constructs with which they were associated. Alice, then, had considerable difficulty in coming to terms with her anxiety at first. It was only in the last session of psychotherapy that she was able to explore some of the deeper meanings that her own death had for her and so to experiment with her own experience.

ALICE: I hadn't realized how great my fear of dying is. I've never even thought about it before, not for me. Both my parents are dead. I had to cope with that, but I didn't let myself dwell on it. If I die . . . when I die . . . what will it mean? For me, the most important thing would be missing my family. I hate to think of not seeing them again . . . not being there to help them. Yes, missing the people I love would be worst. Then, what about me? Where would I be? We just don't know, do we.

The second part of the therapist's two-pronged attack on her anxiety was also not one developed from personal construct theory. Alice was encouraged to deal with her physical tension by the use of differential muscle relaxation (Rimm & Masters, 1979). Her therapist asked her to tense and relax various muscle groups (e.g., her hand and stomach muscles) and to observe carefully the differences between these two states. Special attention was then paid to her relaxing the muscles around her throat and chest where she was able to identify extra tension. In general terms, it was hoped that this newly acquired skill would help her not only to sleep better while she was hospitalized but to relax at will when later dealing with sources of stress. In personal construct terms, another phase of the psychotherapeutic cycle was starting for Alice. This relaxation training was designed to tighten her use of her construct system. This was achieved by having her focus on her own concrete being in the form of the muscles of her body. At the same time, this relaxation training was designed to help Alice recover a pole of a construct that was very important to her. It has already been noted, that, like most people coping with physical illness, she saw herself as helpless. This technique was used, with another that will be described, to keep her in touch with the opposite pole of this construct: "I am in control of at least some parts of my body." While skeptical at first, Alice soon reported some success with this experiment in relaxation.

Alice's depression, like her anxiety, was an appropriate response to her illness. However, it was distressing to herself, the hospital staff who cared for her, and her family. From the personal construct view, the persistence of this depression was the result of the self-limiting constructs she was using (Rowe, 1978). She often repeated, for example: "I'm never going to be able to live a normal life again." This construct was too tight to allow her to function effectively and needed loosening (Epting, 1984). Some of this loosening was accomplished through fantasy. Her therapist asked her to imagine herself in a number of physically undemanding but "normal" situations. While she could not try this out by her own actions, there was only limited loosening. Her therapist therefore asked her to check out her construct with fellow patients who were at a more advanced stage of their rehabilitation program.

They did not validate her construct. As a result she came to be able to loosen it to the point of: "I may have to be careful about myself from now on and not push myself too hard; but there are still things I *can* do." Although this technique is a good example of experimenting with experience in personal construct therapy, it is not unlike the cognitive (Beck, Rush, Shaw, & Emery, 1979) and cognitive behavioral (Meichenbaum, 1977) approaches to depression. Of course Beck and Meichenbaum both admit to being influenced by personal construct theory (R. Neimeyer, 1986). As a result, they share not only therapeutic techniques but also some assumptions they make about clients in therapy. Personal construct, cognitive, and cognitive behavioral therapists, for example, share the assumption that their clients are responding to their interpretations (or constructs, cognitions, or cognitive behaviors) of their world rather than to those worlds themselves (R. Neimeyer, 1985). Such assumptions lead to some similarities in techniques. In their therapeutic relationships, for example, they all regard the client as someone who cooperates with them in the work to be done. Personal construct theory, however, has a more dynamic and better integrated view of the client, who is endowed with the full range of emotions that are an integral part of the construct system.

The therapist also introduced Alice to another technique for dealing with depression, by encouraging her to focus on the more positive or attractive poles of her constructs. Some of these positive construct poles can be developed through the sensitive use of humor, as has been shown by psychotherapists of personal construct (Viney, 1985b) and other (O'Connell, 1975) persuasions. A little gentle teasing of Alice about her concern with helping others and her difficulty in accepting help for herself not only created some of her first laughter and enjoyment since her infarction but loosened more of her too tight constructs about helping. Positive feeling in general, however, is experienced when the interpretations and anticipations of construct systems are confirmed (McCoy, 1980). When Alice was finally able to say "I can still enjoy myself," it was clear that her construct system had become much more effective in helping her understand her condition and plan how to deal with it.

This increased effectiveness was also a result of the therapeutic work designed to deal with her feelings of helplessness. In fixed role therapy (Karst & Trexler, 1970), she experimented with a role in which she felt, not helpless, but, at least in some situations, competent and in control. This role was carefully constructed on the basis of some of her own constructs about helplessness and competence. For example, she described herself as "totally useless." For her, the opposite pole of this bipolar construct was "always able to cope and help others." The role that she played for brief periods was, then, one which was based on a construct that was orthogonal to her own. Her therapist presented it to her in this way.

THERAPIST: I want you to pretend, just for a while, that you are this new person, Mary. Try to forget about yourself and slide into her role. She is a *warm, enthusiastic* person. She is *cheerful* and *optimistic* and has a *practical* approach to life. She *makes friends easily.* When she needs to, she is able to cope and help others. (The underlinings represent Alice's own constructs. The last one presented was the construct that was similar to but different from her construct of helplessness–competence.)

Initially this role seemed very strange to Alice. But her attempts with this technique, first with her therapist and then with her physician, to ascertain her prognosis proved successful. She gradually came to see that she could describe herself, with truth, in the terms of the new role. Limiting the role to her own already existing constructs made this easier for her. She then spontaneously turned to using it to secure the involvement she wanted with her family. This procedure may appear to achieve only the goals achieved by assertiveness training (Wolpe, 1969). They are, however, goals that are much more likely to be retained after fixed role therapy, because there is not only a change in behavior but also fundamental changes in the ways the client used her own constructs. These were the constructs with which the client interpreted and made sense of her behavior.

Another way in which she learned how to revive old constructs of herself as competent was by employing self-reinforcement to modify her life-threatening habit of smoking (Rudestam, 1980). In yet another field experiment, she chose to reward herself with a period of reading her favorite magazines when she had not smoked for periods of 2 hours. She also learned to use her illness-related constructs to prepare herself for better coping with her coronary condition in terms of monitoring her own blood pressure and the side effects of the drugs that were prescribed for her. This technique is much like the social cognitive tool of self-preparation (Mechanic, 1977).

Reduced feelings of helplessness in Alice also led to less frustration and so less anger. There was still, however, appropriate anger to be identified and expressed in a more direct way. Alice was initially unaware of her anger. She learned to recognize this anger by dealing with her body-related constructs. To achieve this aim, her therapist asked her, at quiet times on the ward, to relax and attend to the feelings of her body, and describe their meaning for her (Gendlin, 1981). With this experiment she reported success by the third psychotherapy session.

ALICE: I could feel this lump in my throat. At first I thought it was my heart, but it wasn't. It was as if I had swallowed something that was stuck right down into my chest, and I wanted to push it out—cough, splutter, almost vomit. But what I wanted to get rid of was what had happened to me! Why should I have a heart attack? It's not fair! I've worked hard with the kids and the shop, and I was looking forward to some enjoyment in life! I'm really angry that this has happened.

The other therapeutic technique that was employed involved Alice's therapist in one session with the male members of her family. Her daughter was not included because of her end of high school examinations. Greg expressed much concern for his wife, as did their two sons. The family construct of "Men do not express their feelings" was, however, strongly in evidence. The therapist made no frontal assault on this construct but searched for acceptable related constructs. The most appropriate seemed to be: "Men are not 'mushy,' but they can tell a wife (mother) that they care about her." Alice's husband and sons were also helped to understand that she needed to continue to be a part of their family and so should be included in their decision-making processes (e.g., about their business).

EVALUATION OF THE OUTCOMES OF PSYCHOTHERAPY FOR ALICE

Alice's psychotherapy involved experimenting with her experience. The relevant outcomes of psychotherapy were considered to be Alice's experiences rather than her actions. Assessing the experience of another person is extremely difficult, especially when that person is assumed to be another construing person like you or me (Viney, 1986). When the aim is to measure that experience and not just to deal with it at the level of meaning, the task becomes even more difficult. Content analysis scales have been developed as one solution to this problem (Viney, 1983c). These scales, with predetermined content categories that can be used reliably and have evidence of validity, are applied to verbal communications and have frequently been used with physically ill patients (Gottschalk, Lolas, & Viney, 1986; Viney, 1983b; Viney, Clarke, Bunn, & Benjamin, 1985a, b; Viney & Westbrook, 1981; 1982a, b).

Such verbal communications were collected from Alice on three occasions by a psychologist other than her therapist, using a standard open-ended request. These occasions were on admission to hospital, on discharge two weeks later, and on follow-up 12 months later. The open-ended request was as follows:

PSYCHOLOGIST: Now I'd like you to talk for a few minutes about your life at the moment, the good things and the bad, what it's like for you. Once you've started talking, I'll be here listening to you, but I would prefer not to reply to any questions you may feel like asking until a 5-minute period is over. Do you have any questions you would like to ask me before we start?

Data from the same measures and on the same occasions were also available for comparison purposes from a sample of 108 acutely ill hospitalized adults who did not receive psychotherapy. Their anxiety was measured by the Gottschalk–Gleser Total Anxiety Scale (Gottschalk, 1979), and their depression by the Hostility Inward Scale of the same authors. Feelings of helplessness and competence were assessed with the Pawn and Origin Scales (Westbrook & Viney, 1980). Anger expressed indirectly was measured by the Ambivalent Hostility Scale (Gottschalk, 1979). These accounts of people's current experiences were transcribed and divided into clauses, each one containing an active verb. They were then content analyzed, following the standard instructions for the five content analysis scales described in the next section. Each clause was compared with a set of content-analysis categories that provided verbal cues for each psychological state. Matching clauses were summed. Weights representing the intensity of a state were included for some scales.

For the research program from which these data come, the content analysis was carried out independently by two trained and experienced scorers before they received any information regarding the participants, their treatment group, or whether the transcripts came from the admission, discharge, or follow-up interviews. Interjudge reliability coefficients ranged from .83 to .92. Analyses by t test of a subsample of transcripts showed no significant differences between the mean scores of the two judges.

It may be useful to demonstrate the coding for the content analysis scales. I shall do this with the first statement from Alice that I recorded in this chapter. It is presented again here with clausing and five forms of coding representing the five scales. The Gottschalk–Gleser Total Anxiety Scale has coding categories for six sources of anxiety: Death (1), Mutilation (2), Separation (3), Guilt (4), Shame (5), and Diffuse Anxiety (6). These content categories are given weights according to whether the references in the transcript are to oneself or others (a or b). In Alice's statement, there are only two sources of anxiety to be scored, Mutilation ($2a_3$) and Diffuse Anxiety ($6a_3$). Both are personal statements and so are given the weight of 3. The coding of depression with the Hostility Inward Scale is similar, although its weights indicate the intensity of the feelings expressed. The main categories include self-mutilation (Ia_3), self-blame (Ib_3), discouragement (Ic_3), self-criticism (Ib_2), and disappointment in self (Ia_1). In this excerpt, Alice has only expressed discouragement (Ic_3). The coding for indirectly expressed anger has also been developed by Gottschalk–Gleser so that it is again similar. The coding categories of the Ambivalent Hostility Scale include references to others threatening to kill oneself (IIa_3), others adversely criticizing oneself (IIc_3), others depriving oneself (IIa_2), and situations causing suffering to oneself (IIa_1). Alice spoke of others criticizing her (IIc_3) and others depriving her (IIa_2).

The other two scales, by Westbrook and myself, measure helplessness and competence. These scales have no system of weights and do not differentiate in coding the different types of states described. The Pawn Scale (P) is scored when there are references to lack of intention, lack of effort, and lack of ability, as well as to being controlled by others and to seeing oneself as a "pawn" experiencing unpredictable events. The Origin Scale (O) is scored for references to intention, effort, and ability, as well as to influencing others and to seeing oneself as a cause or "origin." Alice referred to both types of states in this excerpt, but showed more helplessness than competence.

ALICE: /6a₃/
   I'm still so shocked that it's happened. / I always thought it would be Greg
                                        /2a₃/
   and not me / who had the heart attack. / I suppose / I was a bit tired the day
                                        /P/
   before, / and I still can't do much. / Nothing like this has ever happened to
                                        /P/
   me. / I've always been the healthy one. / And I can't seem to find out / what's
                                        /IIc₃/
   going on / now I'm in hospital. / The nurses get sick of me asking them /
                    /IIa₂/   O
   and they won't tell me anything. / I'm still trying to work out / when and how
                                        /Ic₃/
   things happen in hospitals. / And I feel so depressed. / I feel sad for no
   /Ic₃/
   reason, really. /

Alice's anxiety, when assessed by this method, proved initially to be very high (3.00) and a little higher than that of her fellow patients ($\bar{X}$ = 2.65, SD = 1.15) (see Figure 6.1). By discharge, and after psychotherapy, it had fallen considerably (2.20) but then that of the other patients had also, not surprisingly, fallen just prior to discharge ($\bar{X}$ = 2.20, SD = 0.91). However, Alice differed from other patients on follow-up. Twelve months after psychotherapy her anxiety score (1.83) was considerably lower than that of the other ex-patients ($\bar{X}$ = 2.33, SD = 0.96). Lest it be thought that this was due to a greater decrease in external sources of stress for her, her follow-up interview by the independent psychologist revealed that she had experienced another crisis and some continuing worries apart from her own health. Her eldest son had been badly injured in a motor bike accident during the follow-up period, and the family business was having financial difficulties. Her psychotherapy seemed to have helped her cope with her anxiety in the long term, even in the face of these events.

Figure 6.2 shows Alice's level of depression (1.27) initially to be as high as that of her fellow patients ($\bar{X}$ = 1.27, SD = 0.70). As with them ($\bar{X}$ = 1.27, SD = 0.65), her depressed feelings stayed at a high level (1.24) until discharge. The short-term crisis intervention goal set for her in relation to depression was not attained. However, while the patients without psycho-

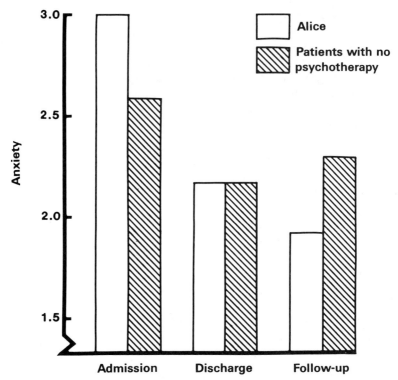

FIGURE 6.1.   Anxiety in Alice and patients with no psychotherapy on admission, discharge and follow-up.

therapy retained their levels of depression at follow-up ($\bar{X}$ = 1.28, SD = 0.78), Alice showed a sleeper effect (0.92). Her depression score had moved from the top half of the distribution of the comparison group to the bottom third. This loss of her depression probably could not be manifested while she was still in hospital, which is a situation likely to promote depression in most people. She seems to have experienced a long-term gain in combating her feelings of depression.

Upon admission, Alice's feelings of helplessness were also high (1.59), like those of the other patients ($\bar{X}$ = 1.64, SD = 0.59) (see Figure 6.3). There is some evidence that they were reduced during psychotherapy (1.31) and were later maintained at a lower level (1.39) than those of her fellow patients (on discharge, $\bar{X}$ = 1.52, SD = 0.59; on follow-up, $\bar{X}$ = 1.54, SD = 0.59). However, when Alice's scores were compared with those of the patients without psychotherapy, there were no marked gains in her position relative to them. Similarly, while her expressions of competence were few on admis-

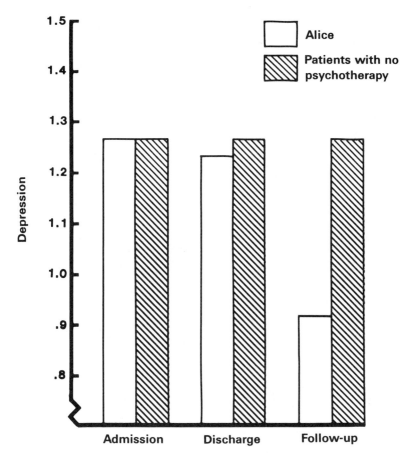

FIGURE 6.2.   Depression in Alice and patients with no psychotherapy on admission, discharge, and follow-up.

sion (0.61), they increased at discharge (1.40) and again on follow-up (1.60) (see Figure 6.4). For the patients without psychotherapy they remained much more stable (on admission, $\bar{X}$ = 1.00, SD = 0.45; on discharge, $\bar{X}$ = 1.06, SD = 0.59; on follow-up, $\bar{X}$ = 1.19, SD = 0.53). When her scores were examined in relation to those of the comparison group, she had moved from being in the top fifth of their distribution at admission to the bottom fifth on follow-up. It was really for feelings of competence only, then, that Alice experienced both short-term and long-term gains.

Alice's indirect expression of anger (0.97) was also similar to that of the comparison group of patients on admission ($\bar{X}$ = 0.96, SD = 0.52). It remained at that level (0.99), whereas theirs increased on discharge ($\bar{X}$ =

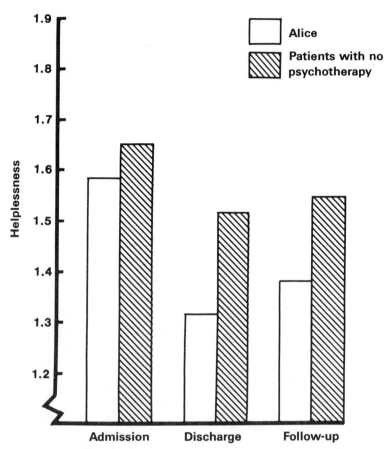

FIGURE 6.3.   Helplessness in Alice and patients with no psychotherapy on admission, discharge, and follow-up.

1.10, SD = 0.47) (see Figure 6.5). Along with the comparison group ($\bar{X}$ = 0.88, SD = 0.46), it declined somewhat (0.82) by follow-up 12 months later. This was not, then, an area in which Alice made much progress. It may be that, while Alice learned to identify her own anger, she did not learn to express it directly as well as indirectly.

These measurement-based assessments of the outcomes of Alice's psychotherapy are informative. However, meaning-based evidence of the success or failure of her psychotherapy must also be considered. She learned several useful techniques for dealing with distressing feelings that she should have been able to use in the future. Yet, it was only when she began to appreciate the ways in which her own construct system were interfering with her effective handling of her cardiac condition that progress could be said to

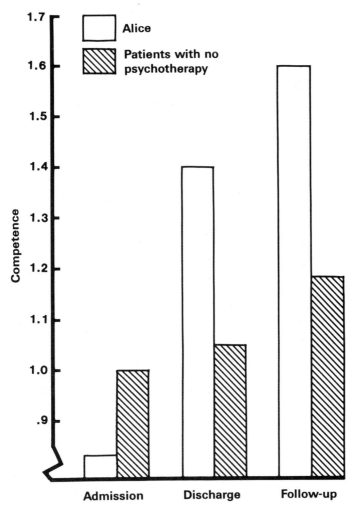

FIGURE 6.4. Competence in Alice and patients with no psychotherapy on admission, discharge, and follow-up.

have been made. By experimenting with her experience, she had come to understand that she was reacting not to her infarction but to her constructs about that infarction. She also came to understand that she had created those constructs herself and could change them when she wanted to do so.

ALICE: You know, I think the most important thing I learned when I was in the hospital and talked with my therapist was that I had to think things through for myself. I was a cauldron of emotions which seemed to overwhelm me. Sharing them with someone was good. But then I began to realize that a lot of it

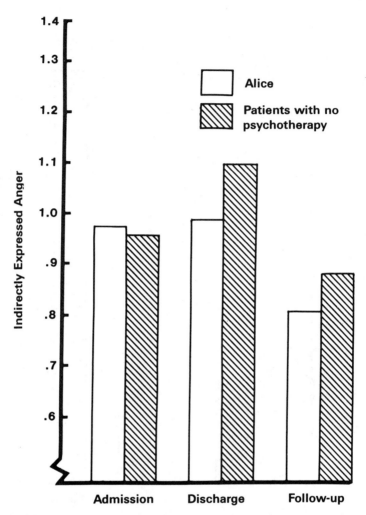

FIGURE 6.5. Indirectly expressed anger in Alice and patients with no psychotherapy on admission, discharge, and follow-up.

was in my own mind. I was getting anxious and depressed because of the way I was seeing things. It was not that I was seeing things that way because I was anxious and depressed. And I came to realize if I was going to cope with my heart condition, I'd better tell it who was boss—me!

Truly therapeutic gains were achieved by Alice, as by other physically ill clients who have been treated with this therapeutic program, only when she was able to say "I have a choice."

REFERENCES

Bannister, D. (1975). Personal construct theory psychotherapy. In D. Bannister (Ed.), *Issues and approaches in the psychological therapies* (pp. 127–146.) London: Wiley.

Beck, A.T., Rush, A.J., Shaw, B.F., & Emery, G. (1979). *Cognitive therapy of depression.* New York: Guilford.

Epting, F.R. (1984). *Personal construct counseling and psychotherapy.* New York: Wiley.

Epting, F., & Neimeyer, R.A. (Eds.) (1984). *Personal meanings of death.* New York: Hemisphere.

Fine, R. (1979). *A history of psychoanalysis.* New York: Columbia.

Gendlin, E.T. (1981). *Focusing.* New York: Bantam.

Gottschalk, L.A. (Ed.) (1979). *The content analysis of verbal behavior.* New York: Spectrum.

Gottschalk, L.A., Lolas, F., & Viney, L.L. (Eds.) (in press). *Content analysis of verbal behavior in clinical medicine.* Berlin: Springer Verlag.

Karst, T.O., & Trexler, L.D. (1970). Initial study using fixed role and rational-emotive therapy in treating public speaking anxiety. *Journal of Consulting and Clinical Psychology, 34,* 360.

Kelly, G.A. (1955). *The psychology of personal constructs.* New York: Norton.

Landfield, A.W. (1980). Personal construct psychotherapy: A personal construction. In A.W. Landfield & L.M. Leitner (Eds.), *Personal construct psychology: Psychotherapy and personality* (pp. 12–21). New York: Wiley.

McCoy, M. (1980). Positive and negative emotion: A personal construct theory interpretation. In H. Bonarius, R. Holland, & S. Rosenberg (Eds.), *Personal construct psychology: Recent advances in the theory and practice* (pp. 187–198). London: Macmillan.

Mechanic, D. (1977). *Medical sociology.* New York: Free Press.

Meichenbaum, D. (1977). *Cognitive-behavior modification: An integrative approach.* New York: Plenum Press.

Neimeyer, R.A. (1985). Personal constructs in clinical practice. In P.C. Kendall (Ed.), *Advances in cognitive behavioral research and therapy* (pp. 275–339). New York: Academic Press.

Neimeyer, R.A. (1986). Personal construct therapy. In W. Dryden & W.L. Golden (Eds.), *Cognitive behavioral approaches to psychotherapy* (pp. 224–260). London: Harper and Row.

O'Connell, W. (1975). *Action therapy and Adlerian theory.* Chicago: Alfred Adler Institute.

Rimm, D.C., & Masters, J.C. (1979). *Behavior therapy.* New York: Academic Press.

Rowe, D. (1978). *The experience of depression.* Chichester: Wiley.

Rudestam, K.E. (1980). *Methods of self change.* Belmont, CA: Brooks/Cole.

Small, L. (1979). *The briefer psychotherapies.* New York: Bruner Mazel.

Viney, L.L. (1981). Experimenting with experience: A psychotherapeutic case study. *Psychotherapy, 18,* 271–278.

Viney, L.L. (1983a). Experiencing chronic illness: A personal construct commentary. In J. Adams-Webber and J. Mancuso (Eds.), *Applications of personal construct theory* (pp. 261–275). London: Academic Press.

Viney, L.L. (1983b). *Images of illness*. Malabar, FL: Krieger.

Viney, L.L. (1983c). Assessing psychological states using content analysis of verbalizations. *Psychological Bulletin, 94,* 542–561.

Viney, L.L. (1985a). Physical illness: A guidebook for the kingdom of the sick. In E. Button (Ed.), *Personal construct theory and mental health* (pp. 262–273). Beckenham: Croom Helm.

Viney, L.L. (1985b). Humor as a therapeutic tool. In A. Landfield & F. Epting (Eds.), *Anticipating personal construct psychology* (pp. 233–245). Nebraska: University of Nebraska Press.

Viney, L.L. (1986). *Interpreting the interpreters: Strategies for a science of construing people*. Malabar, FL: Krieger.

Viney, L.L., Clarke, A.M., Bunn, T.A., & Benjamin, Y.N. (1985a). Crisis intervention counseling: An evaluation of long-term and short-term effects. *Journal of Counseling Psychology, 32,* 29–39.

Viney, L.L., Clarke, A.M., Bunn, T., & Benjamin, Y.N. (1985b). An evaluation of three crisis intervention programs for general hospital patients. *British Journal of Medical Psychology, 58,* 75–86.

Viney, L.L., Clarke, A.M., Bunn, T.A., & Teoh, H.Y. (1985). *Crisis intervention counseling for hospitalized patients*. Sydney: Australian Studies in Health Administration.

Viney, L.L., & Westbrook, M.T. (1981). Psychological reactions to chronic illness-related disability as a function of its severity and type. *Journal of Psychosomatic Medicine, 35,* 513–523.

Viney, L.L., & Westbrook, M.T. (1982a). Patterns of anxiety in the chronically ill. *British Journal of Medical Psychology, 55,* 87–95.

Viney, L.L., & Westbrook, M.T. (1982b). Psychological reactions to chronic illness: Do they predict rehabilitation? *Journal of Applied Rehabilitation Counseling, 13,* 38–44.

Westbrook, M.T., & Viney, L.L. (1980). Measuring people's perceptions of themselves as origins or pawns. *Journal of Personality Assessment, 44,* 157–166.

Wolpe, J.P. (1969). *The practice of behavior therapy*. New York: Pergamon.

Wortman, C.B., & Dunkel-Schetter, C. (1979). Interpersonal relationships and cancer: A theoretical analysis. *Journal of Social Issues, 35,* 120–155.

7
Personal Construct Psychotherapy as a Radical Alternative to Social Skills Training

David A. Winter

Kelly (1970) once joked that the construct of "psychopath" might be applied to those behavior therapists who attempt to modify their clients' behavior while ignoring the constructions that underlie it. He might well have applied the construct not only to practitioners of the skill-deficit model of social skills training, which attempts to teach clients social skills as if they were analogous to motor skills, but also to its products, with their newly developed abilities to manipulate others. The initial introduction of this treatment approach was accompanied by optimistic, not to say extravagant, claims that are still not uncommon. For example, Argyle (1984), after stating that he does "not want to claim too much for SST," goes on to remark that "perhaps 10% of the world's population have quite serious difficulties with common social situations and relationships" which "could be entirely avoided or removed if appropriate SST was available" (pp. 108–109). However, the documented results of training are less impressive, tending neither to maintain over time nor to generalize to settings other than the training situation (Twentyman & Zimering, 1979). This chapter will attempt to explain from a personal construct theory perspective the poor response of clients to social skills training based on the skill-deficit model. I shall then consider whether the alternative models of training for clients adjudged to be deficient in social skills are any more akin to the personal construct psychotherapy approach. Finally, I shall provide an example of the use of this approach with one such client who had previously proved resistant both to a social skills group and to psychodynamic psychotherapy.

AN ALTERNATIVE CONSTRUCTION OF RESISTANCE TO SOCIAL SKILLS TRAINING

For the personal construct theorist, resistance to therapy "is seen less as the client's thwarting or blocking the therapist's moves than as a potentially wise move on the part of the client to pursue a line of meaning that is simply different from what the therapist had in mind" (Epting, 1984, p. 126). A research study of 25 neurotic clients attending social skills groups operating on the skill-deficit model provided an opportunity to explore the line of meaning being pursued by those clients who failed to respond to therapy (Winter, 1985). Treatment gains in these groups were modest in that, although therapists rated their clients as significantly improved, no change was evident on clients' own ratings on their constructs of social competence or on questionnaire measures. Furthermore, the degree of disparity between clients' and therapists' views was indicated by a *negative* correlation ($r = -0.35$) of their ratings of clients' social inadequacy. To explore the possibility that these clients construed social competence in a different way from their therapists, construct correlations in repertory grids that they had completed prior to treatment were examined with a view to identifying the implications of constructs concerning active social interaction, assertiveness, and self-confidence. In 80% of the clients, social competence carried some negative implications in terms of clients' own elicited constructs. Using Landfield's (1971) classification system of construct content, over half of these fell into the categories of Low Tenderness, High Forcefulness, Low Morality, Closed to Alternatives, and High Egoism. Thus, confident, assertive extraverts were construed by individual clients as likely to be, amongst other things, selfish, uncaring, unsympathetic, hard, contemptuous, arrogant, aggressive, demanding, domineering, deceitful, disloyal, dishonest, irresponsible, unreliable, unimaginative, stubborn, pigheaded, bigheaded, and bigmouthed. In order to test the hypothesis that such dilemmas regarding social interaction influenced clients' construing of the social skills group experience, a grid measure of these dilemmas was devised such that the higher a client's score, the greater the tendency for the preferred poles of their social interaction constructs to be associated with their nonpreferred poles on other constructs. Dilemma scores were then correlated with clients' average scores on a Group Climate Questionnaire (MacKenzie, 1983) completed after every group session. As predicted, clients with more pronounced dilemmas were found to perceive the group in a significantly more negative light. In a further sample, those clients for whom social competence carried more negative implications, as reflected in high dilemma scores, construed themselves as less socially competent and obtained higher scores on the Social Situations Questionnaire (SSQ) (Trower, Bryant, & Argyle, 1978), a measure of the degree of difficulty and avoidance of such situations. This might conceivably reflect a strategy by which such individuals maintain some modicum of self-esteem, construing themselves as socially incompetent but receiving the payoff of at least being able to see themselves as humane and virtuous. The dilemma in which they may find themselves ensnared as a result of the way in which they construe social competence is that incompetence may actually represent the preferred choice over the less savory alternatives that would jeopardize more central aspects of themselves.

It is small wonder, then, that these clients were in the main resistant to social skills training. Given their constructions of social skills, many of them may have construed this form of treatment as involving training in selfishness, contempt, and deceit. Indeed, the homework assignments employed in some social skills training programs might serve to validate clients' negative constructions of social competence. For example, it is not uncommon for clients to be asked, as homework, to drive into a garage and, without buying petrol, ask the attendant to check the oil, water, and tire pressures and wash the windows; to buy a dollar's worth of goods and write a check for it; or, in a restaurant, to change the order as soon as the waiter has taken it (e.g., King, Liberman, Roberts, & Bryan, 1977).

MODELS OF SOCIAL SKILLS TRAINING

As with other behavioral methods of treatment, the failure of social skills training to live up to its early promise has been an impetus for a cognitive revolution and the development of alternative treatment models that may appear to take some account of the clients' construing. Linehan (1979) has outlined three such models in relation to assertiveness training. One, the faulty discrimination model, views the client as possessing the necessary skills but as making inappropriate discriminations among situations in terms of when to employ particular skills. Kelly (1955) also regarded the capacity to make appropriate predictions about social situations as central to constructive personal relationships, but emphasized, in this respect, anticipation of the construing of others. Research evidence suggests that failures in such anticipation, and consequent difficulties in forming role relationships, may have their basis in structural features of the construct system such as simplicity of construct organization (Neimeyer & Neimeyer, 1985). Personal construct psychotherapy for clients with interpersonal difficulties of this nature might, therefore, include techniques that encourage loosening and engagement in cycles of construction (Reid, 1979) or approaches that explicitly focus on exploration of the constructions of other people (e.g., Landfield, 1979). Unlike therapies based on the faulty discrimination model, it would not involve assumptions regarding the correctness of certain responses to particular social situations and consequent attempts to instruct clients in how they "should" construe their social world.

Another alternative model of training identified by Linehan (1979) is the response-inhibition model, in which the client's social skills are assumed to be inhibited by anxiety or by maladaptive cognitions. One such treatment method, which bears a superficial resemblance to personal construct psychotherapy in its concern to facilitate reconstruing, is rational-emotive therapy. However, closer scrutiny reveals significant differences between the approaches adopted by the rational-emotive and personal construct therapist, the greater expressiveness and directiveness of the former reflecting the assumption that the therapist's task is to replace the client's irrational thinking by a set of rational perceptions (Dryden, 1984a; Karst & Trexler, 1970; Neimeyer, 1985). Despite this assumption, descriptions of techniques employed by rational-emotive therapists in social skills training would suggest that the clients may not find it easy to maintain a belief that their therapist is a model of rationality. For example, in order to facilitate self-acceptance, rational-emotive therapists have been known to leap to the floor suddenly in a treatment session and bark like a dog, or to encourage their clients to carry out "shame-attacking exercises" such as standing in an elevator facing the other passengers, selling the previous day's newspapers, or trying to buy chocolate in a hardware shop (Dryden, 1984b,c). A more serious criticism of rational-emotive and other cognitive therapies from a personal construct theory perspective is that, as Rowe (1980) has remarked, "there's more to being human than being logical" (p. 9). Indeed, far from being necessarily a sign of psychological disorder and an appropriate target for therapeutic attack, an apparently illogical pattern of construct organization may reflect the capacity to tolerate ambiguity at subordinate levels of the construct system that is afforded the individual who possesses sufficiently permeable superordinate constructs (Sheehan, 1981; Winter, 1983). If, for example, a person contrasts kindness with cruelty but associates both these characteristics with responsibility, this apparent logical inconsistency may be resolved by the use of a superordinate construct that encompasses the notion that one sometimes has to be cruel to be kind.

It may be, then, that the therapist who considers a client's behavior and beliefs to be irrational simply does not have the degree of understanding of the client's construct system necessary to appreciate the client's own logic.

Such a view would reflect Linehan's (1979) rational-choice model, which she claims is "generally held by clients but usually not shared by their therapists," and which, when applied to difficulties in assertion, states that the unassertive person "has the skills, is not inhibited, knows when an assertive response is likely to be effective and, for a wide variety of possible reasons, chooses to behave in a nonassertive manner" (p. 207). Writers such as Trower (1984) who advocate a paradigm shift in social skills training also tend to see the person who persists in apparently unskilled social behavior as making an active choice. Although making no reference to Kelly, Trower's description of the agency approach which he proposes as a radical alternative to the behavioral paradigm, will have a rather familiar ring to it for readers acquainted with personal construct theory. Thus, he states that the approach "conceptualises a man as a social agent who actively constructs his own experience and generates his own goal-directed behaviour on the basis of these constructs" (Trower, p. 4). It is somewhat surprising, therefore, that the treatment method that he favors as representing the agency approach is rational-emotive therapy, for its assumption that the client is irrational and must be instructed to think correctly does not seem fundamentally different from the assumption that the client is deficient in skills and must be taught how to behave socially. Such assumptions ultimately lead to approaches that exhort the client to adopt the therapist's view of the world and are radically different from those that underlie personal construct psychotherapy.

The personal construct psychotherapist, while viewing a client's interpersonal difficulties as stemming directly from their particular constructions of their social world, will assume that these constructions are the client's best available means of anticipating events and that they, and the consequent "social skill deficits," represent what Fransella (1972) has termed the client's "way of life." The therapist will, therefore, not discount the client's view of the world too lightly. As well as helping the client to make more explicit and to test out his existing constructions, the therapist will encourage the client to explore whether alternative constructions might provide a firmer basis for anticipation. Care will be taken, however, not to present this alternative way of life as necessarily the only possible solution to the client's problems but instead as offering constructions that could be tried out as if they offered a more valid understanding of events. Rather than being trained in specific social skills, either behavioral or cognitive, the client will be helped to adopt a broad strategy of approaching social situations with a more propositional style of construing and a concern with understanding the construction processes of others. A primary intention of such an approach is that the client will develop a better elaborated construction of the self as a socially competent person and one that carries fewer negative implications.

SOCIAL SKILLS AND PERSONAL CONSTRUCTS: AN ILLUSTRATION

Having failed to respond to both individual and group analytic psychotherapy, Tom, a 31-year-old bachelor, sought out social skills training and joined one of the groups that was included in the research study discussed above. This proved no more successful than his previous experiences of therapy, and in his posttreatment interview he remarked that "the group didn't help at all. I'm not lacking in social skills. The problem is the feelings behind the social skills." The extent of Tom's dissatisfaction with the social skills group was reflected in his Group Climate Questionnaire responses, which revealed that he construed the group more negatively than did any other client in the sample. Although he was rated by his therapist as somewhat improved, his self-ratings of social adequacy decreased over the course of treatment, his perceived distance from his ideal self increased, and his responses to the Crown–Crisp Experiential Inventory (CCEI) (Crown & Crisp, 1979) indicated a marked increase in neurotic, and particularly in phobic, symptomatology.

Tom's extremely unfavorable view of and lack of response to the social skills group was explicable in that his score on the measure of dilemmas concerning social interaction derived from his pregroup repertory grid was the highest of any of the subjects studied. Changes from pre- to posttreatment assessment in the correlations between his constructs indicated that over the course of the group the negative implications that social interaction held for him tended to increase. For example, he increasingly construed assertive extraverts as "demanding and aggressive." By contrast, those who dislike meeting people and who are negative thinkers were construed as "unselfish." Taking life as it comes, Tom's contrast pole to "worrying," was also associated with selfishness, coldness, inactivity, and lack of intelligence, although less so at follow-up assessment. Given these negative implications of extraversion, assertiveness, and lack of worry, it was scarcely surprising that he saw himself as shy, socially isolated, passive, and a worrier. His perceived dissimilarity to others was reflected in the fact that he placed himself and other persons at opposite poles of his constructs 62% of the time, this being the exact opposite of the normal pattern (Adams-Webber, 1979). Six-month follow-up assessment on the grid and questionnaires indicated further deterioration in his condition. At this point Tom requested additional help for what his general practitioner described as "his long-standing feeling of inadequacy." We therefore decided to commence personal construct psychotherapy on an individual basis and to review his progress after six weekly, tape-recorded sessions. He also agreed to complete a self-characterization before the first treatment session.

The first few sessions focused on controlled elaboration of his complaints, which Kelly (1955, p. 935) saw as "a way of bringing about reconstruction through clarification." Such clarification seemed desirable as both the lack of precision in Tom's speech and the low level of interrelationship between constructs in his grid suggested a rather loosely organized construct system, whose predictive implications would be relatively untestable. Tom's major concern in this initial period was his situation at work. He complained, for example, that "my attitude to work and life is totally different from the people I work with" and that consequently he was rejected and isolated by his colleagues. However, his perceived isolation involved more than a touch of hostility, in Kelly's (1955) sense of tampering with the evidence in order to make it fit with one's predictions. Thus, having obtained his university degree, Tom appeared to have sought out work environments in which he and his colleagues were likely to have had rather different life experiences. He was at present a manual worker and admitted that he saw himself as more "educated," "refined," "sensitive," and "of a higher social class" than his workmates, whom he construed as "ignorant heavy drinkers." In order to encourage less preemptive construing, I asked him if he could see no positive attributes in his workmates. Although replying that they appeared happy and extraverted, Tom went on to associate these characteristics with a "couldn't care less attitude," with insensitivity, and with using "jokiness" in order to avoid intimate relationships. The implication that his depression and introversion might belie a superiority to others echoed a theme from his self-characterization, in which he described how, as children, his friend would spend pounds on new fishing gear, but Tom, with his piece of string on the end of a stick, would catch all the fish. Thus, in both these examples, Tom appeared to derive a certain satisfaction from hiding his light under a bushel and contrasting his own behavior with that of others who were more flamboyant but ultimately less effective.

It appeared, then, that any movement towards becoming a happier and more extraverted person could be fraught with negative implications for Tom. Such dilemmas were further explored by tracing both the negative and positive implications of his complaints as in Tschudi's (1977) ABC procedure (in which the therapist identifies a construct, A, defining the client's problem area; a second construct, B, indicating the disadvantages of the problem; and a third construct, C, indicating its advantages). For example, taking Tom's major complaint, his inability to assert his opinions and to stand up for himself, I asked him what he saw as the advantage of being assertive, to which he replied that it produced "relief of tension." However, that assertiveness also carried negative implications for him, which may in part have led to his difficulties in self-assertion, was immediately suggested by the fact that his contrast pole to being assertive was to be "reasonable." In

response to my questions concerning further negative implications of assertive behavior, he said that such behavior might result in his being perceived
as "a pain in the neck," becoming "personally attacking or physically
violent," or "losing an argument." I asked him what evidence there was to
support his belief that he could be personally or physically violent, and he
admitted that there was none. Taking up his other feared consequence of
assertiveness, I asked why losing an argument would be so disastrous, to
which Tom replied that it would cause him "inner anger" and depression.
When I pointed out that his present strategy of avoiding self-assertion and
consequent arguments hardly seemed to relieve his depression, he laughingly agreed that this was so. We then began to explore the positive
implications of being reasonable, namely that one is liked and seen as "a
good bloke." However, after making this connection Tom immediately
remarked that it was invalid because he was always reasonable but did not
appear to be liked. The "Aha!" quality of this apparent insight suggested
that reconstruing was indeed taking place (c.f., Kelly, 1955, p. 1093). In
order to capitalize on this, I explored with Tom why being reasonable could
possibly lead to one being disliked:

DAVID (D): Could it be that in some way you're being *too* reasonable?
   TOM (T): Yes.
        D: What is it about being very reasonable that people might dislike?
        T: Could be boring perhaps. Frustration I suppose. I'm thinking of an
           answer. I don't know really. Irritating probably.
        D: Is that because someone who's very reasonable never expresses any
           opinion, never disagrees with anything? I suppose if you look far enough
           you can always find a way of agreeing with something, find a reason
           for agreeing.
        T: So people prefer me to disagree because it makes life more interesting. It
           gives them an opportunity to be something, to assert their point of view.
           Perhaps I imagine people are too like myself, don't like arguing.
        D: Maybe, also if you're reasonable all the time, in some way the other per-
           son is forced into being unreasonable by contrast.
        T: This has happened. Some people make a point of choosing the op-
           posite.
        D: Possibly that isn't all that comfortable for them.
        T: But why do they do it?
        D: I don't know. I wonder whether in some way they might not have much
           option if you're being so reasonable all the time.
        T: Perhaps they don't like me being correct all the time.

In addition to interventions such as this, aimed at encouraging him to test
out the validity of constructions underlying his complaints, an attempt was
made to modify these constructions by time-binding, an approach sug-

gested by Kelly (1955, p. 1075) to narrow the range of convenience of a construct by limiting its applicability to a particular period of time. Thus, I suggested that certain of Tom's constructs were anachronisms that he had developed in his childhood in order to anticipate the behavior of a depressive, socially phobic mother. As he described it, his mother rarely spoke either to him or to his father, and on the rare occasions when she did assert her opinions, she would become physically violent. His initial explanation of his mother's behavior was that her life had been a difficult one and that in her silence she was being "unselfish" by not burdening others with her difficulties. I offered him an alternative construction by suggesting that her behavior could be viewed as demanding and controlling, and he subsequently sought evidence for these constructions by directly asking her the reasons for her moodiness. Her lack of response led him to reconstrue her as "the most boring person in the world" and to decide not to visit his parental home again. As he said, it was like "avoiding the plague," because if he were to be with his parents he might, in a sense, "catch" a way of construing and of behaving that was inappropriate to other social situations. In Kelly's terms, there was an element of constriction and foreshortening of the circumspection–preemption–control cycle in this response. That is, Tom could be seen as attempting to find a quick solution to his problems by deciding to exclude an anxiety-provoking element—his mother—from his perceptual field, without really weighing the alternatives. However, I focused on the more positive aspects of his decision, such as the fact that asserting himself in his relationship with his mother had not resulted in the violent consequences that he had anticipated and indeed had made him feel less isolated from people. As he said, "In actual fact, after I had the row, or a few words, with my mother, most people are very pleasant to me, a stark constrast, and I was in quite high spirits actually over the weekend. I suppose I could be a lot closer to people." Tom was also able to reject the considerable similarities that he had previously perceived between himself and his mother, and instead elaborated a more favorable self-construal by contrasting himself with her. He pointed out, for example, that he was more "dynamic" than his mother in that "if something is wrong I will put it right" and that if he wanted something (such as going to university or commencing personal construct psychotherapy) he usually achieved it.

Tom's confrontation with his mother led him to experience some guilt. In Kelly's terms, this could be seen as reflecting the marked departure from his core role that assertive behavior of this type represented. Apart from being guilt-provoking, such behavior and the prospect of further change also led to considerable uncertainty and therefore anxiety. This contrasted with the better elaborated "way of life" that his presenting problems afforded him. Something of this uncertainty was indicated by his statement that he could only become the person he wanted to be if he were "on a firm base first." He elaborated on this point in the following interaction:

T: In a way I'm happy as I am, being the way I am, but it's not getting the rewards that I want.

D: So what would be the rewards that you want?

T: To feel more integrated with other people really. Not to be so alone. I've been living very much alone for a long, long time. Even at university I was alone.

D: I think you really can't have it both ways though. You've either got to decide that you're happy as you are, and what goes along with that is that you are probably going to remain isolated, or you've got to decide to change in some ways, which might mean . . .

T: To change I've got to be on a different planet . . . . And of course change involves being more in focus doesn't it, more in the light.

D: What would that mean?

T: Well, it's going to be a very testing situation, a demanding situation really.

Similarly, the hazards of change, in terms of anxiety and guilt, were apparent in his description of an occasion when he became aware of experiencing feelings of happiness: "I became very self-conscious about them. I was talking a lot but suddenly anxiety came into action and I thought 'Am I going to feel this way in a day's time, and if I came across this person again would I be able to respond, would I still be talkative, or would I become stuck?'"

With a view to elaborating a construction of himself as a more assertive person, and therefore providing the "firm base" which he required for change, I suggested that he write a self-characterization as if he were such a person. However, despite several attempts, Tom felt unable to complete this assignment, saying "I can see your point of view that if you imagine something then when you put it to the task everything's rearranged beforehand. That's how I plan my goals. But I suppose even writing myself down as assertive isn't particularly amicable (sic). I find it difficult to do because there's so little to write about. I'm being someone I'm not." Similarly, except on one occasion, Tom felt unable to engage in enactment during therapy sessions, insisting that he had an immutable personality defect and that, if he were to behave differently, this would only involve "putting on a front." Indeed, he initially maintained that he was suffering from schizophrenia and sought advice from a self-help organization for schizophrenics. However, he admitted that this was because he saw the diagnostic label as providing him with some certainty, whereas if he were to relinquish it his life would be "a mystery." Rather than being seen as resistant behavior that should be overcome, Tom's opposition to my suggestions provided a useful indication that I had underestimated the degree of threat and guilt that change, even when only imagined or role played, might provoke. It also provided an opportunity to point out to him that, in resisting my proposals, he was in fact asserting himself within the therapy sessions but once again without the anticipated dire consequences of such assertiveness.

I asked Tom to make a mental note between therapy sessions of any similar incidents in which he experienced himself or was experienced by others as acting assertively. Here again, my hope was that in discussing the details of these incidents, a viable, more assertive way of life could perhaps be elaborated. In subsequent sessions, he reported several such occasions, mostly involving disagreements with his workmates, his characteristic response to which was to manipulate situations so that "I let them make fools of themselves in the end." He accepted my suggestion that the indirectness of his actions, which on one occasion involved ensuring that disciplinary action was taken against his colleagues, could be construed as deviousness. However, it became apparent that a major obstacle to his asserting himself more directly was his perception that in every argument there is "a right and wrong opinion" and "a winner and a loser," but that winning the argument may depend on the force with which one's opinion is expressed rather than its "rightness." As he would rarely countenance the possibility that another person might have an opinion as valid as his own, he saw little need to attempt to understand the other person's point of view or to argue his case directly, particularly as this might involve losing the argument or having to be "uncool or heavy" in order to win it. It appeared that Tom had considerable difficulty in construing the construction processes of other people, as had been evident during his earlier social skills training, when he was among the least accurate clients in predicting the self-ratings of other group members. I therefore increasingly attempted to encourage more propositional construing by replacing the notion of right and wrong opinions with that of alternative constructions of reality, which could be appreciated by taking the perspectives of other people. Thus, in relation to a difference of opinion with members of his tennis club, Tom noted:

T: I think they disagreed just for disagreeing. Perhaps they just want to annoy me.

D: That seems similar to what you said about your colleagues.

T: I wouldn't do that to another person.

D: I wonder if it's right that they're disagreeing just to annoy you, or is it that you don't really understand what their reasons are because you're so convinced that your position is right?

Similarly, in relation to his difficulties in finding a woman friend and his consequent use of stereotypes in an attempt to gain some understanding of "female psychology":

T: Most girls like a good sense of humor and if I don't provide it someone else will.

D: I wonder if that's true . . . .

T: So why don't I have more relationships? What's the missing ingredient? Perhaps I'm too shy, lacking confidence. What would you say?

D: . . . What I do think is that you can't say that all girls are looking for the same thing.

T: No. But I'm not the only person on earth. It's a very competitive thing, and if someone has a sense of humor they will put themselves across quicker, even if it's just a front, and I'm the loser.

D: If that's what they're looking for. Some people may be looking for someone who's perhaps a bit more sensitive or honest.

T: Yes. So they're just like us, I suppose, really.

After discussion with Tom at the fourth session, it was agreed that I would prepare a fixed role sketch that would emphasize a concern with understanding the viewpoints of others. One of my intentions was that, in enacting this fixed role, Tom would be enabled to experiment with alternative constructions that would be less heavily laden with negative implications. In doing so, he would come to appreciate that he is self-creating and, by behaving differently, able to elicit new reactions from other people. As Kelly (1955) has suggested, by encouraging such experimentation in the world outside the therapy room, the fixed role may also set the stage for termination of therapy.

The role that I prepared for Tom was as follows:

D: Roy Taylor's philosophy of life very much reflects his approach to his favorite sport, tennis: it's not whether a player wins or loses that's important but whether they've played the game to the best of their ability. Whether at work or at play, he believes that if a job is worth doing it's worth doing well, and he brings to everything that he does a certain passion and conviction, which cannot fail to earn your respect. Although you might perhaps think that this would make him appear a little too serious and intense, once you get to know him you soon realize that his main concern is to live life to the full and that this includes having fun as well as working hard. Life doesn't always run smoothly for him, of course, but when he has a disappointment he always seems able to learn something from it, and to look to the future rather than brooding on his present or past misfortunes.

One of his greatest strengths at tennis is his ability to anticipate the moves of the other players, be they his opponents or doubles partners. In other areas of his life, he also always tries to see the world through the eyes of the people with whom he comes into contact, perhaps because he has mixed with people from so many different walks of life. His lively curiosity in what makes other people tick is usually reciprocated and leads him, almost before he knows it, into some very rewarding relationships. He also, of course, has his fair share of disagreements with others, but when this happens he always makes an effort to understand the other person's point of view, even though he might not accept it. Because of this, he has a reputation both for commitment to those causes that are close to his heart and tolerance of the right of others to hold different opinions.

It seemed, however, that Tom was already spontaneously experimenting with new constructions and behavior, and, consequently, it was not until the sixth session that a suitable opportunity arose to show him the fixed role. At this session, Tom came into the therapy room and sat in my chair for the first time, thus vividly demonstrating the behavioral changes that were taking place. That reconstruing was also occurring was suggested by his perception of the fixed role as being like a "character reference" for him: as he remarked, "that's me in a nutshell." In view of these apparent changes, it was decided not to embark on the formal fixed role therapy procedure. Tom did, however, concede the need to "polish" some aspects of the character embodied in the fixed role sketch, such as how to have a lively curiosity in others without being "nosey," and he took the sketch home with him in order to provide a continuing point of reference. Aspects of the role, together with Tom's developing relationship with a woman, were a focus of subsequent therapy sessions, which were held on a less frequent basis.

Assessments with the CCEI and SSQ indicated a marked reduction in Tom's neurotic symptoms and difficulties in social situations over the course of personal construct psychotherapy, in contrast to the changes that had been observed during his social skills training. Repertory grid assessments revealed that changes at the level of symptoms and behavior were paralleled by those in construing, such as reduction of self-ideal self-discrepancy and, perhaps most significantly, reconstruction of social interaction. As an illustration of the latter, it can be seen from Table 7.1 that both the principal dimensions of construing identified by INGRID computer analysis (Slater, 1972) of his pretreatment repertory grid consisted of an amalgam of various aspects of active social interaction, all of which he insisted were somewhat different despite their apparent similarity, together with undesirable qualities such as being demanding and cold. At the posttreatment assessment, however, it seemed that such dilemmas were largely resolved in that constructs concerning active social interaction only contributed highly to the first principal component of his grid and were associated with constructs relating to positively valenced qualities such as warmth and intelligence. The stage was set, therefore, for his becoming more extraverted and assertive without also having to construe himself as more aggressive and less humane.

Commenting on the process of change, Tom remarked:

T: Oh yes, (I'm feeling) a lot better. I think that's because I saw the problem and had to find ways of overcoming it. I wasn't quite sure what the problem was, whether it was me personally, schizophrenia, that sort of thing, or outside factors . . . . I don't know how I got out of it anyway. You must have given me some clear insight that it wasn't me personally. I didn't agree with you initially but I think what happened was that I was getting on well with people socially. That showed the contrast.

D: So where do you want to go from here?

T: I don't think I can really ask for any more.

TABLE 7.1 Constructs with highest loadings (>0.6) on principal components of Tom's repertory grid before and after personal construct psychotherapy

Pretreatment		Posttreatment	
Component I		Component I	
Extraverted *versus* Introverted		Likes people's company *versus* Dislikes meeting people	
Talkative	Quiet	Always cheerful	Depressed
Good mixer	Not a good mixer	Talkative	Quiet
Assertive	Passive	Good mixer	Not a good mixer
Prefers to be center of attention	Shy	Extraverted	Introverted
Always cheerful	Depressed	Positive	Negative thinker
Positive	Negative thinker	Warm	Cold personality
Good company	Solitude	Assertive	Passive
Demanding	Unselfish	Prefers to be center of attention	Shy
		Clever	Average
		Good company	Solitude
		Very active	Not active
		Takes life as it comes	Worrier
Component II		Component II	
Warm *versus* Cold personality		Considerate *versus* Aggressive	
Very active	Not active	Unselfish	Demanding
Considerate	Aggressive		
Dislikes meeting people	Likes people's company		

And again,

T: I think I've become more sociable, perhaps less shy, now. I think I was held back because depressed, miserable, that sort of thing. Because I feel more relaxed and happier inside, I've been developing my social life, so that change brings on further change. I'm getting to know a lot more people, less isolated, and it's having a snowball effect really. I'm seeing more of the opposite sex and there are quite a lot of people phoning me up—"would you like to come to this," "would you like to go to that," which (laughs) never used to happen . . . . Totally different from how I was when I first saw you, I didn't know which way to turn. . . . It needed something to start it all. I'm not sure what it is. Obviously seeing you, talking to you really, and getting round a major problem at work. It's amazing actually because I've only seen you for nearly three months or something like that, but yet I've been seeing other therapists for six months or a year and it seemed to have no effect (laughs). What have you done that they haven't done? I think perhaps you responding to what I say, giving your opinion, has helped a lot, does help a hell of a lot.

CONCLUSIONS

As the technical eclecticism of personal construct psychotherapy may at times suggest a superficial similarity to other treatment methods, this chapter has attempted to address Tom's question of why he responded better to a personal construct theory approach than to alternative therapeutic approaches. If personal construct psychotherapy did indeed prove more beneficial for him, it was perhaps because it involved taking seriously his view of the world, rather than discounting it as invalid, irrational, or as material for esoteric interpretations. Similarly, unlike the various models of social skills training, which could be construed as modern-day versions of codes of etiquette and chivalry (Radley, 1985), alternative constructions were offered to him in an invitational mood rather than as prescriptions for correct social behavior and more rational thinking.

Commenting on Trower's proposed radical approach to social skills training, Schroeder and Rakos (1983) remark that "the emphasis on cognitive restructuring suggests an orientation towards conformity in cognitions, meanings, and ultimately goals" which "highlights the fact that we must be prepared to confront the ethical and political issues involved in endorsing the status quo" (p. 125). To label such an approach radical would scarcely seem appropriate. By contrast, with its credulous approach and its acceptance that there may be many viable ways of construing reality, personal construct psychotherapy offers a genuinely radical alternative to the behavioral paradigm.

REFERENCES

Adams-Webber, J. (1979). *Personal construct theory: Concepts and applications.* Chichester: Wiley.

Argyle, M. (1984). Some new developments in social skills training. *Bulletin of the British Psychological Society, 37,* 405–410.

Crown, S., & Crisp, A. H. (1979). *Crown–Crisp Experiential Index.* London: Hodder & Stoughton.

Dryden, W. (Ed.). (1984a). *Individual therapy in Britain.* London: Harper & Row.

Dryden, W. (1984b). Rational-emotive therapy. In W. Dryden (Ed.), *Individual therapy in Britain* (pp. 235–263). London: Harper & Row.

Dryden, W. (1984c). Social skills training from a rational-emotive perspective. In P. Trower (Ed.), *Radical approaches to social skills training* (pp. 314–346). London: Croom Helm.

Epting, F. (1984). *Personal construct counseling and psychotherapy.* Chichester: Wiley.

Fransella, F. (1972). *Personal change and reconstruction: Research and treatment of stuttering.* London: Academic Press.

Karst, T. O., & Trexler, L. D. (1970). Initial study using fixed role and rational-emotive therapy in treating public speaking anxiety. *Journal of Consulting and Clinical Psychology, 34,* 360–366.

Kelly, G. A. (1955). *The psychology of personal constructs.* New York: Norton.

Kelly, G. A. (1970). Behavior is an experiment. In D. Bannister (Ed.), *Perspectives in personal construct theory* (pp. 255–270). London: Academic Press.

King, L. W., Liberman, R. P., Roberts, J., & Bryan, E. (1977). Personal effectiveness: A structured therapy for improving social and emotional skills. *Behavior Analysis & Modification, 2,* 82–91.

Landfield, A. W. (1971). *Personal construct systems in psychotherapy* (pp. 133–152). Chicago: Rand McNally.

Landfield, A. W. (1979). Exploring socialisation through the interpersonal transaction group. In P. Stringer & D. Bannister (Eds.), *Constructs of sociality and individuality.* London: Academic Press.

Linehan, M. M. (1979). Structured cognitive-behavioural treatment of assertion problems. In P. C. Kendall & S. D. Hollon (Eds.), *Cognitive-behavioural interventions: Theory, research and procedures* (pp. 205–240). New York: Academic Press.

MacKenzie, K. R. (1983). The clinical application of a group climate measure. In R. R. Dies & K. R. MacKenzie (Eds.), *Advances in group psychotherapy: Integrating research and practice* (pp. 159–170). New York: International Universities Press.

Neimeyer, R. A. (1985). Personal constructs in clinical practice. In P. Kendall (Ed.), *Advances in cognitive behavioral research and therapy (Vol. 4)* (pp. 275–339). New York: Academic Press.

Neimeyer, R., & Neimeyer, G. (1985). Disturbed relationships: A personal construct view. In E. Button (Ed.), *Personal construct theory and mental health* (pp. 195–223). London: Croom Helm.

Radley, A. (1985). From courtesy to strategy: Some old developments. *Bulletin of the British Psychological Society, 38,* 209–211.

Reid, F. (1979). Personal constructs and social competence. In P. Stringer & D. Bannister (Eds.), *Constructs of sociality and individuality.* London: Academic Press.

Rowe, D. (1980, August). Logical limitations. *New Forum, 6–9.*

Schroeder, H. E., & Rakos, R. F. (1983). The identification and assessment of social skills. In R. Ellis & D. Whittington (Eds.), *New directions in social skills training* (pp. 117–188). London: Croom Helm.

Sheehan, M. J. (1981). Constructs and 'conflict' in depression. *British Journal of Psychology, 72,* 197–209.

Slater, P. (1972). *Notes on INGRID 72.* London: St. George's Hospital.

Trower, P. (Ed.). (1984). *Radical approaches to social skills training.* London: Croom Helm.

Trower, P., Bryant, B., & Argyle, M. (1978). *Social skills and mental health.* London: Methuen.

Tschudi, F. (1977). Loaded and honest questions: A construct theory view of symptoms and therapy. In D. Bannister (Ed.), *New perspectives in personal construct theory* (pp. 321–350). London: Academic Press.

Twentyman, C. T., & Zimering, R. T. (1979). Behavioural training of social skills: A critical review. In M. Hersen, R. M. Eisler, & P. M. Miller (Eds.), *Progress in behaviour modification (Vol. 7)* (pp. 319–400). New York: Academic Press.

Winter, D. A. (1983). Logical inconsistency in construct relationships: Conflict or complexity? *British Journal of Medical Psychology, 56,* 79–87.

Winter, D. A. (1985). *Constructions in social skills training: The cognitive revolution, radicalism, and personal construct psychotherapy.* Paper presented at 6th International Congress on Personal Construct Psychology. Cambridge, England.

III
Marital
and
Family
Therapy

8
Marital Role Reconstruction Through Couples Group Therapy

Greg J. Neimeyer

Although Kelly's (1955) writings predated the development of group therapy for couples, it is clear that conjoint treatment in a group context is well suited to personal construct theory. In his evident enthusiasm for group treatment, Kelly (1955) likened group psychotherapy to "a large, well-equipped social laboratory with a variety of figures in it, in contrast to a small laboratory with only one other figure in it," and concluded that "the better-equipped laboratory affords an opportunity to perform a greater variety of social experiments" (p. 210). Central to these experiments is the opportunity for partners to formulate and test new relationships with one another in a context that is richly social. The importance of multiple relationships in this enterprise is implicit in Kelly's (1955) recognition that "it is difficult to form new social concepts out of situations which are barren of social relationships" (p. 169). For this reason the group context would seem ideally suited to the reconstruction of intimate role relations, particularly marital relationships, where partners' constructions of one another can be worked with *in vivo* in the group.

Yet, despite this promising fit, Kelly left it for later writers to discuss the application of personal construct theory to conjoint marital therapy, let alone its operation in marital groups. Although much of this work focuses on repertory grid assessments of marital distress (Ryle, 1981; Ryle & Breen, 1972; Ryle & Lipshitz, 1975; Ryle & Lunghi, 1970; Wijesinghe & Wood, 1976), recent work has begun to address issues of conceptualization and intervention (Doster, 1985; Kremsdorf, 1985; G. Neimeyer, 1985; Neimeyer & Hudson, 1985; R. Neimeyer, 1986) in personal construct terms as well. This chapter is written in the belief that personal construct theory has some innovative contributions to make to furthering this literature because the strengths of construct theory converge precisely at the juncture of group and marital therapy—group, because construct theory is so avowedly *inter*personal in its therapeutic orientation, and marital, because Kelly's abiding concern with intimate role relationships is nowhere better fitted than to the treatment of deeply intimate love relationships.

RIGGING THE SHIP

In an effort to experiment with developing a group format for treating marital disorders, I met with two colleagues at the University counseling center to address the parameters of group referral, selection, evaluation, and the like. In our appeal to the literature, we found a rapidly expanding list of relevant references to draw from, most of them quite recent. Although references to conjoint therapy dated to the 1940s, literature on marital group treatment began to accumulate only in the late 1960s (Alger, 1976). But by the time of Gurman's (1973) writings, however, reports of marital group therapy were already outdistancing reports of other innovations in marital treatment. Discussions of marital group therapy are fairly common in the contemporary literature, perhaps reflecting an increased recognition of group therapy as the treatment of choice for many marital disorders (Kaslow & Lieberman, 1981).

From our readings in related family therapy literatures, we decided to incorporate into treatment the use of a live form of supervision involving the three of us as a "consultation team." The team was to operate as a variant of the familiar Greek Chorus (Papp, 1980), working from behind a one-way mirror adjacent to the therapy room. We had agreed in advance with the primary therapists, Dave and Marty, that we would occasionally interrupt the sessions with feedback to the group (through a speaker system), but also that we would meet with the co-therapists during one intermission period in the midst of each of the 11 90-minute sessions. This time would be used to provide them with supervisory feedback and to collaborate with them in designing relevant interventions.

We also talked at length with the co-therapists about the group and its objectives. Since our group was to run about the modal length of most short-term therapies for couples (Gurman, 1971), we developed goals consistent with brief therapy. Most importantly, we viewed therapy as an effort to revitalize productive collaboration between partners in a way that would enable them to continue ongoing revisions of their relationships after group termination. Thus, goals were directed at the process level, at helping partners to develop means of testing and revising their role relationships. Consistent with this objective, our guiding principle as a consultation team was to assist in developing a "therapeutic program around a series of practical experiments which yield validating and invalidating evidence" (Kelly, 1955, p. 500).

As an initial step in the process, we had pretested the four couples selected for the group along three marital relationship measures. Each measure was designed to tap a different aspect of their relationships. The first was the Areas of Change Questionnaire. It consists of a variety of behaviorally specific items (e.g., conducting household chores, visiting friends) along which partners indicate the degree and direction (more or less) of desired changes in their relationship. Total scores (range, 0 to 64) reflect the degree of marital distress. Normative studies suggest that nondistressed couples seek an average of about 7 changes in their relationships, whereas distressed couples seek an average of about 25 changes (for validity and details of scoring, see Weiss, Hops, & Patterson, 1973).

A second measure assessed the degree to which partners shared a common framework for understanding intimate relationships. Stephen and Markman (1983) have argued that an "emergent, conjoint construction of the world may serve as a source of confirmation and reinforcement for partners" (p. 17), and they have developed the Relationship World Index (RWI) as a means to assess this. The instrument is a Q-sort technique consisting of 60 statements describing intimate relationships (e.g., "Relationships should be oriented toward fun"; "Nothing should be left unsaid in a relationship"; "A relationship should not be exclusive or possessive"). Partners independently sort these statements into 15 different piles, ranking them from those they agree with most strongly to those they disagree with most strongly. The instrument's score is expressed as a correlation between partners' rankings (range, −1.0 to 1.0), with higher scores reflecting greater similarity in relationship beliefs and predicting greater relationship satisfaction (Stephen & Markman, 1983). The instrument is compatible with personal construct theory's position that a shared framework for construing relationships bonds partners in a developing and interdependent role relationship.

In addition to the behavioral and relational measures, a repertory grid was also administered to assess (1) the ways in which partners construed other intimate relationships (e.g., parents' relationships, friends' relationships) and (2) the accuracy with which partners understood one another's perceptions. The 10 × 10 reptest was a slightly modified version of the double dyad grid (Ryle, 1985; Ryle & Breen, 1972) in which the ten elements are relationships (e.g., "your relationship with your spouse"; "your father's relationship to your mother," etc.). Each relationship is rated along a series of ten provided constructs (e.g., Trusting 3 2 1 0 1 2 3 Not Trusting), and then re-rated as each spouse imagines his or her partner would perform the ratings. From these ratings measures of partners' similarity and accuracy of construing were derived.

SETTING SAIL

Session 1

All four couples were present for the first session. Married only about 6 months, Ted and Betsy were the first to enter the room. They had presented to the counseling center with concerns ranging from dual career issues to problems with conflict resolution and compromise. Especially troublesome to them was their "parent–child" interactions in which Betsy viewed herself as a "scolding mother" and Ted described himself as a "rebellious kid." Neither was satisfied with "this rut we get in," but neither felt able to alter it. This was clear in the pretest measures where, against the backdrop of fairly similar beliefs regarding intimate relationships (Relationship World Index = 0.54), they felt considerable inequity in their relationship. Betsy especially viewed her own contributions to the relationship as consistently more favorable than she viewed Ted's. Their overall Areas of Change score was 14, reflecting moderate dissatisfaction.

Next were Jay and Karen. Jay was finishing his undergraduate education after a 6-year hiatus as a cook at a local fast-food restaurant. As a recovering alcoholic, he still had what he regarded as "an alcoholic temper," which seemed particularly unbridled in relation to Karen and her children from a previous marriage. Karen wanted to control Jay's temper so that she could feel better about entrusting the children to his care while she worked at nights as a security guard. They showed the greatest dissatisfaction of any of the couples (Areas of Change score = 40) with the least similarity regarding their understanding of intimate relationships (Relationship World Index = 0.36).

Tony and Casey followed with nonspecific presenting concerns. As Casey reflected, "It was just a lot of little piddly things" but an overarching feeling "that we were just drifting apart." Uprooted from her hometown, Casey moved to the university so Tony could finish his degree in computer information sciences, and their relationship had apparently suffered a rough transition en route. We understood their relationship as undergoing a period of *disruption* (R. Neimeyer & G. Neimeyer, 1985) where their previously healthy relationship was no longer receiving its accustomed levels of attention and support. They reported the greatest compatibility in their overall relationship beliefs (Relationship World Index = 0.58) and only moderate levels of dissatisfaction (Areas of Change score = 17), mostly concerning arguments and division of household responsibilities.

The fourth and final couple was Scott and Ann. They entered therapy to make a decision regarding having children. The twist was that each had a different idea as to which was the elaborative end of the construct; Ann actively lobbying in favor of children; Scott steadfastly opposed. Despite the apparently circumscribed nature of their presenting concerns, it was clear that they had somewhat different beliefs about intimate relationships in general (Relationship World Index = 0.43), as well as a number of other more specific concerns about their own relationship (Areas of Change score = 28).

In the first session Marty and Dave (the co-therapists) sat across from one another, with Ted and Betsy, Jay and Karen, Tony and Casey, and Ann and Scott, sitting spouse-to-spouse in between. Following a general welcome by Dave, Marty reminded the members of group guidelines (e.g., confidentiality) and format (e.g., use of the consultation team), already familiar to each couple from their prescreening interview. Dave then began the group in a way that he later described as "dropping a bomb," by issuing a general invitation to members to begin work. In response, members reflexively pasted themselves to the backs of their chairs in an effort to somehow appear inconspicuous, almost as if recoiling from an invisible explosive detonated in the dead center of the group. This was Kelly's (1955) anxiety incarnate, the evident "result of not having sufficient structure with which to deal with a situation" (p. 499). Because group structure reduces anxiety and facilitates early group process (Bednar, Melnick, & Kaul, 1979; G. Neimeyer & Merluzzi, 1982), Dave quickly constricted the group's available field of experience by asking members to say something about "why it's so hard to open the group." Karen was the first to respond by explaining that "We might say something and everyone else would just say, 'Oh, *we* don't have that problem'!" This fear of invalidation hit a responsive chord with other group members, and Marty used it as an opportunity to reframe the fear by uncovering the implicit wish: "So, you're wondering, 'What kinds of problems do we have in common', huh?" Ann quipped, "Don't worry, me and Scott have *all* the problems!" The group was relieved by this interjection of humor (for a discussion of the therapeutic value of humor, see Viney, 1985), and Dave redirected this attention to Karen: "So, you're wondering how you can connect with some of these folks in here, is that it?" "Yeah," she replied, visibly relieved.

This served as an invitation for group members to openly search for consensual validation, for the common threads that would provide them more secure moorings in otherwise uncertain waters. Here, behavior was clearly experimental (see Kelly, 1970), with couples revealing gradually more intimate aspects of their relationships in hopes of eliciting similar experiences from others. This marked the beginning stage of group development, corresponding closely to what Kelly (1955) described as the initiation of mutual acceptance and support. In personal construct theory, acceptance follows from the recognition that someone else is at least willing to try to look at the world from your own perspective. It is regarded as a precondition to the experience of group support, since in order for an individual to feel supported, he or she must feel that at least one other "person in the group is trying to see matters the same way as he does" (Kelly, 1955, p. 1161). Group leadership during this stage consisted primarily of facilitating this acceptance by remarking on similarities among members and providing some reassurance regarding the "universality" (Yalom, 1985) of many of the presenting issues in a way that invalidates the private fear of idiosyncratic pathology. The striking parallel between this early quest for validation in group therapy and that in the larger arena of social acquaintance (Duck, 1977; G. Neimeyer & R. Neimeyer, 1981; 1985) highlights a fundamental continuity in the process of interpersonal relationship development. As Betsy aptly summarized later in the session, "I guess I'd like to hear that we're not the only couple in the world with these problems, so I like to hear other couples say that, too."

Sessions 2 and 3

These sessions signalled a turn toward the second and third stages of group development according to Kelly (1955), stages characterized by the initiation of primary and mutual role relationships. Construct theory understands role relationships as patterns of activity that follow from individuals' understandings of one another. The relationship is limited by the extent to which interactants genuinely understand each other. Therefore, time was spent asking couples to explore the similarities and differences among their outlooks. One early springboard for this discussion was each individual's rankings of the 60 relationship statements from the Relationship World Index (Stephen & Markman, 1983). Individuals differed widely in their rankings of such statements as "Partners should be honest with one another at all times," "Sex is critical to a good marriage," and "Relationships should not be exclusive or possessive." Jay and Karen, for example, had very little similarity in their rankings of the statements ($r = 0.08$) and each was surprised to learn that his or her beliefs were not universally endorsed by other group members. Marty and Dave were careful to engage couples in active inquiry regarding their own, as well as others' beliefs, in an effort to promote role relationships based on as much understanding as possible. Much of this work took the form of laddering (Hinkle, 1965) to more superordinate constructions by asking members to indicate why, for example, they felt that a relationship should (or should not) be oriented toward fun, why (or why not) partners should contribute equally to certain aspects of the relationship, etc. The group discussion around such topics provided a productive and stimulating means of facilitating primary role relationships. By the end of the third group, couples had passed beyond what Yalom (1985) describes as the initial stage of group development and were developing the uneven alliances with one another that form a prelude to the group's later working stage of development.

STORMY WATERS

Session 4

By the third session it was clear that not all members were equally involved in the group process and that Tony and Casey were particularly peripheral. In postgroup supervision sessions, we urged Dave and Marty to consider this exclusionary dynamic. Together we decided that if it appeared to inhibit subsequent group process it might be dealt with by raising the group's level of awareness regarding its operation, since it seemed likely to be most insidious if it continued to operate covertly. In the fourth session, Tony and Casey remained characteristically reticent, so Marty intervened.

MARTY: Dave and I were talking about . . . what was happening last week as far as there seemed to be a group within a group forming . . . and concern about people's reaction to this.

DAVE: Well, it seems like some of us may be opening up more than others.

BETSY: Yeah, I agree with what Dave said.

DAVE: What is the message here? What are you saying but yet not saying?

TED: The message is . . . well us . . . Betsy, Jay, and myself thought maybe that we were sharing more than others; specifically, everybody else really.

DAVE: Ted, what's that like for you?

TED: It inhibits us. We feel . . . well for me, it's hard for me to show myself in front of someone who's not willing to show himself as much . . .

BETSY: To be more direct, with you two (motioning to Tony and Casey), I get the feeling you're trying to look good.

TONY: Do you know it's really funny, but, I have to admit, coming in and meeting all of you, it sounds funny, but it makes me realize how trivial the problems that I've been blowing up really are.

BETSY: (Indignantly) Well, now you've just finished telling me that you don't have any problems!

TONY: (Matter of factly) Well, I don't feel that I do.

BETSY: Well, that's the feeling that I got, too. But I don't believe that.

TONY: (Defensively) Sorry. Casey and I just had a fight this week, does that make us fit in any better (chuckling nervously)?

CASEY: Well I think that our basic problem was . . . was that we were just drifting apart. . . . It's hard to cope when you have two different lives. I feel better just coming here, just knowing there are other couples going through this . . . . We're just quiet. It's not that we're not friendly, we're both just quiet. We're willing to talk, but sometimes I just don't know what to say.

TED: We're not trying to say that you're bad, or anyone's bad, but you said it yourself, your problems don't compare to the rest of the group.

TONY: I feel no compunction against dragging out my dirty laundry, it's just that there is not that much there to begin with and the stuff's not that soiled.

TED: But, in a sense, that inhibits other people, I think . . . . It's hard to bring out problems in front of other people, but it's easier if everyone's in the same boat. One could imagine you sitting there saying "God, they've got problems!"

DAVE: Is that what you imagine, Ted?

TED: Yeah . . . I just feel like you might be judging

TONY: (Interrupting) *Comparing* . . .

TED: *Judging* people's problems, and I don't think that that's good.

TONY: I understand your feelings exactly. But I can say for a fact that I don't judge any person in here. Each person is a unique individual. I keep looking at these things and comparing them to me and Casey . . . I'm learning from it and not judging anybody by it. Is that too general?

CASEY: I think that's right, yeah, we're all learning from each other's problems.

Here Tony and Casey's characteristic style for dealing with difficulties became clearer and began to recreate itself within the group. They are, as Casey describes them, "quiet people," in a way that implies the premium they place on privacy. In the absence of voluntary participation, the group reacts aggressively to Tony and Casey's withdrawal. Tony's reaction is undeniably defensive, but the therapeutic challenge is to determine why this is so and to work with him to explore the implications and limitations of his behavior. This means searching for the hidden rationality, the underlying meaning that informs Tony's resistances, that brings him to deny any problems in his relationship when this is so patently, painfully untrue.

Kelly understood resistance as an indication that "the construct system does not support the kinds of insights we think the person should be able to see" (in R. Neimeyer, 1980, p. 80). It seems likely that Tony experienced the group efforts as attempts to extract a forced confession that would jeopardize a central construction of his, later described as the belief that "things work out better if they run on an even keel; if you don't rock the boat." His reaction, to start bailing out as soon as he experienced the stormy waters lapping up over the gunwales of his boat, is an understandable one—one that makes eminent sense from within his own system of constructions. We understood Tony's habitual defensiveness to disclosure as the elaborative choice he makes along the dimension of "retaining privacy (and perhaps control) vs. divulging personal weaknesses." Rather than asking him to "walk the plank" of his construct, so to speak, we heeded the sage advice of Mark Twain who once remarked that, "Habit is habit, and not to be flung out the window by any man, but coaxed downstairs a step at a time." During the group intermission, we discussed our ideas with Marty and Dave and formulated a strategy to help Tony to experiment with greater expressiveness. This involved asking him to talk more about his experience in the group in a way that would make him better known to others but also protect his sense of privacy.

DAVE: (To Tony) I heard you say that you like to watch but that you're also getting something out of the group.

TONY: Yes. This group has actually been really helpful to us as a focal point for getting together and talking afterwards. It's the sort of talking we used to do . . . but it's something that faded out, and it's something that's brought us quite a bit closer again . . . (A moment later, to Ted, Tony queries) Do you feel any less alienated yet?

TED: Um . . . I'm not sure. I'm glad I brought it out, though. But . . . some other people had some comments, too.

JAY: I definitely feel that by participating, I'm getting some resolve . . .

DAVE: What's the message you're giving to Tony?

JAY: If you've got a problem, let's discuss it. An invitation to work, I guess . . .

SMOOTH SAILING

Session 6

By the sixth session, the group had entered what Yalom (1985) describes as its "working phase." For Kelly (1955) this marks a period of active exploration of personal problems. It is the "phase in which members of the group enact incidents from their own and each other's lives . . . [and deal] with matters of the type which individual psychotherapy explores intensively" (p. 1172). As a prelude to this, Tony and Casey were becoming more actively involved in the group. Tony had begun to disclose more, describing himself as a "fixer, likely to tinker with machines and cars to get them back into good running shape." This immediately alerted us to Kelly's (1955) observation that "a client who loves to pound nails, dig holes, or grease machinery is likely to be using constructs which govern his relationship with people as well as his relation with things" (p. 821). It was not insignificant in this regard that Tony's favorite pastime was "hammering things into shape."

Indeed, his explosive fights with Casey, followed by her angry silence, emerged as their focal concern in therapy. The pattern was predictable for both partners: Casey would be upset over something, and Tony would relentlessly pursue her to open her up to discussion. His discussions only served to drive her still farther away, however, since, in his effort to "hammer some sense into her," he enacted a gross caricature of Rational-Emotive Therapy, exhorting her to realize that her feelings were irrational and ought to be abandoned in favor of more reasonable ones. This, of course, drove Casey still further into her shell as she resolutely determined not to give him the satisfaction of "talking me out of my feelings." This was the familiar pursuer–distancer dynamic (Wile, 1981), and we hoped to help the two of them experiment with some constructive alternatives to it.

In order to do this, we opted for trying to get them to talk about their fights more openly, to elaborate their unspoken feelings, and to explicitly entitle one another to having these feelings.

DAVE: I really feel that I'd like you to be able to fight, to be able to argue really well, to *entitle* yourself to being angry or being scared, to be able to express that, and for it to be an OK, accepted part of your marriage.

TONY: . . . I tend to think that things work out better if they run on an even keel, if you can sit down and discuss them logically. That's what I try to do with her (to Casey), and she reacts by saying a whole bunch about absolutely nothing, and then I blow up fighting, so I get the feeling I'm doing something wrong. I feel guilty about it.

BETSY: I don't think there's anything logical about feelings. How can you be logical about your emotions?

TONY: I don't know, I've always been that way, I guess . . . .

DAVE: But you say that's not working with Casey.

TONY: Well, anytime I get arguing, she responds by clamming up, totally closing up . . . . I really beat my brains out trying to get something solved with her. She'll sit back and I'll say, "Don't you know you're driving me crazy? Don't you know you hurt me?" And she'll just give me a cruel little laugh. And that hurts . . . and that's enough to send me into an absolute fury . . . . And then I feel like I made a mess of it. I feel guilty, like in my last relationship (former marriage). I felt like it was at least as much my fault as the other party involved . . . .

Here, Tony talked about his feelings in his first marriage, his own depression, and the toll it took on his earlier relationship. This was an important disclosure since it alerted us to the likely intrusion of "relationship pentimento" (G. Neimeyer, 1985) whereby the constructions so fundamental to his previous marriage were now showing through and disrupting the composition of his current marital portrait. To test this possibility Marty reflected, "I wonder if Casey's being depressed reminds you in any way of your own depression?"

TONY: Yeah, it does.

MARTY: When she gets depressed it brings that too close to your own depression and, "Whoa, I can't handle that . . . ."

TONY: I remember what it's like to be depressed, and I know for a fact that I hated myself for ever being depressed.

From here it was possible to understand Tony's efforts to dispute Casey's feelings, not as a hostile denial of his own projected depression, but as a genuinely caring attempt to relieve Casey of that heartfelt blackness he knew so intimately. As Wile (1981) notes, this sort of exploration leads to a spontaneous reframing, one that emerges from within the clients' own construction systems, rather than being imposed on them by the therapists. In contrast to the hollow ring of a premature reframing (e.g., "Tony's badgering is his way of saying he cares"), this exploration enables a deeper, fuller appreciation not only of his motives but also of his private misery, self-deprecation, and sense of defeat when rebuked by Casey.

This sequence culminated in group brainstorming for alternative ways they might approach their arguments that would meet both of their needs: Casey's need to feel entitled and justified in her feelings and Tony's need to "be let inside, rather than shut out." Several suggestions were offered, but Tony and Casey ultimately decided to try an approach where she took the initiative to talk with him about her feelings "when she felt ready," and he would respond to her by acknowledging, rather than disputing, those feelings. This was an especially significant transition for Tony since it involved his developing an alternative way of approaching Casey's depression. Previously, he had chosen to "dispute" her feelings because, from his perspective, the alternative was to "ignore her." Kelly (1969a) understood the construct as "a two-way street, essentially a pair of alternatives between which (one) can choose" (p. 86). In this sense Tony's behavior was limited by his available constructions. As long as he continued to operate from within his system, his efforts were frustrated. Significant change was enabled only by efforts to forge *different* ways of interacting. Unable to change significantly from within his system, Tony was left with the fundamental task of therapy: "to construe his way out" (Kelly, 1955, p. 182).

After several weeks of experimenting with this inquiring, supportive approach, Tony reported "feeling more relieved and open now," and Casey acknowledged that she no longer felt "interrogated" by him. Gradually they began to rebuild a relationship that had been disrupted by mutually frustrating and unsatisfying processes of communication.

THREE SHEETS TO THE WIND

Session 8

In the eighth session, Ann was quick to suggest that the group "talk about Scott's and my having children." Scott's response was predictably obdurate: "Why am I here, to be talked into this?"

From previous sessions when issues of childrearing had been addressed only obliquely, it was clear that Scott was fearful of a direct discussion of having children and that part of this followed from his guilt associated with having earlier promised Ann one child, a promise he was now reneging on. But this time his stonewalling made even more evident the threat he associated with the topic. Kelly (1955) understood threat as an awareness of an imminent change in one's central identity processes, those core role perceptions by which the person *"maintains his identity and existence"* (original emphasis, p. 482).

In order to set the stage for discussing core role issues regarding childrearing, we (the consultation team) met with Dave and Marty to plan strategy. We all felt, as Dave put it, "Like we're walking on eggshells when we talk with Scott about having kids." This alerted us to the need to shore up Scott's defenses before further exploration, by providing him measured doses of reassurance. Reassurance was communicated to him "so that his behavior and ideas (would) . . . temporarily appear to him to be consistent, acceptable, and organized" (Kelly, 1955, p. 699). The two complicating factors were that we wanted to actively involve the group in providing the reassurance and to do so without estranging Ann, whose perspective also needed to be addressed. To do this we decided to have Ann and Scott move to the center of the group and sit facing one another. Group members were asked to line up behind either Scott or Ann, "whoever's side you feel like you can identify with more fully." We chose this wording to encourage group members to develop their role relations with Scott and Ann and to circumvent the relatively impermeable construction implicit in taking a "pro-baby" vs. "anti-baby" stance. Scott and Ann were then asked to briefly state why they did (or did not) want a baby and then yield their chair to the person in line behind them who would support their position with another statement that further developed their perspective. This process continued until every member of the group had participated.

In talking with Ann and Scott afterwards, each of them identified a particularly salient statement of their feelings from among those offered by their supporters. Ann recalled Karen's statement that "I want a baby, because it would help us fulfill our lives," whereas for Scott, what resonated most deeply was Betsy's statement that "I don't want a baby, because it'll change my life and I'm scared."

The ensuing discussion focused on this feeling and began to elaborate the complaint (Kelly, 1955) in relation to other, larger issues in Scott and Ann's relationship. Foremost among these was their chronic substance abuse, primarily alcohol, but also a variety of opiates and amphetamines. Neither was willing to view him or herself as drug dependent, though both admitted that their relationship was founded on mutual drug use and that both (but especially Scott) regularly drank until they were "sailing with three sheets to the wind."

The relational aspect became clearer as Ann reported successful periods of abstinence from alcohol, during which Scott continued drinking, having failed to maintain his commitment to sobriety. At this point, we began to appreciate the likelihood that Ann anticipated being able and willing to exchange her "alcoholic lifestyle" for a "parental lifestyle," whereas Scott could not. Ann's aggressive elaboration of her perceptual field in this way, by capably admitting the possibility of extensive core role revisions, appeared to threaten Scott's ability to retain control over his own core role structure. Particularly apt in this regard is Kelly's (1955, p. 509) recognition that

> The aggressive person . . . keeps plunging himself and his associates into social adventures which unduly complicate their well-ordered lives . . . [other persons] see, in their impending reciprocal identification with him, a major shift coming up in their own core role structures. That is threat. One might say that the aggressive person in this kind of setting is perceived as threatening, not because of what he does or because of any desire to be harmful, but because of what his behavior signifies in the lives of his associates.

In order to explore this threat further, Marty and Dave began a discussion about the relationship between alcohol and childrearing. Betsy joined in and then Scott responded.

SCOTT: I think it's a big problem for me, like Betsy was saying, talking about the alcoholism lifestyle; say, the "party lifestyle" vs. the "parent lifestyle"—I see a big wall right there; party on one side, parent on the other. But I still want to party. I seem to be very one-sided about it. I can't see the two surviving together.

Here Scott outlined the dichotomous and impermeable nature of his construing, raising his own level of awareness regarding the either-or type dilemma outlined by Ryle (1981): either I party or I parent, but not both. The "party lifestyle" is impermeable to any of the new elements Scott associates with childrearing (e.g., centering activities around the child, being responsible), and the "parent lifestyle" does not admit many core elements of his existing lifestyle (e.g., being "free," partying, being self-centered). The lines are drawn clearly, and the direction of his "elaborative choice" is a foregone conclusion. Recognizing this, Marty focused on the implications of this conflict.

MARTY: (To Scott): Comes back to the fear that I don't want to put myself in the position where the baby's more important than the party . . . . The fear of having to look at what my life would be like without the party aspect.

ANN: (After a very loud silence) . . . I think you're right.

SCOTT: Could be, I'm trying to think . . . I'm confused about . . . The thoughts are in a jumble.

Scott's reaction here is particularly noteworthy. Marty has taken him to the edge of his internal abyss and invited him to peer over to see what his "life would be like without the party aspect." His reaction—confusion and anxiety—betrays either an image of himself so sketchily drawn that it is unacceptably uncertain or one that draws very distinct, but deeply threatening, implications for change. Kelly (1969b) had characterized threat as "the experience that occurs at the moment when we stand on the brink of profound change in ourselves and we can see just enough of what lies ahead to know that so much of what we are now will be left behind forever, once we take that next step" (p. 156). Staying with this feeling of threat, Marty continued:

MARTY: I sensed a panic . . . .

SCOTT: I've felt this all along. How can I deal with this? And I never seem to get anywhere with it . . . . Whenever we get real close to the side of me that says, "OK, I'll have a kid," the party side of me grabs me and says, "Hold it!"

MARTY: That's that last minute panic sort of thing.

TED: It's real emotional . . . a lot of being real scared. You go through this big change . . . that's kind of scary if someone likes to stay controlled.

DAVE: Are you saying that Scott's sort of like that? He seems very controlled and yet, it means saying, "I'm out of control"?

SCOTT: I feel like I'm trying to tie the fear and the alcoholism thing together. If I continue to drink and then become a parent, then I will be raising "alcoholic kids" and the chain will continue . . . But if I don't have a kid, it won't get the kid.

MARTY: I almost hear you saying that if I don't have a kid, then I don't have to face the alcoholism.

SCOTT: Yeah, you're right, it does force me to look at it, because I see becoming a parent continuing the hereditary chain of alcoholism . . . I see how my childhood was, and here I am. It puts a big fear in me.

Scott's identification of his "fear of fatherhood" represents what Kelly (1969b) described as that "transitional moment when the confusion has partly cleared and we catch a glimpse of what is emerging, but with it are confronted with the stark realization that we are to be profoundly affected if we continue our course. This is the moment of threat. It is the threshold between confusion and certainty . . . . It is precisely at this moment when we are most tempted to turn back" (p. 152). And this is precisely what Scott, in a very subtle way, chooses to do.

In this sequence, even as Scott began to explore his feelings relating to fatherhood, he also revealed his very subtle use of hostility in the service of protecting his existing self-structures from the threat of extensive revision. In hostility, rather than revising existing structures to better fit preceived reality, the individual "takes further active steps to alter the data to fit his hypothesis" (Kelly, 1955, p. 512). In this case, Scott's refusal to have a child may represent a hostile means of preserving his existing core role structure.

This is clearer if we consider Scott's conundrum. He has two options. First, he could have a child. This would satisfy his sense of obligation to Ann, but it would also either plunge him into massive guilt or threat: guilt following from the distinct possibility that he would not revise his "party lifestyle" and thereby recapitulate the kind of childrearing he associates with his own alcoholic father; threat over the equally painful possibility that childrearing would necessarily force revisions in his core role processes, thereby jeopardizing the integrity of his existing structures.

The second option, of course, is to not have a child. This would enable him to preserve his existing structures, simultaneously avoiding the anticipated guilt of incompetent fatherhood and the threat of essential core role reconstruction. On the down side of things, reneging on his promise to Ann to have one child makes him "feel guilty as hell" in that it dislodges him from his view of himself as an honest and trustworthy mate. One way to reconcile the entire situation is to take the seemingly magnanimous route of claiming that it's not fair *to the child* to be born to an alcoholic parent, and this is precisely the option he chooses.

But this is an understandable choice on Scott's part, given the perceived alternatives available to him. Particularly since fatherhood would radically reconstitute his only enduring, intimate role relationship (with Ann), his intransigence on the issue is functional. Regrettably, Scott and Ann did not move much beyond this point in the group, owing in large part to our inability to engage him in core role reconstruction (see R. Neimeyer, Chapter 4, *this volume*). This highlights Kelly's (1955, p. 513) caveat that "the therapist must make sure that the hostile person has at least the rudiments of a new core role with respect to some people, perhaps with respect to himself . . . before he starts a wholesale reinterpretation of the world."

Session 10

By the 10th session, Betsy and Ted had begun to work actively on revising their role relationship. Their mutually accusatory pattern was still troublesome to them, however, and they asked the group for help. In describing this pattern it was clear that their relatively minor criticisms gradually escalated into the runaway arguments so characteristic of mutually angry partners. This pattern of interaction is typically dealt with in one of three ways: by encouraging partners to avoid fighting, by teaching them to restrict their expressions of anger to more acceptable forms, or by focusing on the underlying issues that fuel their fire.

The first approach follows from the belief that "the venting of anger is inappropriate in a love relationship" (Mace, 1976, p. 35). As a result, partners are asked to renounce their anger as inappropriate and instructed to report their anger rather than express it. A similar orientation to response prevention is advocated by Ellis (1976) who suggests that partners avoid expressing their anger by counting to 10, going to a movie, or exercising some other means of distracting themselves from volatile expression. But this approach has serious disadvantages from a personal construct perspective because it minimizes the partners' opportunity to learn more about the underlying meaning, or significance, of their anger.

The same is true of the second approach to anger management in which couples are encouraged to express their anger but only within "acceptable" boundaries (e.g., "fair fighting," Bach & Wyden, 1969). The objective is to render arguments so rule-bound that they are essentially detoxified, thereby minimizing their impact on the relationship. Again, the central issue regarding why partners are so angry to begin with remains unanswered.

The third orientation most closely approximates some of the concerns a construct therapist might have. Here there is recognition that the apparent anger carries deeper level implications for the partners, that behind "the smoke screen of anger" lies the "raw fire of hurt" (L'Abate, 1977, p. 14). The therapist's first task is to determine the particular ways in which partners are hurting. Some of those ways became evident in Marty's questions to Ted and Betsy:

MARTY: Do you feel like you're both pretty critical of one another?

TED: I feel that we are. I feel that I'm less critical than Betsy. I think I give her more respect to make her own decisions, or more courtesy in that area, to make her own decisions.

BETSY: I think he's right.

When Ted says that he feels he gives Betsy "more respect . . . more courtesy, to make her own decisions," he is indicating the particular areas in which he feels disqualified or invalidated in relation to her. Later discussion with Betsy revealed that when Ted failed to do his chores, despite her persistent reminders, she felt as if he wasn't listening to her and didn't really care what she said. This left her feeling even more angry and hurt. At more superordinate levels, then, Ted and Betsy seemed to be asking for much the same thing: to be cared about, listened to, and respected. By reflecting this to them, Marty and Dave began to help them develop a relationship based on collaborative empiricism, since they were left with the unresolved question: "If we want the same things from each other, why are we arguing so much?"

This is precisely the position, an inquiring partnership, that is often so productive in revising role relationships. In order to help them develop answers to their questions, we designed a casual enactment (Kelly, 1955). Enactments are informal role plays designed to "give the client a chance to experiment" by trying "on a part in order to see what it is like" (Kelly, 1955, p. 1165). Enactments are aimed at discovery rather than demonstration. They are "designed, like a good experiment, to give the experimenter and his colleagues a chance to observe its outcomes" (p. 1166).

In this case, Ted and Betsy were asked to choose an issue that they often fight about (paying bills) and to spend a few minutes discussing it as they would at home. The only twist was that they reverse roles in their discussions with Betsy portraying Ted and vice versa. In keeping with Kelly's (1955) suggestions, we moved quickly into the enactment:

DAVE:	You're Ted right now, Betsy.
BETSY (As Ted):	Well, I've been doing pretty good with the bills lately . . .
TED (As Betsy):	Well, yeah, but the basket back there is full of the one's you haven't looked at yet.
BETSY (Slipping out of role):	But that's *your* basket! . . . . Oh, no, that's right, I'm supposed to be Ted . . . . Um (regaining composure) . . . but I don't know the system. I don't know how they're arranged.
TED (As Betsy):	If you'd just sit down with me sometime and go over it then you would know.
BETSY (As Ted, pause):	Well, I said to you that I'd like to sit down and have you show me the filing system in the box and you've never shown it to me before. So . . . you know, I've been writing checks for the ones on the table.
TED (As Betsy):	But you don't file them.
BETSY (As Ted):	Well you never showed me the filing system.
TED (As Betsy):	I don't feel I should have to show you stuff.
BETSY (As Ted):	Well, you set the whole system up. How am I supposed to know . . . .
TED (As Betsy):	It's not very hard to figure out. The bills are in the pocket where it says "bills," and the files are in the box on the dresser. All you have to do to file them is look through the box and file the bills. That's all there is to it.
BETSY (As Ted):	Well, maybe if you set up a schedule of duties then we could do it.

At this point the enactment seemed to reach a period of closure, so Dave intervened to halt it and to discuss what Betsy and Ted had learned from the intervention.

DAVE: (To Betsy) What was it like being in Ted's role?

BETSY: Pretty hard . . . Well, I was thinking of things I wanted *him* to say.

DAVE: That you wanted Betsy (gesturing to Ted) to say? Like what?

BETSY: Like how come *I* always have to set up the schedule?

MARTY: I got the feeling that it was a lot easier for Ted to play your part than for you to play his.

BETSY: That's because he didn't do a very good job of representing me.

This enactment and its subsequent processing sparked a number of clinical hypotheses for us. Particularly evident was the difficulty Betsy experienced in adopting Ted's perspective. We understood this as possibly signalling the development of an asymmetrical role relationship (G. Neimeyer & R. Neimeyer, 1985) between Ted and Betsy, one based on different levels of understanding. "While one person may play a role in a social process involving the other person," Kelly (1955, pp. 98–99) observed, "the understanding need not be reciprocated." In this case, the role is enacted on the basis of the available constructions, "even though this understanding may be minimal, fragmentary, or misguided" (Kelly, 1955, p. 98). The dissatisfaction related to these discrepant levels of understanding has been documented elsewhere (G. Neimeyer & Hudson, 1985) and can be understood as a special instance of disrupted relationships (R. Neimeyer & G. Neimeyer, 1985). In disrupted relationships, once satisfactory partnerships begin to drift apart such that original levels of support and validation are not adequately sustained.

But we were also struck with the particular salience of Betsy's critical commentary in this interaction and began to speculate about the relationship between her criticisms of Ted and the apparently asymmetrical nature of their role relationship. Our working hypothesis was that Betsy's *understanding* of Ted was jeopardized by her *evaluation* of him—that her habitual criticisms restricted her understanding. Because we viewed this criticalness as central to their relationship, and it was now operating *in vivo,* we intervened impulsively. Impulsivity is characterized by a foreshortened period of circumspection prior to action. In other words, we quickly narrowed down our hypotheses and made a choice that committed us to the following confrontation.

CONSULTATION TEAM: (Over the speaker to the group) Excuse our interruption, but the consultation team just wanted to make the observation that Ted seems incapable of doing *anything* right in the relationship. He's even incapable of role playing Betsy.

BETSY: (Visibly affected) I think that's kind of harsh. I just said that Ted is getting better lately, that he's been doing more around the house.

DAVE: Ted, how do you feel about the feedback the consultation team gave you. They buzzed in here and said, "Seems like Ted can't do anything right." How did that hit you?

TED: Well, . . . my first reaction was that I felt like defending Betsy. That was my first reaction. And then I felt like sometimes that's really true . . .

DAVE: That *feeling* (emphatically).

TED: That feeling that I can't really be left to do anything on my own. That's pretty aggravating. And it makes me feel that I'm walking on needles a lot of times. Like, man if I don't go through the day without screwing up then there's going to be another example that I'm not doing things right.

DAVE: Have you ever told that to Betsy?

TED: I think I have before. That I feel uneasy, and I have to watch my step. And if I take the wrong step, or I don't do things the way Betsy thinks they should be done, then there's going to be some kind of trouble. Yeah, so in that respect I think that maybe they made a good point.

DAVE: (To the rest of the group) How do you feel about the way that Betsy was just confronted by the consultation team?

KAREN: I think it was kind of hard, too.

SCOTT: You know, maybe it was a truthful statement, but it does sound kind of shocking.

BETSY: What, that Ted can't do anything right?

SCOTT: (To Betsy) Yeah, I think what they're . . . if it will take some of the shock effect off that . . . they're trying to get down really underneath to say that maybe subtly that's the way you feel.

BETSY: Yeah, it is, I know, it's in there. It's really in there. Like, I can see that I don't really trust him (to do chores) and he knows it and it makes him feel bad.

SCOTT: You said you don't trust him sometimes, right? It gave me the feeling that that's a real deep undertone.

BETSY: (To Ted) Yeah, and it does go real deep. If sometimes you feel like I'm looking down on you, it's because I am. If you feel like I'm treating you like a child, it's because I am sometimes.

Here, Betsy gives direct expression to some of her relationship constructions. Particularly evident is the way in which the relationship negativity is maintained contemptuously, in this case by Betsy's confirming her own constructions as a mature and responsible adult by contrasting them with Ted who is cast in the role of an immature, irresponsible child. As McCoy (1981) has noted, contempt can be viewed as positive from Betsy's standpoint insofar as it confirms the validity of her existing system.

What concerned us here was not that Betsy was making unreasonable demands on Ted but that her approach to satisfying very legitimate needs (to feel mature, responsible, competent) were foiled by the very efforts she launched to achieve them. This conceptualization is similar to those of ego-analytic therapists (e.g., Wachtel, 1977; Wile, 1981) who are more likely to view partners as deprived of ordinary adult satisfactions than as gratifying regressive impulses. In this case, Betsy's criticisms, which, by Ted's admission he reacted to "like a rebellious kid," represented efforts to extract perverse validational evidence in favor of very reasonable needs. The problem was not that she expressed criticism, not that she was "too needy," but that the process she chose in her quest for confirmation was self-defeating in relation to Ted. In order to better understand the relationship between her criticism and her needs, we opted to use a laddering procedure (Hinkle, 1965) for eliciting the superordinate implications of her "being critical."

DAVE: Betsy, we've been talking about your tendency to be critical, and about the way Ted responds to it. What sense do you make of all this?

BETSY: I know I have a problem. And that's why this is very difficult to deal with. The problem is that I'm very critical of the people that I really care about . . . that goes for me, too. I'm very critical of myself. Sometimes I beat my head against the wall trying to get things done.

DAVE: You said that you're critical of the ones you love, including yourself, right?

BETSY: Yeah . . . .

DAVE: Why is that? Why do you figure you're critical of *them?*

BETSY: Well, I don't really know.

DAVE: OK, let's do it this way. What's the opposite of being critical of them, of pushing them?

BETSY: Leaving them alone, I suppose.

DAVE: So you'd rather criticize them than to leave them alone, is that it?

BETSY: Yeah, 'cause if I left them alone, they'd just sit there, doing nothing.

DAVE: Oh, so you hope for them to do *something* as a result of your being critical?

BETSY: Yeah, I hope to get them moving, to motivate them.

DAVE: OK, so you're *critical* of them in order to *motivate* them, that makes sense.

BETSY: It's the same thing I do with myself. I'll get really down on myself until I finally do what I need to get done.

DAVE: And do you also hope to motivate Ted in the same way?

BETSY: I guess so, but I never thought really thought about it like that.

Here Marty and Dave opted to accept the possibility that self-criticism was motivating for Betsy but to question its usefulness with intimate others. This was a preliminary attempt at *person binding* (Kelly, 1955, p. 1077) by limiting the range of convenience of Betsy's constructions to certain elements only (i.e., herself). The effort was aimed at supporting the potential utility of a construction within certain boundaries but sharply delimiting its range of convenience beyond those boundaries. The net effect of binding is to reduce a construction to impermeability, rendering it inapplicable to all but a single context. Kelly's (1955, pp. 1074–1077) discussion of various forms of binding makes it clear that "while it might seem better in such cases to test the construct and discard it altogether, such a revision . . . may have a devastating effect upon the organization of the personality" (pp. 1076–1077). In this case Marty and Dave anticipated the likely resistance that would follow from an assault on Betsy's system directly, so they opted to first bind the construction and then to test the utility of alternative constructions outside the proposed boundary.

To do this they developed a restricted role sketch in which Ted and Betsy would experiment with a different kind of role relationship. During this one-week experiment, they were to enact a "student–teacher," rather than a "parent–child," relationship. But it was to be a special kind of student-teacher relationship, one in which the student (Betsy) was to actively try to understand (rather than evaluate) the motivations, feelings, and thoughts of the teacher (Ted) by asking open-ended questions until she could not only anticipate Ted's actions but also his feelings on a day-to-day basis. This sketch was then enacted briefly in the session. Betsy's comment afterwards, that "That sure is a different way of talking. It even *feels* different," was encouraging, while Ted's remark, "Yeah, I feel powerful!" was a bit more worrisome. Still, they were asked to try out the enactment at home each evening and report back during the next, and final, session of the group.

ALL ASHORE

The final group began with discussing Ted and Betsy's enactment. Ted reported an immediate sense of relief, explaining that he felt more able to be himself around the house than he had in months. Interestingly, he also found himself taking Betsy's role occasionally, "trying to find out how she felt and stuff" in a way that represented a spontaneous elaboration of his script. Betsy's reactions were mixed, feeling at times restricted by the role and at others "a little uneasy about it," since "it feels so foreign." This uneasiness was interpreted as an indication of anxiety, which is regarded as a precondition to change. Because the group was ending, Betsy and Ted were not asked to continue the enactment but to consider the possibility that there are many different ways to enact their role relationship. As a concrete suggestion they were asked to "list five different couples you know" (friends, family, other group members) and to ask "how these others might react in various circumstances that you find yourselves stuck in." The effort was directed at helping them to continue their efforts to differentiate a broader range of relational alternatives whenever they confronted difficulties rather than to respond with their habitual one.

The remainder of the final group was devoted to dealing with termination issues; to reviewing progress in the group, identifying its salient "critical incidents," and reinforcing an understanding of the process of change. Particular emphasis was placed on the continuation of "personal experiments," efforts to test alternative ways to handle marital problems and to discuss the results of these joint projects with one another. Partners were also asked to discuss their best understandings of the changes in their relationship throughout the group in an attempt to help them articulate and reinforce their own implicit relationship theories in a way that might facilitate their continuing prediction and control of their interpersonal process.

OUTCOME

In general, the effects of the group were quite favorable, with the possible exception of Jay and Karen who separated shortly after its termination. They considered this a trial separation in order to better anticipate the effects of divorce. On follow-up, Jay indicated that he had experienced tremendous support from the group but felt unable to become the type of husband Karen wanted. Karen expressed no change in Jay and for that reason felt her treatment goals had not been achieved. Jay and Karen had entered treatment with the highest levels of dissatisfaction and the lowest levels of shared beliefs regarding marital relationships. Our sense was that the group helped to underline these differences and for that reason served to expedite their separation. But the implications of their decision to separate were uncertain for us, in part because none of their posttreatment measures were returned.

By contrast, Casey and Tony were quite satisfied with the group and reported having attained 75% or more of their treatment goals. They continued to share considerable overlap in their basic beliefs about the nature of intimate relationships and significantly reduced the number of changes they wanted to make in their relationship (from 17 at pretreatment to six at posttreatment). Tony reported "feeling closer than we have in some time," and Casey felt "relieved to know that we can talk about things again."

Scott and Ann also expressed satisfaction with the group, each reporting that they attained about 50% of their treatment goals. This was reflected in the reduction in the number of issues that concerned them in their relationship (from 28 to 15) and in the increased compatibility of their overall system of beliefs regarding relationships (from 0.43 to 0.59). While their focal conflict regarding having children remained, neither felt the same level of urgency regarding their decision making. Both decided to continue treatment focusing on substance-abuse issues.

Finally, Betsy and Ted showed the greatest treatment gains, reporting having achieved more than 75% of their treatment goals and reducing the number of desired changes in their relationship significantly (from 14 to 4). A corresponding increase was evident in their overall similarity of beliefs regarding relationships (from 0.58 to 0.77), perhaps suggesting their development of "an emergent conjoint construction of the world" (Stephen & Markman, 1983, p. 17). Grid-based measures also documented positive changes over time, with both partners showing greater understanding of the other's perspective (c.f., Smail, 1972; Wijesinghe & Wood, 1976) and Betsy reporting greater equity in the relationship. These changes were supported by their own feelings that the group had helped them "get out of a rut" and begin to understand and discuss their relationship rather than "nag and hound each other until we get into an argument."

SUMMARY

The purpose of this chapter has been to illustrate the application of personal construct therapy in a marital group. Regarding marriage, Kelly (1955) remarked that "there is no greater tragedy than the failure to arrive at those understandings which permit this kind of role relationship" (p. 100). The group offers unique advantages as a vehicle for developing these understandings, and I have tried to emphasize these in this chapter. But the decision to chronicle the development of the group, emphasizing salient marital interactions within each session, has necessarily limited the attention given to other, equally important, aspects. In particular, the underemphasis on group dynamics has perhaps mistakenly conveyed the impression that personal construct therapy operates primarily as conjoint treatment in a group context. Contrary to this impression, many of the curative factors that operated within the group occurred among the couples themselves and were a unique product of their interpersonal interaction. Because "the opinions of other people operate as validators of one's personal constructs" (Kelly, 1955, p. 176) the group provided a particularly rich opportunity for testing a variety of constructions within a heterogeneous context. Similarly, the opportunity to enact multiple role relationships and to experiment with the development of new role relations were properties unique to the group. Moreover, implicit in the discussion of group development is the recognition that the group had a life of its own, its own identity and developmental trajectory above and beyond each of its dyadic constituents (c.f., G. Neimeyer & R. Neimeyer, 1985). This was especially clear when members reported some months after termination that they found themselves asking "what the group would say to me" about various change attempts or personal experiments. In this way the group served as a continuing referent for supporting additional relationship changes.

But these aspects have been underemphasized in this chapter, together with other issues such as the development of the co-therapy relationship, the operation of the consultation team, and the nature of our supervisory relationship with the co-therapists. Each of these is an aspect that was subordinated in our focus on the operation of the group itself, despite the fact that these are important topics of discussion in their own right.

As a final point of emphasis, it is worth noting that this approach is only one of many conceivable tacks that personal construct therapists might take in couples' group therapy. If this chapter has succeeded in its efforts it will have conveyed the fact that construct therapy is technically eclectic within a theoretically consistent framework. Basic to its approach to couples is its emphasis on interpersonal inquiry, collaborative empiricism, and personal responsibility in a way that promotes partners' continued experimentation with the revision in their role relationships.

REFERENCES

Alger, I. (1976). Multiple couple therapy. In P. Guerin, Jr. (Ed.), *Family therapy: Theory and practice* (pp. 364–387). New York: Gardner Press.

Bach, G. R., & Wyden, P. (1969). *The intimate enemy: How to fight fair in love and marriage.* New York: William Morrow.

Bednar, R. L., Melnick, J., & Kaul, T. J. (1979). Risk, responsibility, and structure: Ingredients for a conceptual framework for initiating group therapy. *Journal of Counseling Psychology, 21,* 31–37.

Doster, J. A. (1985). Marital violence: A personal construct assessment. In F. Epting & A. Landfield (Eds.), *Anticipating personal construct psychology* (pp. 225–232). Lincoln: University of Nebraska Press.

Duck, S. W. (Ed.). (1977). Inquiry, hypothesis and the quest for validation: Personal construct systems in the development of acquaintance. In *Theory and practice in interpersonal attraction* (pp. 379–404). London: Academic Press.

Ellis, A. (1976). Techniques of handling anger in marriage. *Journal of Marriage and Family Counseling, 2,* 305–315.

Gurman, A. S. (1971). Group marital therapy: Clinical and empirical implications for outcome research. *International Journal of Group Psychotherapy, 21,* 174–189.

Gurman, A. S. (1973). Marital therapy: Emerging trends in research and practice. *Family Process, 12,* 45–54.

Hinkle, D. (1965). *The change of personal constructs from the viewpoint of a theory of construct implications.* Unpublished doctoral dissertation. Ohio State University, OH.

Kaslow, F., & Lieberman, J. E. (1981). Couples group therapy: Rationale, dynamics, and process. In P. Sholevar (Ed.), *The handbook of marriage and marital therapy* (pp. 347–370). New York: SP Medical and Scientific Books.

Kelly, G. A. (1955). *The psychology of personal constructs (Vols. 1–2).* New York: W. W. Norton.

Kelly, G. A. (1969a). Man's construction of his alternatives. In B. Maher (Ed.), *Clinical psychology and personality: The selected papers of George Kelly* (pp. 66–93). New York: Wiley.

Kelly, G. A. (1969b). The language of hypothesis: Man's psychological instrument. In B. Maher (Ed.), *Clinical psychology and personality: The selected papers of George Kelly* (pp. 147-162). New York: Wiley.

Kelly, G. A. (1970). Behavior is an experiment. In D. Bannister (Ed.), *Perspectives in personal construct theory* (pp. 255-269). London: Academic.

Kremsdorf, R. (1985). An extension of fixed-role therapy with a couple. In F. Epting & A. Landfield (Eds.), *Anticipating personal construct psychology* (pp. 216-224). Lincoln: University of Nebraska Press.

L'Abate, L. (1977). Intimacy is sharing hurt feelings: A reply to David Mace. *Journal of Marriage and Family Counseling, 3,* 13-16.

Mace, D. R. (1976). Marital intimacy and the deadly love-anger cycle. *Journal of Marriage and Family Counseling, 2,* 131-137.

McCoy, M. M. (1981). Positive and negative emotion: A personal construct theory interpretation. In H. Bonarius, R. Holland, & S. Rosenberg (Eds.), *Personal construct psychology: Recent advances in theory and practice* (pp. 95-104). London: Macmillan.

Neimeyer, G. J. (1985). Personal constructs in the counseling of couples. In F. R. Epting & A. W. Landfield (Eds.), *Anticipating personal construct psychology* (pp. 201-215). Lincoln: University of Nebraska Press.

Neimeyer, G. J., & Hudson, J. E. (1985). Couple's constructs: Personal systems in marital satisfaction. In D. Bannister (Ed.), *Issues and approaches in personal construct theory* (pp. 127-141). London: Wiley.

Neimeyer, G. J., & Merluzzi, T. V. (1982). Group structure and group process: Explorations in therapeutic sociality. *Samll Group Behavior, 13,* 150-164.

Neimeyer, G. J., & Neimeyer, R. A. (1981). Functional similarity and interpersonal attraction. *Journal of Research in Personality, 15,* 427-435.

Neimeyer, G. J., & Neimeyer, R. A. (1985). Relational trajectories: A personal construct contribution. *Journal of Social and Personal Relationships, 2,* 325-349.

Neimeyer, R. A. (1980). George Kelly as therapist: A review of his tapes. In A. Landfield & L. Leitner (Eds.), *Personal construct psychology: Psychotherapy and personality* (pp. 74-100). New York: Wiley Interscience.

Neimeyer, R. A. (1986). Personal construct therapy. In W. Dryden & W. Golden (Eds.), *Cognitive behavioral approaches to psychotherapy* (pp. 224-260). London: Harper & Row.

Neimeyer, R. A., & Neimeyer, G. J. (1985). Disturbed relationships: A personal construct view. In E. Button (Ed.), *Personal construct theory and mental health: Theory, research, and practice* (pp. 195-223). Beckenham, England: Croom Helm.

Papp, P. (1980). The Greek chorus and other techniques of family therapy. *Family Process, 19,* 45-57.

Ryle, A. (1981). Dyad grid dilemmas in patient and control subjects. *British Journal of Medical Psychology, 54,* 353-358.

Ryle, A. (1985). The dyad grid and psychotherapy research. In N. Beail (Ed.), *Repertory grid technique and personal constructs: Applications in clinical and educational settings* (pp. 190-206). Cambridge: Brookline Books.

Ryle, A., & Breen, D. (1972). A comparison of adjusted and maladjusted couples using the double dyad grid. *British Journal of Medical Psychology, 45,* 375-382.

Ryle, A., & Lipshitz, S. (1975). Recording change in marital therapy with the reconstruction grid. *British Journal of Medical Psychology, 48,* 39–48.

Ryle, A., & Lunghi, M. W. (1970). The dyad grid: A modification of repertory grid technique. *British Journal of Psychiatry, 117,* 323–327.

Smail, D. J. (1972). A grid measure of empathy in a therapeutic group. *British Journal of Medical Psychology, 45,* 165–169.

Stephen, T. D., & Markman, H. J. (1983). Assessing the development of relationships: A new measure. *Family Practice, 22,* 15–25.

Viney, L. L. (1985). Humor as a therapeutic tool: Another way to experiment with experience. In F. Epting & A. Landfield (Eds.), *Anticipating personal construct psychology* (pp. 233–245). Lincoln: University of Nebraska Press.

Wachtel, P. L. (1977). *Psychoanalysis and behavior therapy: Toward an integration.* New York: Basic.

Weiss, R. L., Hops, H., & Patterson, G. R. (1973). A framework for conceptualizing marital conflict: A technology for altering it, some data for evaluating it. In L. A. Hamerlynch, L. C. Handy, & J. Mash (Eds.), *Behavior change: Methodology, concepts, and practice* (pp. 309–343). Champaign, IL: Research Press.

Wijesinghe, O. B. A., & Wood, R. R. (1976). A repertory grid study of interpersonal perception within a married couple. *British Journal of Medical Psychology, 49,* 287–293.

Wile, D. B. (1981). *Couple's therapy: A nontraditional approach.* New York: Wiley.

Yalom, I. D. (1985). *The theory and practice of group psychotherapy.* New York: Basic Books.

9
Change in the Family Construct System: Therapy of a Mute and Withdrawn Schizophrenic Patient

Harry G. Procter

> To what extent do you consider the hypnotic state and the psychotic state to be similar?
>
> M.H. Erickson: A pansy in a tomato bed is a weed, just as a tomato in a pansy bed is a weed.

THEORETICAL BACKGROUND

Since the early 1970s I have been engaged in the development of a rigorous and comprehensive psychology of the family that would rest on a firm philosophical basis. It would be useful at a theoretical level, giving a language of description and explanation. It would provide research methods capable of testing hypotheses about processes of problem formation and resolution in families. And most of all it would be useful in formulating and conducting psychotherapy and systems intervention. And by making sense of any particular school of therapy and its strategies under a single theoretical umbrella, it would allow the utilization of a tremendously broad range of therapeutic methods without falling into the trap of eclecticism.

Kelly's (1955) psychology of personal constructs seemed to be an ideal tool to begin this process. Construct theory seemed to answer many of the problems of psychoanalytic and behavioral psychologies (Procter, 1978). Yet construct theory needed revision and extension itself when it came to examining the processes so richly described by family researchers and therapists.

The central organizing concept of the approach is the family construct system. Kelly had outlined how the individual derives a system of constructs, but it is clear that when people habitually relate together over an extended period of time a system of shared constructs emerges that is an entity in its own right. Each individual may have a unique position in the group system of construing, but these positions become dependent on each other in a dynamic equilibrium. This family construct system will develop as Kelly described—through elaboration, revision, cycles of reconstruction, fragmentation—as the family members struggle to make sense of their reality. But there are also changes and processes less easy to describe in Kelly's intrapsychic language.

For we are talking here about the interaction of construct systems, which is a different level of analysis. Each family member's choices and actions are governed by the way they understand and see things—the fundamental postulate. But their constructs are validated (or not) by the evidence at their disposal—each other's actions and choices. Bill can be irritated with Peter, because he seems not to be pulling his weight in the family. Peter withdraws and goes mute, because Bill's irritation is evidence to him that he doesn't understand, that he won't understand.

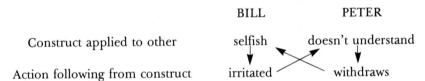

But the two of them do not have to see things like this, they do not have to be like this. The whole situation maintains itself in a self-fulfilling way. Systems like this can demonstrate sudden and discontinuous change. Reconstruing and change in the level of action occur simultaneously. How the pattern is revised depends on what other alternatives are available in the family's set of resources. Readers interested in pursuing this model further are referred to Procter (1978; 1981; 1985a, b).

CASE HISTORY

This is a case of construct-oriented work with a family in which one member, Peter, had become mute. He had been demonstrating paranoid symptomatology and had stopped talking and eating when he was admitted to psychiatric hospital after a crisis. He sat through the first four sessions completely immobile, staring fixedly into space.

Family work is probably the treatment of choice in these cases. Interveiwing the other members allows the therapist to gain detailed information. As sense is gradually made of the situation and new construction of the events occurs, the patient's presence, albeit silent, allows participation in the therapeutic process. This is the second case of this kind that I have reported in which a sudden return to normal occurred immediately after one of the therapy sessions (see Procter, 1985a).

The Browns, of rural British background, consisted of the parents, an adopted elder sister Ruth, aged 37, and her husband Bill. Peter, aged 35, had been married before. Up to his admission to hospital in March, he had been living with his common-law wife Tracy and their daughter Zoe, aged two. Tracy would not attend the sessions, but the younger brother Jim (22) and his wife Jean did come.

My involvement started in July after various physical treatments had been attempted without success. When I first met Peter, he was going downhill rapidly, refusing to eat. Two brief meetings were held in the acute ward with Peter, his father, Ruth, and Bill. Bill was a very aggressive, overbearing character and had quite frightened the hospital staff. But an agreement was made to see the family in the clinic, with live supervision from a team (Procter & Stephens, 1984). This is the beginning of the first session.

HARRY PROCTER (HP): I've spoken to Bill and Ruth a couple of times and you (father) in Tone Vale. I was wondering if I could start off with you, Mrs. Brown . . . just how you understand the problem, how you see it . . .

MOTHER: Well, what I don't understand is why doesn't Peter eat his meals at the hospital.

HP: Well . . . that's going to be a question, obviously, that we're going to want to have a look at. How much have you been seeing Peter since he's been in hospital—you've been ill yourself.

This is an error on my part. I implicitly ascribe the construct "ill" to Peter. It would have been better simply to state, "I understand you've been ill."

MOTHER: Well, I've been ill myself, and I haven't been to the hospital, not since about the middle of May, and Peter seemed to be eating his meals then.

HP: Will you describe to me what happened on that occasion? What—when he starts talking, what was going on?

MOTHER: He wasn't talking in the hospital. But we had him home for the weekend then and he was talking a little.

HP: And . . . what did you make of the situation at that time?

MOTHER: Well, he was talking something sensible, but sometimes he'll talk rubbish.

HP: When did you first become aware that there was a problem?

MOTHER: Well, I'm going back several years ago.

HP: So, what do you understand the problem to be then? It's been going on a while. What is the problem?

MOTHER: Well, he used to lock things up and used to blame people for what they didn't do, and people were following him and things like that. And he used to blame me for what I didn't do and he sort of caught me hold of the throat and was going to murder me. That was more than two years ago.

HP: What did you used to do when that sort of thing used to happen?

MOTHER: Well, I went to the doctor, and I saw Dr. Carmichael. And I told him that I thought Peter should have treatment. The doctor, he wouldn't come to the house and—Peter wouldn't go to the doctor.

We find that the mother is construing the problem as an illness, with its associated medical solution. She will have her own unique meaning for "ill" of course, but at this point I move on to Jim.

HP: Jim, how do you see the problem?

JIM: It's very . . . what's the word?

FATHER: Complicated.

JIM: Unusual.

HP: What did you observe?

JIM: Well it all stemmed from when he got divorced, I think.

HP: What year was that?

JIM: Five years ago? Well he used to go working—I don't see him very much anyway. Maybe ten times a year. And he used to be saying people was after him. He worked at the brewery and relations of his ex-wife worked at the brewery. And he used to reckon that people was after him in—where he worked . . . .

HP: And how was it before that? I mean, you know, did you have any inkling that that marriage was in difficulty?

JIM: For a couple of years yes, I think, because he used to go out with other girls anyway. We more or less all knew that it was going to end sooner or later because it was so open, you know. But it's since then that it's got worse and worse.

With Jim there is a shift in construing; he has a historical frame. "People being after him" may have a real basis. Peter's betrayed wife's friends at work may actually have been threatening him.

HP: Jean, thanks for coming today. What have you observed with your own eyes? What do you see as going on?

JEAN: Peter was very talkative before, and we went to a wedding in October, and we saw Peter about three times shortly after the wedding and spent most of the time at the wedding together, and we hadn't seen him for a long time then. He said a few odd things at the wedding, but on the whole he was quite good at the wedding.

In the interaction that follows, the therapist seizes on this construct "talkative" and explores it. Up to this point the atmosphere in the session had been strained and tense, particularly with Bill. Suddenly there are guffaws of laughter. This gives an idea of the usefulness of this kind of approach. It generates information, lightens the atmosphere, and suggests the importance of shared family constructs in human problems (Procter, 1981; 1985a, b). I first noticed the power of this type of questioning when eliciting constructs with families in a repertory grid project (Procter, 1978). Later, the Milan team discussed a similar methodology (Palazzoli, Boscolo, Cecchin, & Prata, 1980).

HP: You say that Peter was talkative before. What, of the three children, Ruth and Jim and Peter—Ruth, you're adopted aren't you?

RUTH: Uh-huh.

HP: (To Peter and Jim) But the two of you are not adopted.

JIM: No.

HP: But still thinking of the three of you, the three children in the family, who would you say normally is the most talkative of the three of you? (Laughter all round.)

FATHER: It's Ruth (patting her on the knee). She talks sense, mind you, she talks sense! I never heard her talk a word of rubbish.

HP: Who's the next most talkative? The outsiders may be able to judge better.

When there is a strong polarization in a family as here (Peter as "ill" versus the rest of them as "sensible") it is often useful to divide up the family in orthogonal ways: males–females, children–parents, adopted–not adopted. Here I provide "insiders–outsiders" as a way of preparing for Bill's anticipated domineering entry. Ruth accepts my construct:

FATHER: Well, I don't know—it's a job to tell.

RUTH: Hang on a minute, Pop.

HP: What would you say, Bill or Jean?

JEAN: Well, I think, when I first met the family, Jim was always deemed the quiet one.

HP: Jim was the quiet one?

JEAN: Uh, at that time. Peter was always fairly boastful over his horses and things, not really boastful, but, I mean, he had horses and he would talk about them.

HP: Yes. (To Mum) Do you go along with that, that Ruth's the most talkative, Peter's next, and then Jim?

MOTHER: Yes, yes.

HP: Yeh? (Checks with Ruth, then Bill) Of the five of you, who was the most talkative, Ruth again? Where do the two parents fit into that? (More laughter—Jim and Mum point at Dad.)

FATHER: Sometimes I got to do the talking. (More laughter.)

HP: And who's more talkative, Ruth or her father?

RUTH: Pop.

FATHER: I don't think I'm too bad!

HP: And, um, Mum, where does she fit in?

FATHER: Just occasionally she gets a bit worked up.

HP: And is she more talkative than Peter or Jim?

FATHER: Oh, I think Peter was more . . .

RUTH: No, Peter was more talkative, definitely.

HP: He would normally talk more than his mother?

RUTH: Yes.

HP: And would Jim be quieter than her?

RUTH: Jim has always been known as the quiet one in the family.

FATHER: He thinks deeply.

MOTHER: He thinks, but he doesn't do a lot of talking.

The family seem comfortable with this mode of questioning, so I proceed to explore similarities.

HP: I mean who would you say of the three of them . . . who does Ruth take after more? Mother or Father? I mean, I know that you were adopted, but still you learn a lot from your parents.

FATHER: Oh yeh.

HP: Who's Ruth more like?

MOTHER: Well, Jim is more like myself.

HP: Yeh? In what way?

MOTHER: Well, he thinks and plans things more, he doesn't rush into things.

HP: That sounds like useful stuff.

MOTHER: Yes.

HP: And you do too?

MOTHER: Yes.

HP: And who would you say that Peter takes after more, normally?

FATHER: Well, I don't know what to say about that . . .

HP: Bill, what would you say?

BILL: Well, Peter was . . . when I first met Peter I would have said, like Mother's just said, that Jim, when I first met the family as a whole . . . Jim and Mother are the sort of quietest two . . . I'm talking about when I first met them. Peter and Pop are both excitable, they're both excitable. Pop's excitable. Peter was excitable.

HP: (To father) Is that a word you would go along with?

BILL: Well, it's my personal opinion. Pop would get worked up very quickly, Peter would get worked up very quickly . . . . Again talking as an outsider it would, from what I've heard, from what I've heard now, it would probably be better from me and Jean, to say more than anyone else because . . .

HP: You can give a view from the outside.

BILL: Well, the thing is, you see, from what I've gathered, I'd say that between—they've heard this lot before so that it's no problem to me— they pampered Peter, they tolerated Ruth, and they didn't bother with Jim.
(Tense silence as this critical material sinks in.)

HP: Jean, do you agree with that?

JEAN: Yes.

HP: What does Bill mean, do you think, when he says that they pampered Peter?

JEAN: Well, when I first met Jim, Peter had a brand new motorbike, and the money had come from his father. And Jim told me that they hadn't even bought him a pushbike when he was younger. So, you know.

FATHER: But um, well if I could . . . (shrugs).

BILL: It sounds hard the way I said that.

HP: It's "complicated" (laughter).

HP: Did you say "tolerated Ruth?"

BILL: Yes. That sounds, it's the only word I can think of. It sounds hard—it's not that they didn't love her or anything like that, don't get me wrong, by saying this, but that's the way I see it, you know, I can't think of another way to describe it, quite honestly. I don't say that they didn't want her there or anything like that. It's just that, it's just my impression that Ruth's . . . you know, that Peter was pampered, Jim was left out, Ruth was there, but Ruth's always been very forward, with her ways and everything like that, so therefore, perhaps "tolerated" is the wrong word but I can't think of another one.

Later Ruth recounts:

RUTH: Well, Jim and I always had to go to school, we couldn't . . . when Peter didn't want to go to school, he didn't have to go. He'd get Mum to write a note to say he was poorly. And he'd get away with things like that. And if he didn't want to do something he didn't have to do it.

HP: Yes.

RUTH: But Jim and I couldn't get away with it.

HP: Mother do you feel closer to, who do you feel closest to of the three of them?

MOTHER: Well, I've always tried to make Peter, and bring him up the same as Jim and Ruth. But his Dad used to give in to him and let him get away with things that I didn't want for him to . . . I didn't want for him to have a motorcycle. I said have a bicycle. I said he can go where he wants to on a bicycle, and he won't be running the roads, he'll not be able to go away, and he'll be able to go to work instead of putting his mind on going for joyrides.

A major difference between the parents has emerged so to protect them (and the therapy) from potential invalidation I ask them about Peter's marriage, a thematically related but safe area, which Jim had brought up as being the onset of the problem.

HP: Uh-huh. Which of you was most upset or surprised when you heard that Peter and Yvonne were splitting up?

MOTHER: Well, I wasn't surprised. I wasn't surprised at all because I knew that there was going to be trouble. Because Peter, he was going around, he had a lorry, he had a horse, he was . . . mixing with girls and, at the same time, I didn't want for him to do it, I wanted for him to buy his house and be like Jim.

Mother wants Peter to be like Jim, the quiet deep-thinking one in the family. Peter has certainly taken her literally this time.

It is worth noting how, even in a relatively short space of time, questioning about constructs allows an extremely rich picture of the family to emerge. There is a long-standing jealousy by the other siblings, supported by their spouses, of the way Peter was treated with greater favor by the parents (in their eyes), Bill being the chief spokesman in this. He seems to be acting on their behalf. Mother responds to this accusation by pointing to her husband as the one who spoilt Peter. He rarely gets a chance to speak though. In these early sessions there was tension between Bill and Father. At the first meeting, Father warned me, whispering as we were going in, "Bill is tough, you know."

In this approach, the members' unique positions are explored in line with Kelly's therapy. But an emphasis is also put on the way these views are interdependent, part of a wider gestalt or jigsaw of shared family constructs. A rough approximation to each's position is discovered, and, in spiral manner, one returns again and again getting a more and more accurate fix on their personal meanings and implications. This is exploratory but therapeutic too. As the therapist gains understanding, the members indirectly discover things about each other's perspectives. They have often been assuming they agree when they differ and vice versa. It is a dialectical process of enhancing commonality and individuality. When a similarity of views is established, it poses ways in which they differ. Likewise, differences of opinion, sharpened and clarified in the session, often lead to the discovery of how much, in fact, they share.

The discussion went on to the events immediately preceding Peter's admission to hospital. Two weeks before, they had taken Peter to the doctor, who gave him medication and wanted to see him in a fortnight. After this, Peter, Tracy, and the baby had moved back to near Tracy's parents some miles away. When the fortnight was up, Bill drove all the way over to their house and said to him "Peter, you're due to see the doctor. If you're not ready in three minutes, I'll give you a reason to see a doctor." He threatened to break his arm, but still Peter refused. A crisis developed, culminating in the psychiatrist being called. Peter was compulsorily admitted to hospital. He had been mute and catatonic ever since.

We went on to discuss the goals of the work. Bill and Ruth would not allow Peter to go back to his parents. They had no room to have him themselves. So where was he to go? Jean wondered if there was some kind of hostel for psychiatric patients.

We agreed to meet for a series of sessions and closed with a comment on how close and jovial they had been and how much they obviously cared about Peter. I told them there was probably an important reason why Peter wasn't talking, something painful or frightening, and that we should work on this slowly and thoroughly. For the time being, therefore, he should stay in hospital and not be encouraged to talk. Even if he were to start talking, during a visit, they were not to encourage him. This kind of paradoxical measure, inspired by the brief therapy team (Watzlawick, Weakland, & Fisch, 1974), is extremely useful for consolidating improvements and promoting further change by blocking existing hostile solutions. Kelly (1955) described this kind of approach as "reassurance"—providing a temporary rationale for the client's choices so that they appear consistent and acceptable.

In the next sessions, more family history was collected: Mother's own spell in psychiatric hospital and Ruth's previous marriage and divorce. Bill had also been divorced, and there were worries about his son Simon. Bill was also having quite serious heart problems, needing to take things easy. When I had been sympathetic about Peter's disappointments in marriage in the first meeting, Bill retorted angrily, "well, who *hasn't* been through a broken marriage, that's no excuse!"

The first three sessions were devoted to deepening and elaborating our (and their) understanding of their construing system. People act in groups not only according to their construing of each other's views (the sociality corollary) but also according to how they construe relationships (Procter, 1978;

1981). This includes not only dyads as in personal construct work in marital therapy (G. Neimeyer, 1985; R. Neimeyer, 1986; Ryle, 1985) but also larger combinations. I formulated the group corollary to cover this area: To the extent that a person can construe the relationships between members of a group, he or she may take part in a group process with them (Procter, 1978; 1981).

Some of the display of the family member's relationship construing is verbal. Already I had discovered that Bill and Ruth considered the parents to have waited on Peter, Jean and Mother elaborating on this (the motorbike issue). All seemed to agree that Ruth and her father were close. They also showed this behaviorally—in their proximity and physical contact (shown only in this pair).

Much of the work of therapy entails asking about situations rather than eliciting verbal labels. Haley (1963) pointed out how few words there are in the language for relationships compared to the number for describing individuals. But constructs are communicated through action.

> HP: (To mother) They're saying you waited on Peter too much?
>
> RUTH: She does a lot more things. And Peter would come and say, "I want my shoes cleaned, I want this done." But I wouldn't do it. I'd say, "Now there's your shoes, Peter, you do it, you clean them." And he'd do it. If Mum told him to clean his shoes, he wouldn't do it, he'd ask her to do it.
>
> HP: So if your Mum said, "Clean your shoes, Peter," what would you do if he refused?
>
> RUTH: If he refused, I'd say he can jolly well clean them. Put them down, let him clean them.
>
> FATHER: Then there would be a bit of an argument.
>
> RUTH: Yeh, but if I wasn't there she'd go on and do it for him.

From glimpses like this, we begin to build up a total picture: Ruth construes the Peter/Mother pair as needing her to be present for its correct functioning. Father sees this threesome as a continual argument between the women about how to deal with Peter and calms them down. Mother sees father as spoiling Peter, and so on. The picture is tested by asking for further examples, checking their words, how they would prefer it and so on.

There is also room sometimes for *not* defining relationships. I deliberately "drifted away" from a direct consideration of the parent's marriage. Preemptive, "nothing but" construing of the parents' marriage is a common problem when there is a difficulty in children leaving home (including when children fail in their own marriages and return to the family of origin). The son or daughter may construe the parents' marriage as incompatible, believing that "they never communicate," but these views are typically derived from very partial evidence—from when they are themselves present or from the secret complaints of one of the partners. By avoiding a consideration of the area it may be easier for shifts in the relationship to be achieved.

FOURTH SESSION

At the beginning of the fourth session, in mid October (4 months after therapy had begun), I saw Peter alone for a few minutes, quietly summarizing what I knew of the situation and explaining the therapy. This was done to confirm him as an individual and to see if he would respond without the others being present. Private time with Peter could also be useful when presenting a position to the others. He did not give a glimmer of a response.

Much of the remainder of this family session was spent talking about Tracy, with complaints that she was taking all Peter's things. Bill wanted me to write to Peter's solicitor. I had asked Tracy to come, but although she said she would, she failed to appear. I told them that we thought that the therapy should be kept separate from any legal aspects of the case.

Personal construct theory poses the hypothesis that in having a symptom a patient is making a choice. In the model I have developed (Procter, 1978; 1985a), this ongoing choice is seen as part of a pattern of concerted action by the group of people involved. Choices are made not simply to elaborate one's own system of constructs (the choice corollary) but to elaborate the shared family construct system. Specifically, I assume that Peter's withdrawal was a preferable alternative to others he envisaged. However, since he was mute this could only be inferred from a careful examination of the contextual reality. It seemed that his behavior allowed differences between the others, which he might have anticipated to escalate uncontrollably, to be suspended while they worked together to help him.

At this point in the therapy, the team felt it was time to start sharing these thoughts with the family:

> HP: We've been having some thoughts over the time we've been working with you. I'll try and explain our thinking . . . We don't consider Peter to be ill, we consider him to be deliberately keeping quiet for the following reasons. We think that he is quite aware of what he is doing, alright, and that he's doing it for generous purposes. We think that this has actually been going on for a tremendous length of time and that he has been sacrificing himself, sacrificing his development and his own life in order to help the rest of you. We think he has sacrificed . . .

> FATHER: What . . .

> RUTH: Just a minute, Pop.

> HP: . . . one marriage, and then another, not an actual marriage, but another marriage, that he's allowed them both to come to grief in order to help in

a number of different ways. To help you, Mrs. Brown, to help his mother in giving you, in earlier times, the company of a son. And you see, the thing is, that he knows that by continuing with this and keeping quiet he is able to allow the rest of you to keep close and to have a common concern, a common goal, to be able to share a lot. (Father and Bill move to speak.)

RUTH: (To father and Bill) Look, listen, just a minute, no . . .

HP: You see, Bill, by keeping quiet he knows that, if he starts talking, what will have to happen is he'll come home, and he'll have to involve the rest of you in a lot of worries and strenuous activity for his mother. So we think that he is deliberately keeping himself in hospital in order to help spare you the burden and the strain of having to deal with . . .

BILL: But if he was to start talking, looking after himself, then he wouldn't burden anybody, would he?

FATHER: Course he wouldn't!

BILL: I mean he's not keeping the family close, the family was close before he decided not to talk and that. That's a load of tripe, that is!

FATHER: If he was to talk . . .

BILL: That's a load of tripe, that is.

RUTH: Just a minute, let Jean say what she wants to say.

BILL: You say, Jean.

JEAN: No, I just wanted to say that I disagree with what he says. I totally disagree.

FATHER: Peter's a burden where he is, down there.

JEAN: It's nothing—we want to see him well. I mean he's not helping us by staying in hospital. We've always been close.

FATHER: He can walk out tomorrow . . .

HP: He knows that if he was to come out he would have to . . .

BILL: He'd have to do something for himself!

HP: . . . that his mother would be involved in worry and strain.

JEAN: We were all happy when he was married and working.

BILL: (Overlap) What the hell's she doing now?

RUTH: Mum's been more worried since March. I mean, I had an absolutely frantic phone call just before he was admitted, because they were worried. And he was more of a worry then, when he was married to Yvonne. He was . . . true? You were worried . . . Mother? . . . Mum?

FATHER: Are you listening?

MOTHER: Yes, I'm listening.

BILL: I think he's doing it for purely selfish motives. That's what I think. Nothing to do with us, he couldn't give a damn about us, I'm sorry.

HP: Well, we'll have to continue this next time, continue these thoughts. But our thinking at this point was that we should be respecting Peter and allowing him to stay in the hospital at this time.

BILL: Well, perhaps if Peter thinks, if your team thinks that Peter is helping us all by staying in hospital then perhaps it might be a good idea if we said,

"Well, Peter, if you think that's such a damn good idea, you stay in the hospital, keeping away from us all, you stay in hospital my son! We won't bother to go and visit you." Now perhaps that will make him happier still, if he thinks he's making us happy by acting the way he's doing now, then we'll turn round and say "Well right, I tell you, if you want to be really deliriously happy (laughter) we won't visit you at all!" Then he'll get better straight away. I think he's being quiet purely for selfish motives. I just think he's . . .

HP: That's the point at issue, that we think that he's actually keeping quiet for generous motives.

BILL: Well, I think exactly the opposite. I just I don't see that at all.

FATHER: Well, I think it's more like it's his second home, now he's getting used to it down there. "Might just as well stay there, I'm being fed and bedding and everything. I've got nothing to worry about."

BILL: Breakfast, carted round, brought up, given things . . . you know . . . his mother worrying about him, his father worrying about him, Ruth worried about him, I worry, Jean worries.

HP: You mustn't underestimate the generosity of this move to go to a psychiatric hospital . . . .

As can be seen, this intervention unleashed an extraordinary reaction. Bill's construing of Peter is laid completely bare, "selfish" as opposed to my "generous." Bill, Jean, and Ruth (Jim was absent) joined together in indignant rejection of our thoughts, and, significantly, Father joined them in this. Mother, however, remained silent and thoughtful. Peter made no response. I simply stuck to my guns. When we saw them again a month later, there was a surprise in store for us.

FIFTH SESSION (ONE MONTH LATER)

(HP, Ruth, Jean, Peter, and Jim enter.)

HP: Sorry to have kept you waiting.

PETER: I feel a lot better now, I go swimming, badminton, YMCA, everything . . . play football. I've been coming home to stay a few days at Mum and Dad's.

(Mother, Father, and Bill enter.)

HP: Sorry to have kept you waiting. We were running a bit late this morning. Come on Peter, you were saying?

PETER: Well, I said I'm a lot better, I been going swimming and playing table tennis, darts, badminton, football and everything, having a good time. I've put on a stone in weight. I've been coming home and staying for a few days at Mum and Dad's. Just feel a lot better in myself, you know. I haven't got much more to say at the minute (laughs). More happy and cheerful.

FATHER: That's what counts, that counts for a lot.

MOTHER: You've been doing your Land Rover.

PETER: Oh yeh, I've been up one day at Tracy's. Been working on the Land Rover. I'm going to start putting all the engine back in there. Got all the engine taken out. Started the job months ago, I never finished it. I feel like doing it again now so I just started working on this vehicle . . . I've been going down at weekends . . . two weekends I been down there. I haven't stayed down there, I just go down there for the day. Tracy comes out and gets me, picks me up and drives me down there and everything.

HP: Yes.

MOTHER: You've been doing decorating.

FATHER: Painting and decorating.

PETER: Oh, I've been painting and decorating, done some painting and decorating, haven't I? Washing up, doing the housework.

FATHER: Bit of gardening.

PETER: Done some gardening, haven't I?

FATHER: Oh yes.

PETER: Keeping busy.

HP: And you've stayed, you've been in the hospital but you've gone out for . . .

PETER: Yeh, I've gone out and stayed home for about four or five days.

HP: That's with your Mum and Dad?

PETER: Yeh.

HP: (To Mother) Tell me more about how he's been when he's been at home.

MOTHER: Well, he's been like anyone else. He's been washing up, wiping up, and did a bit of washing for himself. Then he turned around, and when it was dry he got the ironing board and iron and ironed it for himself. Help to get the meals, do the vegetables, and do a bit of hoovering, and did some decorating for me and make his own bed . . . .

(Later)

HP: Have you got any idea how you managed it, how you managed to make these changes?

PETER: I've been sat down for so long now I just feel like it's time I done something. I just feel I've been sitting about for so many months now. I look back on these months now and think "what a waste of time!" (Laughs.) I suppose I just haven't felt up to it till now and I guess it's time I got on, got back to work. I had a letter from the job center, I phoned them up. They said until I get signed off, I can't really do anything about it, you know . . . .

HP: Anyone else got any thoughts on how the change has been achieved?

BILL: Well, after . . . last month, when you told me . . .

RUTH: That's when it started, from that day.

BILL: When you told me that I forced Peter into hospital. That was your words . . . "forced."

HP: I don't think I said that.

I had said nothing of the kind. Interestingly, they seem to have construed my statement that Peter chose to be there as them forcing him there.

BILL: Oh you did. That's right, isn't it Ruth.

RUTH: Well, not "forced," but you said words to that effect.

BILL: You look at that video, it was "forced." That's when I lost my rag with you . . . I lost my rag, I went out of here, I took Peter over there, and I made Peter, told Ruth to get on home with them. I had Peter in the car. I never lied to Peter by the way, he knows that. I tried to do all I could for him. And all the way back over to our place . . .

HP: This is after the last meeting here?

BILL: This is after our last meeting when I went a little bit—I wish Jim had been here actually.

JIM: Yeh, I'm sorry I missed it really.

BILL: Because, the things I said last week, last month . . . I meant every word I said last week, last time, by the way, what I did say. And then I took Peter out of here and took him home to our place and on the way over I told him I wasn't interested whether he spoke to me or not. And I told him, as far as I was concerned, that you lot over here had been treating him wrong right from the word go. Because you were under the impression that he was a voluntary patient of Tone Vale Hospital, and that as far as I was concerned, and the rest of the family, he could go down that bloody hospital and he could stay there and he could rot. And if he didn't start talking soon then that's exactly what would happen to him and he'd better prove himself . . . (To Peter) Bear me out what I said on the way over . . .

PETER: Yes, that's true.

HP: (To Peter) Did you reply to him at that point?

BILL: No he didn't.

PETER: (Overlaps) No, I agreed, didn't I?

BILL: He didn't answer me. I wasn't going to let him answer me . . . . I won't have being messed about by . . . by you or the people in there or the people down Tone Vale, nurses down at Tone Vale . . . I wasn't going to be messed about by nobody else. And I won't let the family be messed about either, so we either started talking or he stayed there and he rotted there. Now whether that brought it on, I don't know.

RUTH: I think it did because when we walked back into Tone Vale, he was a different person . . . .

(Later)

MOTHER: And he's been different and talking ever since and he's been coming home and . . .

RUTH: Generally mucking in with the family, hasn't he. In fact more so now than what he was. I said to Bill, after Bridgwater Carnival, I know we've all been in here. And we've been at home at different times, all of us. But to actually have a family occasion, and I think Jim will bear me out, where we've all enjoyed ourselves, where we've had supper and a few drinks . . .

FATHER: The carnival night.

RUTH: Carnival, we were all together and I think that that was the first time that Peter joined us for an evening like that in quite a few years.

JIM: Years, yeh.

RUTH: Wasn't it Jim? And it was a nice, it was a proper family, because he hasn't for Christmases and things, he wouldn't join us, would he? This last Thursday . . .

PETER: That was a good evening out, I thoroughly enjoyed it (laughter).

FATHER: Yes he had four pints of beer!

RUTH: I had to keep my eye on him! (much laughter) . . . he helped me get the food ready. He helped organize it.

PETER: Long time since I had a drink.

MOTHER: I couldn't get him out of the chair (laughter) . . . .

RUTH: Anyway it was a whole family get-together last week. It was alright. It was like we all used to be years ago.

FATHER: So anyhow, I think things have really got together at last. Thank goodness . . . .

HP: What's your explanation?

BILL: He found out it's no bloody good trying to con us anymore. (Mother laughs) . . . bit of con . . .

FATHER: He was rough . . .

BILL: He was rough to begin with, but if he'd been treated right to begin with, I don't think he'd have been down there that length of time.

PETER: Tell you what, I was worried about first of all. I had to have ECT, I didn't like that.

BILL: Well, you wouldn't have had that if you'd talked, would you?

PETER: I was more worried about ECT all the time. I didn't like it at all.

HP: Have you got any theories about this, Jean?

JEAN: Well, after the last meeting we went back to the flat. And I'm afraid we all had a good laugh at your theory. And Peter laughed with us. And I think that was the beginning of coming out of it . . . We thought it was such a ridiculous thing that you'd thought up about his giving up his, his, you know, his life with his wife, and his life with his girl friend for the sake of the family that we, we . . .

BILL: Couldn't believe it.

JEAN: Couldn't believe it. And he laughed with us, you know. We didn't know what to do but laugh. We just didn't agree with it at all. And he laughed with us.

HP: That was on the Thursday?

JEAN: That was the Thursday.

BILL: When we went over to our flat.

JEAN: He definitely seemed brighter from that moment on . . .

PETER: What it really was was moving. Right in the middle of moving houses. Then we needed extra money and the money wasn't there and Tracy wanted to move. And I think that's what brought a lot of it on. And she wasn't happy. We should never have gone to Penton to live in the first place, not really. To be quite honest, if we'd gone to Worth to live and she'd been living near her family we'd never have been here in the first place, I don't think.

HP: If Tracy was here and I asked her how she saw things, what would she say?

PETER: More or less the same thing. Tracy didn't like living at Penton. She was lonely, no friends. Now her brother and sister are living next door. Tracy is a family girl, close to her family.

Three further sessions were held with this family, one a month later and two 5 and 6 months later. Improvements were maintained and follow-up 2 years later found Peter well, living with his parents and seeing Zoe regularly. In the meantime, Bill himself had sought help for a problem—anxiety in expressing himself.

DISCUSSION

It was argued in an earlier paper that a reconstruction of a problem offered to a family should be capable of being subsumed by a superordinate construct shared by the family members (Procter, 1981). It is relatively easy to see how change is effected in cases where the provided construction is accepted by the family, as in the other case mentioned (Procter, 1985a). The others start behaving towards him differently, he reconstrues them, acts differently, and a new family construct system emerges.

Clearly, it worked differently in Peter's family. The family rejected the provided construct of "generous" as a description of Peter's motives. But it must still have been understood and subsumed by them for them to throw it out so violently and reassert contrasts—that he was "selfish," "pampered," etc. The hospital and therapists were then seen as the pampering ones, rather than the parents, or the father.

They were able to come together against me—"you lot." And "Peter laughed along with us." The polarization changed from a within-family distinction to one drawn between them and us, establishing a new boundary. Father and Bill very noticeably agree now in their rejection of my idea. Possibly this allowed old wounds about Ruth's adoption and the perceived unfairness of the parents' pampering of Peter to be forgotten. Peter's problems and their resolution may have been functional in allowing a proper negotiation to occur about Ruth's divorce and Bill's entry into the family. In the second session, Ruth had said, after discussing her earlier marriage, that she had not talked before about her divorce in front of her parents, "in case of worrying them." After Peter's recovery a general improvement in the family relationships was reported.

In line with Kelly's metaphor, I like to think of the family as a team of scientists, each struggling bravely to understand and solve the problems that face them, learning from their own and each other's experiments. The members vary in their approaches. Mother with her medical position, perhaps the most sympathetic to Peter, was hampered by constriction—she construed the problem almost exclusively in terms of eating. Bill, with his moral position, showed classic Kellian hostility, although, who knows, his perseverance may have been crucial in the end. Father was characterized by looseness—going with the wind. Peter's position remains unknown—unfortunately, we failed to ask him what he thought of our idea of his generous concern for his mother and the family unity.

Therapy can be seen as helping the family team get moving again, after getting stuck in their project. We (the clinic team) offered our hypothesis, and they chose unanimously to reject it. This perhaps allowed them to resolve their differences through rejecting a contrasting alternative that they did not wish to accept.

REFERENCES

Haley, J. (1963). *Strategies of psychotherapy.* New York: Grune & Stratton.

Kelly, G. A. (1955). *The psychology of personal constructs (Vol. 2).* New York: Norton.

Neimeyer, G. J. (1985). Personal constructs in the counseling of couples. In F. Epting & A. W. Landfield (Eds.), *Anticipating personal construct theory* (pp. 201–215). Lincoln: University of Nebraska Press.

Neimeyer, R. (1986). Personal construct therapy. In W. Dryden & W. L. Golden (Eds.), *Cognitive behavioural approaches to psychotherapy* (pp. 224–260). London: Harper & Row.

Palazzoli, M. S., Boscolo, L., Cecchin, G., & Prata, G. (1980). Hypothesizing-circularity-neutrality: Three guidelines for the conductor of the session. *Family Process, 19,* 3–12.

Procter, H. G. (1978). *Personal construct theory and the family: A theoretical and methodological study.* Unpublished doctoral dissertation, University of Bristol, England.

Procter, H. G. (1981). Family construct psychology: An approach to understanding and treating families. In S. Walrond-Skinner (Ed.), *Developments in family therapy* (pp. 350–366). London: Routledge & Kegan Paul.

Procter, H. G. (1985a). A construct approach to family therapy and systems intervention. In E. Button (Ed.), *Personal construct theory and mental health* (pp. 327–350). Beckenham, Kent: Croom Helm.

Procter, H. G. (1985b). Repertory grid techniques in family therapy and research. In N. Beail (Ed.), *Repertory grid technique and personal constructs: Application in clinical and educational settings* (pp. 218–239). Beckenham, Kent: Croom Helm.

Procter, H. G., & Stephens, P. K. E. (1984). Developing family therapy in the day hospital. In A. Treacher & J. Carpenter (Eds.), *Using family therapy* (pp. 133–148). Oxford: Blackwell.

Ryle, A. (1985). The dyad grid and psychotherapy research. In N. Beail (Ed.), *Repertory grid technique and personal constructs: Application in clinical and educational settings* (pp. 190–206). Beckenham, Kent: Croom Helm.

Watzlawick, P., Weakland, J., & Fisch, R. (1974). *Change: Principles of problem formation and problem resolution.* New York: Norton.

10
A Constructivist Approach to Parent Training[1]

Dorothy E. McDonald
James C. Mancuso

This chapter includes (1) the theoretical framework underpinning a personal construct parenting program, (2) discussion of the structure of such a program, and (3) case study material designed to demonstrate the complementarity of the program and other family therapy models. Case study materials presented here represent examples gleaned from parent training work with high-risk, multiproblem families. The authors believe, however, that a personal construct approach to parent skills training can be used by any clinician working with parents who act on the basis of faulty information about the parental role, who display parenting skills inadequate to meet the range of needs of their child, who demonstrate difficulties in child-management, and who report conflictual parent–child relationships. American society has developed mechanisms to intervene when children are at physical or psychological risk and holds the belief that parental behavior is implicated when children's basic needs are unmet or when children fail to conform to society's behavioral expectations. Our society makes the moral statement that it is good to intervene in family dysfunction. As theorists and practitioners we have a responsibility to insure that our theory-based parenting interventions help family members become effective problem-solvers.

1. We would like to acknowledge the efforts of Anne Byron, Thomas Houlihan, Mario Riccio, Kim Eryusal, Helen Hayes, and Kenneth Handin, members of the staff of St. Catherine's Center for Children for their continuing advancement of the Constructivist Parent Training Program presented here, and to Shirley P. Schwarz for her assistance in completing the ParRep Analyses.

ESSENTIAL ASSUMPTIONS OF A CONSTRUCTIVIST PARENTING PROGRAM

In this chapter, we will present a constructivist parent training program that has been developed at Saint Catherine's Center for Children, Albany, New York (Mancuso & Handin, 1983). This program differs from mechanistic or behavior modification programs in which the trainer frames procedures and assesses outcomes in terms of cause-effect sequences in social interaction. A constructivist parent training model would not proceed as if more or less cause (parent behavior) produces more or less effect (child behavior). A constructivist's perspective would not urge the therapist to guide parents to construe parenting practices along a permissive–restrictive continuum. A constructivist clinician views every parent as a "scientist" (Kelly, 1955, p. 4), as a person who constantly hypothesizes about and construes the behavior of others. A training program based in personal construct theory would prompt parents and children to alter unproductive behavior patterns by leading parents to consider the impact of their childrens' beliefs about themselves, others, and the world on their hypothesis making. In a constructivist parent training program, parents explore the process through which persons build an implicit theory about the world. Specifically, they are assisted in considering their own belief system, including their beliefs about the task of parenting their children. Following this sojourn, parents participate in interactions with their children, with prompting to consider the beliefs held by their children regarding these interactions. The goals of the program are (1) to decrease parent–child conflict, (2) to enhance the parent-child relationship, and (3) to promote the growth and development of the children. Parents are led to gradually shift their focus from the child's actions to the child's construing and the ways in which the child's constructions lead to the behavior. This focus on the cognitions of the adult and the child maximizes the parent's ability to fashion the most productive (growth producing and relationship-enhancing) interaction with their children. Involvement with a constructivist training program prompts parents to extend the evaluation of their parenting practices beyond that which "works." The therapist facilitates an analysis of how his or her practices guide the child to acquire a construction of self, or others, and of social interaction.

We will begin by outlining the assumptions of a personal construct parenting program. This will include a review of Kelly's (1955) essential propositions for constructivist psychotherapy.

To begin with, one must make explicit the often implicit knowledge that participants in parent training programs have regarding the role of being a caregiver to a child. In construct theory terms, "A role is an on-going pattern of behavior that follows from a person's understanding of how others who are associated with him think about the task" (Kelly, 1955, pp. 97-98). This concept of role is adopted in order to explain the apparent consistency of a person's behavior over time as well as to explain the consistency of behavior across persons. According to Kelly's (1955) fundamental postulate: a person develops beliefs and builds self-guiding constructions in order to anticipate environmental feedback. One strives for a match between what one predicts will happen (the way one expects others to react to his/her role enactments) and what actually does happen (the reaction one receives to her/his performance). A person builds a role or schema of "parent" in order to predict the feedback that occurs when interacting with the child she or he has undertaken to rear. From this perspective, it is important to consider the quality of this feedback during a person's occupation of the parent role.

Return for a moment to Kelly's definition of role. According to this concept, a person plays the parent role when the role enactment reflects the constructions used by other persons involved in childrearing. For the parent role, as with any social role, a person may organize input generated from external standards or prescriptions. That input can become one means by which an individual determines which ideas and behaviors to incorporate into the role enactment. Mancuso, Heerdt, and Hamill (1984), in considering how a person "transitions" to the parent role (p. 292), note that parent role standards are created by society and its constituent parts. For example, the parent role reference group may be made up of family, friends, neighbors, church, school system, mental health and human service professionals, etc. The feedback the parent needs to consider may come from one or several of these subgroups and, in a very powerful way, from the behavior and responses of his or her children to the parenting strategies.

In common terms, feedback that follows from the functioning of the system guiding a person's parenting practices may be perceived as either positive or negative, as either validating or invalidating. The parent who understands the constructions of the reference group and uses these in his or her role enactment will have successfully anticipated many of the group's reactions to her or his enactments. The parent role enactments will be validated. By contrast, the parent who has built a role construction at odds with the social group's construction will fail to anticipate accurately, and the group's responses will invalidate the parent role enactment.

Invalidation may be conceptualized as a discrepancy between anticipatory construction and ensuing input. Failure to anticipate accurately produces a physiologic reaction, called arousal or, in other language, emotion. Thus, emotion signals to an individual that he or she can consider altering the parental role construction. A constructivist views behavior change following invalidation as an attempt on the part of the role player to enact an alternative version of the role (Carver & Scheier, 1981).

From this view, a person's development of the parent role is an evolutionary process that entails (1) acquiring the elements of the role, (2) attempting to enact the role, (3) receiving feedback that validates or invalidates the role, (4) experiencing the arousal ("emotion") that follows a discrepancy between feedback and anticipatory construction, (5) considering the adequacy of such constructions, and (6) changing the constructions that guide one's parenting practices.

The design of the constructivist parent training program presented here is founded on the assumptions enumerated above. As indicated, those assumptions reflect the position laid out by Kelly. Kelly (1955) espoused the belief that the provision of opportunities for "make believe," "probably man's oldest protective screen for reaching out into the unknown" (p. 373), enables the creation of new role constructions. Kelly proposed that an atmosphere of experimentation should help the client to "try on" new constructs and role definitions in a safe, insular environment. This safe therapeutic space must not only provide a setting for trying out novel ideas but must also provide "validating data" to facilitate construct change. The therapist therefore assumes a responsibility for helping the client to "fabricate for himself constructs which will serve his personal purposes and enable him to meet the particular kinds of situations which confront him" (Kelly, 1955, p. 321). The clinician, having reviewed case history and testing data, listens carefully and credulously to the client's perspective of the problem. The resulting conceptualization identifies the ways in which the client anticipates, as well as his or her capacity to reconstrue. Therapist-designed experiments should allow the client to "try on" the kinds of constructs that enhance his "person-perceiving system" (Mancuso et al., 1984, p. 290), thereby enabling a better understanding of the construction systems of those who make up his reference group.

DESIGN OF A CONSTRUCTIVIST PARENT TRAINING PROGRAM

The Parent Skills Training Program at St. Catherine's Center for Children guides parents to a better understanding of (1) the standard proposed for the parent role by our society, (2) their own parent role construction, and (3) the construction systems of their children. Parents and their children participate in 12 weekly, agency-based 90-minute family activity sessions conducted by a parent trainer. During each session the parent and children are videotaped in play or interaction designed to give them opportunities to try on some new constructs and to practice new ways of relating to each other. The parent has access to "tools" (i.e., information about child development, ideas about developmentally appropriate activities) necessary for conducting video-taped parent-child "experiments." The video-tapes are viewed together by the parent and therapist, sometimes with the children present as well. This provides opportunities to guide parents in the process of identifying their children's constructs, as evidenced by behavior during the interaction.

During the video-tape review the parent trainer maintains the role of guide to the parent who operates as an explorer. The therapist tailors the training to maintain moderate, controlled discrepancy between the client's constructions and the feedback from the flow of events, as a later example will illustrate. In short, the therapist becomes the novelty or arousal regulator for the parent and the children, enabling them to experience a moderate degree of validation or invalidation during experimentation. A manageable degree of discrepancy (producing the experience of a moderate arousal state) allows parents to confront the discrepancy between the anticipations and the feedback provided by the interaction with their children. The parent trainer enhances the client's experimental perspective and investigative role by listening and questioning. The trainer draws the parents' attention to evidence of discrepancy or validation during video-taped interactions by using techniques such as Sigel's distancing behavior (Sigel, 1977). The distancing technique places the cognitive demand on the client, most often through the use of open-ended questions. It draws the clients' attention to contradictions or inconsistencies in behavior and then involves the client in reviewing and better understanding the nature of these inconsistencies. During review of video-taped sessions, the trainer leads the parent in considering harmonious or disruptive interactions as evidence of the use of similar or different anticipatory beliefs by themselves and their children (Mancuso & Handin, 1983, p. 184).

Following from Kelly's sociality corollary, constructivist parent training presents the parent with the hypothesis that a successful parent recognizes and anticipates differences in adult-child construing of events and reflects this knowledge in parenting behavior. This means presenting children with resolvable discrepancies (Mancuso & Handin, 1983). This point is particularly salient for parents who avoid reprimand or who enact reprimands that fail to bring congruence between their own and their children's constructions. In these cases, parents are encouraged to consider whether or not their behavior may be creating an excessive degree of discrepancy for the child. Parents are prompted to try on appropriate reprimands and other behaviors that indicate that the child's perspective has been considered (moderate novelty principle). The therapist continually supports parents in their task of elaborating their parental role concepts—to think beyond child management to the promotion of child development through the enhancement of the parent-child relationship.

As families begin in the parent training program, then, the trainer begins to develop a view of the parents' construct systems. The trainer consults case history and referral information, considering this as a possible chronology of the life events of a client and as one, or several, possible perspectives on the behavior of the client. The therapist is cognizant that case history and evaluative information regarding a client also reflect the beliefs of the person who prepared this information. The constructivist parent trainer, therefore, reviews collateral material but pays particular attention to data gleaned from interaction and interviews with the clients. Data collected from the clients' own problem statement and from statements about their immediate needs have a high degree of salience for the trainer. Evaluative tools that offer a representation of the client's beliefs about the role of parent and parenting performance assist the trainer in formulating ideas about the clients' construct system. The trainer maintains a credulous attitude in listening to the explanations of the world offered by the client, because, even though those versions of history may be divergent from reports prepared by members of the reference group, they reflect the clients' present and future anticipations of events. Kelly (1955) supported this posture, stating:

> Because we would be concerned with his channelizing constructs and not merely his (the client's) terminal acts, we would, in accordance with our sociality corollary, be taking the first step toward establishing a role for ourselves in relation to them (p. 321).

The personal construct trainer, then, offers "technical assistance" to the client in his process of conducting the experiments that will lead to reconstruction.

A METHOD OF ASSESSING PARENT ROLE CONSTRUCTION SYSTEMS

A process built on Kelly's (1955) repertory grid approach was developed to evaluate the parent training program. Mancuso and his co-workers (Mancuso, 1987; Mancuso & Handin, 1980) have reported elsewhere on the development and use of the Parent Repertory Grid (ParRep grid). In order to insure common understandings, however, it must be noted at this point that the repertory grid analysis does not reflect a cause-effect paradigm and will not produce a simple measurement of attitudes.

In addition to providing an assessment of parent role processes that is compatible with the theory guiding the program, the use of the parrep grid provides a unique way of focusing the training of the parent training staff. The grid technology offers a face valid representation of many of the concepts underlying constructivist views of psychological processes, because it clearly illustrates the concepts of dichotomous construing and hierarchical organization in the construct system. Additionally, the constant exploration of the burgeoning grid technologies (Mancuso & Shaw, 1987) conveys to a parent training staff the notion that the trainer, like the parent, also acts as an experimenter who constantly changes her or his constructions of events.

CASE ILLUSTRATION

Family Status

The Bell family was composed of six members: Nan, the 34-year-old mother; Frank, her 12-year-old son; Sharon, her 9-year-old daughter; Gina, her 8-year-old daughter; and Debbie, her 3-year-old daughter. The biologic father of Sharon, Gina, and Debbie lived in the household but did not participate in the parent training program. Frank had several friends with whom he interacted. Sharon and Gina had few friends living nearby and were isolated in the neighborhood.

Presenting Problem

The Bell family became involved in family treatment due to continuous parental difficulty in the area of child management. Clinical evaluations of both children recommended that the family become involved in family treatment designed to enhance parent functioning in order to insure the safety of the children and the growth and development of all family members.

Family Functioning

Primary responsibility for household management and childrearing had been delegated to Nan, who reported that she was frequently overwhelmed by the dual demands of housekeeping and childrearing.

Both parents reported having strong attachments with their children. The children, particularly Frank and Gina, were highly self-directed and frequently resisted parental direction. Nan stated that she was unable to "control" her children and avoided limit-setting and reprimand. The children demonstrated some confrontive behaviors that appeared to be designed to engage their mother and encourage her to enact the parent role.

Family Problem Statement

As presenting problems the family identified the lack of limit-setting and the lack of obedience as features of family life that needed to change in order for everyone to be more safe and for the family and its members to accomplish their developmental tasks.

Interventions

Assessment. Following family counseling and advocacy services, the Bell family agreed to participate in parent training services in order to accomplish the changes they had identified as necessary. Participation in the program began by Nan responding to a version of the Parent Repertory Analysis (ParRep). In this case the examiner randomly chose and laid before the client one of the 14 parent role descriptors that constitute the ParRep parent role set (see Table 10.1). She was asked to consider carefully the role description, and to try to set in her mind as complete an idea of the parent role as she could construct. The examiner then selected one of the 16 child rearing statements (see Table 10.1), and Nan was asked to indicate the extent to which the person in the role description would believe the statement. She was asked to make her decision in terms of three levels of belief—(0) wouldn't believe the statement at all, (1) would tend to agree with the statement, and (2) would definitely believe the statement.

Nan's completed ParRep grid, which contained 224 such judgments (14 role descriptions by 16 belief statements), was subjected to multidimensional cluster analysis. Figure 10.1 displays the mapping of the cluster analyses that were performed.

Consider some of the indices that the display provides (see Figure 10.1). Note first that the index of similarity that is used in this analysis (see Rosenberg & Jones, 1972) summarizes the level of similarity of two roles in terms of how similarly the various persons would perceive each of the belief statements. The distance measure becomes larger as the two described role persons diverge in their acceptance of the belief statements. If the respondent judges that two role persons would accept all the belief statements to approximately the same level, then a low distance measure would index the similarity of those two persons. For example, Nan ascribes very similar beliefs to Parent Role 12 (SATISFYD) and Parent Role 10 (CH-ALONG). If the respondent judges that two role persons hold the 16 beliefs quite differently, then the analysis would yield a very high distance measure between those two role persons. For example, Nan judges that Parent Role 04 (YOUATBEST) would view the belief statements very differently than would Parent Role 08 (CHBRAKRU). As a result, the index of similarity (the distance measure) between those two roles is very high.

Within Nan's system the similarity of the belief statements would also be quantified in terms of the ways in which the respondent ascribes them to the role occupants. If all role persons were seen to believe two of the statements in the same way, then the index of similarity would be very high. In the present results, plotted in Figure 10.1, one can see that, according to Nan, all

Table 10.1 Parent role descriptions and parenting belief statements included in ParRep analysis

---

Parent Role Descriptions

---

01. Frank Gable gets along beautifully with his children. Frank and his children can work out anything that might trouble them. What would Frank say about this? (GETALONG)

02. Picture Sally Smith. Sally has raised a child who really sticks to what needs to be done. If Sally's child starts to put together a puzzle, or to learn something . . . she sticks right to it. (CPERSIST)

03. How hard would it be for *you* to believe this statement? (YOU)

04. If you were the very best mother you could be to your child, what would you say about this statement? (YOUATBEST)

05. Mary Jones is the best mother there could be. (BEST)

06. Three or four couples are at a little gathering, they are talking about their young children, talking about how to raise the children. How hard would it be for these couples to believe this statement? (GRUPCONS)

07. Bob Wilson has really tried to raise his children so that they do things the first time they are asked to do them. (CHCOMPLY)

08. Jim Klinger has a fifth grade child who can't seem to do the right thing. Jim's child fights the rules more than anybody in fifth grade. When Jim was raising his child, how hard would it have been for him to believe this statement? (CHBRAKRU)

09. Ruth Kramer is a mother who knows the best thing to do when children get upset. (CALMWELL)

10. Faye Dunn has raised a child who doesn't get along with other people outside of the family. Faye's child just has trouble getting along with other people. (CH-ALONG)

11. Barbara Moore has a child who can't stand being in new situations. Barbara just hasn't helped her child to put up with anything new—new food, new places, new people. Barbara's child really fusses whenever the family tries something different or new. (CH-NOVEL)

12. Sue Doyle really feels satisfied with herself as a parent. Sue feels that she does a good job. She's very happy being a mother. (SATISFYD)

13. Joe Hooker is the kind of parent who doesn't always try hard to get his children to do what they are told to do. He's kind of easy on them. (EASY)

14. John Powers is a man who is known to be very fair with his children. John's friends and all the other kids always say, "John Powers is fair in whatever he asks his children to do." (FAIR)

Child Rearing Statements

---

01. A child who learns to do what his father says to do will grow up to be a person who won't get into trouble. (OBEYFATH)

02. The child who has done something really bad deserves a really hard punishment, and the child who has done something that is not so bad deserves an easier punishment. (PUNFITCR)

03. A child should settle down whenever he's told to settle down. (SETLDOWN)

04. When a child has done something that a parent doesn't like, talking to the child works better than punishing the child. (TALK-PUN)

05. Even though parents must teach their child to follow rules, the child can be a friend to his parents. (BEFRIEND)

06. When a child is having temper tantrums, it helps to give him/her a good swat on the rear. (SWATCALM)

07. A 10-year-old and 4-year-old are no different when it comes to punishment. If the 4-year-old breaks something, he/she gets the same punishment as the 10-year-old who breaks something. (PUNALSAM)

08. There are a lot of children who end up causing trouble, even though the parents are really good parents. (SOMEBAD)

09. It doesn't hurt to let a child disagree when a parent tries to explain something that the child did wrong. (LETCHDIS)

10. Always try to tell a kid what is going to happen before it happens. (FOREWARN)

11. Punish a child whenever he/she does not do what he/she is told to do. (DOWATOLD)

12. Once a parent makes a rule, a child should never be allowed to break the rule . . . no matter what. (NOBRKRUL)

13. If you are trying to teach a child something, like how to put on his/her shoes, let him/her work it out his/her own way. (LRNBYDNG)

14. A parent makes it clear to his/her children that they will be punished whenever they do something stupid. (PUNISCLR)

15. When it's time to put a child to bed do things in the same order each night—like, a bath first, then a snack, then a story—the same order each night. (ROUTINE)

16. Let a child tell what he/she thinks when his/her parents ask him/her to do something. (LETCHTEL)

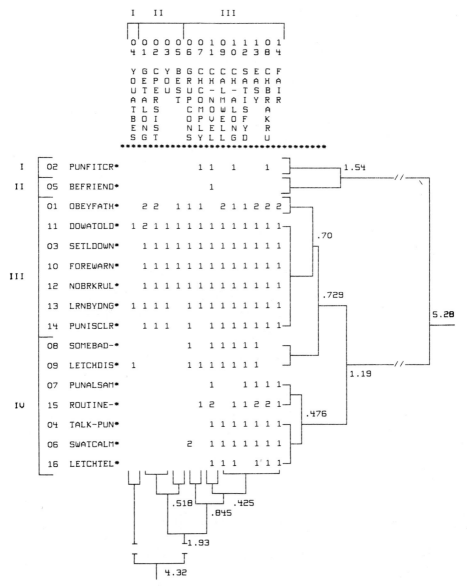

FIGURE 10.1. Permuted, two-way display of cluster-analyzed roles and beliefs from ParRep matrix completed by Nan at the beginning of her parent training program involvement. Major clusters of beliefs (on the rows) are labeled on the left. Major clusters of roles (on the columns) are labeled on the top. The tree diagrams on the bottom and on the right side trace through the clustering process, with the numbers at the stems indicating the δ measure between those events that come together at that joining.

parent role occupants would tend to agree with belief statements 03 (SETLDOWN), 10 (FOREWARD), and 12 (NOBRKRUL). Only Parent Role 04 (YOUATBES) would reject those beliefs.

The two dimensional display of the belief statements and parent roles neatly shows the patterns underlying her parent role construing system. In creating that display, we generally have followed the practice of keeping separate those clusters of roles (beliefs) that contain pairs of clusters whose similarity is indexed by a distance measure of less than 1.0. For example, all the roles in Role Cluster II and Cluster III, when compared to each other, would yield distance measures of less than 1.0. One can conclude then, that Nan groups parents into two broad categories. A third parent role (YOUATBES) stands as an "outlier." After observing the belief clusters one can easily describe the character of Nan's two main parent role clusters. One can observe that the parent belief statements also fall into two main clusters (with one separate outlier). Nan sees the socially acceptable parents as belonging to one broad cluster, Role Cluster II; and despite the evidence of her children's unsatisfactory behavior, she includes herself in that group. Her view of parenting has led her to see the parents of less satisfactory children as another grouping. Note, however, that parents like CALMWELL and the FAIR parent are grouped with the EASY parent and the parent of the rule-breaking fifth grade child. Her conception of herself at her best proves difficult to understand. She indicates that in that role she would then have to believe none of the parent belief statements.

When she began the parent training program, Nan perceived two broad types of parents: (1) "hard" parents, who believe the statements that advocate being "tough" on children and who reject the statements that give children status as persons; and (2) "messy" parents, who endorse both kinds of belief statements. Further indication of the character of her parental construct system can be extracted by observing the kinds of statements she considers to be similar. As indicated, Nan judges that offering a child forewarning of events that are about to take place is similar to insisting on a child's self-control on demand. She also judges that a belief that one should talk rather than punish shares strong similarity to the belief that one should swat an aroused child in order to calm him or her. It is also worth noting that in Nan's judgment, a fair parent (FAIR) would hold the same "messy" set of beliefs as does the parent of a fifth-grade child who cannot follow the rules (CHBRKRUL). It is not hard to conclude that Nan approached her parenting activities with a limited construction system that would restrict the range of alternatives available in guiding her relationships with her children.

Treatment. Following review of referral information, case history data, problem statement, ParRep analysis, and observation of an assessment video-tape, the parent trainer developed her conceptualization of the constructions of the Bell family. Based on this conceptualization, the therapist constructed parent training experiments designed to (1) guide Nan in developing an understanding of the perspective of children; (2) create opportunities for her to practice using her knowledge of the child's perspective in parent–child interaction; (3) assist her in elaborating her constructions of the role of parent; (4) provide data demonstrating that consideration of the child's perspective leads the child to respond more positively to the parent; (5) guide her in developing safe, effective reprimands that lead her children to reconstrue their behavior and consider the adult view of an event; (6) generate opportunities for the Bell children to experience Nan as a resourceful parent who assists them in understanding and operating in their world; and (7) enable Nan to maintain herself in a position of authority and, at the same time, experience enjoyable, satisfying interactions with her children.

The session activities were chosen to provide on-going opportunities for family members to express and integrate divergent perspectives and for Nan to devise feedback and, when necessary, reprimands that would enable her children to develop more effective self-guiding constructions about social interaction.

In order to demonstrate constructivist parent training, an interaction from one of the Bell family's sessions will be discussed. Particular attention will be paid to the questions and statements that might be offered by the parent trainer during video-tape review.

Video-tape Analysis.   Each of the 12 sessions was videotaped for review. During the fourth session, the family was instructed by the trainer in playing a board game. The game required each player to answer questions related to social interaction and social problem-solving in order to move around the board. Nan was given the role of explaining the rules, assisting Frank, Sharon, and Gina in playing the game, and maintaining a harmonious play environment.

Nan explained the rules of the game in a clear fashion, sitting very close to the table and making eye contact with her children. As each child chose a card, Nan offered alternative questions to be answered. The tenor of the game was serious, and Nan placed an emphasis on finding the "right" answer. At approximately the mid-point of the game, Gina was unable to understand the question on her card and asked for clarification. Nan offered another question, but Gina still did not understand and asked her mother what she should say. Nan replied that she should not offer any more help to Gina as she had to "answer her own questions."

Discussion of the above parent–child interaction during video-tape review was facilitated by statements and questions such as the following:

THERAPIST (T): It seems like you were worried about giving answers to the children. Could you tell me what you were thinking when Gina asked for help?

PARENT-
THERAPIST (P-T): Parent and therapist reach a concensus that Gina was "stuck" (couldn't answer the question) and needed more help from her mother.

T: When your child is "stuck," how can you help her without doing it for her?

P-T: Parent and therapist clarify the difference between doing things *for* children (Nan's EASY parent) and working *with* children to enable them to do as much as possible for themselves.

T: It seems like when you said "You have to answer your own questions," Gina might have thought that you weren't willing to help her. What do you think about that?

P-T: Parent and therapist conclude that Gina may have felt Nan was unwilling, but that Nan responded in that fashion because she was unsure how much help was too much help.

T: If Gina believes that you were not interested in helping her, what might she do the next time she needed your help?

P-T: Parent and therapist agree that Nan could have returned to the strategy that she had employed in the beginning of the game, asking a series of increasingly simpler questions until Gina was able to understand the meaning of the questions.

T: How would the ideas that Gina developed about you as a helper be different if you had offered a series of other questions until Gina could understand the concept?

T: If you helped her to solve that problem, how might that affect what she would do the next time she needs your help?

T: If Gina believes that you are interested in the way she is thinking, and you usually help her when she is "stuck," how will that affect the way she listens to you and follows your directions?

The above example of a possible parent-therapist interchange is offered to demonstrate constructivist parent training strategies for guiding the activity of the parent. The discussion of ideas and beliefs during video-tape review provides the data for the subsequent parent-child experiment. Parent responses to therapist questions serve as practice for subsequent sessions during which feedback on parent-therapist hypotheses would be provided by the responses and behavior of the children.

Evaluation. Following participation in the training program, Nan again completed a ParRep grid in order to assess whether change in her beliefs about the role of parent and her enactment of the role of parent could be demonstrated. Figure 10.2 suggests that Nan's system changed radically during the interval between the first and second administration of the ParRep grid. The system depicted in Figure 10.2 is not necessarily a representation of the system of an "ideal" parent, but it does show movement for Nan. The change implied by comparing Figure 10.1 and Figure 10.2 is

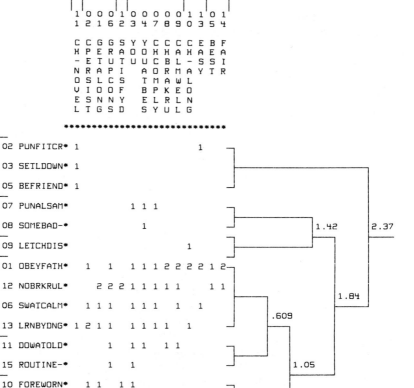

FIGURE 10.2. Permuted, two-way display of cluster-analyzed roles and beliefs from ParRep matrix completed by Nan at the close of her parent training program involvement. Major clusters of beliefs (on the rows) are labeled on the left. Major clusters of roles (on the columns) are labeled on the top. The tree diagrams on the bottom and on the right side trace through the clustering process, with the numbers at the stems indicating the δ measure between those events that come together at that joining.

fairly radical, and we are willing to ascribe such change to Nan's involvement in the parent training program.

As Figure 10.2 shows, Nan now has expanded the list of beliefs that would be rejected by most parents. It is not easy to understand why this has happened. One guess about the meaning of this change is that the belief statements that Nan now rejects were beliefs that she earlier ascribed only to parents included in her "Messy Parents" category. Perhaps now she thinks something like the following: "Only a really messed up parent could believe those things, and there really isn't a person who could be stupid enough to believe those things."

If one keeps separate those clusters that contain pairs of roles which are indexed by a distance measure of less than 1.0, then three broad role clusters emerge from her second ParRep grid. Roles 11 (CH-NOVEL) and 12 (SATISFYD) tend to stand as outliers, and the clusters marked V and VI are kept separate in the display, though they barely pass our criteria for remaining separate. It is clear that the clusters displayed in Figure 10.2 represent a scrambling of the clusters that emerged from the analysis of Nan's first grid.

If one treats Role Clusters II and III as one broad cluster, one sees that the parent roles that Nan once included in her "Hard" parent grouping now accept more of the "Soft" parent beliefs. The second broad cluster (Role Cluster IV) of parent roles in Nan's system tend to accept a series of the "Hard" beliefs and to reject all others. Nan continues to show considerable difficulty in thinking about the parent roles of those who occupy the third broad cluster (composed of V and VI) of parent role. She seems to indicate that these role figures (three of which she previously included in her "Messy Parent" category) would endorse several of the particularly "Hard" beliefs but would reject all other beliefs.

It is clear that in this second administration Nan classed the belief statements differently from the ways in which she classified them the first time. Though she still links together beliefs that might seem incongruous, she does tend to group together those beliefs that give important status to the child's constructions of events (the beliefs in Clusters V, VI, VII). At the same time, she now more clearly sees similarities between those child-rearing beliefs that attempt to coerce children into accepting the constructions of the parent.

If one observes the content of the role clusters, it is clear that Nan begins to think of the BEST parent as a member of a category which includes other parent roles that might appear as negative parents. We have observed that this pattern occurs frequently in the systems of parents of children who are judged to be poorly socialized. One might conjecture that these parents think of "best" entirely from their view of the child's perspective. They assume that a child "always tries to get away with murder;" and it seems that they believe that, from the child's perspective, BEST parent would be FAIR and/or EASY.

Note also that Nan now categorizes herself at her best with the roles CHBRAKRU and CALMWELL. Additionally, SATISFYD parent has shifted from the "Messy Parent" grouping into the socially acceptable grouping. In general, Nan now seems to understand more clearly that playing a role in relation to her children will depend on her ability to construe the construction systems of the children.

Generalizing Constructivist Conceptions

Investigators of the processes of parenting have long been willing to entertain the assumption that the "attitudes" of a parent will strongly affect the outcomes of child-rearing activities (Baumrind, 1967). The constructivist parent training program described in this chapter focuses directly on the construction systems of the clients and, as such, targets relevant parental "attitudes" as foci of intervention. But the ParRep approach is also designed to search out the hierarchically organized structures that underlie a person's parental attitudes, and it is the function of the total structures of the parent that must be the concern of parent training programs. "What constructions can a person organize to frame the role enactment of self and of others?" "What alternative constructions can a person assemble as he/she observes invalidation of his or her role enactments?" "How permeable would a person's existing role construction system be?" Such are the questions that are open to exploration from a constructivist approach to considering a person's expertise in framing problems of parenting.

The content of the system, of course, would also be of considerable importance, particularly as one thinks of the permeability of a learner's system. For example, in that Nan construes the EASY parent, the FAIR parent, the SATISFIED parent, and the parent of the fifth-grade rule-breaking child as being essentially identical, we can expect that she will change her conception of fairness only at great psychological cost. To change her idea of fairness will require change, as well, in her construction of being an easy parent, and of those behaviors which lead to rule-following. Thus, we would expect that certain changes in the content of Nan's constructs will allow her to function more adequately as a parent. Nevertheless, the content cannot be treated outside of the context (the organizational structure) in which that content is embedded, and a trainer who focuses on that structure works from a perspective that differs greatly from the perspective of the trainer who thinks of a parent's attitudes only as a cause of a child's behavior.

REFERENCES

Baumrind, D. (1967). Child care practices anteceding three patterns of preschool behavior. *Genetic Psychology Monographs, 75,* 43–88.

Carver, C. S., & Scheier, M. F. (1981). *Attention and self-regulation: A control-theory approach to human behavior.* New York: Springer-Verlag.

Kelly, G. A. (1955). *The psychology of personal constructs.* New York: W. W. Norton.

Mancuso, J. C. (1987). Analyzing cognitive structure. An application to parent role systems. In J. C. Mancuso and M. L. G. Shaw (Eds.), *Cognition and personal structures: Computer access and analysis.* New York: Praeger Press.

Mancuso, J. C., & Handin, K. H. (1980). Training parents to construe the child's construing. In A. W. Landfield and L. M. Leitner (Eds.), *Personal construct psychology: Psychotherapy and personality* (pp. 271–288). New York: John Wiley.

Mancuso, J. C., & Handin, K. H. (1983). Prompting parents toward constructivist caregiving practices. In I. E. Sigel and L. M. Laosa (Eds.), *Changing Families* (pp. 163–202). New York: Plenum Press.

Mancuso, J. C., Heerdt, W. A., & Hamill, R. (1984). Construing the transition to parent roles as a constructive process. In V. L. Allen & E. van der Vliert (Eds.), *Proceedings of NATO Symposium on Role Transitions* (pp. 289–300). New York: Plenum.

Mancuso, J. C., & Shaw, M. L. G. (Eds.). (1987). *Cognition and personal structures: Computer access and analysis.* New York: Praeger Press.

Rosenberg, S., & Jones, R. (1972). A method for investigating and representing a persons implicit theory of personality. *Journal of Personality, 22,* 372–386.

Sigel, I. E. (1977). *Parents as teachers of their own learning disabled children.* Educational Testing Service, submitted grant proposal.

11
Family Somatics: A Personal Construct Approach to Cancer

Vincent Kenny

THE WORD-MADE MAN

Kelly's image of persons is that they are active processes or forms of action who are busily engaged in the construction of their own reality. Kelly was keen to illuminate this image and spoke of the difference between using nouns or verbs to characterize human experience. He warned against getting caught in the linear structure of the English language, specifically in the "subject-predicate trap." "Western thinking . . . takes the very practical view that a word is beholden to the object it is used to describe. The object determines it." However, Kelly (1969a) takes the view that "the word is beholden to the person who utters it, or, more properly speaking, to the *construction* system, that complex of personal constructs of which it is a part" (p. 74).

The psychology of personal constructs emphasizes the notion that you are your constructions to use Bruner's (1956) phrase. Constructs are not something you "have" but rather constitute your very existence. They are not merely descriptions or predictions but, further, prescribe what actions or roles to take in any series of events. Therefore, what we construe is what we do. Kelly's theory of learning is that "you become what you do," that is, your construct system evolves a coherence (Dell, 1982) in the direction of your practiced actions or repeated role enactments. We may summarize the above as follows: (a) you are your constructs, (b) you do what you construe, and (c) you become what you do. In this way we conserve our "fit" (von Glasersfeld, 1984) with the world while retaining our own integral coherence. Constructs are our means of relating ourselves to our reality. In

190

family medicine, many physicians are beginning to see the power of a shift from nouns (stasis) to verbs (process) and are ceasing to speak of the patient as "having hypertension" but rather of the patient "hypertensing" or even "doing hypertension." Similarly we may speak of complainants doing anorexia, doing psychosis, or doing cancer. In all of these, we may observe the cyclical recursive process of the construing system where "we do what we construe" and "we become what we do." However, it must be made clear that construing has little to do with cognition. Kelly (1969a) points out that, "The personal construct we talk about bears no essential relation to grammatical structure, syntax, words, language, or even communication; nor does it imply consciousness. It is simply a psychologically construed unit for understanding human processes" (p. 87). Here Kelly takes a clear monist position on the mind–body problem. He wanted at all costs to avoid fragmenting the human person. It is the whole person who construes, not merely his or her thinking brain. This position allows Kelly (1969b) to state that much of our construing is at a low level of awareness, and within personal construct psychology (PCP) he describes the preverbal construing process being manifested where the complainant "is struggling to make new sense out of some experience that lies just beyond the reach of his semantic language. But it can be observed in some degree at even less accessible levels, levels that lie even beyond the reach of his primitive semiotic speech" (p. 198).

It is largely within this rather inaccessible arena of preverbal constructs (PVCs) one must operate in doing psychotherapy with cancer complainants. Kelly (1955) phrases the therapeutic dilemma in dealing with preverbal constructs in this way: "It is like handling a live fish in the dark; not only does it wiggle but it is slippery and hard to see" (p. 1082). From the foregoing it will be clear that in PCP there is no theory of cancer per se but rather a theory of persons as wholes and of how we go about the business of changing ourselves and reinventing our humanness.

INITIAL PRESENTATION

The person in question, Una, was a 30-year-old unmarried woman who was living apart from her family with her 8-year-old daughter and was referred by her shiatsu (Japanese massage) teacher, because she had a conflict about whether or not to have a hysterectomy in the light of a recently diagnosed cancer of the cervix. In our initial conversation, she made it clear to me that the conflict was not that she was ambivalent about having this operation, but that she decidedly did not want it while her family were insisting that she must have it. She reported being subjected to sustained and strong pressure from her family, from her family doctor, and from the surgeon in question (who was also a family friend). In exploring the question of having versus not having the hysterectomy, it became clear that for Una, death was not a threat but rather an event she could welcome. She had almost died eight years previously in childbirth and lived only by virtue of the emergency procedures of the resuscitation team at the hospital. She could clearly recall the experience of dying as a warm sensation of floating away in an accepting darkness.

Family Structure and History

Una was born the last of three children with one sister five years older and one brother three years older than she. Both parents were teachers. Una describes her experience in the family in the following written portrait which she entitled "My place in the family."

> UNA: My sister always bossed me around. She envied me, felt she'd been hard done by . . . My brother was a weakling, Mommy always came to his defence, I think he saw me as a rival for her affections . . . I could never be better than him at anything. When learning to swim we had a race, they cheered at the edge of the pool, and when I won I thought they would congratulate me. They ignored me and said how his swimming was improving. I couldn't believe it. I think I was always careful not to be good at things he was doing, to play my role I had to stay behind him, my mother always told me I was my father's pet. But then he used to beat me for the slightest provocation. He wasn't capable of showing affection and just wanted everyone to behave as he wanted. If he did like me, he only liked the *idea* of the little blonde haired blue-eyed girl; because I was not this perfect child (though I tried) he used to beat me.

In this and other passages, we find that Una's attempts to positively and aggressively elaborate her evolving construct system were systematically invalidated and rechanneled. We particularly note that any explicit competition with her brother was futile and that her only refuge from mother's rejection was a father who was dangerously volatile and frequently beat Una. The following extract from Una's therapy diary makes her untenable position in the family more clear.

> UNA: When we were children, my brother and I, the worst thing that could happen would be for Daddy to lose his temper, something we were led to believe he had no control over. When he did lose it and beat me, or us, we were then told how bad he felt about it and how he had retired to bed with a headache. So immediately we are taken away from our own feelings of fear and pain to feel sympathy for him who has inflicted it on us. So my mother is covering up for his irresponsibility. She was also transmitting her own dislike of him in these situations, yet feeling duty-bound not to take sides with us against him, which he was always complaining of, particularly in relation to my brother who he is jealous of, saying if she interfered it only made him worse, and she would end up bearing the brunt. Mother would then get headaches and retire to bed. I

used to sit on her bed and put my hand on her forehead and wish I could make the pain go. Often when she had retired to bed my father would also go and lie down, because if she wasn't going to cope then he certainly wasn't either. Once she went helpless he did too.

Here again we have clear statements relating to (a) The double-bind of her father punishing her because he loved her, that is, she was expected to feel loved when beaten, instead of feeling rejected, hurt, etc. (Watzlawick, 1977); (b) the mother refusing to bear "the brunt" of her husband's anger and deflecting it onto Una, while taking a protective attitude to her son of whom the father is jealous; (c) the creation of guilt in Una and her brother as somehow to blame for the whole event; and (d) the symmetrical (competitive) relationship between the parents, both of whom refused to cope at the same time; this forced Una into the caring responsible role, attempting to cure her mother's "suffering face"; this was an unrealizable objective.

Family Construct Chreods

This family construct pattern had been transferred down a number of generations, where both the construct channels of movement and the elements (people) moving along such channels were replicated in an uncanny fashion. The following examination of the immediate family tree helps to illustrate this pattern. Una's maternal grandfather and her own father both lost their respective parents when young. Her ex-boyfriend, Colm (the father of her daughter, Kate), lost his father when young. These three men were all violent with "uncontrollable tempers." Una and her mother (Joan) shared the same family pattern: they were the youngest of three with an older brother and sister. Una hates Joan as Joan hated her mother. There are many patterned connections across the generations where the cast of characters and roles remains invariant, attesting to the power of these transgenerational construct chreods (this word deriving from Greek meaning a "necessary path," hence I use it to emphasize the recursive self-recreating power of such constructs that preempt other channels of movement). Joan "found" a substitute for her violent father by marrying a violent man. She replicated her brother and sister in Una's brother and sister. She relates to her grandchild, Kate, as her mother related to Una. She is hated by Una as she in turn hated her mother. She rejected Colm, as her parents rejected her own husband. Joan alienated Una, as Una alienated Kate. What is most striking about this family construct system is that nobody wants to be a parent, and everyone wants to be a loved child. The consequence is that no one feels loved, and everyone resents having to care for any other person. This vicious circle goes on unbroken where the symmetrical competition is to seek to be loved and to seek not to have to be a caring parent. This gives us the major axis of "to be nurtured/passive/child-like versus to give succor/active/parent-like." Superordinate to this is the construct "to need caring for versus to be a caregiver." Also superordinate is the construct "dependent versus autonomous."

SUMMARY OF INITIAL PROBLEM PRESENTATION

Una had cervical cancer and refused to have an operation to excise it. This attitude was strongly contested by her family. At this initial stage Una was unsure as to whether or not she wanted to live or die. She wanted some help in clarifying this issue and also in regard to the implications of refusing surgery.

A radical PCP framework for approaching an understanding of cancer complainants would include the following constructions: The person is actively doing/creating/bringing forth cancer. Early disturbances in parental relationships lead to developments in early role enactments of "being ill" where the child learns to relate herself to parents through the development of a construct subsystem cohering around "dis-ease" and illness. On presentation the person often has an extreme preoccupation with past events while the future is largely blank or unanticipated. Particularly there is little or no anticipated future self. This is very significant from Kelly's point of view as our primary aim is the anticipation of future events. Since the person seems to abandon any investment in anticipating a future self, then, in terms of the cycle of experience (see R. A. Neimeyer, Chapter 1, *this volume*), she ceases all major self experimentation—there being no anticipation with which to begin the cycle. Neimeyer (1985) points out that many of the severest human problems (e.g., schizophrenia) tend to result from difficulties with the anticipation phase of this cycle. Our constructs prescribe future role enactments for us and help us delineate a future psychological space within which we can exist. If there are few future self-anticipations this makes it difficult for the person to relevantly locate himself in the future. Looked at another way, this is the prescription of a specific future role enactment, that is, to be a dead person. We need to look no further than the literature on voodoo death (Cannon, 1957) to appreciate the power of the assumptive construct system to channel one's processes into death.

In the months and years before developing cancer, such persons may have persistently engaged in vivid visualization of themselves being ill, often imagining themselves in a hospital bed surrounded by sympathetic friends. This seems to be their final use of the cycle of experience for radical personal change. That is, having actively invested in the anticipation of a future (diseased) self and having subsequently become ill (i.e., validated their anticipation) they revise their construct system by reconstruing themselves as the disease construct system. In achieving this organized identity (cancer victim) the system concurrently develops mechanisms for its propagation and conservation. For example, the experience cycle having been used to achieve a self-destructive identity is, through its own conclusion, preempted from being used for any further constructive self-elaboration. Having been used to arrive at a certain position it is thrown away like Wittgenstein's (1971) ladder, marooning the person on a chreodic channel. The cycle is now used for a tightening of coherence of cancer identity. That is, the more he does cancer, the more he becomes cancerous, etc. The person comes to relate himself to the world primarily through the disease-construct-system. Therefore the best fit that the person reaches with his world is one which will ultimately destroy him; that is, the construct system coheres paradoxically around an organization that has created the conditions for its own destruction. Maturana (1983) points out that we remain viable "autopoietic systems" (from *autos* = self, and *poiesis* = creation, hence self-producing) as long as we conserve our "structural coupling" (relating one's self to the world) with the medium while conserving our own organizational invariance (i.e., our core constructs or self-maintenance processes). Cancer patients, by relating themselves to the world through systems for disease, pay the ultimate price, that is, the loss of autopoietic organization (death).

ELABORATING THE COMPLAINT

The Meaning of Cancer

The constructivist therapist is mindful that "a client can express himself only within the framework of his construct system" (Kelly, 1969a, p. 83). Thus, I always start within the coherence of the person's system. For example, whether or not Una construed cancer as self-induced at the outset is immaterial. My initial objectives were to unpack Una's construing processes in relation to cancer and to her family construct system. The following is an extract from the diary I asked her to keep during therapy. Diary writing was an important part of the continuous therapeutic effort to articulate the PVCs implicit in Una's complaint.

UNA: I think the effects of a hysterectomy would be extremely traumatic and would probably leave me without the necessary energy to continue to change, it would also I believe weaken my immune system further, by taking away something it should be trying to eliminate itself, it removes the immediate threat but also leaves it more vulnerable and open to attack. If part of me has to die so that another may live, does my womb mean more than my entire body? If I have done this to myself then I can undo it. Belief. I have always been afraid of the things I believe in, in case they may not be acceptable to others—sounds crazy, but I have not been able to accept that part of myself that believes. When I'm feeling positive and full of energy everything is fine, even coming close to being grateful for having cancer . . . see how I seem to need an excuse to be myself—be myself or else.

In this extract, we may note the construal that if she has generated this cancer then through her own agency she should eliminate it. Further, she suggested that doing cancer provided her with an opportunity for independent action as opposed to a reliance on the administrations of others. She commented that if her parents died it would be a relief since "I let them get too far in on me." She also mentioned that the only way she could express her unhappiness when young was psychosomatically.

To further aid the articulation of PVCs Una was requested to provide a written summary of each session. As part of one summary she included the following list of reasons as to why she had developed cancer.

> UNA: Fear of exclusion/fear of causing upset/fear of the separateness of my vision/ fear of other's anger/fear of confrontation/fear of being visible/fear of externalizing inner perceptions/fear of taking responsibility/fear of being defeated/fear of letting go/fear of my own anger/fear of its effects/fear of being without my unhappiness and having nothing to hold onto/fear of break through/fear of the unknown.

From the point of view of the experience cycle these fears highlight a variety of difficulties at several of its phases. Una's own anticipations (autonomy of vision) are not elaborated very well, beyond those predicting unhappiness. She does not invest in any alternative outcome (the unknown is threatening). She does not encounter events very willingly (avoids confronting or upsetting others). Invalidation is also avoided (not wishing to risk defeat), and there would seem to be very little opportunity or inclination to constructively revise her outlook. (If she does, it is through relying on others' opinions or reconstructions and not on her own "separateness of vision"). These are the reasons she cites to explain how she developed cancer. We may postulate that, in the absence of "positively" elaborating her system, she "destructively" elaborates her system, since no system can "stand still" but must evolve. Thus, elaborating a cancerous system is her way of attempting to validate her construct system as a whole.

In further conversations she described the sense of being out of control of her life. Through a necessary process of constriction (the narrowing of her perceptual field) Una gives the opportunity for despised others to be in control of her life. This form of constriction, leaving the control of one's life in the hands of others, may well be reflected in the nonverbal construing system where the proliferation of cancer cells is also "out of control." This is for her the choice point. Her "out-of-controlness" can again be "solved" by an external agent, for example, the surgeon who will invasively intervene in her life. However, it is at this point precisely that she chooses to refuse external interventions. She chooses to use cancer as the focus of her attempts to regain control over her experience. She wants to attempt to end her destructive self-elaboration and begin a positive and independent elaboration. Thus we have the apparent paradox of having to do cancer in order to begin life.

The Corporate Family

From our explorations we noted that her family largely tried to ignore her wishes and also showed some envy of her. I found their reaction puzzling, so I decided to explore the family construct system more closely. I asked Una to draw the outline of a human body and, using this as a metaphor, to map the family members onto the body in terms of the symptoms recurrently experienced by each member. The following is the mapping produced.

Her mother recurrently experiences migraine headaches, stomach ulcers, arthritis of the hands, neck, and knees, and eye pain. Una construed this to mean that Joan was the "head" of the family who controlled everything. She saw her as the "brains of the corporation" whose influence extended everywhere from the central core to the far extremities of the system. Being the head, she could also render the family system "blind" to where it was going or what was going on. The father has a heart complaint and "weakened" legs. Una describes him as the "heart of the matter" who threatens to undermine Joan's "head-ship" by another coronary that will stop the family system dead in its tracks. Her sister experiences neuralgia of the face, while Kate has ear difficulties. They are both subserved to Joan's wishes and used to obscure issues and create confusion. Una's brother has had severe asthma since childhood, often necessitating hospital admission. As the lungs of the system he focuses attention sharply when he "cuts off the air supply." Una describes herself as the reproductive organs of the family (cervical cancer) and thus threatens the continuity of the family system.

From these discussions we noted that illness was prevalent among the whole family, that there was a symmetrical competition for attention through illness events, that the system members related themselves to others primarily through illness experiences, and that Una recalled "feeling special when sick, something definite to be." She went on to say "I can beat them all, cancer gets many more points . . . but what is the prize? Death. I have put a lot of effort into dying and being noticed by my absence . . . Denying my life because it didn't agree with or conform to their own hellish existence . . . If you're healthy you're outside the family scope."

The organization of this family into a system is achieved through what we may call (following Maturana, 1985) "Conversations for Illness." The family network of conversations reveals the interactions the members enter into in order to constitute a certain type of system (Kenny, 1985a). In this case, the constitutive relations flow along PVC channels of somatic symptoms that each individual uses to channel his/her own processes. Since any system must conserve its organization (core constructs) if it is to retain its identity then the task of therapy (whether individual or family) is to destroy such organizational invariance. In Una's case, both her individual and family organizations must be disintegrated so that the family members can act alternatively. To achieve this I must, from the outset, interact orthogonally with Una, who in turn must learn to interact orthogonally with the family system. To be orthogonal is to approach the system from its periphery through axes redundant to the constitution of the organizational invariance of the system (Maturana, 1985). In other words, I must relate through construct channels that are superfluous to the constitutive relations, that is, those dimensions not constitutive of the system's organization. In this way, I may disconfirm the sytem and avoid becoming part of the family problem rather than being part of the solution. I must therefore proffer a suitable blend of the intriguingly alien with the reliably familiar while composing an alternative lexicon (to that of disease) for conversations both within the therapy sessions and within the family system.

While Una's cancer is moving her toward an autopoietic disintegration (death) the therapeutic task is to try to attain a destruction of organization that is not an autopoietic disintegration but a psychological or constructive disintegration. From Una's point of view she is the "family's sexual reproductive system" and therefore the family's method of self-propagation. Hence the family panic since they will no longer be able to "reproduce" their current identity. They will "die" as the current family system, that is, that characterized through construct dimensions of anger, violence, disease, etc. Una must choose between the loss of a literal womb (her own) and the loss of a metaphorical womb (herself). If her own womb is extirpated the family conserves its "womb" and its system intact. If she refuses surgery and cancer advances to the point of her own death, then the family loses its "womb," and it disintegrates. There is a third option, namely, to refuse surgery but to change her personal organization to such a degree that doing cancer becomes unnecessary to the constitution of her own system's identity to the point where she can no longer help constitute the family organization. This is the therapeutic choice.

SPECIFIC INTERVENTIONS PLANNED

Intrapersonal

With cancer patients I find it important to have a multi-level approach to the construing system, often involving the physical, psychological, and spiritual domains. This is not to imply that these are separately existing fragments of the person but rather are different logical levels of the same phenomenon. With Una this multi-layered approach was particularly suitable since she was already engaged in a number of activities that I could use for elaborating her construct system. The physical/somatic experiments could be embarked upon within the context of her shiatsu (body massage) sessions together with changes in her macrobiotic diet. The spiritual explorations could be pursued within her interest in Tibetan Buddhism, and the psychological (especially the preverbal) areas could be elaborated within her practice of meditation and, of course, the weekly psychotherapy consultations. Space limits me to a discussion largely of the family dimension.

Interpersonal/Familial

While Kelly describes a construct as capable of being overpermeable (i.e., an overgeneralized approach to life creating much ambiguity) it is possible to describe the whole construct system organization as being overpermeable and therefore having no effective boundary with the outside. Since a construct may be viewed as a discrimination or a way of drawing a boundary line between elements, we may say from Una's experience that she had little effective boundary between her system and that of other people, especially her family. She had always been in a position of listening to outside advice and ignoring her own autonomous ideas. With very depressed autonomy and overpermeability she had difficulty knowing where she began and others ended. In the family pattern she played Joan's role with her own daughter, and so on. It was difficult for her to define an autonomous construct organization that uniquely identified her as separate from the "molecular soup" (Varela, 1984) of the family in which she was extremely enmeshed. Her escalation of the family conversation for illness to the point of cancer had paradoxically placed her outside the family game of disease and allowed her to create a clear boundary differentiating herself from the family in her willingness to die and refusal to use medical agents to prolong the family conversation. Thus, the development of cancer may be construed as a boundary-making strategy. In such cases, I find it useful to follow this movement and to artificially create some literal or metaphorical boundary that clearly isolates the person. This strategy is to remove the need to maintain the somatic discrimination (cancer) as a boundary-marker and also to deliberately provoke the observer role in such patients to the point where they can begin to consciously experiment with boundary-making within the family network of conversations.

EMBARKING ON EXPERIMENTS

I decided to begin therapeutic experiments in the here and now, accepting Una's tendency to avoid anticipating the future in any clear way, and also to diminish her preoccupation with past injustices experienced within the family. To do this I asked her to elaborate her meditative techniques in particular ways and to begin working on a visual image that she could use within Simonton et al.'s (1981) general method of combating cancer. Together with conventional medical interventions this involves activating the patient's positive expectancies using a variety of meditative procedures, deep relaxation, and visualization of the immune system destroying the cancer cells. Concomitant with these changes Una began to draw boundaries between herself and her family. This took the form of a unilateral change in her way of helping to constitute the family conversations. For example, through casual enactments we devised alternative conversations for various contexts including a radical diminishing of contact with her family. Just as the therapist must demonstrate versatility in role relationships with the patient (by eluding her transferences), so also Una began to extricate herself from her existing enactments within the family system and generate a useful degree of impermeability.

The Family Conversations

> UNA: In relating to my parents I discovered that once I stopped playing the role, distanced myself from them, I didn't feel the weight of responsibility for their problems, didn't feel involved in their lives anymore, was able to view them in a different way. Realized how negative my mother is, seeing the negative side of everything, afraid. I felt able to shut them out when I need to, out and off. I feel no longer underneath their influence, and am amazed at the feeling of having been under them, swamped by them. My mother doesn't like not being in control.

In this extract from Una's diary, we see the powerful effects of triggering the observer role (Kenny, 1985b) in that (a) it can interrupt her usual part in the family network of conversations ("didn't feel involved"), (b) it allows her to note and dislike more detailed aspects of the pattern, (c) she begins to reconstrue her mother, (d) she can explore the contrast to being "swamped by them," and (e) the issue of "control" emerges clearly for her.

Questions Raised by the Experimental Answers

Kelly believed that the best experiment raised more questions than it gave "final" answers (which tend to preempt any further questions). Therapeutic experiments have a way of leading the co-experimenters forward through the experiential domain to the next "burning issues." Such questions often appear in the form of unforeseen consequences or implications of the previous experiment. One main problem Una experienced after cutting down her family contacts was with Kate who missed seeing her grandparents. She became extremely demanding and difficult for Una to cope with as the following extract shows.

> UNA: I have the feeling that Kate is dragging me down. I despise her for this, her very presence angers me, her games enrage me, and her continuous whining and constant demands drive me crazy. She wants to subjugate me to her will. I don't want to be close to her. She wants to be close in a role, not with "me." I despise her for giving me a role and expecting me to play it out—the same as in all my relationships.

Here we notice Una transferring onto Kate the feeling that Kate is trying to control her, and her response now is to apply her newly-found solution to her controlling family, that is, to cut herself off and become distant. This of course acts like a vicious circle, because the more Una tries to escape from Kate, the more will Kate escalate her efforts to become visible to her mother. Kate is trying to evoke the "mother role" in Una, who in turn wishes to avoid being cast into any role whatsoever by anyone. Levenson's (1985) ideas of carcinogenic relationships are consistent with this picture, and the need to dislodge Una and Kate from the family construct chreods (difficulty in giving and receiving affection) was paramount.

Una and Kate

Una almost died when giving birth to Kate. In our discussions together, we noted that they were more like sisters than like mother and daughter. This is partly due to the family construct system where everyone wants to be cared for like a child and no one wants to be the caregiver-parent—we noted above the vicious circle of how Una gets angry when Kate tries to evoke a mother-role in her, etc.—and partly due to Una's sense of having been born, or reborn, from death at the same time as Kate, making them "twins" psychologically speaking. Many of their arguments together had become very stylized and predictable. To break up this pattern I found it useful to use Kelly's technique of controlled elaboration which is used to make the system more internally consistent, communicable, testable, and ultimately more effective. Kelly's (1955) view of psychotherapy as a form of experimentation is illustrated very well in using controlled elaboration through prescribed activities (p. 994). Interestingly, Kelly (1955) illustrates one type of controlled elaboration through prescribing the symptom, thereby foreshadowing a strategy that would later become common practice in family therapy (Weeks & L'Abate, 1982). In this case, one must ask the patient to carefully experiment with doing the symptom in a prescribed manner, at a certain time, under certain conditions, etc. I saw Una and Kate together for four sessions and told them that I needed to understand their arguments better, to which end I requested that Kate attempt to make Una angry every day for one week upon coming home from school. We discussed together several methods that would normally guarantee her mother getting angry (e.g., refusing to change her school uniform, slamming the door, etc.), and she was instructed to use any of these methods for one half-hour and then end the experiment. Una was asked to observe which particular methods Kate was using at any one time and to note her feelings about each. Controlled elaboration used in this way tends to interrupt the spontaneously emerging pattern by making it deliberate and therefore no longer spontaneous. More specifically, I tried to block her impulsive action through the acceleration of the CPC cycle (involving casting about for alternative approaches to a problem, preempting on one, and then choosing to behave on that basis) is blocked. By placing both protagonists into the role of observers we raise their level of cognitive awareness and tend to lengthen the circumspection and preemption phases of the cycle before the control (or action) phase is reached. Indeed, in this case, neither Una nor Kate could achieve the action phase as before, that is, neither could get angry or upset. Rather, they ended each experiment laughing together at their newly found paralysis (of the anger mechanism). Both participants tend to remain at the circumspection phase and face the elements of the situation propositionally or in a multidimensional fashion. This allows the elaboration of alternative pathways of interaction.

CONTINUITY OF PROBLEMS AND PROBLEMS OF CONTINUITY

Change does not occur in a linear manner. The transition between the old construct system disintegrating and the construction of the new system is a time of oscillation between what was and what could be. Our need for accurate anticipation or fit with our future often drives us back to reevoke the earlier system, despite the fact that its anticipations may ultimately be self-destructive. When attempting to elaborate a new system we have a double dilemma with anticipation. First that we are (relatively) unable to anticipate future events (since the new system is little elaborated) and, second, we are unable to anticipate the emerging construct system itself, both in terms of what the "map" will actually look like when we have elaborated it and how well it will function to get us from A to B. We have already seen the significance of problems of anticipation for cancer patients. Thus, the recurrence of therapeutic problems is to be taken as a sign of and an opportunity for the necessity of further elaboration of new structure.

Family Conversations

Throughout therapy the family continued to escalate its pressures on Una to "be sensible" and to rejoin the group's conversations for illness in the prescribed way. They tried to achieve this with many conversations for the disqualification of Una, that she was "mad," "self-destructive," "committing suicide," "wrong-headed," did not know what was best for her, and so on. Such conversations were very threatening to her and naturally slowed her elaborative processes which depend on moving through the creativity cycle, that is, from loosened construing to tight and back to loose again. Following encounters with her parents, Una often felt "suicidal, defenseless, hopeless, caught in the same trap, negating everything I had done up to now. Felt very angry at my helplessness, wished the cancer cells would hurry up and finish it all."

The pressure exerted by her parents attests to the degree of panic experienced within the family organization. Later, the pressure escalated within the family conversation for illness as we see in this extract.

> UNA: When Kate phoned my mother she found that my father was in hospital. Superb timing. Reminds me again of always having the wind taken out of my sails. But not this time Daddy, I'm not playing. I feel strongly removed, find it all even funny, almost relieved at the obviousness of the whole situation—I'm not emotionally involved, I don't feel guilty.

Here we see Una's reconstruction of herself within the conversation for illness. Having become an observer of this conversation and developed a language to describe it, she reaches a stage of being able to precisely anticipate the conversational network itself as a whole or simple unity. Moreover, by apprehending this unity she does not have to shift to experiencing the system as a participant who, by decomposing the apprehended (simple) unity into a composite unity, would become enmeshed in conserving the family organization. Instead she feels "relieved at the obviousness," is not emotionally involved, and feels no guilt. From Kelly's point of view, the issue of guilt is very important here since its absence indicates a radical readjustment of her anticipations of herself. She now predicts that she should behave in a manner orthogonal to the family network of conversations and no longer has to be a constitutive component of it. Following this reconstruction, Una was led to a rapidly elaborating view of her relationship with her mother and the dangers this presented for her. The following passage illustrates her new thinking in this area.

> UNA: When I spoke to my mother on the phone yesterday I felt her hostility towards me. I feel that she thinks I don't deserve to be well, I also feel that she probably doesn't want me to be well because then she will have no power over me. A healthy person cannot play our family game.

In these conversations, Una illustrates how her construct system for doing disease is firmly anchored in the context of others' expectations of her (sociality) and how doing health is extremely difficult, and even incompatible, with this network of conversations for illness. She herself will also be threatened by a new construct system for health, since what she is (and knows how to anticipate) is a self-identity-system organized around illness. It is the destruction of this organization that therapy is concerned with. The attempts to reconstrue her family and their network of conversations continued to pose difficulties as each family member exerted pressure on her in turn. For example "My sister (Mary) sees it as a chance to be brought back into the family, but I don't feel part of the family . . . My sister thinks that if I refuse the operation I leave myself too far out beyond help and also refusing the love and help of the family." It is important not to forget the extraordinary courage of a patient in this situation: Una is taking perhaps the largest risk a human can take, i.e., the ability to trust the system to ultimately promote health and positive growth. In such a case, the support of the therapist is a very delicate and crucial issue.

The fact that she is still trying to keep a foot in each construct system, that is, the old system and the newly emerging structure, is revealed in the next statements.

UNA: My emotions seem to be a locking-in process for me, though in the last week there has been such, at times, unbearable opening up and shattering of my old image, it seems there is no escape, my emotions insist on a change, desire it, and I hold on tentatively to a bird that is determined to fly, fluttering its unfolding wings, writhing to be free.

Overall we see a growing awareness that her old system of relating herself to the world is increasingly redundant with the concomitant need to aggressively elaborate her new structures. This is made clear even at times of extreme conflict when we would expect her to revert to her old patterns at least some of the time.

Reconstruction of Grandmother: Anticipating the Past

Throughout the sessions Una had mentioned her grandmother, who had died several years previously, very little and then only to describe a hypochondriacal selfish old lady who seemed at best irritating. However, during one shiatsu session all of this changed. Una made an important reconstrual that was pivotal in leading to many others, including that of her mother. She uncovered positive memories of loving and being loved by her grandmother. As she noted, "I think I didn't let myself know I loved her, because my mother wouldn't have approved. My mother has never approved of anyone I thought I loved." This type of reconstruction is typical of what happens in much of psychotherapy when the patient is essentially anticipating the emergence of an alternative past that is being retrospectively constructed in the present moment. Having built such construct bridges with their newly invented history, the person is free to anticipate a novel future based on this novel past. In this case, Una discovered or brought forth her Granny from her preverbal repertoire and thus created for herself an ally, a loved figure who found Una lovable. She discovered a new guilt, having discovered her grandmother, and it was her attempts to remove this guilt that leads our story forward toward completion.

In the subsequent weeks, she discovered that her mother had never placed a tombstone on the grandmother's grave but had left it neglected for years with only an anonymous number identifying it. This so incensed Una that in confronting her mother about this she came to understand that her own mother had never loved nor wanted Una. Most of these feelings surfaced during shiatsu sessions. This journey into her tacit construing continued, and she was able to increasingly articulate elusive areas of knowledge/feeling in therapy. Her preverbal system or "felt sense" (Gendlin, 1982) was elaborated to the point where it became easier to remain in touch with this "intuitive sensitivity" (Smail, 1984) and to avoid the traps of self-deception, that is, what she told herself about her tacit knowledge. As she said, "Out of the family, into myself. Out of my mind, into my body—so what's next?"

TRANSCENDENCE

Having reconstrued most family members, including herself and Kate, Una had radically altered the family conversations for illness to the point where her own father was asking Una's advice about whether or not to have his operation. The danger here was that the family could begin a new "conversation for health" and elect Una into the expert role where she could continue her "caring" for them in this new disguise. She managed to avoid this danger, at least in the context of her family. After successfully and happily extricating herself from the family network, Una created a new existence for herself and Kate in Scotland. In her letters, she mentioned that her new boyfriend, Jack, had also cured himself of abdominal cancer through meditation and diet. While Jack did not seem to qualify as someone on whom she could readily transfer her old constructs about relationships (i.e., he was gentle, not violent, etc.) and generally seemed to extricate himself from her transference efforts, I nonetheless began to wonder whether she had transferred the more general family relationship pattern of the conversation for illness/health. In later letters, this anticipation seemed to have been correct. One year later she wrote the following observations.

UNA: I always seemed to be hurt by my relationships with men. This one started off wonderfully, I felt I had so much space, warmth, caring, love, and understanding. I wanted him to change and felt I could help, so I pushed, became too involved, narrowed down my world. The more I gave, the more he felt I gave nothing, the more I gave. Most of my energy going into this.

Una gave a very clear description of how a recently discarded structure can rematerialize in new guises and contexts. Through a relationship set up around the conversation for disease, which began ostensibly as a symmetrical striving for self-healing, it transformed itself into a complementary relationship where Una was the changer and Jack the one to be changed. Whereas her construct organization was now one replete with constructs of movement, his was organized around invariant identification with pain. It was a small shift from this changer–to be changed dichotomy to completely recover Una's role as caregiver to those family members demanding to be looked after or cared for as dependent children. Again, the depletion of her energy, the constriction of her life activities, and the experience of overpermeability ("feeling the physical pain of it for him") were recognized as danger signals that led her to terminate the relationship.

Una has since consulted a number of Tibetan medical physicians who, using their blend of Western and Oriental medical techniques, told her that they could detect no traces of any cancer. She continues to follow her diet and meditative purification practice. In her most recent reports, she describes the happy and healthy life that she and Kate are enjoying.

DISCUSSION

Una's struggle for personal change advanced at many levels: intrapersonally with the elucidation of preverbal construing through meditation, diet, and shiatsu, and interpersonally through the extrication of herself from the conversation for disease, first with her family and laterally with Jack in Scotland. The development of her vivid visualization talents and her verbal articulation of preverbal processes were powerful catalysts to change. Una got herself to the position where almost any event (external or internal perturbations) could be used by her to trigger more structural changes. Through the recovery of her granny she realized that she could love and be loved, and there quickly followed the difficult acknowledgment that her mother had not loved her. When she could open herself to her tender, warm feelings her relationship with her daughter was radically changed. She no longer construed Kate as trying to manipulate her into a constricting role. Una was successful in her therapeutic efforts because she reorganized her construct system largely along the superordinate lines of the "desirability of change." With such movement constructs she is most unlikely to become stuck in her growth processes in the future.

From this presentation it is clear that the Kellian view of psychotherapy is not one in which the therapist "applies a treatment to a patient" but rather is one of co-experimentation. The aim of personal construct therapy is not merely to get people back on their feet again but rather to get them moving along personal dimensions that will lead them into a constructive future. I end with this quote from Kelly (1969c) about his clients, which I believe illustrates the way people change.

At last they were somehow able to demonstrate that what I did to them did not make them well or compel them to conduct themselves with propriety. It was their behaviour that eventually made them well, just as their original distress had been an ill-fated undertaking of their own contrivance. They were not patients who submitted to my treatment—at least the ones who got well weren't—but clients who made some use of me (pp. 18–19).

REFERENCES

Bruner, J. (1956). You are your constructs. *Contemporary Psychology, 1,* 355–356.

Cannon, W. B. (1957). Voodoo death. *Psychosomatic Medicine, 19,* 170–190.

Dell, P. (1982). Beyond homeostasis: Toward a concept of coherence. *Family Process, 21*(1), 21–41.

Gendlin, E. T. (1982). *Focusing.* New York: Bantam.

Kelly, G. A. (1955). *The psychology of personal constructs (Vols. 1–2).* New York: Norton.

Kelly, G. A. (1969a). Man's construction of his alternatives. In B. Maher (Ed.), *Clinical psychology and personality* (pp. 66–93). New York: Wiley.

Kelly, G. A. (1969b). In whom confide: On whom depend for what? In B. Maher (Ed.), *Clinical psychology and personality* (pp. 189–206). New York: Wiley.

Kelly, G. A. (1969c). Ontological acceleration. In B. Maher (Ed.), *Clinical psychology and personality* (pp. 7–45). New York: Wiley.

Kenny, V. (1985a, October). *An introduction to the ideas of Humberto Maturana: Life, the multiverse and everything.* Invited paper presented at the Instituto di Psicologia, Universita Cattolica del Sacro Cuore, Rome.

Kenny, V. (1985b, August). *Autopoiesis and alternativism in psychotherapy: Fluctuations and reconstructions.* Paper presented at the Sixth International Congress on Personal Construct Psychology, Churchill College, Cambridge.

Levenson, F. B. (1985). *The causes and prevention of cancer.* London: Sidgwick and Jackson.

Maturana, H. (1983). What is it to see? *Archives of Biological and Medical Experiments, 16,* 255–269.

Maturana, H. (1985). *The Maturana dialogues.* A Two-Day Conference on "Man and mind: Process and perception," City University, London.

Neimeyer, R. (1985). Personal constructs in clinical practice. In P. C. Kendall (Ed.), *Advances in cognitive-behavioural research and therapy (Vol. IV)* (pp. 275–339). New York: Academic Press.

Simonton, O. C., Simonton, S., & Creighton, J. (1981). *Getting well again.* New York: Bantam.

Smail, D. (1984). *Illusion and reality.* London: Dent.

Varela, F. (1984). The creative circle: Sketches on the natural history of circularity. In P. Watzlawick (Ed.), *The invented reality* (pp. 309–323). New York: Norton.

von Glasersfeld, E. (1984). An introduction to radical constructivism. In P. Watzlawick (Ed.), *The invented reality* (pp. 17–40). New York: Norton.

Watzlawick, P. (1977). *How real is real?* New York: Vintage.

Weeks, G., & L'Abate, L. (1982). *Paradoxical psychotherapy.* New York: Brunner/Mazel.

Wittgenstein, L. (1971). *Tractatus logico-philosophicus.* London: Routledge and Kegan Paul.

IV
Group
Therapy

12

Personal Constructs in the Group Treatment of Incest[1]

Pamela C. Alexander
Victoria M. Follette

Incest is becoming recognized as a major problem in the United States. Finkelhor (1978) and Russell (1984) have found evidence suggesting that one out of five women in the United States has been sexually victimized as a child, and approximately one-third of these women have been victims of father–daughter incest. Although sexual abuse is by no means limited to females, Finkelhor (1978) noted that the incidence is lower among males, and the abuse is more likely to be perpetrated by someone from outside the family. Therefore, as the focus of this chapter is upon incest (as opposed to sexual abuse), discussion will center on the effects of incest on women. Common long-term effects of father–daughter incest include interpersonal problems with both men and women (evidenced by depression, loneliness, and marital problems), a poor self-concept, and an increased risk of subsequent victimization (Browne & Finkelhor, 1986). Although reactions to incest are diagnostically defined in DSM-III as posttraumatic stress disorder, the effects are much more complicated and chronic, because they take place within the family context. In fact, it is difficult to separate the long-term effects of the incestuous experience from the long-term effects of growing up in a family system that is sufficiently dysfunctional to permit the occurrence of incest. Whatever the source, subsequent problems are frequently re-

[1]The present report was based upon a study funded by NIMH grant No. MH 40477-01 and by the Center for Applied Psychological Research granted through the Centers of Excellence Program of the State of Tennessee.

flected in the incest victim's interpersonal perceptual style fostered in her family of origin. Because personal construct theory emphasizes the individual's perceptual style, we find it useful to conceptualize both the long-term effects of incest and the family socialization with which they are associated from a personal construct perspective.

This chapter will attempt to (1) describe the development of the incest victim's constructs in her family of origin, (2) relate these constructs to the kinds of problems often manifested by incest victims, (3) demonstrate the utility of a personal construct perspective in the group treatment of incest victims, (4) represent the relationship between constructs and symptoms through reference to a group of women recently seen for treatment following a childhood history of incest, and (5) illustrate more subtle aspects of group process through the use of group transcript material.

Personal construct theory states that an individual seeks to make sense of the world by developing certain psychological constructs or dimensions that provide a basis for organizing perceptions and predicting future behavior and events. Subsequent events and interpersonal encounters can serve to either validate the predictive assumptions or invalidate them, thus necessitating some restructuring of the constructs. However, several characteristics of the initial constructs can influence the interpretation of those subsequent events and thus affect the validation/invalidation process. Constructs can be so loosely organized that they do not facilitate any interpretation of a seemingly confusing world or so tightly organized that they greatly limit the possible interpretations of any event and thereby defy invalidation. Similarly, constructs can be used in a very simplistic or preemptive manner (e.g., "All women are weak and all men are strong") or in a more complex or propositional way (e.g., "Mother is somewhat weak in this type of situation but stronger in that type of situation"). Finally, constructs can reflect either organized and logical thinking or idiosyncratic and distorted thinking. The latter can significantly interfere with an individual's attempt to empathize with others and impair other people's abilities to empathize with her.

INCESTUOUS FAMILY STRUCTURE

Procter (1981) has described a family construct system as the negotiation of a common family reality. He acknowledges that family members do not necessarily have to be in agreement; in fact, they could be at opposite poles but still "share a finite set of avenues of movement." Several characteristics of incestuous families are frequently identified that can be related to Procter's description of a family construct system. First and foremost, incestuous families can be described as isolated and relatively closed systems (Alexander, 1985; Tierney & Corwin, 1983). If they are not actually physically isolated (Lustig, Dresser, Spellman, & Murray, 1966), they tend to be socially isolated with few outside contacts, limited friendships, and an avoidance of interaction with community groups and agencies. Minuchin's concept of boundaries can be related to Kelly's use of the term "permeability" to describe how unlikely it is for a family with such a tight external boundary to observe and incorporate enough new elements to allow for the development of a complex and highly differentiated family construct system.

Just as the boundary around the incestuous family system is typically rigid and fairly impermeable, the boundaries between subsystems within the family tend to be loose and ill-defined. Parent and child roles are not clearly differentiated. In fact, they are frequently reversed, with parents looking to their children for the nurturance and parenting that they themselves never received (Blick & Porter, 1983; Herman & Hirschman, 1981; James & Nasjleti, 1983; Lustig et al., 1966). The obvious result of these blurred boundaries is the incestuous act itself and its pervasive effect. It is difficult for the children in the family to develop healthy expectations or constructs of "father," "mother," and "parents," given that their own parents obviously do not subscribe to accepted notions of these constructs.

The only clear role differentiation that does typically exist in the incestuous family is one based on a stereotypic notion of sex differences. In fact, Herman (1981) stated that the most salient characteristic of an incestuous family is its patriarchal structure. Fathers tent to be authoritarian and abusive at home, while deferential, even ingratiating, away from home. Mothers tend to maintain the beliefs that a woman is defenseless, that marriage must be preserved at all costs, and that a wife's duty is to serve and endure. Families are thus marked by a traditional sexual division of labor. It can readily be inferred that such a family structure not only reflects but also promotes polarized, sex-typed construing.

The effects of growing up in this type of family structure are pervasive and significant. An important function of the family unit is to provide the child with an array of experiences and perceptions and with a consistent family construct system with which to classify and organize these perceptions. In the incestuous family, access to a variety of personalities is severely limited by the nature of the isolation of the family unit. Furthermore, the variety of emotions, behaviors, and roles overtly expressed by individuals within the family is restricted to simplistic sex roles. Any subtle deviations from these roles (e.g., instances of assertiveness in a mother or sensitivity in a father) are minimized or even denied. The child becomes deficient in reading subtleties in others' behaviors and in her own behavior and is quite justified in regarding interpersonal relationships as confusing and unpredictable.

LONG-TERM EFFECTS OF INCEST

It is easy to see how the long-term effects of incest (interpersonal problems, poor self-concept, and increased risk of victimization) develop from this family structure. Take, for example, the interpersonal problems frequently observed in the adult survivor of incest. Her relationships with men and women seem to be characterized by a highly polarized view of the sexes. Herman (1981) described the father–daughter incest victim as the "archetypally feminine woman" who tends to "overvalue and idealize men" thus ceding to them a great deal of power. Since the constructs of sex and affection overlapped greatly in her relationship with her father, she may sexualize all relationships with men. The effect is to contribute to her increased risk for subsequent sexual victimization.

Another typical kind of intimate relationship in which an incest victim finds herself is one characterized mostly by negative emotions in which each partner validates his or her own self-concept by contrast with the other. For example, the woman may be able to maintain her self-image as a victim by seeing her partner as a victimizer. R. Neimeyer and G. Neimeyer (1985) note that this kind of negative relationship tends to be marked by contempt, guilt, and threat. Unfortunately, this may keep the relationship resistant to change. This joint construct begins to appear remarkably similar to the family construct found in the woman's family of origin.

Relationships with women are equally problematic for the incest victim. Given her highly polarized view of women as weak, irrelevant, and dependent, other women come to be viewed as significant only in terms of being potential rivals for the affection of men. This stereotypic view has three important effects. First, it precludes the development of emotionally supportive friendships with women. There can thus be little alleviation of the incest victim's feelings of loneliness, isolation, and depression if men are seen as emotionally inaccessible and women are seen as too untrustworthy. Second, the incest victim's view of herself and other women as "helpless in the face of men" mitigates the likelihood of being able to appropriately express anger towards men. Instead, it encourages displacement of hostility to herself and other women. Finally, this view of women may contribute to a competitive, rather than a protective, relationship with her own daughters for the attention of a man in the home (Herman, 1981). The result is often a self-fulfilling prophecy, and the cycle of incest is maintained.

One final problem experienced by the incest victim deserves mention. Not only has she been traumatized as a child or adolescent, but she also tends to retain the guilt and sense of responsibility for her own abuse. Just as she has generally not had the experience of seeing her parents as "parental," she has reciprocally not had the experience of seeing herself as "childlike." In fact, she had probably assumed not only the "adult" function of sexual partner to her father but also other "adult" functions as well. Therefore, she has had no basis for associating the construct "responsibility" with the element "parents" instead of with the element "children." Consequently, the incest victim often assumes either that she was somehow responsible for the abuse or that her mother was irresponsible in not fulfilling her father's sexual needs. In either case, the blame and responsibility is frequently directed by the incest victim toward herself—for being the victim or just for being a woman. Russell (1984) has suggested that one result of this internalized self-blame is an increased risk of subsequent victimization. Renshaw and Renshaw (1977) have noted that it is associated with an increased likelihood of anxiety and depression. Therefore, the poor self-concept and self-blame typically seen in the incest victim is an important construct that makes her vulnerable to subsequent troubles.

GROUP TREATMENT FOR INCEST

The use of group psychotherapy for adult victims of incest has emerged as one of the most effective methods of treatment for this population. In particular, a short-term, time-limited group format seems to have a number of advantages especially germane to incest victims. By its very nature, a short-term group minimizes the possibility of regression and highlights the strengths of the participants, both important considerations for women who tend to see themselves as helpless and powerless (Goodman & Nowak-Scibelli, 1985). A short-term group format counteracts two problems present in the incestuous family of origin; the family's denial is counteracted by focusing on the incest, and unstated or confusing expectations are precluded by clear time boundaries (Goodman & Nowak-Scibelli, 1985). A short-term group facilitates bonding quickly. This may be an advantage for women who tend to be socially isolated, although a rapid push toward intimacy can be problematic in itself. Finally, a short-term group provides a concrete structure for dealing with very difficult and painful emotions (Herman & Schatzow, 1984).

As might be expected from the previous discussion of the effects of incest, common themes that tend to emerge in such groups include shame and guilt, feelings of isolation, stigmatization leading to a negative self-image, anger and resentment toward parents, sexual dysfunction, and relationship distress (Deighton & McPeek, 1985; Goodman & Nowak-Scibelli, 1985; Herman & Schatzow, 1984; Tsai & Wagner, 1978). Consequently, common goals of treatment include the relief of guilt and a decreased sense of isolation (which emerges partially from the cohesiveness of a homogeneous group). In addition, most treatment providers emphasize the importance of examining those family issues that tend to result in repeated dysfunctional interactions in future relationships (Deighton & McPeek, 1985; Tsai & Wagner, 1978). Goodman and Nowak-Scibelli (1985) note the important, although complicated, task of emphasizing the perpetrator's responsibility for the abuse while also discouraging scapegoating and acknowledging the incest victim's loyalty to her family. Herman and Schatzow (1984) also stress the importance of this goal by discussing the necessity of developing a new cognitive framework that the incest victim can use in viewing her family, herself, and other important relationships.

PERSONAL CONSTRUCT THEORY AND GROUPS FOR INCEST VICTIMS

In his discussion of group psychotherapy, Koch (1985) refers to Kelly's discussion of commonality and sociality, which Kelly describes as essential to an understanding of group process. Commonality, which is similar to Yalom's (1975) concept of universality, provides consensual validation for group members. This process is especially important for incest victims in that they may frequently enter a group without having previously disclosed the abuse. Commonality thus provides the reassurance that one is not so different from other people and also explicitly negates the directive that the incest should continue to remain a secret. In this way, commonality provides the psychological security required for the eventual consideration of new and alternative constructions (Koch, 1985). However, a prolonged and exclusive validation also has its dangers, since the incest victim often tends to define every aspect of her existence in terms of her incest experience, thus justifying and predicting a future cycle of victimization.

After a basis of similarity has been established, the group members have to acknowledge and deal with their differences. Since differences between people were usually seen as sterotypic and extreme in the incestuous family of origin, the ability to understand and incorporate in one's construction specific and subtle points of difference is generally underdeveloped in the incest victim. Therefore, a second and equally essential goal of group psychotherapy becomes the clarification and discussion of differences in the constructs of group members in order to facilitate sociality or the ability to "subsume someone else's constructions of experience."

CASE STUDY OF AN INCEST GROUP

The following case study illustrates the utility of a personal construct perspective in the treatment of incest. The therapy described was a 10-week time-limited group which met for one and one-half hour sessions each week. The group consisted of two female co-therapists and seven women who had all sought group therapy for problems that they related to a history of father–daughter incest. The women's names have been changed as have been many important identifying characteristics in order to assure their confidentiality.

The women were assessed prior to and following the group therapy on a variety of instruments including the Beck Depression Inventory (Beck, 1978) and the Social Adjustment Scale (Weissman & Paykel, 1974). The Social Adjustment Scale scores are based on a semistructured interview that assesses functioning in a variety of areas of living. In addition, each subject completed a repertory (rep) grid after the first and ninth sessions of the group. This rep grid assessed their perceptions of each other, the two group therapists, themselves, and their ideal selves. The 10 constructs provided on this grid were selected because they had been found to be relevant to group process in other personal construct studies of groups (c.f., Neimeyer, 1985). The constructs were dominant/submissive, shows feelings/hides feelings, depends on others/others depend on her, good relations with men/poor relations with men, attacking/comforting, intelligent/unintelligent, sincere/insincere, mentally ill/mentally healthy, cold/warm, vulnerable/not vulnerable. These constructs were used in a ratings grid format (G. Neimeyer & R. Neimeyer, 1981) to flank 13-point scales on which the various elements were rated.

Analyses of these grids included the change in absolute discrepancy between the self and the ideal self from the first administration to the second nine weeks later. Another measure that seemed particularly useful for a description of the group process was the correlation at posttest of a group member's rating of her ideal self (on all 10 constructs) with her ratings of other group members on those same dimensions. This correlation thus constituted a subjective evaluation of other group members and can be seen as relevant to an understanding of subgrouping and alliances. As this psychotherapy group constituted only seven members and was part of a larger treatment study, inferential statistics based on the grids and other measures would not be meaningful. However, the grids did provide a basis for a more detailed clinical analysis of the group process.

Many of the symptoms displayed by individual group members, as well as important themes that emerged in the group, can be related to certain ways of construing that are common among incest victims. A transcript taken from a group session demonstrates the relevance of personal construct therapy to altering the constructs of these women. Finally, the information derived from the rep grids can be seen to provide valuable insights into the process of this group.

Vivian

Vivian was a unique member of the group both in terms of her history of abuse and in the role that she was to fulfill for the group. At a very young age,

Vivian was placed in her father's bed by her mother. The abuse eventually progressed from fondling to intercourse. Her abuse was somewhat different from most incest victims in that there was no pretense of secrecy within the family. Vivian felt that it was clearly her role to take her mother's place as her father's sexual partner. In addition, she felt that she was forced into the position of mothering her own mother.

Vivian tended toward a use of concrete constructs that she used in a polarized manner. One apparently superordinate construct was the victim/perpetrator contrast. She saw herself as trapped, a perpetual victim, first of her father and then of her husband. During the first session of the group, she identified her husband of 30 years as the source of many of her current problems. She reported that he was not only a convicted rapist but that he had also sexually abused their daughter.

Darlene

Darlene seemed to be an interesting contrast to Vivian. She appeared to be a strong independent person who was quite capable of making it on her own in the world. She also had a very traumatic childhood that involved both physical and sexual abuse. By the time Darlene began the group, she had reportedly overcome many of her previous problems, which included severe bouts of depression and a very unsatisfactory marriage.

Darlene also provided an interesting set of contrasts in the group itself. She was quick to offer support and understanding to others in the group and could be counted on to offer an empathic response. However, she described another side of herself that was never exhibited in the group—a cold, mean-spirited, aggressive, and physically violent women who would reject any attempts of others to get close to her. Unfortunately, this polarized discrepancy in Darlene's self-concept did not come to the awareness of the group early enough for it to be satisfactorily resolved. Perhaps as an indication of this unresolved issue, Darlene did not attend the final group meeting.

Sandy

Sandy had experienced sexual and physical abuse by multiple perpetrators in her childhood. Family interactions had been characterized by extremely violent episodes that seemed to drastically color her adult perceptions of the world. Sandy's poor marital adjustment seemed in great part to be a function of her inability to tolerate emotional and physical intimacy. She was extremely isolated and actually described herself as "a hermit." Early in the group, she was generally withdrawn and rarely spoke. However, she did resonate strongly to any expressions of anger from other group members.

This resonance did not take the form of empathy but rather provided a basis for her expression of a parallel story with an angry theme. Anger seemed to be a core component of her construct system, which is understandable given her developmental history.

Sandy revealed that she experienced a great deal of anxiety both in the group and in her daily life. Bannister (1975) notes two types of responses to anxiety. The individual may either become withdrawn in an attempt to narrow her perceptual field, or she may become aggressive in an attempt to more actively explore her own conflictual feelings. Sandy demonstrated both types of behaviors in the group. At times, she expressed a great deal of confusion in response to material that lay outside the range of convenience of her construct system. The effect of the confusion was to allow her to retreat and to narrow her perceptual field. Alternatively, she would angrily pursue a group member whose own issues might be too similar to her own. A turning point for Sandy seemed to occur when she no longer needed to resort to these extreme strategies but instead was able to interact with group members in a more moderated manner.

Ann

Ann had been sexually abused by her brother and by her father. Additionally, she had been raped by someone known to her one year prior to entering the group. The rape resulted in a long drawn-out court battle that was still in a state of appeal during the time of her group participation. Ann had recently moved from her hometown in order to escape the public exposure. She reported feeling isolated and depressed at the pretherapy evaluation. Hostility seemed to characterize many of her relationships and may have served the function of precluding more meaningful role relationships (Leitner, 1985). Ann frequently used a process of triangulation in which she would ally with one group member (for example, Sandy) in an attempt to create a contrast with another group member (for example, Carol). Data from group grids, however, suggested that Ann's alliances may have been based more on negative perceptions of herself and another group member than positive attraction. For example, Ann rated both herself and Sandy almost as different from her ideal as she had rated Vivian. Although this process of triangulation was not always successful in creating actual alliances, it did serve to give Ann an illusion of power and control. Unfortunately, it also had the effect of distancing her from any meaningful interactions with other group members.

Sharon

As opposed to Ann, who was an active and involved group member, Sharon remained somewhat peripheral in her group participation. Sharon was a college student who was comfortable dealing with intellectual issues but was almost completely unable to relate on a more affective level. Sharon had only vague memories of being fondled by her father. However, her experiences in her family of origin were not that discrepant from those of other group members. Upon telling her mother about the fondling, Sharon's mother had accused her of lying. Furthermore, after having been told repeatedly by her mother that the only reason she had been born was because "the condom broke," Sharon had little basis for construing her mother in anything other than negative terms. Due to her own uncertainty about the abuse as well as her mother's persistent invalidation of her experience, Sharon presented a picture not unlike other incest victims. Sharon displayed an extreme form of confusion (i.e., a dissociative reaction) when talking very specifically about the abuse or about her mother.

Donna

Donna was similar to Sharon in a number of ways. She, like Sharon, reported a less severe history of abuse and experienced confusion in connection with the abuse. Although she was the only Black member of the group, her identification with the group on the basis of being an incest victim seemed to supercede any racial differences. Although she was an active participant in the group, the therapists felt that many of her accounts did not actually represent an attempt to obtain information that would either validate or invalidate hypotheses based upon her construct system. They instead seemed to constitute a form of story-telling, and it was not always clear how the group could help her with these experiences.

Carol

Carol entered the group with a very different self-concept than other group members. Although she had experienced a long history of sexual abuse that included intercourse with her father, she described herself as having overcome any negative effects of this experience. She presented herself as a cheerful, confident, competent individual who was always able to be of help to others. This inability to articulate goals for participation in the group suggested her reluctance to question her construction of reality and to experiment with new behaviors. It also precluded identification with other group members who were more motivated to change. As the group progressed, some of Carol's dysfunctional behaviors became evident. She consistently arrived to the group sessions 15 to 30 minutes late, often with the smell of alcohol on her breath. She described dating a man who had previously raped her, although she indicated that she felt she had adequate control over the situation. While Carol described herself as having a plethora of friends, she actually had much less social support than other group members.

GROUP PROCESS

Although certain similar themes emerge in most groups of incest victims, it is our experience that groups vary greatly in the emotional tone and specific treatment of issues. This is partly due to the diversity in composition of the groups, which limits the range of possible role interactions. However, it is also affected by events, occurring as early as the first group session, that can create certain expectations for the group members as to how they should behave and interact in subsequent sessions. A significant event in the life of this group was Darlene's crying in the first session as she was describing her history of abuse. Although the effect for her may have been to make her more cautious throughout the remainder of the group, it did have the effect of setting the tone for a very disclosing group through the validation of their common experiences.

The first important theme to emerge in this group was the issue of ambivalence toward mothers. Vivian was a generation older than most other group members and set herself apart from the group even further by focusing on the age differential and her role as a mother. Group rep grid data indicated that Vivian was seen as the most discrepant from everyone's ideal. Although this group perception was partly a reaction to Vivian's myriad of problems, it may also have been a reflection of group members' distancing from a mother figure. The reaction of the group to Vivian was at first puzzlement and then irritation. Group members began to respond to her as daughters and spoke openly of their anger and frustration at her for staying with an abusive husband and not adequately protecting her own daughter. In this way, the norm of focusing on relationships in the room was quickly and concretely established, thereby providing a laboratory setting for exploring new roles and constructs. The effects of these "mother–daughter" interactions were striking and ultimately very useful. Sharon, in particular, was forced to develop a more differentiated perception of her mother as she eventually came to understand Vivian. The group actively encouraged Vivian to focus on her desires in her family as opposed to simply subsuming them under those of her husband and daughter. This focus on mothers and daughters also allowed a consideration of the construct "protectiveness." Although this initially seemed to be related most closely to the role of "mother," group members began to apply the construct to other roles. Ann, who was an elementary school teacher, debated over how to deal with several children in her classroom whom she suspected of having been abused, and Sharon expressed concern about her nieces visiting her father. Much later in the group, this increased identification with "mother" allowed the extension of the construct "protectiveness" to protection of oneself. Several group members were encouraged to evaluate the judgement they had used in certain situations where there had been some risk of danger.

The issue of control emerged in response to group members' disclosures about feelings of helplessness in dealing with problems outside the group. Ann, for example, spoke of still having to give her father a wide berth when walking near his chair to avoid being grabbed by him. Donna spoke of still being subject to her father's authoritarian and patriarchal decisions. As the therapists continued to emphasize how group members could take control, different resolutions were achieved. In a strikingly parallel set of examples, Donna disclosed that she had decided to purchase her own plane ticket home for Christmas as a statement to her family of her independence, while Ann recounted accepting money for a plane ticket home from a man she barely knew.

Group members thus served as definite contrasts to each other in spite of the similarity of their experiences. Not being able to trust oneself (a concern expressed by everyone in the group) resulted in the reluctance of some group members to trust anybody and the tendency of other group members to be too trusting. Similarly, although termination of the group seemed to be a difficult issue for the group as a whole, the variety of reactions to it was interesting. Ann's indignation at the group therapists for not acquiescing to demands for continuation of the group seemed to be more of a reflection of lingering feelings of powerlessness and isolation outside the group than actual attachment to the group. Sandy seemed to experience genuine sadness, since she was losing a safe testing ground for changes she was making in her construction of anger. While Vivian expressed gratitude for being accepted by the group, Darlene ran from the group's attempts to get closer to her during the final sessions. Carol seemed relieved that the group was ending and she would thereby escape further confrontation. Sharon and Donna seemed satisfied with the progress they had made but appeared ready to move on.

TRANSCRIPT OF GROUP SESSION

The following interchange occurred in the seventh session. It demonstrates the relevance of a personal construct approach in explaining the kinds of construing that lead to continued problems for these women. The interventions by Susan and Mary, the co-therapists, challenged the group participants to question their constructs and to view themselves and each other in a more differentiated way.

SUSAN: Darlene, we were talking a little before group. Mary and I were noticing that somehow we never get around to talking to you that much.

DARLENE: Well, that's true, I guess. I don't know what to say.

SUSAN: You've been very good about being supportive of other people and in some ways, it's easy not to ask you how you're feeling. That's something we've been concerned about. You mentioned a while ago that your husband's been wondering about the group because you've been having a hard time at home and some stuff with your mother, and we've never really talked about that.

DARLENE: Well, my problem with my mother is almost identical to some of the others in here, and I was just listening to see how everyone else is handling it. I don't know how to, and I don't know if I want to. But I don't think I want her back in my life. I've always been different than most people. I can cut a relationship and never go back. Most people can't do that. But when I'm through, I'm through, and I don't want her back in my life. That's the confusion or contradiction. I don't know what to do about it.

(Darlene notes the commonality among group members with respect to their views of "mother." Eliminating people from her environment can serve the function of preventing others from invalidating her core constructs.)

MARY: What kind of goal would you have? I guess I'm a little confused . . . .

DARLENE: The contradictions there? (Laughs.)

MARY: No. I follow that completely. My question is where do you have a need to have some resolution about your mother? What kinds of things are bothering you?

(The therapist is acknowledging Darlene's ambivalence toward her mother; however, she is also questioning whether Darlene needs to view her mother on some dimension other than "contact vs. no contact." In other words, the dimension of contact/no contact does not have to be identical to resolution/no resolution.)

DARLEEN: I think her unfairness. I just want to shake some sense into her, that she should quit blaming me. She should get her head straightened out and quit blaming me or hating me. She blames me, and I don't think I deserve that, but she will not talk about it. She will not talk about it. You can't force her. I thought about writing her a letter.

SUSAN: Do you think you'd be able to ask us for something if you needed it? How come you end up hanging back a lot?

(The therapist is bringing Darlene's conflict with her mother back into the group. This is especially important since the possibility for Darlene to resolve the conflict with her mother by talking about it to her personally seems unlikely.)

DARLENE: I don't know. I've just never been able to ask anybody for anything. I can give, but I can't ask.

MARY: (To the group) What do you all think about that? (Long pause.)

DARLENE: (Laughs) O.K. Support me. I supported you all.

SANDY: About what she said about her mother or what?

DARLENE: Anything. Just whatever comes to mind. There I go again.

SANDY: I like the letter idea.
(Pause.)

SANDY: Why are you all looking at me?
(Sandy is evidencing a constricted response to a threatening subject.)

DARLENE: I'm real good with words, but I can't talk worth a darn. I can get my feelings out on paper.

ANN: I think you're a pretty good talker.

DONNA: Well, do you want to be in contact with your mother, or do you want to resolve things?
(Donna is putting constructs that may be unrelated for Darlene on the same dimension—i.e., "contact with mother" vs. "resolution.")

DARLENE: No, I don't want contact. I just took the blame for a long time, and I don't want to anymore. I've been in a combat zone for a long time.

ANN: I was kind of stuck on your contact with your mother. I heard about a woman who divorced her mother. She had to do that to say "This is final." She thought it was helpful. I thought, "Divorce your mother—how sacreligious!"
(Ann is introducing an alternative construct, although she herself rejects it.)

SANDY: That's weird that you said that. I've thought of divorcing my father.

DARLENE: I just told my mother, "Get out of my life and stay out. Don't come around here anymore." My husband said, "Boy, she's going to be curious what you don't want to talk about." My mother knows me and she knows when I'm through, I'm through. There's never been a relationship there anyway.

DONNA: Do you find people don't support you generally?
(Donna is abstracting from the specific to the general.)

DARLENE: I don't ever ask for it. I don't expect it, and I push people back. If people get close, I run them off.

MARY: All of them?

DARLENE: All of them except my husband. I'm going to hang on to him.
(Darlene describes a construct of "giving support vs. receiving support." She seems to differentiate herself from other people with respect to receiving support except as it relates to her husband.)

SUSAN: Do you feel like that in here?

DARLENE: I'm conscious of the fact that once this is over, I won't ever see anyone in here, so it doesn't bother me. I'm like this. I'll help someone in here if they need it, but as soon as I see they are strong and want to help me, I'd get rid of them. That's a terrible way to put it. (Laughs.) No offense.
(Darlene rejects the idea that anyone in the group could ever give her support. Her validation process works so well that she is precluding any opportunity for this expectation of lack of support to be invalidated.)

MARY: Do you like it that way?

DARLENE: I guess so. That's one reason I want so bad to be a novelist. I'm a loner.

SANDY: Do you have any close friends?

DARLENE: I've got lots of surface friends, but when they get close, I get rid of them. I get ugly. I get violent. I'm vicious.
[Darlene is equating rejection of support (a core construct for her) with other extremely negative constructs.]

ANN: How did your husband get close to you?

DARLENE: I don't know. He hung in there. He saw something good under there and hung around.

MARY: So he passed the test—was worthy of your trust?

DARLENE: Exactly. He hung around when no one else would. I wouldn't put up with that from someone.
(Carol walks in.)
(Carol appears once again to be functioning as a distractor in the group.)

DARLENE: (To Carol) Where were you, short stuff?

CAROL: I was looking for something.

MARY: Go ahead, Darlene.

DARLENE: I was done.

MARY: I hate to just scoot off the topic, because I feel we would do a real disservice to you by not talking about this. I get a sense that because this group is time-limited, it would be a much safer place for you to take a step beyond where you are right now with relationships.
(The therapist is referring to the use of the group as a laboratory for experimenting with new interpersonal behaviors and alternative constructions.)

DARLENE: That's what I had counted on. That it would get me beyond whatever it is that I need to get beyond. You nailed me.

MARY: How do you get beyond it?

DARLENE: I don't know. My life just went downhill this year. I broke off with my brother, then my father struck again. Then I broke off with my mother. Everything's just hitting. All of a sudden, I'm not the black sheep. My mother leaned on me all her life. She took and took and never gave.
(Darlene is referring to her father's recent molestation of a neighbor girl. The crisis for Darlene appears to be related to her no longer seeing herself as the black sheep of the family. Consequently, she has lost her basis for relating to her family, since her prescribed role no longer fits.)

SUSAN: How was it that other things have been getting worse?

DARLENE: A lot of stuff started before the group. Then it got worse as the group started and I heard everyone else. A piece of my life is in every one of the girls in here. In some way, I can relate to everyone, and it was all coming to a head, and I was taking it out on my husband because he was the handiest. But it's got to get worse before it gets better.
(By seeing commonalities between her experience and that of everyone else in the group, Darlene is more able to integrate different aspects of herself.)

MARY: How did you take it out on your husband?

DARLENE: I was snappish and couldn't sleep. I'd walk the floors. I was hating the whole world.

SUSAN: That doesn't fit for me with how I see you in here.

DARLENE: You mean you can't imagine me as a total bitch? I am. I'm vicious. I'll fistfight.

SANDY: You seem warm and wicked to me.
(The therapist attempts to invalidate Darlene's perception of herself, and Darlene reacts strongly against that invalidation. Sandy modifies that self-construct slightly—maybe just enough for Darlene to be more willing to accept it.)

DARLENE: I am until someone gets close. You should see people when I turn on them.

CAROL: But you take it out more on friends?

DARLENE: No, I'll tell anyone off. I'll tell someone in a restaurant, "Don't snap that gum around me. Spit it out."
(Ann spits out her gum. Group dissolves into laughter.)

MARY: You know what strikes me about this is all the comments seen to be one extreme or the other.
(The therapist refers to Darlene's use of slot-rattling, i.e., her vacillation between opposite poles of some constructs.)

DARLENE: Yeah, I'm extreme and I'm violent. I'd be easily capable of murder.

SUSAN: How come we never see any of that anger in here?
(The therapist again questions Darlene's rather extreme self-construct.)

DARLENE: Because you're not threats to me. I'm not going to pursue a relationship with you.

Even though the focus in this transaction is primarily upon one individual, many of the family characteristics and long-term effects frequently associated with the experience of incest are illustrated. For example, the devaluation of women commonly seen in a patriarchal family structure is apparent in Darlene's exclusive focus of her anger and rejection on her mother with hardly any mention of her father. She also describes the role reversal typically seen in the incestuous family in references to how her mother leaned on her and "took and took" without ever giving. The role reversal is also apparent in Darlene's perception of feeling blamed by her mother (even as a child) for behavior initiated by her father. The effects of this family construction are reflected in Darlene's negative self-concept, her polarized views, and her tendency to maintain the impermeable boundaries of her family of origin by actively avoiding and rejecting new experiences and alternate constructions. Although specific experiences may vary, these reactions to incest are so common that the interventions made for Darlene are undoubtedly relevant to the other group members.

Outcome of the Group

Several measures derived from the grids were used to evaluate change as a function of treatment. For all group members, comparisons of the ratings of the therapists with each member's ideal led to significant correlations (usually in the 0.90s). This suggests that the group members had confidence in the therapists and sought to emulate them, although it is also possible that the group members were tending to idealize the therapists. Possibly as a function of group members' confidence in the treatment, outcome measures were generally positive. Most significantly, the reduction in the absolute difference between the rating of self and the rating of ideal self from the first to the ninth session was substantial for all group members except for Darlene, who actually saw herself in a more negative light at the end of the group. The validity of this measure was also suggested by similar changes in scores on the Beck Depression Scale and on the Social Adjustment Scale. Darlene's lack of improvement (and possible deterioration) over the course of the group appeared to be related to attempts by group members to encourage in her a very different self-construction that she perceived as threatening to her core role structure. Unfortunately, her construct system may have been too impermeable to allow immediate integration of this alternate construction. Six-month follow-up evaluation will determine whether the challenge to her self-construction led to a more differentiated and more satisfying view of herself as she had more time to integrate it.

CONCLUSION

The long-term effects of incest have received increasing attention in the literature as an important problem deserving the attention of the clinician and the researcher. In this chapter, we have described commonalities in the characteristics of incestuous families (impermeable external boundaries, role confusion, and stereotypic sex roles) and the resulting long-term effects of incest (polarized views of men and women leading to relationship problems with both and a sense of guilt and responsibility for the incest leading to subsequent victimization). We have also presented a rationale for the utility of personal construct theory in providing a framework for conceptualizing and treating the problems associated with incest.

Case histories of group members were presented, along with a discussion of prominent themes that emerged over the course of therapy. A transcript illustrated these themes as well as interventions used to introduce alternate constructions. The group therapy setting thus seems to provide an excellent opportunity for these women to explore new ways of construing in a less threatening environment.

REFERENCES

Alexander, P. (1985). A systems theory conceptualization of incest. *Family Process, 24,* 79–88.

Bannister, D. (1975). Personal construct theory psychotherapy. In D. Bannister (Ed.), *Issues and approaches in the psychological therapies* (pp. 127–146). New York: Wiley.

Beck, A. T. (1978). *Depression inventory.* Philadelphia: Center for Cognitive Therapy.

Blick, L. C., & Porter, F. S. (1982). Group therapy with female adolescent incest victims. In S. M. Sgroi (Ed.), *Handbook of clinical intervention in child sexual abuse.* Lexington, MA: Lexington Books.

Browne, A., & Finkelhor, D. (1986). Impact of child sexual abuse: A review of the research. *Psychological Bulletin, 99,* 66–77.

Deighton, J., & McPeek, P. (1985). Group treatment: Adult victims of childhood sexual abuse. *Social Casework,* 403–410.

Finkelhor, D. (1979). *Sexually victimized children.* New York: The Free Press.

Goodman, B., & Nowak-Scibelli, D. (1985). Group treatment for women incestuously abused as children. *International Journal of Group Psychotherapy, 35,* 531–544.

Herman, J. L. (1981). *Father–daughter incest.* Cambridge, MA: Harvard University Press.

Herman, J., & Hirschman, L. (1981). Families at risk for father–daughter incest. *American Journal of Psychiatry, 138,* 967–970.

Herman, J., & Schatzow, E. (1984). Time-limited group therapy for women with a history of incest. *International Journal of Group Psychotherapy, 34,* 605–616.

James, B., & Nasjleti, M. (1983). *Treating sexually abused children and their families.* Palo Alto, CA: Consulting Psychologists Press.

Koch, H. (1985). Group psychotherapy. In E. Button (Ed.), *Personal construct theory and mental health* (pp. 302–326). London: Croom-Helm.

Leitner, L. M. (1985). The terrors of cognition: On the experiential validity of personal construct theory. In D. Bannister (Ed.), *Issues and approaches in personal construct theory* (pp. 83–104). London: Academic.

Lustig, N., Dresser, J. W., Spellman, S. W., & Murray, T. B. (1966). Incest: A family group survival pattern. *Archives of General Psychiatry, 14,* 31–40.

Neimeyer, G. J., & Neimeyer, R. A. (1981). Personal construct perspectives on cognitive assessment. In T. Merluzzi, C. Glass, & M. Genest (Eds.), *Cognitive assessment* (pp. 188–232). New York: Guilford.

Neimeyer, R. A. (1985). Personal constructs in clinical practice. In P. C. Kendall (Ed.), *Advances in cognitive-behavioral research and therapy, (Vol. IV)* (pp. 275–339). New York: Academic.

Neimeyer, R. A., & Neimeyer, G. J. (1985). Disturbed relationships: A personal construct view. In E. Button (Ed.), *Personal construct theory and mental health* (pp. 195–222). London: Croom-Helm.

Procter, H. (1981). Family construct psychology: An approach to understanding and treating families. In S. Walrond-Skinner (Ed.), *Developments in family therapy* (pp. 350–366). London: Routledge and Kegan Paul.

Renshaw, D. C., & Renshaw, R. H. (1977). Incest. *Journal of Sex Education and Therapy, 3,* 3–7.

Russell, D. (1984). *Sexual exploitation: Rape, child sexual abuse, and workplace harassment.* Beverly Hills, CA: Sage.

Tierney, K. H., & Corwin, D. L. (1983). Exploring intrafamilial child sexual abuse: A systems approach. In D. Finkelhor, R. J. Gilles, G. T. Hotaling, & M. A. Strauss (Eds.), *The dark side of families.* Beverly Hills, CA: Sage.

Tsai, M., & Wagner, N. N. (1978). Therapy groups for women sexually molested as children. *Archives of Sexual Behavior, 7,* 417–427.

Weissman, M. M., & Paykel, E. S. (1974). *The depressed woman.* Chicago: The University of Chicago Press.

Yalom, I. D. (1975). *The theory and practice of group psychotherapy* (2nd ed.). New York: Basic Books.

13

Construing People or Weight?: An Eating Disorders Group

Eric J. Button

For some years now I have worked with people whose lives seem to be almost dominated by concerns about the need to be the right body weight. These people are mainly women, perhaps reflecting response to a generally higher level of concern about appearance in the female population (Garner, Garfinkel, Schwartz, & Thompson, 1980). Such concern is reflected in a general evaluation of slimness, if not thinness, as good and fatness as bad. At a behavioral level this is manifested by considerable popular interest in dieting, exercise regimes such as aerobics, and food in general. For most people, such pursuits may be regarded as relatively harmless and often constitute something approaching a hobby, as well as contributing to an industry: "the slimming business." Although diet and exercise consciousness can have health-enhancing features, when taken to extremes they can become a problem. A conservative estimate suggests that at least 5% of young postpubertal females in more affluent societies could be regarded as suffering from an eating disorder, with substantially higher figures often quoted for milder forms of eating restraint. I regard the primary characteristic of the eating disorder group as their preoccupation with the need to be thin to a degree that it is virtually the only thing that matters and is associated with considerable distress and persistent efforts to control weight that can sometimes be of a most bizarre nature. Two main kinds of eating disorder have been identified: anorexia nervosa and bulimia nervosa ("bulimia" is the more usual term for the latter in the United States). In anorexia nervosa, there is considerable self-induced weight loss and a wide range of associated physical and psychological symptoms. In bulimia nervosa, there are similar attitudinal features, but the person's weight is within "normal limits" or is over-weight. Efforts to avoid food have not been as successful as in anorexia nervosa, and the person engages in frequent enormous eating binges followed by self-induced vomiting and/or purging. Such persons often out-wardly appear "normal" but may experience considerable distress, disgust, bouts of depression, and a variety of adverse physical consequences. In recent years, there has been a growing interest in eating disorders in both the general public and the medical-psychological literature. This is manifested by frequent media presentation, international conferences (e.g., Szmukler, Slade, Harris, Benton, & Russell, 1985), the rapid escalation of publications (both scientific and popular), and the growth in treatment suggestions and outlets, including self-help (see Garner and Garfinkel, 1985). The personal construct literature on eating disorders is relatively limited, but there have been several studies using repertory grids that offer important theoretical and practical insights into the nature of these disorders (Crisp and Fransella, 1972; Fransella and Button, 1983; Fransella and Crisp, 1970, 1979; Mottram, 1985; Neimeyer and Khouzam, 1985; Weinreich, Doherty, & Harris, 1985).

In my own work evolving from a personal construct framework (Button, 1980; 1983b; 1985a, b), partly derived from grid research and partly from clinical experience, I have come to the view that the core of the psy-chopathology in eating disorders is a "quest for control" (Button, 1985a) in the context of a failure to anticipate in the person context. More precisely, the way in which people with eating disorders construe people is such that their expectations of people are continually invalidated. This is particularly so in relation to their construction of themselves. They turn to weight and related issues as offering some hope of validation and control. It is my view that they receive partial support for this approach, and it is only when it appears to be in danger of crumbling that they are open to treatment, although they may be extremely apprehensive of giving up their ways—understandably so, in my view, given what to them is a lack of any apparent alternative. It may be evident that this kind of formulation echoes personal construct formulations of other disorders, and indeed I have argued (But-ton, 1983a) that there may be similar underlying causes to all psychological disorders, with specific symptoms determined more by social factors (e.g., alcohol and criminality may be a more likely source of validation for a male). What is specific about eating disorders is the choice of "evidence"—namely weight, food, and appearance-related constructs. It follows from this kind of conceptualization that any attempt at treatment will be unsuccessful in the long-term if the person has not developed an alternative framework or con-struct system for understanding people. Thus, symptomatic treatment, including behavioral and cognitive treatment, will only lead to enduring change if the person can learn to anticipate people without relying solely on weight as a guideline. Clearly, a major obstacle to achieving this is the threat of possible chaos and it seems likely that a trusting therapeutic relationship is an essential ingredient. For some time I have endeavored to work along these lines on an individual therapeutic basis, but there seemed to me to be good grounds for exploring the feasibility of a group approach. In planning to do this, I was particularly influenced by Landfield and Rivers' (1975) Interpersonal Transaction Group with alcoholics. Research using this approach has demonstrated that it promotes precisely the kind of psychological understanding of others that is apparently lacking in the clinical population I am describing. This chapter is primarily focused on the experience of running such a group for young women who present with an eating disorder. The group was led by myself and Margaret Campbell, a psychotherapist with considerable experience in group therapy.

ASSESSMENT OF PRETREATMENT CONSTRUING

We advertised amongst local sources of referral that an "eating disorders group" would be taking place. It was emphasized that the group, although based on previous research, was a new venture and hence experimental in nature. It should be stressed, however, that although assessment and evaluation was built into the group, we were not attempting a controlled treatment trial: the latter would be relevant at a later stage in the light of experience of our first efforts to explore possible change in construing.

In addition to symptomatic assessment (see below), a form of repertory grid was individually administered pregroup in order to assess person construing. Each subject was asked to name those people who were or had been important in their lives, with an emphasis on their being a cross-section of people, not all liked or good friends. The mean number of elements elicited was 10.5 (range 7 to 14). Through a series of triads including two of these elements plus the supplied element "me," personal constructs were elicited by asking subjects to name as many important similarities or differences amongst the elements that they could identify: the mean number of constructs elicited was 14.9 (range 8 to 21). The final stage involved completing a grid by asking subjects to rate all elements in terms of all constructs on a seven-point scale. Grids included the following supplied elements: "me as I would ideally like to be" (ideal self), "me as I think others see me," "me as I imagine I would be without an eating problem." Unless already offered by the subject herself, the following constructs were also supplied; "thin-fat," "attractive to the opposite sex–unattractive to the opposite sex," "in control–out of control." Along with the symptomatic measures, grids were repeated after the tenth group session, at the end of treatment, and a year after initial assessment. In these repeat grids, group members were added as elements; in addition, subjects were invited to add elements and constructs that had become important to them since the last assessment point.

As will be well-known to many readers of this book, repertory grids yield large amounts of data, and any description of a person or group of person's grids must inevitably be selective. The grids have been analyzed partly by means of Slater's Ingrid program (Slater, 1977) but also in terms of various other measures devised by myself. My primary interest in the grid data is in what they reveal about how the group members were construing people. Some indication of this can be gained from the interrelationships between the elements, using Slater's element distances (in which smaller numbers indicate greater similarity): Whereas "me" was seen as generally very similar to "as others see me" (mean distance 0.56), there was an opposite relationship between me and "ideal self" (mean distance 1.33). The latter finding may be regarded as indicative of a generally poor self-esteem and is very similar to Mottram's (1985) mean of 1.32 for a group of anorexics vs. 0.70 for a group of controls on the same measure. This negative self-esteem was particularly apparent in Helen (self-ideal distance 1.67), a very thin young woman who claimed to want to put on weight but had repeatedly placed obstacles in the path of any therapeutic facilitation of weight gain. On most constructs she placed herself at polar opposite to her ideal self, with constructs such as "weird," "no enthusiasm to do things," "out of control," and "selfish" particularly salient in defining herself.

Whilst having a generally negative self-esteem, group members expected that "me without an eating disorder" would be very similar to ideal self (mean distance 0.51). For example, Theresa's main concern about herself was that she was introverted and wished to be outgoing. She associated her introversion with her binging and being overweight and anticipated that if she didn't have an eating problem she would become outgoing. One other grid measure of particular concern is subjects' relative psychological isolation from others, which is revealed by the mean distance of 1.19 between "me" and all nonself elements. Although there were invariably some people who they regarded themselves as similar to, they tended to feel different and isolated from most people. This sentiment is reflected by Rachel who on follow-up recalling herself before the group said, "I felt desperately alone but would not allow myself to feel liked or cared about by anyone."

A clearer picture of the clients' self-image can be formed by considering the personal constructs most clearly defining the self and others. On examining the first principal component, it was striking that only one person had a weight-related construct loading highly, whereas interpersonal concerns were quite prominent (e.g., "independence," "lack of confidence," "introverted"). In most cases, the "self" and "as others see me" were seen negatively and contrasted with "ideal self" and "me without an eating problem." At the same time, other people were more likely to be construed positively. For two subjects, however, their dissatisfaction with themselves only emerged on the second component. Sally generally evaluated herself positively on the first component, with the construct "will talk things over-sulks" particularly defining the positive and negative poles of the component. On the second component, however, she indicated she'd like to be less "frightened of getting hurt." Debbie also showed a generally positive evaluation of herself on the first component, stressing her ability to "understand other's problems," but on the second component revealed that she would prefer to be less inclined to "let things worry" her.

THE GROUP

Selection

Our main criterion for acceptance was that the person was prepared to look at her problem in psychological terms. Of those referred, eight young women were accepted and agreed to participate. Several people were not included for such reasons as inappropriateness of the group modality, travel problems, and dubious motivation. Age ranged from 19 to 30. Weight varied considerably from 34 to 110 kg (75 to 242 pounds): three were clearly underweight, three overweight, and two were of more average weight. The three obese subjects were all bulimic and had a poor self-image associated with their weight. Three had been diagnosed as anorexic and two bulimic. With the exception of one obese binger all scored within the anorexic range on the Eating Attitudes Test (Garner & Garfinkel, 1979), and all but one subject said they thought of food "most or all of the time" on a symptom checklist devised specifically for the group. Eating problems were generally long standing (range 2 to 18 years) and all of them had already had some previous unsuccessful psychological or psychiatric help.

Interpersonal Transaction Group Format

The group ran for 20 weekly sessions of one hour. During the first 10 sessions a substantial feature of the group was the use of "rotating dyads" (Landfield & Rivers, 1975). The main characteristic of rotating dyads is of short (5 to 10 minutes) paired interactions in which each person is required to find out about the other in terms of some specific theme. For example, in the first session the relatively nonthreatening theme of "what you enjoy doing" was selected. Other themes included "situations where I feel in control and situations where I do not feel in control" and "people who have been important to me and people who might become important." Group members were paired randomly initially but on subsequent occasions subjects were allocated to pairs in such a way as to ensure that everyone was paired with everyone else at least once. Initially the group leaders were just paired with each other, but later they also paired off with the clients. These dyadic interactions, however, only formed part of the group, and part of each session was taken up with a group discussion that could focus on issues arising out of the dyads or any other issues which came up. In fact, the dyads were discontinued on the 10th session by mutual agreement as there was a general feeling that more time was needed for whole group discussion. The general philosophy of trying to understand others was maintained throughout, however, irrespective of whether the medium was dyads or whole group. Thus the major emphasis was on the development of "sociality" (i.e., trying to see things from other people's point of view and by implication trying to help others see our point of view).

Group Process

From the standpoint of the overall orientation of the group, it is natural that a major focus in the group should be on the issue of similarity and difference in constructions of people. From the outset, themes of similarity and difference were echoed by many group members. In the first session, a common theme was apprehension about being different from others, followed by comfort from finding others who shared something in common. For example, in the plenary session of the first meeting, Kay revealed that she generally felt different from others and valued meeting others "in the same boat." Theresa was also stressing commonality in commenting "we're all using food—whether for comfort or rejecting it." It is likely that such superficial features as weight and eating concerns were a prominent source of initial apparent "validation," and it was interesting how the two most obviously "anorexic" people (Kay and Debbie) formed a kind of alliance with each other. However, similarity and difference on other constructs soon came to transcend weight. Dyadic interactions on nonweight themes seemed to facilitate this, with Rachel commenting after her second session dyad on "situations where you feel at ease or ill at ease," that people who appeared opposite in terms of weight might turn out to be quite similar. Such examples are consistent with the view that group members seek consensual validation in ways that parallel the process of acquaintance in the wider social arena (Duck, 1973, 1977; G. Neimeyer & R. Neimeyer, 1981). In fact, as Koch (1985) suggests, the security that such confirmation provides may be essential if subsequent change is to take place. Certainly, by actively encouraging "sociality" through focusing on each others' construing rather than their weight, we were opening up the possibility of elaboration through "extension" rather than exclusively by "definition."

This difference of emphasis towards people rather than eating and weight was generally accepted in the group, but one person in particular (Helen) repeatedly tried to bring the subject back to weight and tried to make group leaders conform with such expectations. In fact, in the 17th session she stormed out of the group after I had resisted giving her "answers" about eating behavior but did return the following week. It seemed that Helen's construct subsystem for construing people was extremely limited and polarized and perhaps, whenever faced with social "evidence" that was difficult to construe, she would call on the familiar ground of weight-related constructs. In spite of her "hostility" to moving away from her weight concerns, she did eventually shift after the group terminated and has continued with individual help in which she has been increasingly prepared to focus on her interpersonal difficulties, with weight becoming more peripheral. She is now more openly concerned with questions like whether people like her and more specifically the possibility and risks of an intimate relationship with a man. In so doing, the limitations of her existing constructs are obvious, but she is beginning to elaborate far beyond the expectation that she will be automatically rejected because of her weight.

People who are new to construct theory often form the mistaken impression that its "cognitive" emphasis excludes emotion. Of course, it has been stressed elsewhere that emotion is intimately bound up with construction (Bannister, 1977), particularly in respect of change in construing. Although the expression of feelings was not actively sought in a kind of cathartic way, it is not surprising that the above incident was by no means an isolated affair. Difficulty in expressing feelings was a common concern, and although some subjects seemed to be trying hard to contain their feelings, on several occasions subjects either broke into tears or expressed similar feelings of sadness in other ways. Anger was also in evidence and was more often than not expressed towards group leaders. Anxiety was a particular source of concern for Kay, who described feeling this in social situations in general, including the group. In fact, in the fifth session, she appeared to have a near panic attack and asked for the window to be opened because she felt "funny." She recovered from this incident and persevered, often making a positive contribution to the group. But her difficulties persisted and after missing a later session, she wrote saying "I am finding life harder and harder to cope with—when it means talking or mixing with other people (even though I know everyone in the group is quite harmless)." Finally, after the 12th session, she wrote to say she just couldn't face coming any more. It could be argued that her anxiety was a reflection of difficulty in anticipating other people, and possibly she may have been more suited to individual therapy.

The most powerful evidence of emotional change in the group was that demonstrated by Harriett, who towards the end of the group, took an overdose in the context of depressive mood, something she had been prone to previously. At the time, she denied a link with the group, but on considering her comments on follow-up some months after the group ended, I think this is open to question. Harriett had been overweight for some years and saw this as the cause of her difficulties. Depressive symptoms recurred after the group, and she lost a considerable amount of weight, thus getting direct experience of being slim. She still lacked confidence, however, and commented that even if she did get down to her ideal weight, that wouldn't be the solution. In her words, "The *eating* is the problem—the weight is the *consequence*. I suppose I have come to see that I had isolated myself and cut myself off through secretive eating." One might speculate, thus, that Harriett's suicidal behavior in the group may have reflected awareness gained from the group of the limitations of her constructs about weight, with the impending loss of validity of the major focus of her construing. Her comment at follow-up highlights this—"At least I knew where I was going (when aiming to lose weight)." Although Harriett's overdose and depressive symptoms were regrettable, I don't believe we should simply conclude failure. In fact, she completed the group and decided to pursue family-oriented therapy, something she had resisted earlier. She commented at follow-up that what she felt she needed most help with was more "understanding and sharing" within her family, recognizing that she had previously used food to avoid this potentially threatening area. Harriett's experience is a powerful reminder that the process of change is by no means a smooth affair. One possible implication of this may be that whilst this kind of group may be valuable for opening up new ways of construing people, it should perhaps best be viewed as *part* of a therapeutic process, which in most cases needs to be supplemented by individual sessions that may help the person to integrate the implications of the group experience.

Although the focus has been primarily on the group, we should not forget the importance of what goes on outside the group. In fact, an interesting phenomenon was the spontaneous development of a postgroup group. Myself and my co-group leader routinely met afterwards, but it soon became evident that our "patients" were doing the same thing. This was neither encouraged nor discouraged by us, although it was discussed in the group, and it was agreed that this was something they found valuable but not as in competition with the main group. In addition, social networks evolved between group members, so that communication between them outside the group became a valuable additional source of "evidence" about people. This was particularly evident at the mid-group and post-group assessments, with comments often made about other group members arising out of extra-group experience. For example Debbie commented at the mid-group assessment how interesting it was to see how differently people might behave outside the group: she remarked, for instance, that whilst Caroline was very quiet in the group, when walking to the bus with her afterwards she had been very chatty. This contextual "evidence" seemed to be bringing to question some of her assumptions about the meaning of quietness. One should also add that relationships with other people outside the group (parents, boyfriends, colleagues, etc.) were often a focus of concern for members. As group leaders, our aim was to help members elaborate their construing of others through such experience—to try to understand the other rather than to stick with their initial construction of the person.

CHANGES WITH TREATMENT

As is typical of follow-up studies, there were drop-outs. As mentioned above, one of the anorexic patients, Kay, dropped out shortly after halfway, saying she couldn't face the anxiety she felt on being with people. Sally, one of the bulimics who had been an active member of the group, also dropped out after the 14th session, having shown some impatience with the resistance of some of the group members. She seemed to have acted on her construction, "It's up to me to work at things—you can't expect other people to solve your problems." Interestingly, however, she subsequently made several urgent requests for further individual help, but on each occasion she failed to sustain an ongoing therapeutic relationship. In fact, she showed many features of "impulsivity," what Kelly describes as a foreshortening of the circumspection phase of the CPC cycle (Circumspection-Pre-emption-Control). This seems to be linked with her predominant usage of "all or nothing" construing, something that she readily acknowledged in herself. It is not difficult to see how this kind of construing inhibits development beyond the superficial phase of a relationship, and it is notable that her difficulties were particularly marked in the area of relationships with the opposite sex, which she both wanted and felt very vulnerable about. She clearly used binging as a way of avoiding such difficulties, and when I last saw her was openly ambivalent about giving it up.

In terms of formal assessments, although all eight were reassessed at midgroup, six returned for the end of group assessment, and only four completed the one year follow-up. Although eating behavior was not the focus of treatment, it is of interest to note any changes in this area. Of the six group members on whom postgroup assessment was available, three showed no substantial change, whereas three showed improvement. The nonimprovers were two anorexics and one very socially withdrawn obese patient. Two of the obese patients showed marked improvement, with one being asymptomatic by the one year follow-up. One of the bulimics, Caroline, was still binging by the end of the group but felt it was just a habit, and she no longer enjoyed it. Although not seen at one year follow-up, indirect evidence from her mother confirmed her improvement. It is concluded that three clients improved symptomatically, three didn't, and in two cases there was insufficient data to judge therapeutic change. One of the latter, however, the anorexic who had dropped out because of her anxiety, did write to say she was feeling better now but did not wish to "drag up memories."

Grid Changes

The most dramatic change in construing, in a similar vein to the author's study of anorexics (Button, 1980; 1983b), was of a structural kind. Less extreme and more moderate self construing had been shown in the above study to be a positive prognostic factor. It was therefore decided to examine measures of extremity in group members. A simple measure was derived from counting the number of ratings in three categories: (a) 1's and 7's, (b) 2's and 6's, and (c) 3's, 4's, and 5's. These can be regarded as representing decreasing extremity. The mean percentage of such ratings was calculated for each self element and for nonself elements ("others"). From the second grids onwards, separate extremity scores were also obtained for construing of group members.

Table 13.1 displays the percentages of extreme ratings (1 and 7), and it can be seen that there is a marked change between first and later grids. In the case of self elements, it can be seen that on first grids on average 40% to 50% of self ratings are in the most extreme category, whereas by the end of the group and at follow-up the figure is generally between 10% and 20%. In the case of "self" and "self as others see me," there seems to be a progressive reduction in extremity of construing from the time of the second grid (mid-group). In respect of "ideal self" and "me without an eating problem," however, the trend is not evident until the third grid (immediately after the end of the group). This might suggest that the group had provided them with moderating feedback about themselves and how others see them quite early on, whereas changes in their goals take longer to become manifest.

Table 13.1   Percentage of constructs on which self elements are rated extremely

	Pregroup (N = 8)	Mid-Group (N = 8)	Postgroup (N = 6)	1 Year Follow-Up (N = 4)
Me	45.1	33.8	18.6	12.6
Me as others see me	40.6	24.5	15.7	16.0
Ideal self	51.5	47.4	24.5	17.9
Me without eating problem	45.9	43.2	17.6	12.6
Others	28.5	26.1	15.7	13.0
Group members	—	14.5	8.5	10.8

Their construing of other people shows a similar trend of decreasing extremity, although it is notable that they start off at a lower level of extremity than when construing selves. By the end of treatment, in fact, they construe others at a similar level of extremity as themselves. In this respect, the construing of group members is of interest in that from their very first inclusion they are construed relatively moderately (with only 14.5% extreme ratings). It could be argued that this is a function of lack of knowledge of the person, but this seems doubtful, as they become even more moderate by the time of the third grid. It is suggested, therefore, that their encounters with the other group members have challenged their extreme constructions as well as encouraging reappraisal of their self-construction. By the end of the group there is evidence that this has extended to their construction of other people outside the group. The experience with this group thus provides further evidence for the role of extreme or polarized construing in psychological disorder. In addition to eating disorders, it has been implicated, for example, in depression (R. Neimeyer, 1985). One hypothesis currently being examined by the author is that such construing may reflect a tendency to see people in fixed terms rather than in contextual terms and be a characteristic of those prone to psychological disorder in general.

Although the above general trend is very striking, there were of course individual differences on this measure. It was notable that, in line with my anorexic research, those three group members who improved symptomatically (Caroline, Rachel, and Theresa) all started out with relatively low levels: they also ended up with even lower scores on this measure. It is of interest that even the drop-outs (Sally and Kay) and the nonimprovers on clinical grounds (Helen and Harriett) also showed reductions from high to more moderate extremity of self-construing. The exception was one of the anorexics (Debbie) who started off with zero level of extremity for all selves and a near zero level for nonselves. She showed very little change on this measure, although she did show a modest increase in the use of such ratings in construing others. Perhaps her initial complete absence of extreme construing is itself a matter of psychopathological interest, and it may be that the ability to construe some people extremely is a healthy sign.

As a result of this moderating effect of self-construing it is not surprising that there was a lessening of the previously described negative self-image for the group as a whole (last grid "self-ideal" distance mean 1.16 versus initial mean of 1.33). But this overall average masks the wide individual differences that parallelled the above changes in extremity of self-construing. For example, Theresa showed a dramatic improvement in self-image (1.77 to 0.65 from first to last grid), whereas Debbie showed a reverse trend (1.14 to 1.38). A similar finding applied to the "self–other" distances, with less polarization between self and others (last grid "self–others" distance mean 1.08 versus initial mean of 1.19, with again wide individual differences).

Selected Excerpts

While grid data has the attraction of offering a degree of objectivity, what clients have to say provides a much richer insight into the experience of change. All of the group members made comments about their experience of the group, but one person, Rachel, a physically disabled young woman who was also severely overweight, produced a detailed written retrospective account about two years later, and I include extracts from it here that I think you will agree are highly illuminating.

RACHEL: The first change that I would like to discuss is one of self acceptance. Before and during the 6 months of treatment the view that I held of myself was a totally negative one. This feeling of "self-hatred" was not confined to my appearance or my eating disorder but permeated every aspect of my existence . . . . I was absolutely convinced that although I might appear to be a "nice" person on the surface that in reality there was something highly undesirable about the "real me," which I must hide from the world. One of the reasons for this was that no matter how hard I tried (and I did try), I did not seem able to attain perfection. It was my belief that only perfect people had any right to have their needs met and in order to be perfect one should not only be slim but severely underweight . . . . I think that about six weeks into treatment I began to realize that there was no hope of me reducing my weight unless I was prepared to let go of some of the attitudes and ideas that had led me to eat compulsively in the first place . . . . Leading on from this came the realization that thin people were no more perfect than I was. I had the chance to get to know some people who were very underweight, and from this I was able to see how the type of person that you were did not depend upon your weight. I was able to see that being thin would not solve all my problems as I had once thought it would. This idea is one upon which I based my entire thinking life, and to let it go caused me much grief and pain. It was not for some months after I'd finished the group that this pain began to subside and I was able to begin to think in a constructive way. After leaving the group I recall feeling very angry and cheated. I felt that the only reason I had for living, i.e., my dream that I would some day be thin and happy, had been stolen from me—I had intended to exchange this dream for reality, but to have it stolen and be left with nothing just felt like the end of my world. I could see no reason for living, at that time my existence was very bleak. Looking back I can see that I had learned enough to know that I did have other options in life, and I now know that I gave up the dream of my own free choice—in order to move onto a life of many more choices.

I am now able to set myself more realistic goals (unrelated to weight), and the satisfaction I feel when I have reached them gives me the extra confidence that I need to go to new and more exciting goals. In contrast to before attending the group, I now love being alive, I love all the choices and decisions, and above all I love being in charge of my own life. I feel somehow that my being able to try now where I couldn't do so before is a result of having the confidence to express my real feelings more clearly . . . . I think that it is true to say that I had been using food as a tranquilizer, and now that I have attempted to stop using them it is as if a blindfold has been removed. Everything feels so new and bright . . . .

> Whilst I realize that I still have a severe weight problem I now feel that I
> am approaching a point where I can consider making some choices about
> how and if I wish to tackle the issue.

Rachel's statement illustrates a number of points. The role of extremity of
construing is revealed in her reference to seeking perfection. The meaning of
weight is revealed in her belief in thinness as defining perfection and in contrast having a highly negative view of herself as very overweight. She did,
however, succeed in reconstruing and clearly now sees many other avenues
in her life that she wishes to pursue. Although not directly referred to above,
this particularly concerned more intimate relationships with others, with
weight becoming a relatively peripheral construct. The encounter with the
people of varying weights in the group clearly played a part in this
reconstruction, but the process was clearly a painful one. Like Harriett, she
also experienced depressive feelings, apparently reflecting loss or what Kelly
might describe as "guilt," as one is dislodged from "core" constructs about
oneself and one's world. It is regrettable that all of the group members
weren't able to move on in the way that Rachel as well as Theresa and Caroline were able to. Perhaps Debbie's comments are relevant here. Debbie
had been anorexic for a number of years, with the death of her mother in an
accident apparently a pivotal etiological factor. She had considerable grief
about her mother and seemed to be primarily seeking parental-type
relationships. At mid-group she remarked, "All I don't want is to be fat . . . .
I don't want to grow up . . . . I want to stay a little girl . . . people taking me
under their wing." By follow-up she had shifted somewhat, with more
emphasis on her also looking after others (particularly young children),
rather than just being looked after herself. It seemed, however, that this was
primarily what Kelly called "slot-rattling," and she had not fundamentally
revised her constructs. There thus seemed no immediate prospect of aban-
donment of her anorexic life: "I have a way of life now and it would be difficult to adapt to a new one."

CONCLUDING COMMENTS

Change is neither easy nor impossible. In this study, it is clear that change in
construing did take place, but this in itself is not the end of the story, and
reconstruing is by no means synonymous with recovery. It seems likely that
such group experience as we provided can at best act as a catalyst that opens
up the possibility of new ways of viewing people and one's life and at the
same time encourages one to build and consolidate one's understandings of
people. Two additional lines of approach seem worthy of consideration for
the possibility of improving treatment. First, serious attention needs to be

given to the management of the emotions that perhaps are the result of discovering the questionability of previous assumptions about people. Secondly, it could be argued that cognitive-behavioral treatment of the disturbed eating behavior could go hand-in-hand with efforts to facilitate the development of person construing.

Finally, I have one regret, which is that we did not incorporate measures designed specifically to tap possible increased "sociality": reconstruing in one's own terms may indeed be progress, but ultimately it may be more crucial to social functioning to be open to "reading" the constructions of others. However it is equally important that people communicate their own constructions to others. By developing in both these ways a person makes progress towards relationships in which all perspectives are respected, thus allowing for the possibility of a truly creative involvement between people, unhindered by preemptive constructions, such as those that stem from weight preoccupation.

REFERENCES

Bannister, D. (1977). The logic of passion. In D. Bannister (Ed.), *New perspectives in personal construct theory* (pp. 21–37). London: Academic Press.

Button, E. J. (1980). *Construing and clinical outcome in anorexia nervosa*. Unpublished doctoral thesis, University of London.

Button, E. J. (1983a). Personal construct theory and psychological well-being. *British Journal of Medical Psychology, 56,* 313–321.

Button, E. J. (1983b). Construing the anorexic. In J. Adams-Webber & J. Mancuso (Eds.), *Applications of personal construct theory* (pp. 305–316). Toronto: Academic Press.

Button, E. J. (1985a). Eating disorders: A quest for control?. In E. Button (Ed.), *Personal construct theory and mental health: Theory, research and practice* (pp. 153–168). London: Croom Helm.

Button, E. J. (1985b). Women with weight on their minds. In N. Beail (Ed.), *Repertory grid technique and personal constructs: Clincial and educational applications* (pp. 61–74). London: Croom Helm.

Crisp, A. H., & Fransella, F. (1972). Conceptual changes during recovery from anorexia nervosa. *British Journal of Medical Psychology, 45,* 395–405.

Duck, S. W. (1973). Similarity and perceived similarity of personal constructs as influences of friendship choice. *British Journal of Social and Clinical Psychology, 12,* 1–6.

Duck, S. W. (1977). Inquiry, hypothesis and the quest for validation: Personal construct systems in the development of acquaintance. In S. Duck (Ed.), *Theory and practice in interpersonal attraction* (pp. 379–404). London: Academic Press.

Fransella, F., & Button, E. J. (1983). The "construing" of self and body size in relation to maintenance of weight gain in anorexia nervosa. In P. L. Darby, P. E.

Garfinkel, D. M. Garner, & D. V. Coscina (Eds.), *Anorexia nervosa: Recent developments in research* (pp. 107–116). New York: Alan Liss Inc.

Fransella, F., & Crisp, A. H. (1970). Conceptual organization and weight change. *Psychosomatics and Psychotherapy, 18,* 176–185.

Fransella, F., & Crisp, A. H. (1979). Comparisons of weight concepts in groups of (a) neurotics, (b) normal and (c) anorexic females. *British Journal of Psychiatry, 134,* 79–86.

Garner, D. M., & Garfinkel, P. E. (1979). The eating attitudes test: An index of the symptoms of anorexia nervosa, *Psychological Medicine, 9,* 273–279.

Garner, D. M., & Garfinkel, P. E. (Eds.). (1985). *Handbook of psychotherapy for anorexia nervosa and bulimia,* New York: Guildford Press.

Garner, D. M., Garfinkel, P. E., Schwartz, D., & Thompson, M. (1980). Cultural expectations of thinness in women. *Psychological Reports, 47,* 483–491.

Koch, H. (1985). Group psychotherapy . In E. J. Button (Ed.), *Personal construct theory and mental health* (pp. 302–326). London: Croom Helm.

Landfield, A. W., & Rivers, P. C. (1975). An introduction to interpersonal transaction and rotating dyads. *Psychotherapy: Theory, research and practice, 12,* 366–374.

Mottram, M. A. (1985). Personal constructs in anorexia nervosa. *Journal of Psychiatric Research, 19* (2–3), 291–295.

Neimeyer, G. J., & Khouzam, N. (1985). A repertory grid study of restrained eaters. *British Journal of Medical Psychology, 58* (4), 365–367.

Neimeyer, G. J., & Neimeyer, R. A. (1981). Functional similarity and interpersonal attraction. *Journal of Research in Personality, 15,* 427–435.

Neimeyer, R. A. (1985). Personal constructs in depression: research and clinical implications. In E. J. Button (Ed.), *Personal construct theory and mental health* (pp. 82–102). London: Croom Helm.

Slater, P. (1977). *The measurement of intrapersonal space by grid techniques. Vol. 2: Dimensions of intrapersonal space,* London: Wiley.

Szmukler, G. I., Slade, P. D., Harris, P., Benton, D., & Russell, G. F. M. (1985). Anorexia nervosa and bulimic disorders: Current perspectives. *Special Issue of the Journal of Psychiatric Research, 19* (2/3), 83–521.

Weinreich, P., Doherty, J., & Harris, P. (1985). Empirical assessment of identity in anorexia and bulimia nervosa. *Journal of Psychiatric Research, 19* (2/3), 297–302.

14

The Use of Personal Construct Theory in Groups

Sue Llewelyn
Gavin Dunnett

In this paper, we hope to outline and then to develop a number of ideas for and approaches to the treatment of clients using group psychotherapy, from a rather novel perspective. This treatment approach has been developed through the application of one established theoretical approach (personal construct theory) in another established treatment mode (group psychotherapy). To the authors' knowledge, this approach has rarely been used to date as a therapeutic tool in any systematic way, nor has it in this capacity been subject to extensive empirical research.

Both personal construct theory and group psychotherapy are of course well-established fields of enquiry and practice, and some of the techniques of construct theory have been used in the measurement of change occurring in groups (for example, Fielding, 1975; Koch, 1983a, b; Watson, 1970, 1972; Winter, 1985). Further, some exercises developed from construct theory have been used, particularly in structured groups (for example, Landfield, 1979; Landfield & Rivers, 1975; Procter & Parry, 1978). Nevertheless, there appear to be few detailed reports of group psychotherapy aimed at a clinical population conducted specifically from within a Kellian framework. Hence, this chapter is intended as an introduction to the use of personal construct theory in group settings as a therapeutic strategy and will emphasize the theoretical rationale for the strategy, rather than presenting at great length the outcome of any particular intervention. Nevertheless, two shorter case illustrations are included at the end of this chapter, and a detailed account of a group using personal construct theory led by the authors is available elsewhere (Dunnett & Llewelyn, 1988).

THE NEED FOR AN ALTERNATIVE MODEL OF GROUP THERAPY

The argument in favor of the development of a personal construct theory approach to groups is both pragmatic and theoretical. Firstly, such an approach is suitable for short-term groups, which are likely to grow in importance in the coming years. In his discussion of therapeutic intervention in institutions, Erickson (1981) pointed out that a short-term approach is the only really feasible one for use in the majority of psychiatric care settings nowadays, noting that: "The days when the backward housed chronically hospitalized patients are gone, but the chronic patient has not disappeared. Instead, she has become a revolving door patient" (p. 140). In addition, short-term therapy may be more appropriate in a situation of financial restraint coupled with increased demand for many inpatients as well as for patients who remain within the community. Yet the precise nature of that intervention seems to be crucial; it does not seem to be good enough simply to transfer without modification to the short-term context the models and strategies that may be effective in the long-term context. For example, a study by Kanas, Rogers, Kreth, Patterson, and Campbell (1980) concluded that insight-oriented group psychotherapy is not likely to be effective in the early stages of hospitalization; and Smith, Wood, and Smale (1980) suggest that "it is supportive non-analytic therapy which may be most appropriate with this population" (p. 111). Maxmen (1984) points out that "the evidence supporting the efficacy of group therapy for psychiatric in-patients is disappointing" and comments that "either the methods for evaluating inpatient groups are inadequate; no type of group works; or more loosely structured, psychoanalytically oriented groups are ineffective" (p. 355). Hence a new model for these types of groups seems indicated.

A second argument supporting the need for an alternative model of group therapy is the increasing willingness of nursing staff and other paramedical groups to become actively involved in the psychotherapeutic treatment of patients. Recognizing the need for more psychological therapy to be made available to more of their patients, nursing and occupational therapy staff, with or without training and supervision, may attempt to establish short-term group therapy loosely based on a psychodynamic model and not surprisingly, they often meet with little success. Yet, there are very few models currently available on which a short-term approach can be developed, although some do exist, for example, Budman, Randall, and Demby (1981) and Maxmen (1984). But, in general, the combination of a lack of understanding of anything beyond a rudimentary grasp of psychodynamic principles, together with a perpetually changing staff and patient population means that group interventions often result in dismal failure.

There is however a third reason for the increasing use of short-term, nonanalytic group therapy as a treatment of choice, which is more theoretical in nature. One of the notable features of short-term therapy is that it relates events occurring within the group more directly to the members' lives outside the group than does more conventional long-term group therapy, in which the "therapy experience (is) to be considered the most important event in their lives" (Yalom, 1975, p. 119). Unlike long-term groups, short-term group psychotherapy is focused upon current relationships and present life difficulties, without excessive attention being paid to the genesis of particular problems and with minimal attention being paid to any manifestation of transference. In the approach advocated by short-term group therapists such as Budman, Randall, and Demby (1981) and Maxmen (1984), the emphasis is upon the need for specific focus in the therapy. Hence, it is recommended that the sessions should be highly structured around particular foci and oriented towards solving particular life problems or crises rather than towards a reorganization of the whole personality. According to Budman and Gurman (1983), "The brief therapist views cure as inconceivable" (p. 281). Further, the aim of short-term therapy should be the alleviation of current sources of distress: "The brief therapist takes the patient's presenting problems seriously and hopes to make changes in some of the areas that the patient specifies as important" (Budman & Gurman, 1983, p. 281). According to Budman, Randall, and Demby (1981), although it is obviously the therapist's responsibility to help the patient to understand the nature of those difficulties, nevertheless the orientation should be on the resolution of current difficulties that have a clearly identifiable focus. Interestingly, Budman and Gurman (1983) cite research evidence that errors in technique (i.e., failure to structure the sessions) lead to negative outcome.

AN ALTERNATIVE MODEL: PERSONAL CONSTRUCT THEORY

Because of evidence of this sort, we would like to suggest that an approach is needed for group therapeutic interventions in settings such as acute, inpatient psychiatric wards, outpatient clinics, and community based programs, that nevertheless maintains some theoretical coherence that many broadly based or eclectic short-term groups seem to lack. We suggest that such an approach can be found within personal construct theory, although we shall also describe a number of developments of the theory that seem indicated beyond the original formulation by Kelly (1955).

Kelly's (1955) theory of personal constructs was primarily devised for use in individual psychotherapy. It is concerned with seeing an individual through his or her own personal perspective and focuses on the continuous flow of experiments that the person makes to predict and understand the surrounding world. The theory is positive about change and creates an environment in which both therapist and client can work together to understand and modify the client's personal system of construing. Personal construct theory encourages the client to take experiments away from therapy and into the real world to try them out, returning to the therapist to explore the results and plan future attempts. It is fundamentally goal-directed, since the process of elaborating predictions by experiment demands a purpose or goal for embarking on the procedure. It does however allow for a wide range of experimentation, ranging from the practical to the abstract, and does not prescribe any particular method to do this. Rather, the specific methods to encourage the process of elaboration and reconstruing come from the interaction between the therapist and the client themselves and may take many forms. Above all, this model is one which the client can continue to make use of long after short-term therapy has ended. This of course means that it is eminently suitable for use in short-term intervention for specific problems, and it also reduces the dependency on the therapist. Considering these principles in the light of the preceding discussion about groups, it does appear that personal construct theory would have a lot to offer short-term group psychotherapy, if the model can survive the transition from individual to group format.

It will have become clear that amongst other features, some of the basic elements of the personal construct theory approach are that it is personal, is based in the present and not in the past, sees movement and change as an essential characteristic of human beings, and applies as much to the therapist as to the client. Hence, it sees each person as having their own unique way of making sense of the world that structures their current ways of interaction but which can always be modified and changed in the future. These features are crucial to the process of active experimentation that the personal construct theory therapist encourages. There seems to be no reason why such features should not apply equally well to the group format. Yet most construct theorists have not made this transition. Why?

Paradoxically, this is possibly because of the particular way that Kelly (1955) himself envisaged the elaboration taking place, which many therapists may find difficult to follow in practical, rather than theoretical terms. Towards the end of Kelly's seminal work (1955), there is an outline of the implications of the psychology of personal constructs for group psychotherapy, which is presented in terms of both theoretical implications and brief descriptions of practice. Here, Kelly outlines both the functions and techniques to be used in group therapy, which he suggests is a particularly effective treatment opportunity for clients to develop more appropriate channels for the anticipation of events. He points out that the group setting provides an especially fruitful base for experimentation and the testing of hypotheses concerning the social world. By this he means that the group is "like having a large well-equipped social laboratory" (Kelly, 1955, p. 1156), which enables the client to develop a satsifactory and comprehensive social role and to learn how to discriminate appropriately in his or her application of constructs to others. Further, it "provides a way of shaking out (constellatory and) preemptive constructs" (Kelly, 1955, p. 1157), thus allowing the client to develop more sophisticated judgments of himself and others. Lastly, it provides a variety of sources of validational evidence for clients' experimental explorations of a new social role and permits the dispersion of dependency amongst group members. Hence, group therapy provides for the client "a broader initial base, both for experimentation and for his new role" (Kelly, 1955, p. 1156).

So far, so good. But while the theoretical formulation probably makes a lot of sense to personal construct theory therapists, the specific method of application is not one that we, for example, have found particularly easy to use. We shall nevertheless describe it, since our own elaboration very clearly builds on both Kelly's theoretical formulation and his practical suggestions. The precise methods that Kelly recommends are fixed role therapy and enactment, which are aimed at assisting clients in the exploration of their personal systems of construing. This is recommended for a variety of reasons. First, the process of enactment allows the client to begin to explore the ways in which he or she sees the world in comparison with others. This in turn can lead to an acceptance that others have alternative ways of construing. Second, it provides a supportive environment in which clients can learn to become active experimenters. Third, and most crucial, the client is given the opportunity to discover something about the world or the self. Kelly points out that although role play or enactment are very effective means of bringing about such experiences, they can also be produced by supportive discussion. But whatever means is used, the emphasis is on active experimentation in the group, in order to allow the client to work through a number of distinctive stages in the group. These are as follows.

First, the client is introduced to enactment both in order to give the client a chance to get used to the notion of role playing and to experiment with his or her own social role. The effect of this is to allow all of the group members to feel supported by other members of the group.

Second, this enactment develops from emotionally nonthreatening situations to more pertinent, personally difficult situations where important role relationships are introduced into the role plays. The aim of this stage of the treatment is to encourage the client to subsume the constructs of other participants, so that he or she is able to elaborate his or her own system of construing. At this point, clients may well experience threat and hostility as they begin experimentation with their construct systems.

Third, the group moves on to a process of group interaction that involves what Kelly calls "mutual enterprise," in which clients use their understanding of each other to propose and carry out experiments.

These experiments initially involve only interactions within the group but develop, in the fourth stage, into role plays (or discussion) involving incidents from the client's own lives outside the group. At this point the group members are seen as assisting each individual in the process of experimentation outside the group.

In the fifth stage, clients are encouraged to try to examine the construal processes of others outside the group, through which the client can "extend the lessons he has learned about role relationships with a particular group of persons and apply them to other persons outside the group and to humanity in general" (Kelly, 1955, p. 1175).

The sixth and final stage of group psychotherapy is characterized by the clients becoming involved in mutual exploration and experimentation with people outside the group and thus using the group chiefly as a "safety net."

Throughout the stages outlined above, the therapist encourages the application of the client's experiments in the group, to the client's own social world outside the group, and has particular responsibility to ensure that individual clients generalize the role relationships that they have developed within the group to others outside, thus encouraging permeability of construing.

MODIFICATIONS OF PERSONAL CONSTRUCT THEORY FOR USE IN THE GROUP SETTING

As has been described above, one extremely important aspect of the personal construct theory approach to groups is the insistence on the transfer of the findings of experimentation within the group to the client's world outside the group. It is this feature that we felt made it particularly suitable for application in a short-term setting. However, as we have already indicated, we felt somewhat uncomfortable with the specific elaboration outlined in Kelly's original work in 1955, in particular the emphasis on enactment. Our intention, therefore, has been to develop a method of group therapy that takes into account the need to maintain a specifically focused approach, which is tied in to the social situation of the client outside the group and which also maintains a coherent theoretical approach appropriate to a heterogeneous group of clients. Hence we have developed our own modification of a personal construct theory approach to group therapy. Such work is experimental in a Kellian sense: the group provides an opportunity for participants, including the leaders, to explore the implications of their particular construct systems, to examine the implications of specific pre-emptive or constellatory constructions, and to bring to the group results of experiments taking place both inside and outside the group setting.

In our modification of Kelly's ideas about group therapy, we have adapted a number of different techniques for use during the group's development. First, emphasis is placed on the speedy establishment of cohesiveness, as indicated by Yalom (1975) and others. This is achieved in early sessions of the group through the use of simple warm-up games or other group-based exercises. Second, self-disclosure is encouraged by subdividing the group into pairs, who are then asked to share particular areas of concern with each other. These are then related to the rest of the group by the partner, thus encouraging both cohesiveness, and the facilitation of permeability of construing. Third, the usefulness and flexibility of systems of construing or of particular constructs are examined by looking at interactions between group members. The Kellian concept of hostility (the distortion of the "evidence" to fit a person's theories) is introduced to group members and distinguished from the more productive concept of aggression (the expansion of the construct system to take account of the new evidence). Fourth, clients are encouraged to develop a stance of active experimentation towards their difficulties and to use the group sessions as a format for trying out new strategies in relating to other people. This is done both individually and also collectively through the use of a group grid, which facilitates individuals' understanding of their social role. Members are also introduced to the concept of "slot-rattling," which involves a sudden "flip" of a construct so that what was white becomes black and vice versa. When applying this to personal change, the individual learns that it is not necessary to overthrow everything they once were in order to change themselves, but, rather, that modification is usually more feasible and desirable than revolution. Fifth, a small amount of self-disclosure on the part of the leaders is used to model the process of experimentation. Last, group members are encouraged to look outwards to current life problems, and to set one another "homework" tasks, thus ensuring transfer of the experimental approach to "real life" outside the group. The success or otherwise of the "homework" is then reported back to the group, and in this way group pressure is used to encourage the internalization of change (as suggested by Kelman, 1963).

CASE ILLUSTRATION 1

The following case description illustrates some of the benefits and problems encountered when using personal construct theory in a group setting.

A fuller description of the membership of this group is available elsewhere (Dunnett & Llewelyn, 1988) so it will not be repeated here.

Apart from the leaders, the group consisted of seven members, all of whom were outpatients, although three had previously had inpatient treatment. The main concern of this group was to provide both the impetus and structure for experimentation. This was done in the early stages by providing a number of structured experiences allowing for gradual and safe self-disclosure. This included a brief period of enactment in which group members role played a partner in the group, thus encouraging members to subsume the constructs of others. This exercise involved a certain amount of discomfort, as personal anxieties were aired in the group for the first time.

During the general discussion following this exercise, Roger, a 34-year-old "man-of-the-world" who possessed plenty of superficial charm, but who nevertheless experienced considerable difficulties in maintaining close relationships with women, offered a cigarette to Holly, another group member. This she refused. Holly was a 25-year-old woman, whose difficulties centered on her lack of self-confidence and inability to assert herself in relationships. At the time, she was involved in a somewhat masochistic relationship with a man who did little but find fault with her and which she felt unable to terminate or alter. When Holly refused the cigarette, Roger tried to persuade her, and Holly continued to refuse, although confessing that she was "dying for a smoke." In explanation, she told the group that "I haven't got any to offer back, so I would have felt terribly guilty taking one." In addition, she said that she felt uncomfortable because Roger had only offered a cigarette to her and not to other group members.

As therapists, we decided to use this incident to encourage members to examine the usefulness of the constructs that they were using towards one another. Roger explained that he had thought that Holly had been uncomfortable during the previous discussion and had offered her a cigarette in order to "help" her. At Holly's refusal, he had experienced a feeling of annoyance, together with a confirmation of his prediction that women rejected him unless he made enormous efforts to "charm" them. He also felt surprised that his strategy of picking out one particular woman for special attention had not succeeded and, as a consequence, discovered that he was feeling very uncomfortable. Holly, who believed that everything had a price tag attached to it, realized that she was simply obtaining confirmation for her belief. The price, in this situation, would have been the disapproval of the rest of the group. The previous group discussion, in which Holly had been revealing negative aspects about herself, was perceived by Roger to be very difficult. To Holly, being offered a gift by Roger was a far more difficult situation. For Roger, a strategy of deflecting attention from his own discomfort by behaving gallantly towards another in distress was a well-practiced tactic, even when unsuccessful.

In this interaction, both participants were behaving in ways that were familiar and consistent with their personal construct systems, albeit with unproductive consequences. Roger had been able to cast himself into the role of generous if misunderstood giver, while Holly could see herself in the role of the "undeserving pauper" who couldn't have what she wanted, either because she couldn't pay for it, or because everyone else would hate her for getting it.

We then asked both Roger and Holly to test out the hypotheses that they were operating with and to see whether they could devise alternative ways of making sense of their own and each other's behavior. We wanted then to examine the possibility that they had each misconstrued the other and also the rest of the group and that they could gain a more productive perspective on the world by a readjustment of their pattern of construal. In other words, we were asking them to shift from being hostile (contorting the evidence to fit the theory) to being aggressive (active elaboration of their construct systems). However, our hypotheses that the group was ready for such exploration at this point proved to be incorrect. It was too early for such exploration, and our attempts fell on stony ground, as neither client felt able to embark on any form of experimentation. Hence, they clung on to their predictions with a clear demonstration of hostility.

However, the incident was not forgotten, as it resurfaced in the subsequent session. During the second half of this session, Roger referred back to the "cigarette incident" and began to explore how misunderstandings occur in personal relationships and how intentions can be misconstrued by others. Meanwhile, Holly began to consider whether she was in fact as undeserving of positive "gifts" from others as she had thought. The following week, Holly was prepared to take part in a role play in which she stood up to her undermining boyfriend, and by the end of the series of group sessions, she had terminated the relationship. Both clients had only been able to risk the active elaboration of their system of construing when they felt more able to risk the consequences of loosening up: in other words, when the group was more cohesive and supportive to such an elaboration.

CASE ILLUSTRATION 2

In the second illustration, a different type of group will be described. This group consisted of one leader only, with six members, all of whom were taking part in a short residential course aimed at the exploration of the uses of personal construct theory in a group setting. This group has also been described elsewhere (Dodds, 1985). The group meeting took place in a small room, some distance away from the dining areas, which meant that refreshment breaks had to be taken in the meeting room, and group members had themselves to provide coffee, tea, milk, etc.

On the evening of the second day, Becky, a 40-year-old social worker, told the group that she should like to try to be more assertive with her friends and family. The group suggested that she should, as a form of "homework," experiment with the task of refusing to comply with the requests that others always seemed to be making of her. The following morning, just before the meeting, the leader asked Becky, who was seated in the dining area, to fetch some milk for the day's meeting. This Becky agreed to do, but just as the leader was leaving the room, she recalled her "homework" and called to the leader that she would "rather not" fetch the milk. The leader, undeflected, told Becky that she must sort it out and left. Becky then tried unsuccessfully to persuade other members who were also present in the dining area to do so but eventually ended up fetching it herself.

This incident (which had not in fact been engineered deliberately by the group leader) then formed the basis of an examination of Becky's behavior, why she had yet again failed to assert herself, and how it was that other group members (including the leader) had "chosen" her to be responsible for meeting the group's needs for refreshment. Becky was asked to explore, first, the implications of being assertive within her own construct system and, second, to devise alternative ways of behaving that did not involve compliance. At first Becky was unable to imagine anything other than a "slot-rattle" or complete reversal of her existing ways of behaving, which she felt would be unacceptable to herself and her friends and family. But, through role play she was helped to see how other ways of interacting were in fact possible that did not involve "slot-rattling." In this instance, a different way of behaving entailed refusing to accept the task (of fetching the milk) that she had been assigned by the leader, in a clear and assertive way, rather than accepting and trying to back out of it at the last moment. In the group, Becky was able to test out her hypotheses that others would dislike her and that they would see her as uncaring by experimenting and observing the results. The fact that her first attempt (her homework) had "failed" allowed her to learn more about the precise means by which her new behaviors could be put into practice. The presence of other group members meant both that she could use other group members as models and also that she could test out the implications of her new behavior in this "well-equipped social laboratory."

RELATIONSHIP OF KELLY'S MODEL OF GROUP THERAPY TO OTHER MODELS

In many ways, this approach to short-term therapy is not dissimilar to other approaches where the relationships between individuals are used by the therapists as a resource for promoting personal change. But one or two differences are apparent. First, the emphasis on generalizing to the client's world beyond the group is in clear distinction from some other varieties of group therapy where discussion of issues outside the group is seen as avoidance of the crucial aspects of the group functioning, or even flight (see, for example, the work of Bion, 1961; Foulkes, 1965). Second, the leaders in the group are seen as additional data for the client's own experimentation whose view of "reality" is no more accurate (or sacrosanct) than that of the client or other clients. Therapists are also seen to model the process of experimentation. Third, and perhaps most crucial, what this approach to therapy offers to the client is a methodology by which the client can begin to understand very simply that the ways in which he or she construes the world place limitations on that world (see the dilemmas, traps, and snags described by Ryle, 1979) and hence on that world's potential. Concepts such as "hostility" or "slot-rattle" are easily understood by most clients and allow individuals to make sense of and, in many cases, take control of their own behavior. The group setting makes those concepts even more powerful, as the existence of alternative ways of construing the same thing are only too evident to each personal construer.

Of course there are also a number of aspects of personal construct theory as applied in the group setting that are similar to other models. For example, although given different labels, the therapeutic strategies described by Kelly clearly correlate with some of the factors identified by researchers such as Maxmen and Hanover (1973), Steinfeld and Mabli (1974), Butler and Fuhriman (1983), and Bloch and Crouch (1985), among others. For instance, it might be argued that the factors labeled by Yalom (1975) as "learning from interpersonal actions" and "acceptance" are identical to those proposed by Kelly as the "base for experimentation" and "the variety of validational evidence," which are said to occur at various stages of the group development. Equally, the "mutual enterprise" could be said to be effective through the operation of both "universality" and "altruism."

Furthermore, the processes by which change actually occurs may not in fact be very different across different theoretical formulations. There is increasing evidence (Frank, 1979; Stiles, 1983; Stiles, Shapiro, & Elliott, 1986) that the factors responsible for change in individual therapy are likely to be both extremely varied and, simultaneously, quite straightforward. That is, clients seem to be helped by a variety of aspects of what being in therapy provides, such as having support, encouragement, and a new way of thinking about things. In addition, it is quite possible that the precise techniques or theories used are not in themselves of any great importance, over and above their worth as a rationale for doing things differently and their persuasive content. There is no reason why this should not also apply to group therapy. This may help to explain why differing methodologies tend to produce very similar outcomes (Luborsky, Singer, & Luborsky, 1975).

CONCLUSION

Personal construct theory is particularly well placed to provide short-term group therapists with a theoretically coherent structure on which to base their interventions. Although it can be argued that the process and outcome of a group run along these lines is not, from some viewpoints at least, likely to be very different from that of a group run along more conventional lines, we nevertheless believe that personal construct theory does have a number of distinct advantages over more traditionally led groups. These include the emphasis on personal experimentation, which the client learns as a strategy towards living in the future as well as in the present, and, in addition, the emphasis on expanding the range and versatility of constructs, which means that the client is able to bring more of his or her own world under personal control. The approach is reasonably easily learned by novice therapists and clients alike and has considerable explanatory and predictive power. The use of the other group members as co-experimenters provides support for the gradual elaboration of constructs, so minimizing the dangers of either over-rapid dilation of the system or of a hostile tightening of the system. Lastly, the experimental stance of the leaders means that they too should be more prepared to be adaptable and flexible in response to the needs of the specific individuals, rather than using the group as data to bolster belief in any particular theory. This in the long run can only be of benefit both to specific clients and also to the development of therapeutic practice in general.

REFERENCES

Bion, W. (1961). *Experiences in groups*. London: Tavistock.
Bloch, S., & Crouch, E. (1985). *Therapeutic factors in groups*. Oxford: Oxford University Press.
Budman, S., & Gurman, A. (1983). The practice of brief therapy. *Professional Psychology, 14*, 277–292.
Budman, S., Randall, M., & Demby, A. (1981). Outcome in short-term group psychotherapy. *Group, 5*, 37–51.
Butler, T., & Fuhriman, A. (1983). Curative factors in group therapy: A review of the literature. *Small Group Behavior, 14*, 131–142.
Dodds, J. (1985). PPA summer training conference report: Applying construct theory in groups. *Changes, 3*, 138.
Dunnett, G. N., & Llewelyn, S. P. (1988). Elaborating personal construct theory in a group setting. In G. Dunnett (Ed.), *Personal construct psychology in clinical settings*. London: Routledge and Kegan Paul.
Erickson, R. (1981). Small-group psychotherapy with patients on a short-stay ward: An opportunity for innovation. *Hospital and Community Psychiatry, 32*, 269–272.

Fielding, J. M. (1975). A technique for measuring outcome in group psychotherapy. *British Journal of Medical Psychology, 48,* 189–198.

Foulkes, S. H. (1965). *Therapeutic group analysis.* New York: International Universities Press.

Frank, J. D. (1979). The present status of outcome studies. *Journal of Consulting and Clinical Psychology, 47,* 310–316.

Kanas, N., Rogers, M., Kreth, E., Patterson, O., & Campbell, R. (1980). The effectiveness of group psychotherapy during the first three weeks of hospitalization. *The Journal of Nervous and Mental Disease, 168,* 487–492.

Kelly, G. A. (1955). *The psychology of personal constructs.* New York: Norton.

Kelman, H. (1963). The role of the group in the induction of therapeutic change. *International Journal of Group Psychotherapy, 13,* 399–342.

Koch, H. (1983a). Changes in personal construing in three psychotherapy groups and a control group. *British Journal of Medical Psychology, 56,* 245–254.

Koch, H. (1983b). Correlates of changes in personal construing of members of two psychotherapy groups: Changes in affective expression. *British Journal of Medical Psychology, 56,* 323–327.

Landfield, A. (1979). Exploring socialization through the Interpersonal Transaction group. In P. Stringer & D. Bannister (Eds.), *Constructs of sociality & individuality* (pp. 133–151). London: Academic.

Landfield, A., & Rivers, P. C. (1975). Interpersonal Transaction and rotating dyads. *Psychotherapy: Theory, Research & Practice, 12,* 366–374.

Luborsky, L., Singer, B., & Luborsky, L. (1975). Comparative studies of psychotherapy. *Archives of General Psychiatry, 32,* 995–1008.

Maxmen, J. (1984). Helping patients survive theories: The practice of an educative model. *International Journal of Group Psychotherapy, 34,* 355–368.

Maxmen, J., & Hanover, H. (1973). Group therapy as viewed by hospitalized patients. *Archives of General Psychiatry, 28,* 404–408.

Procter, H., & Parry, G. (1978). Constraint and freedom: The social origin of personal constructs. In F. Fransella (Ed.), *Personal construct psychology 1977* (pp. 157–170). London: Academic.

Ryle, A. (1979). The focus in brief psychotherapy sessions: Dilemmas, traps and snags as target problems. *British Journal of Psychiatry, 134,* 46–54.

Smith, P. B., Wood, H., & Smale, G. C. (1980). The usefulness of groups in clinical settings. In P. B. Smith (Ed.), *Small groups and personal change* (pp. 107–153). London: Methuen.

Steinfeld, G., & Mabli, J. (1974). Perceived curative factors in group therapy by residents of a therapeutic community. *Criminal Justice and Behaviour, 1,* 278–288.

Stiles, W. (1983). Normality, diversity and psychotherapy. *Psychotherapy: Theory, Research and Practice, 20,* 183–189.

Stiles, W., Shapiro, D. A., & Elliott, R. (1986). Are all psychotherapies equivalent? *American Psychologist, 41,* 165–180.

Watson, J. (1970). A repertory grid method of studying groups. *British Journal of Psychiatry, 117,* 309–314.

Watson, J. (1974). Possible measures of change during group psychotherapy. *British Journal of Medical Psychology, 45,* 71.

Winter, D. (1985). Group therapy with depressives: A personal construct theory approach. *International Journal of Mental Health, 13,* 67–85.

Yalom, I. (1975). *The theory and practice of group psychotherapy.* New York: Basic Books.

V
Special
Applications

15
Framing Career Decisions

Larry Cochran

Helping a person to make a career decision is a deceptively simple affair. For example, one might help a person to identify alternatives, examine evaluative criteria, and use a reasonable decision strategy. However, the clarity of such steps is complicated in actual practice. First, the major aim of decision counseling is often not to just make a decision. The major aim might be to learn how to decide, to consolidate an orientation, or even to dissolve the need for a decision. Second, in practice, it soon becomes apparent that there are numerous potential steps that might be added to a decision model. A client might resolve conflicts, set priorities, validate judgements, or integrate a conception of his or her life. Moreover, whatever the steps of a decision might be, they are accomplished within a personal context that complicates decision making. For example, the completion of a decision step such as setting value priorities might be influenced by self-esteem, maturity, motivation, significant others, resources, and any number of factors. Often, one must detour from basic decision-making strategies to supportive tasks that become preconditions for further development.

Within this context, models of decision-making differ considerably in scope as well as focus. For example, classical decision theory is restricted primarily to the use of a rational decision strategy, to the neglect of other aspects. Trying to enhance esteem in order to increase the range of viable options would fall outside the model. Many approaches to decision counseling are similarly restrictive (for a broad review, consult Horan, 1979), although each offers valuable contributions.

Personal construct theory is compatible with most approaches to career development (Herr & Cramer, 1979) and decision-making (for example, Janis & Mann, 1977); it also offers a fairly comprehensive and coherent basis for decision counseling, one that seems nicely suited to providing guidance within the complexities of actual practice. Although personal construct theory offers a variety of novel contributions to career counseling (e.g., the career grid; Cochran, 1983a), I would like to concentrate upon what I consider to be its most distinctive advantage for decision counseling; namely, framing a decision rather than simply making a decision. From the perspective of personal construct theory, framing a decision is not just a prelude to deciding. Rather, it represents a central task in itself—a pivotal achievement. Before grasping the significance of this contribution, it is necessary to review briefly how a career decision is regarded and the role that framing plays within a construct theory approach to decision counseling.

LIFE RESEARCH

Kelly's (1955) theory is grounded in the analogy of the person as scientist. From this viewpoint, a career decision is a tentative start to a major experiment in living. In approaching a career decision, a decider has a more or less organized set of beliefs about a career, based upon interpretations of the world, the self, and particular occupations. These beliefs (values, ambitions, and the like) constitute what might be termed an implicit or lay theory of career. From this personal theory, a person forms hypotheses (expectations, predictions, judgments, and just plain hopes) that will be put to the test in trying to implement a decision. There is nothing fixed about a career decision; it is contingent, provisional, promissory, fallible, and in short, quite experimental in nature. One tries it out and hopes for the best. Trying a decision out in training, education, or actual work is the experiment proper. The experiment yields results that validate or invalidate one's theory, encouraging a person to extend and/or revise the theory, often in preparation for another experiment involving a different career path.

Given this viewpoint, the aim of career decision counseling is to facilitate productive experiments in living. A career decision is not viewed as one experiment but as the beginning of a series of experiments. Consequently, the major question in career counseling is whether a person is capable of conducting fruitful life experiments and benefiting from the results. By heightening a person's capacity to conduct useful experimentation, the individual is more apt to attain a greater sense of meaningfulness, satisfaction, productivity, and happiness. The logic of this view is similar to the logic of developmental counseling generally, particularly as described by Super (1984). There is no one intervention to be followed, in this view, but different interventions that depend upon the particular strengths and weaknesses of the client (Neimeyer, Nevill, Probert, & Fukuyama, 1985; Super, 1983).

Suppose a client made a career decision and entered an occupation that was unsuitable for a variety of reasons. The client might be miserable, discouraged, disappointed, disillusioned, and depressed, among other things. However, from a construct theory perspective, the first job venture is not yet a failure. Certainly, it is unfortunate that one's decision did not work out better, but it is not a failure on that account. An experiment is really a failure only when one has learned nothing from it, if one has no better basis for venturing forth anew than he or she had before. In contrast, if the person were able to use the results of this experiment to consolidate a more workable theory for the next try, then it would be regarded as a success.

Suppose a client made a career decision and entered an occupation that was suitable in a variety of ways. The client reports satisfaction, contentment, confirmation, and a general optimism. From a construct theory perspective, such a report would be encouraging, but it would not yet be considered a complete success. For example, the person's next four years in work might be merely a repetition of his or her first year, with little novelty or development. Optimism dwindles. Boredom rises. In this case, the experiment has moved toward stagnation.

Whether the topic is career counseling or something quite different like thought disorder, the general aim of a personal construct theory approach is the same. People who enter counseling or therapy are regarded as "stuck" in some fashion. The task is to help them become unstuck. Kelly (1955) phrases this as the elaboration of one's personal construct system, and elaboration occurs as one makes fruitful experiments in living. In other terms, the aim is to maximize intrinsic motivation (Deci, 1975), to steer between stultifying boredom and overwhelming chaos. The most common word for this between-state is "challenge."

DECISION FRAMES

To make a career decision, a person employs a set of vocational constructs (such as interesting/uninteresting) that are interrelated, constituting a hierarchical system that might be variously termed a "frame," "scheme," or "theory." This set of vocational constructs is embedded within a larger network of constructs concerned with oneself, the world, and how life is to be lived. For example, job security has no value in itself. Rather, it is a vehicle for the instantiation of broader value constructs that involve a person's vision of the good life, given restrictions of oneself and the world. As another example of the relationship between the vocational construct system and its larger, interpersonal system, Waas (1983) found that information about the personal characteristics of people in occupations allowed individuals to differentiate among those occupations more than did information about the occupations themselves. Neimeyer (1985) has argued that vocational and interpersonal systems are intimately connected, not only in terms of their content, but also in terms of their structure. In support of this reasoning, Lawlis and Crawford (1975) found that women who were more cognitively complex in interpersonal relationships tended toward nontraditional careers more than women who were less cognitively complex. They interpreted this finding as indicating that, "interpersonal complexity is a factor in vocational choice" (Lawlis & Crawford, 1975, p. 226). A decision scheme appears, in this light, as a more or less fallible translation of other construct systems into vocational constructions.

People enter career counseling in varying degrees of disharmony. That is, their decision schemes manifest more or less relationship, harmony, and integration. Aims (values, desires, etc.) might be fragmented and scattered, conflicting, vague, superficial, incongruent with capacities and motives, or lacking in priority. They might be largely tacit and unexamined, negatively directed, or short-sighted. Framing is concerned with identifying and integrating aims into a more harmonious whole. To consolidate a frame, some aims (an aim here is the positive pole of a construct) might be discarded as incompatible with the whole, some placed at the periphery, some deemed complementary, and some united to form the center of one's theory. From a disharmonious variety, the central task is to create a more explicit frame that can be translated into a workable plan. To consolidate a decision frame is to consolidate in vocational terms a person's general plan of living.

While a counselor might focus upon a number of areas to foster more productive life experiments in a career, the central focus is a person's decision frame or implicit career theory. The frame is the basis for experiment and for interpretation of the results. It is like a working model, subject to extension, refinement, and revision as one learns more in living it out. However, a fault in the frame is apt to emerge as a fault in the experiment, leading to entrapment rather than elaboration. It is for this reason that the decision frame is regarded as more important than the actual decision a person makes.

The following cases illustrate various faults in framing a decision and ways to correct them. In these cases, there has been no attempt to select flashy ones or ones that turned on a single phrase. Rather, the cases were selected more to represent the ordinary work of daily practice. For any one presented, there are numerous cases similar to it. In this way, I hope to convey something of the flavor of what it is to conduct career counseling from the perspective of personal construct theory.

SLOW DEATH IN THE ACCOUNTING DEPARTMENT

Jim, approaching 30 years old, was in distress over his career. In undergraduate work, years before, he had majored in business administration. When nearing graduation, he had taken a Strong–Campbell Interest Inventory, which showed that he had much in common with people in banking. Consequently, he sought and landed a job with a national bank. As part of junior executive training he was rotated through various departments over a course of several years. Apparently, life was fine until he was rotated to the accounting department. After a few weeks he became irritable and then disgruntled. His work day now felt endless, and soon he began to question his career choice. Was banking really suitable for him? After another eight months, he quit his job. For the next few years, he floundered in jobs merely to earn a living, wondering what steps to take to get his career in motion once again. He had no idea why he lost interest in banking after such a promising start.

Jim was a product of a "test 'em and tell 'em" approach that dominates a great deal of practice. That is, the client is tested, and the tests are interpreted in light of whatever little is known about the client. If the client is attracted to recommended occupations, one can count another success. This primitive version of trait-factor counseling assumes that the aim of career decision counseling is an appropriate decision or match between person and occupation. That is, the person–occupation match is reasonable, and the person seems to want the particular occupation. Jim's case shows one of the many glaring weaknesses of this vapid practice.

Jim was so uninformed about himself that he became stuck when faced with the first career adjustment of any significance. He had not made explicit nor consolidated a frame for decision. Jim had neither considered nor weighed even the most obvious of constructs against others. His particular problem was that he was exceedingly extroverted, and accounting required long hours all by himself. It felt like solitary confinement, yet he could not articulate the difficulty in any way that allowed him to act constructively. The solution to the immediate problem was simply a review of the accounting situation in view of his extreme extroversion. The solution to the larger problem was an exploration of himself in relation to situations. For example, given a set of activities one enjoyed and a set one did not enjoy, a person can identify likes, values, and strengths that are personally optimal. In short, one can begin to make explicit a vision of the good life and relate this vision to work. There are a great variety of techniques for explorations such as this (Herr & Cramer, 1979), ranging from written or spoken autobiographies to sounder test interpretations that trait-factor theorists originally advocated (Williamson, 1939). Jim returned to banking more able to describe the roles in which he could perform well and the roles in which he would not. He returned with a more differentiated view of work that might allow him to make wiser choices and adjustments (Bodden, 1970).

Of all the faults in a frame, Jim's fault is perhaps the most basic and most common. Without a more explicit consolidated theory of one's personal career, it is difficult to communicate its nature to others, dialogue with oneself, assess the suitability of an occupation in a refined way, make adjustments, problem-solve, or assess deficiencies in one's frame. One is not in a position to use the evidence of experience to venture forth anew.

We fall prey to that which we do not construe. What we construe sets the bounds on our freedom to make things happen differently. If one construes with some degree of validity, he or she is in a position to anticipate accurately and to exercise some control over the course of events. Events that lie outside our scope of construing happen to us. We exercise no control, nor can we anticipate, and effective action presupposes an anticipation of consequences. For example, a person might neglect the geographical implications of a decision and so fall prey to them when they occur. A person might so focus on salary and status to the neglect of meaningful purposes that work is unexpectedly made into a benevolent form of slavery. A person might believe that the hard work presumably necessary for success excludes friendship (too time-consuming) yet be surprised by an inescapable emptiness that might follow. We fall prey not only to what we do not construe but to unexamined implications of our construing. A person might construe minute aspects of living and leave larger patterns to chance. Having little time for family might simply be a consequence that unexpectedly arises. In framing a decision, we influence the scope of the control we can potentially exercise.

LIFE BESIDE A DREAM

Upon graduation from high school, Jane thought wishfully of entering university to prepare for a career in the helping professions. She had thought a lot about social work, but also counseling psychology, personnel management, and a variety of occupations requiring more education. However, the thought of actually going to university and working in her interest area was painful. In her anxiety, she retreated, abandoned university plans, and became a secretary. She worked in a downtown office, dreaming of what it would be like if she went to university. Several years later she noticed that her friends, who had gone on and were graduating, seemed so interesting, so confident, so optimistic, while she languished. Now, the old ambition has arisen once more with force, and she feels she must come to a decision. Should she stay a secretary, perhaps going into word processing? Should she quit her job and enter university? Or should she just go travelling?

In order to help a person frame a decision, I often use a career grid (Cochran, 1983a), in which a set of occupations are rated on a set of career constructs. Occupations are generated by brainstorming, consultation, study, testing, and the like, depending upon the time available. Constructs are generated in a variety of ways, most prominent of which is Kelly's (1955) triad method. Given selections of three occupations, a person is asked: "In what important way for making a career decision are two of these occupations similar yet different from the third?" Then, using a rating system (I prefer a five-point scale), a person is asked to rate occupations on each construct in turn. To complete a career grid is to complete the major steps of a decision (Horan, 1979). One generates alternatives, generates constructs or evaluative criteria for judging alternatives, rates alternatives on each construct, and then uses the grid representation to evaluate occupations thoroughly, weighing the advantages and disadvantages of occupations against one another. A career grid is also an attempt to represent a person's decision frame, providing a way to examine the frame more directly.

Jane's career constructs clustered into two related groups, one involving social consciousness and human relations, the other involving intrinsic rewards of work. In the first cluster, she preferred dealing directly with people in a way that involved real contact and informality rather than a formal show, social concern rather than frivolity, and in which she would help people develop their potential rather than remain unconcerned or removed. In the second cluster, she preferred creativity, independence and responsibility, and challenge in work. Satisfaction related to constructs in both clusters. What stood out as a major fault of her frame was conflict. In those occupations in which she would be more creative, be in real contact, be independent and responsible, be challenged, and be satisfied, she would also experience a painful lack of confidence. To diminish the awkward agony of a self-conscious lack of assurance, she had initially opted for work that she regarded as "mechanical," "boring," "frustrating," "staged" (rather than a sense of the real), and "under the direction of a watching boss." Her first job entry in the adult world involved a decision to avoid the negative rather than reach for the positive, generating a virtual paralysis of life and career development. There she hoped her assurance might grow, but it did not. Now years later, just the thought of entering university or acting in the role of a human service worker can still fill Jane with both dread and welcome.

Conflict among career constructs is common in my experience and in available research (Cochran, 1983b; Cochran & Giza, 1986), and there are many ways to manage it. Conflict can sometimes be dissolved by valid judgments, by discovering an alternative in which the conflict is absent, or by focusing upon central values that make peripheral conflicts fade in significance. Sometimes, conflict can be resolved by altering, elaborating, or loosening rigid meanings, by establishing value priorities, and by a careful decision about the roles of each value in the life one envisions. In the present case, conflict could be solved by personal change and development. That is, if she became more confident or at least learned how to minimize discomfort, the conflict might either lose potency or be eliminated as a conflict.

Why not abandon deciding and simply help her to become more confident? While this certainly might be advantageous in some cases, it would not have been advantageous in this one. A vague confidence in general is different than specific confidence in relevant tasks. To place her decision on hold once more seemed short-sighted and potentially self-defeating. After all, she could avoid a decision just as well by working on her confidence as by travelling, which she was seriously considering. Also, there is both clinical evidence (Greenwald, 1973) and research evidence (Janis & Mann, 1977) to suggest that if a well-deliberated decision precedes an effort to change, the person is apt to remain more committed and less vulnerable to small setbacks. The issue is not just a matter of confidence, and there is no guarantee that she would ever feel confident enough. From Maslow's (1968) perspective, the decision is one of deficit motivation versus growth motivation. From Kelly's (1955), it is one of security versus adventure, whether to avoid negatives or risk approaching positives of life. This decision involves a fundamental difference in a plan of life, regardless of one's actual alternatives. She is faced with a fundamental choice about the kind of life she will lead that transcends the actual alternatives she has in mind.

As conceived here, the counseling task was to help Jane make this decision. One way was to help her construct a balance sheet of the advantages and disadvantages of going to university versus staying as she is (Janis & Mann, 1977). Aside from deepening and broadening awareness, this method forces a person to note the advantages of one's present situation. As Tschudi (1977) noted, people tend to be blind to the advantages of the present. Certainly, secretarial work had little opportunity to reveal its merits to her, given her dream. In this instance, however, the balance sheet was not rich enough for the task. Rather, it provided a grounding for laddering up to higher values. Laddering (Hinkle, 1965) is a way to elicit deeper, more central constructs, a way to move from subordinate to superordinate issues. The laddering discussion began in the following way, "The basic choices seem to be going to university versus staying as is, and you are more inclined toward university. Now why would you prefer to go to university in contrast to staying as is?"

JANE: I would feel like I was getting somewhere.

LARRY: In contrast to?

JANE: Not getting anywhere.

LARRY: Why would you prefer to get somewhere rather than not get anywhere?

JANE: If I was progressing, I would be developing my own potential rather than not developing.

Given whatever construct elicited, the same question is posed once more. Laddering continues until the elicited construct is so self-obvious that the client cannot imagine further justification is necessary. If the task is framed as an exploration of meanings and comment is encouraged, laddering becomes more like a structured conversation rather than just a matter of questions and answers. Her ladder was as follows:

Going to University	Staying as is
1. Get somewhere	Not get anywhere
2. Develop own potential	Not develop potential
3. Exciting	Boring
4. Makes me interesting	Less interesting
5. People would like me	People would not like me as much
6. I would like myself	I would not like myself as much
7. Growth and changing	Stagnating
8. Developing assurance	Stay unassured
9. Happy	Unhappy

What emerged from laddering was not simply a meaningful series of implications, although that is evident enough, but a personal theory of change, of how to become unstuck. First, change settings from ones that do not facilitate movement to ones that do. Second, in the new setting, experience the excitement of going somewhere and developing one's own potential. Third, this change will ramify to make her more interesting and likable, both to herself and others. Fourth, if she is developing in a more affirmative setting, she will be released or stimulated to grow and change, and in particular, to become more assured. This will culminate in a happier life.

As a theory of personal change, her ladder is quite reasonable. Certainly, one could help her to refine aspects, to forearm or caution her against unrealistic expectations, and so on. However, her theory involves a workable plan of change that might be strengthened by elaboration rather than extensive revision. Whether the plan eventually results in her dream occupation has become somewhat secondary. There are a variety of occupations that might be suitable, once she begins exploring. The essential point is that her plan allowed her to begin experimenting with life, elaborating her career theory and frame for decision as the evidence of her life experiments was evaluated.

From beginning to end, the aim of counseling was to search for an adequate frame for conducting life experiments. While the techniques could be viewed as ways to heighten awareness, to explore, or to make the implicit explicit, the goal is never just awareness or explication, but workable and potentially fruitful models of reality that can guide new ventures in living. People become stuck when their constructions of life serve more to encage rather than frame (Ryle, 1975). The counselor's task is to discover or invent transformative aspects of a person's construing that allow the person to become unstuck. Once this is accomplished, one can help prepare people to benefit from a plan, initiate alternative ways to attain certain aims (such as being liked), guide the person through experiments, and in general, support and encourage the plan.

WHOSE LIFE TO LIVE?

The client was a bright 20-year-old university student named Carol. She entered counseling with considerable confusion about her career plans. Discussion resulted in a torrent of considerations with no clear pattern. The same terms seemed to shift in meaning, arising in different contexts with different meanings. At one point, there would be a reasonably clear stance toward career and at another point, there would be a different one. The interview was dominated by the sheer profusion of thoughts she expressed, which were confused and confusing.

The career grid was introduced as a way to help sort out her thoughts and to organize them. Once 10 career constructs were elicited and used to rate her 10 most viable occupations, a pattern began to form in the way constructs were related. To clarify the pattern, 10 more constructs were added by laddering each previous construct one step. It might be noted here that completing a career grid is not like taking a test. It is like a structured interview, and, within the structure, counselor and client are free to exchange comments, focus on topics, elaborate a point, and so on. The career grid is valuable not just because of results but also because the process itself is facilitative. People are forced to think broadly and specifically, to make distinctions, and to clarify vague notions. As they proceed, people tend to try to make sense of their own ways of construing. For clients who are confused, the activities required in completing a grid can be quite beneficial in themselves.

Constructs were clustered into groups in which each construct related to every other construct. Clustering resulted in one large group and two small groups. The large group was related to the two small groups through a mediating construct. Indirectly, through this mediating construct, the large group was in conflict with the two smaller groups. The small groups constituted an opposing meaning scheme in relation to the large group.

Setting out the opposing meaning schemes allowed Carol to understand what was happening during deliberation. At one time, using the large group, she could be clear about what she wanted to do. At another time, using the small groups, she could be clear. However, one undermined the other, altering the very meaning of her terms. In moments in between, when she attempted to integrate her considerations, she was thrown into confusion.

The strategy of counseling was to practice the opposing meaning schemes, to discover something about how they arose, and then to act on whatever way out of the impasse emerged. Practicing is a matter of construing occupations and one's career solely from the perspective of a harmonious cluster. "Given this group of ideas only, how would you evaluate your occupations? What kind of life would you live? What would be the highlights of your career? Does it fit what you want?" Viewed in this way, practice is like Kelly's (1955) concept of "controlled elaboration"; it is a way of taking command of a viewpoint. Once the person has more control, then one viewpoint is viewed in terms of the other. "From this perspective (indicating a group of constructs), how do the ideas of the other group appear? How would you evaluate this way of seeing things?" In this way, a person practices control over the different meanings, noting differences as well as similarities or potential bridges between the two. As command was fostered, we were able to discuss how these meanings arose in her life. That is, where did they come from?

The large cluster involved positive poles such as "imaginative," "use own ideas," "stimulating," "more meaningful," "have personal input," "more free and broad," "richer, challenged," "more important," and "feel more useful." These qualities required a field that was less defined and broad of scope. This cluster seemed to arise from her experience. That is, she was bright, intellectual, and imaginative. She liked theory and research, to play with ideas. This meaning scheme favored academic or investigative occupations such as economist, biologist, and law-politics.

The two small clusters involved positive poles such as "personal sacrifice" (of time, effort, etc.), "giving of yourself," "direct personal service," "emotional involvement with people," "more contribution," and "long-term effects or benefits for others." These qualities arose largely, in her view, from her parents' expectations and ideals. Both professionals, they advocated the old-time standards of a dedicated, selfless servant of mankind. This meaning scheme favored professions such as medicine, nursing, and special education. That is, of what use is economy, biology, and law-politics? Do they help anyone directly? From the perspective of her experience, the professional viewpoint appeared to be exceedingly severe and narrow.

Although she approved of and admired the constructs of professionalism, she became doubtful that they were really appropriate for her. When she imagined living the code of her parents, she felt confined. She began to explore some of the severer judgments and was helped to pose more fruitful questions. For example, is it really true that economists do not benefit anyone? How might an economist make a contribution, be involved, or offer service? If some theories are too abstract, is there a possibility that one might develop theories that are more practical and beneficial? What would make her feel useful and meaningful as an economist, biologist, or lawyer-politician?

Partially, my shift to questioning was intended to facilitate exploration. Partially, it was intended to soften or loosen meanings so that bridges might be developed between the opposing schemes. Largely, the intent of questioning at this point was to throw Carol's future into question. She had gained command of two rival viewpoints, and it was time to begin experimenting. Questioning is an important prelude for cultivating an experimental attitude.

When a person is deliberating, it is difficult to maintain perspective. Perspective can be lost as one becomes involved. One is unable to reflect very well upon what he or she is doing, and reflection is necessary to make sense of confusion. By representing the confusion within Carol's decision frame and practicing the opposing perspectives, her confusion was reduced. Indeed, this pallid description hardly conveys the joy and relief she experienced nor the inquiring state that emerged. From this release she began to conduct experiments. For example, she pursued her academic work differently, talked to people about their work, and tried things out for herself. One of her occupations was work as a model, and she tried modeling. While she was able to confirm that it was too meaningless for her, it was exciting and she earned money. Over the next year, she would stop by occasionally to let me know of all the things she had tried, what she had learned, and how she was exploring her occupational possibilities. She had some time before a decision had to be made and was planning to explore as much as she could. Perhaps the most distinctive quality that I noticed about Carol, after relief from confusion, was the utter enthusiasm she radiated. Later, to enthusiasm she added what might be called autonomy or assurance about herself, her decisions, plans, and actions.

IN THE NAME OF STUPIDITY

Cindy, a woman in her late twenties, entered counseling with a request to take an intelligence test. When the education system was so desperate for teachers that they required only a high school degree with some university work, she applied and went to work as a teacher. She apparently functioned adequately in the job and liked it. Then one day, Cindy had a chance to peek in her personnel file and found that her intelligence score was around 90. She could not tell me later if this was a raw score, a standard score, or even what test was involved. Nevertheless, what it meant to her was that she was subnormal, somewhat retarded. From then on, she lived with this secret that set her apart from her colleagues and students. Didn't the hard work of preparation indicate she was slow, since some colleagues prepared very little? Wasn't she uncertain of what to do sometimes? Diligent but never too sure of herself (after all, she did not have a B.Ed.), the secret began to color her experience of herself and her life. She was but passing as an acceptably intelligent person, who might be discovered and exposed. Perhaps she should get out of teaching and into an occupation she was more able to manage?

Two features were salient when I saw Cindy. First, her gathering and weighing of evidence from life experiences were appalling. She was like a nurse I had worked with who believed that she crumbled under pressure. Since the nurse worked in a highly demanding specialty, I wondered why she was able to function so well. She responded that it could not be that demanding since she could do it without crumbling. But if she trained to be an operating room nurse, which she really wanted, she would surely crumble and expose her weakness to everyone. That she should crumble under pressure was so tautologically fixed that no evidence could challenge it. Similarly, evidence had become irrelevant to my client. Although there was enough doubt that Cindy came to see me, the evidence of her experience had been neglected as she tended to concentrate upon her assumed stupidity.

Second, she had been cultivating the standpoint of a subnormal person for years, and what one attends to elaborates. It was no longer just a matter of correcting a mistaken belief but of revising a way of living. In friendship, for example, she tended to take the part of an inept little sister, dependent upon a big sister. In classes at university, she had questions but was afraid to voice them.

After a variety of rationales to avoid giving her an intelligence test and to engage her in a working partnership of more duration, she agreed to work with me over the school year. (As she was on study leave from school, she had one year of university to complete before returning to work.) Our task for the year was to learn more about how one goes about acting intelligently. For example, she felt stupid in a class. Well, how can one feel intelligent? What do people do that is intelligent? Once that is determined, one can try to act intelligently. Cindy felt stupid sometimes in relationship with her "big sister" friend. Consequently, her friend was brought in and informed of the project. Although a discussion of how she contributed to the problem took on the flavor of a confrontation, she came to appreciate the difficulty and was willing to try to alter her role. During the year, I provided direct instruction on how to enhance Cindy's capability for learning, modeled problem solving, and directly supported her efforts in whatever way I could. We role played, planned, envisioned, imagined alternative scenarios, and the like. The specific techniques are quite secondary. For any one I used, I could just as well have used another. Of central importance is the larger strategy for which specific techniques are merely tactics.

We became co-researchers on life. For each venture, we framed ideas and clarified hypotheses and questions. We carefully selected settings in which her ideas could be reasonably tested. We rehearsed the actions that would launch the experiment. We discussed the kinds of evidence that must be gathered before prematurely foreclosing the experiment with judgements. Then, we evaluated the evidence in preparation for further ventures. Evaluation is partly a matter of accurate judgment, as cognitive therapists stress (e.g., Beck, 1976). However, from a construct theory perspective, it is also partly a matter of frutifulness. If a glass is half empty or half full, there are two judgments that accord with evidence, but a large difference in the fruitfulness of those judgments. The actual practice of co-research with a client is not as neat as this paragraph suggests, but it certainly involves the elements noted.

The fault in her frame was a dominant construct that stifled and distorted her frame of living. Through repeated experiments in acting more intelligently, Cindy was able to loosen and elaborate the idea of intelligence, allowing it to become just a part of her personal theory. While she did not quite make the honor roll in university, her grades were quite respectable, and she received supportive comments from professors and students. The issue of stupidity did not evaporate suddenly. Rather, it receded. As the question of intelligence lost force, the need for a career decision was eliminated. She returned to teaching with a more diverse view of intelligence, a greater appreciation of her capacities, and a release from domination that would allow her to explore other dimensions of experience.

PHILOSOPHIES OF LIVING

To apply personal construct theory in the area of career counseling is a fascinating undertaking. Beneath the repetitious litany of stated career constructs involving salary, interest, and ability, among others, there is a concern for how life is best to be lived. No one wants salary in itself, for instance, but rather wants what a salary stands for. Salary might be a way to acquire goods of life, to become secure, to have status among others, to gain power, or to have more to give. In some sense, typical vocational constructs are symbols into which one invests a latent philosophy of living, what I have previously termed a personal career theory. Career counseling becomes a discipline in which a counselor works directly with a philosophy of living, both in design and implementation. As a description of this enterprise, applied philosophy would not be far wrong, even if it is a little presumptuous (however, see Koestenbaum, 1978).

While personality theories might help in this area, philosophy helps far better for it has debated for centuries the merits of different philosophies of living. Stoicism, platonism, epicureanism, eudemonism, and the like all concern defined approaches to living well, and variants of these philosophies are precisely what one meets in career counseling. Consider, for instance, a conflict between salary and talent. Practically, one can envision life with more or less salary and with more or less cultivation of one's talents. Philosophically, however, the issue might pose the question of whether it is best to acquire goods or to be good, having versus being. Paul Gaugin's life, as one example, turned on this very issue, among others. Denouncing the evils of civilization, he quit his job as a banker, left his wife and children, and sought to live as a primitive while he cultivated his art. Philosophies of living are not arid abstractions with no connection to actual living; they are the very ground from which our plans of life emerge.

Personal construct theory does not offer an adequate philosophy of living. It is more of a metatheory of the kinds of theories people have. To heighten awareness of issues and their significance, it would be better to study, for instance, Kierkegaard, Sartre, or ancient Greek views of the good life. However, what personal construct theory does offer is an elaborate theory of the way people become stuck and might be helped to become unstuck, whether they are modern stoics, eudemonists, or epicureans. As a basis for attempting to correct faults in decision frames that stifle experiments in living from the start, it is invaluable. It provides not so much definitive answers to career counseling, as conceived here, but rather a reasonable basis for elaboration.

REFERENCES

Beck, A. (1976). *Cognitive therapy and the emotional disorders.* New York: International Universities Press.

Bodden, J. L. (1970). Cognitive complexity as a factor in appropriate vocational choice. *Journal of Counseling Psychology, 17,* 364–368.

Cochran, L. (1983a). Seven measures of the ways that deciders frame their career decisions. *Measurement and Evaluation in Guidance, 16,* 67–77.

Cochran, L. (1983b). Conflict and integration in career decision schemes. *Journal of Vocational Behavior, 23,* 87–97.

Cochran, L., & Giza, L. (1986). Conflict in the career decision schemes of high aspiration youth. *Canadian Journal of Counselling, 20,* 136–145.

Deci, E. (1975). *Intrinsic motivation*. New York: Plenum.

Greenwald, H. (1973). *Decision therapy*. New York: Wyden.

Herr, E., & Cramer, S. (1979). *Career guidance through the lifespan*. Boston: Little, Brown & Co.

Hinkle, D. (1965). *The change of personal constructs from the viewpoint of a theory of implications*. Unpublished doctoral dissertation, Ohio State University.

Horan, J. (1979). *Counseling for effective decision making*. North Scituate, MA: Duxbury Press.

Janis, I., & Mann, L. (1977). *Decision making: A psychological analysis of conflict, choice and commitment*. New York: The Free Press.

Kelly, G. (1955). *The psychology of personal constructs*. New York: Norton.

Koestenbaum, P. (1978). *The new image of the person: The theory and practice of clinical philosophy*. Westport, CT: Greenwood Press.

Lawlis, F., & Crawford, J. (1975). Cognitive differentiation in women and pioneer-traditional vocational choices. *Journal of Vocational Behavior, 6*, 263–267.

Maslow, A. H. (1968). *Toward a psychology of being* (2nd ed.). New York: Van Nostrand Reinhold.

Neimeyer, G. (1985). *Personal construct systems in vocational development*. Paper presented at the 6th International Congress on Personal Construct Psychology, Cambridge University, England.

Neimeyer, G., Nevill, D., Probert, B., & Fukuyama, M. (1985). Cognitive structures in vocational development. *Journal of Vocational Behavior, 25*, 191–201.

Ryle, A. (1975). *Frames and cages*. London: Sussex University Press.

Super, D. (1983). Assessment in career guidance: Toward truly developmental counseling. *Personnel and Guidance Journal, 61*, 555–562.

Super, D. (1984). Career and life development. In D. Brown & L. Brooks (Eds.), *Career choice and development* (pp. 192–234). San Francisco: Jossey-Bass.

Tschudi, F. (1977). Loaded and honest questions: A construct theory view of symptoms and therapy. In D. Bannister (Ed.), *New perspectives in personal construct theory* (pp. 321–350). New York: Academic Press.

Waas, G. (1983). Cognitive differentiation as a function of information type and its relation to career choice. *Journal of Vocational Behavior, 24*, 66–72.

Williamson, E. (1939). *How to counsel students*. New York: McGraw-Hill.

16
Designing a Fixed Role Therapy: Issues, Techniques, and Modifications

Franz R. Epting
Andres Nazario, Jr.

In this chapter, we will be exploring some of the issues involved in designing and implementing a fixed role therapy. Of the therapeutic techniques developed within personal construct theory, fixed role therapy is by far the best known and most frequently described. For this reason we will present only a brief description of the basic technique, just enough to serve as an anchor and clear referent for the issues and concerns we wish to consider. There are a number of places one can find a more detailed description of the basic technique (Adams-Webber, 1981; Bonarius, 1970; Epting, 1984) including, of course, the original presentations of the technique by Kelly (1955, 1973).

BASIC TECHNIQUE

The fixed role procedure is based on the general assumption that clients can profit from undertaking a comprehensive change in their life patterns for a brief period of time. Instead of working on one issue at a time in order to facilitate gradual change, the client is invited to immediately adopt an alternate personality structure by role playing a character somewhat different from the present self. This alternative characterization is based on a self-description that the client provides the therapist in response to the following instructions:

THERAPIST: I want you to write a character sketch of Harry Brown (client's name), just as if he were the principal character in a play. Write it as it might be written by a friend who knew him very intimately and very sympathetically, perhaps better than anyone ever really could know him. Be sure to write it in the third person. For example, start out by saying, "Harry Brown is . . . " (Kelly, 1955, p. 323).

Based on this self-description, a therapist using fixed role therapy then constructs an enactment sketch that is designed to provide the client an opportunity to approach life, with its difficulties and joys, in a different manner than the client might have tried before. This enactment sketch is presented as a role sketch of a "new person" (with a new name) that the client is invited to "become" for approximately a two-week period of time. Examples of what two clients have produced to the instructions are provided below, preceded by brief descriptions of their presenting problems, and followed by enactment sketches written for each client.

KATHERINE

Katherine was a 40-year-old woman who initially came to therapy with her family. The presenting problem was her 16-year-old daughter's acting out behaviors. She had three other children, and she had divorced their father seven or eight years prior. She had recently remarried, and soon after entering family therapy she decided to divorce her husband of just a few months. The family sessions were soon discontinued, since Katherine had taken charge of her family and the presenting problem had been solved. A year or so later Katherine returned for individual therapy. Although she felt she had made some progress since her last divorce, she now felt confused about her future and generally "stuck." It was at this point that she was asked to engage in an experiment with the therapist, which began by writing a self-characterization in the form of a letter to the therapist, from the standpoint of one of her close friends. She began as follows:

KATHERINE: Katherine is working hard to find out what she wants and how to obtain it. She fights a lot of hang-ups along the way but she keeps "slugging" and somehow knows that she will accomplish her goal.

The paths to be taken toward this end are often unclear for her. This lack of clarity is often due to confusion caused by internal pressures, needs, drives and desires. Sometimes she will be motivated by a desire just to get away and have some fun even though it might sacrifice time needed by her children. Being able to act on her sense of priorities is not always easy for her.

Matters which concern money and career goals present another situation where things become muddled. With career choices, she may end up doing nothing, and with money she will alternately pay essentials only and then splurge on nonessentials. In this area, part of the confusion stems from pressures from family on a too-lean budget. Budgets, by the way, elude her though she is certainly capable of handling one.

Her confusion also creeps into her relationships with people—at work and at home. She will misinterpret what she is told at times—reading either too much into it or distorting what was said by rephrasing the message. The result is that she feels hurt, defensive, or unappreciated—often without cause. The "this or that" dilemma even filters into her choice of clothes—every aspect actually. It is frustrating for her and she wants to be more focused and self-confident and self-directed. Please do not assume that Katherine is wishy-washy or easily swayed. Not so, she does consider all sides. Sometimes, though, it appears that even the best reasoning takes a back row seat.

The end of her marriage to Paul (her second husband) has proven to be a turning point. She is dedicated more than ever to a goal based around self-assertion and self-reliance. Although the paths are (as before) not clear, a sense of direction is well established. She tries to be a loving, understanding, and helpful person and succeeds more often than she allows. When she has been harsh or unfair she will let it worry her at times way out of proportion.

This is about all I can go into now. She is dedicated to getting "there" and I hope that you will continue to help her. She deserves the feeling of accomplishment and self-worth that she will obtain. She deserves to shine and stand out as the unique, creative, and compassionate woman she is.

Sincerely,
Her friend

Katherine's Role Sketch

THERAPIST: Trish is a bright, articulate woman deriving a great deal of satisfaction from life at the present time. From her father, Trish learned certain cautiousness that comes in very handy at times. From her mother, Trish learned a little bit of lack of regard for money and a carefree attitude about the world. Trish is maturing, she has left behind the struggles of many years and feels a sense of command of her own destiny. Trish can be impulsive, and at times she may act out in a manner that displeases her, but Trish does not analyze her behavior, she perceives these incidents as fuel to replenish her well of experiences. Trish has a sense of direction that allows her to know where she is going in life, and when something or someone gets in her way, being a creative woman, she maneuvers and finds a detour that puts her back on course. There are many sides to Trish, she is not totally fulfilled, yet she is satisfied. She is somewhat shy, yet she can assert herself quite well. She is a feeling person, yet she does quite well with her thinking. She is a woman striving to leave a mark in the world, yet she can't slow down and contemplate.

MELANIE

This second case involved Melanie, a 25-year-old student. She had been in and out of therapy on several occasions. At the time of the initial contact she had come in because her parents had established professional help as a condition for their continued financial support while in college. She had dropped out of college several times, had moved to different cities, and had always returned home to a crisis. The therapeutic goal was to do family work with Melanie individually, since her family lived in another city and was not available for therapy. The clinical hypothesis established by the therapist was that Melanie was triangulated in the family conflict and that her dysfunction had a purpose for the family system. After a few months of working with Melanie in relation to her family system, the therapist suggested bringing in the family for one session. Although she did not refuse, she panicked at the idea and went into a series of mini-crises for the following two or three sessions. The therapist was concerned about a setback and decided to invite Melanie to put aside the family work for a few weeks and engage in a project that required the participation of both therapist and client as experimenters (i.e., fixed role therapy). As the first step in the process, Melanie wrote the following self-characterization:

MELANIE: Melanie is the most sympathetic of friends. She always goes out of her way to support and help those she cares about. If there's a real crisis in your life she would give you the shirt off her back and travel to the ends of the earth for you. But sometimes, in the lull between such storms she becomes less attentive and forgetful. She never means to hurt feelings or to take advantage, she just seems to have other things on her mind and thus will forget to call you back or follow through or remember birthdays and things like that. She's too busy spinning her wheels with her own life and never seems to get organized. Melanie's a good listener and usually gives good advice but never can apply it to herself. She's not very practical and tends to let her emotions rule her actions more often than she should. Though often times this can get her into trouble because she doesn't think ahead, it also can be exciting and fun.

I worry about her sometimes because she can be so intimidated by people. For some reason she doesn't feel like she measures up with adults and doesn't do well in crowds or big parties at all. When she has the confidence she can tune into people really well but many times she feels too intimidated to relax and enjoy herself.

Melanie has a lot of trouble with her parents. They don't communicate very well and it really bothers her. She goes back and forth from wanting to please them and be accepted by them to feeling resentful and angry at their inability to accept her. They come down really hard on her at times and she can't always blow it off or forget it.

Melanie's Role Sketch

THERAPIST: Betty is a youthful woman, friendly and life-loving in many different ways. She is loving and caring with herself and others. She cares for herself by always attending to her own needs, prioritizing them, and working hard at making sure they are met. This allows plenty of time to attend to others, something from which she derives great satisfaction. She is a *doer,* too. She participates in numerous activities both socially and academically. She does well in school and does not become discouraged or overwhelmed when the academic pressures increase. On the contrary, she loves the challenge and meets it with resolution and hard work.

At times Betty gets angry easily. And when she does, she doesn't hold back. She faces the source of her anger and at times blows more steam than she needs to. In this sense, she is more like her father. Occasionally, she will ask him about his expertise in anger management. Lately, Betty has grown distant from her mother. She certaily loves her, but given that she (Betty) is exploring many new aspects of womanhood, she wants to make sure that closeness with her mother does not handicap her objectivity in family life as a different woman. Betty is career-oriented and aspires to some power and control in the business world. In matters of love, Betty is a "softy," and she allows many men to get close to her heart, but she is also selective in terms of whom she is going to commit herself to.

Above all, Betty seeks fun and entertainment and she is very responsible about locating the situations and activities which will satisfy this desire for fun and excitement.

As the enactment sketch is presented to the clients, it is important to elicit their reactions to it and to modify it so that it becomes a credible character to enact. One helpful analogy is to consider the relationship between actor and director in a play. The script (the enactment sketch) can be acted and directed differently according to those involved. The therapist indicates that there will be a number of opportunities for the client to try out this new role both with the therapist and in outside situations. It is important that the therapist help create the atmosphere of role playing by trying the role himself or herself. After sufficient practice between therapist and client, the sequence of subsequent sessions is usually carried out in the following order:

1. The first session involves the client trying out the new role with the therapist, who enacts the part of a teacher, boss, or supervisor. These figures are somewhat important but not very personally or emotionally significant to the client. Once the client achieves proficiency in such interactions with the theapist, we assign her the task of enacting the part with an actual authority figure as between session homework.

For some clients this first experiment is carried out smoothly and easily. For others, it is a somewhat scary experience, and they may come back to the next therapy session stating that they were unable to complete the task. At times mere reassurance may prepare the client for a new attempt, but there have been cases in which it has been necessary to take the role to one lower step. For instance, since Melanie's primary conflicts were in relationship to those in authority over her, she was unable to begin her role at this level. Therefore, the therapist sent her to the shopping mall to windowshop as Betty and to interact with several salespersons while in the new role. Once she was able to successfully accomplish this task, she was able to move on and try the role with a teacher.

2. The second session is designed around an interaction with a good friend or personally significant other.

Although most clients have an initial strong reaction to this step because of their fears of being "found out," it is often experienced as a surprisingly easy task, and most clients report great satisfaction with the positive feedback they get from their good friend or significant other.

3. The third session truly deepens the personal significance of the situation, for it involves an interaction with the client's spouse or lover. In each case, the client is urged not to reveal to the other person that the client is, in fact, playing a role. It is thought that if the other person knew, the situation might become artificial and insignificant.

4. In the fourth session, the client is given the opportunity to practice with the therapist and then enact the fixed role with a parent. The client might call or write the parent while in the fixed role or have the opportunity to have a face-to-face interaction.

This seems to be one of the most difficult of steps. Even clients who are able to complete the previous tasks without much difficulty sometimes hesitate and resist this fourth task. Many clearly express that it would be impossible for them to carry out the role with the parents. Others tend to indicate, as a way of resisting, that they keep minimum contact with their parents and therefore it is not necessary to enact the role with them. In making a phone call, some clients have gone through with their role and upon hearing the voice at the other end have apologized and stated they forgot why they were calling.

5. In the fifth session, the client is invited to engage in activities that would involve ultimate values in some way. The client might try praying or meditating while in the fixed role or try to make sense out of some religious writings or church services while in the fixed role.

6. The sixth and final session is devoted to an assessment and evaluation of the fixed role enterprise. The client is invited to take back his or her own name and identity and attempt to make sense out of what has taken place over the past two weeks. The client tries to decide what if anything from the

fixed role might be useful as a part of everyday living. At this point the therapy goes back into the usual pattern of client–therapist interaction.

This final session is a very valuable one. It is important to review the process and keep the session lighthearted. This session offers the opportunity for client and therapist to have fun and review those early stages of the role playing in which both felt awkward with the new role. The review is important because many times clients experience very positive reactions from those with whom they have interacted. A specific case was Katherine's first enactment with a supervisor. She was working in a restaurant as a waitress. Something had happened in the previous shift, and Katherine was called to the boss's office and was fired. Katherine's reaction was to feel embarrassed and leave, without defending herself. As she approached the doors of the establishment to leave, she remembered the role she had been practicing. She immediately assumed the role of Trish and went back to the boss and argued her point. The boss apologized and rehired her, and for Katherine the success of this enactment provided tremendous momentum to move further with the experiment. In review of this enactment with Trish, Katherine felt so positive about the changes the role brought to her that she asked the therapist if she could keep the sketch in her purse for those times in the future she might not feel secure about her own role.

Therapy with Katherine was terminated some time after this sixth session. On a six month follow-up, Katherine stated that for awhile she was delighted knowing that she carried Trish with her all the time as they have become good friends but that later on she decided to burn the script since she no longer needed her.

CONDITIONS AND CHARACTERISTICS

We shall now turn our attention to a number of conditions and characteristics that we believe are important in designing and carrying out a fixed role therapy. Certainly the list below is not a complete list of significant concerns, but simply represents our present understanding of how this technique might best be used.

1. Fixed role therapy is presented to the client as a joint experiment. It is important to emphasize the experimental nature of the approach and for both therapist and client to participate equally in "rounding-out" the enactment sketch. It is very important for the therapist to fumble with the role, make mistakes, and let the client see this struggle in role playing. The therapist and the client take turns at playing the enactment sketch in the therapy room prior to the client's carrying it into real situations (i.e., with

teacher, supervisor, boyfriend, parent, etc.). This promotes the idea of co-investigators engaged in an egalitarian relationship (Kelly, 1973). It is important to create a playful attitude toward the therapeutic enterprise. This helps the client take on the enactment sketch with enthusiasm.

2. Fixed role therapy can best be accomplished in the context of a safe secure relationship with the therapist—one in which the pallative techniques of acceptance and support have been used. In some ways, fixed role therapy can be a very demanding and threatening therapy, and the client needs to feel understood by the therapist. It has been our experience that the most difficulty is encountered with the technique when the client does not know the therapist very well or is still too threatened by the therapeutic situation to begin to become experimental and adventuresome with the therapist. The best time to begin fixed role therapy is when the client first starts not to take herself so seriously and starts to become just a little amused by her predicament.

3. Fixed role therapy can often be fruitfully employed when an impasse has been reached in the normal course of events in a therapy. It is often introduced as something different that has not been tried up to that point in the therapy. It operates to take the burden off the client for producing material to be worked on in the therapy. It might be introduced like this. "It does not appear that we are moving very fast in the therapy just now. Why don't we try something a little different from what we have been doing up to this point?" Of course, fixed role therapy could be selected in advance as the treatment of choice, but it often comes in handy at the point of being stuck in the therapy.

4. One attractive aspect of fixed role therapy is that it does not require a great deal of introspection and self-disclosure on the part of the client. In this procedure, the therapist is likely to risk as much as the client. Instead of the usual focus on the client, the focus is on the task at hand. This procedure is task-centered and can be centered on a specific problem. The client does not have to feel so vulnerable and obligated to "produce material." Adams-Webber (1981) has also noted that fixed role therapy does not promote the kinds of dependencies that lead to a heavy transference in the relationship with the therapist. The task-centered nature of the procedure serves to focus attention on the world outside the therapy room and the enterprises in which the client can be engaged. In this way, the client does not easily become reliant on the clinician as a single source of help.

5. Fixed role therapy in many instances may be an opportunity for clients to experiment with what they already feel themselves becoming or secretly want to be. It is a way of encouraging and supporting a process of becoming by helping the person undertake some specific projects that facilitate this process. As clinicians helping to write the enactment sketch, we are concerned with the question, "What are the client's best possibilities?" The

question is not what would make the client "well." If this is the question then the whole enterprise can deteriorate into a set of behavioral prescriptions (Kelly, 1973). In writing the enactment sketch, the content of the material included is not necessarily what either the therapist or client might want the client to adopt. In this way, it is very different from a traditional behavioral therapy. The enactment sketch is simply designed to afford the client the opportunity to explore some alternatives to the usual approach to life's complexities. These alternatives are often entered into for their own sake—just to provide the experience of being able to change. In designing the enactment sketch, it is generally a good idea not to include too many different themes, perhaps one main theme with two subthemes. If the initial enactment sketch is made too complex, it is difficult for both the client and therapist to keep it clearly in mind. As the therapy progresses it is easy to expand this initial elaboration. This initial sketch should not be totally different from the client's present stance and should include "clay feet." This is to say that the sketch should not be of a perfect person. Some statement should be made about how the new character makes mistakes and the kind of mistakes that are usually made. Kelly (1955) also recommended that some aspect of the sociality corollary should be included. This usually takes the form of saying that the new character spends some time thinking about how other people see their world—the ability to take the perspective of the other.

6. In conducting a fixed role therapy, some attention needs to be paid to what the client is undertaking and how much of a risk is involved to the client and other people. A good rule of thumb is to instruct clients not to undertake anything that will put themselves or other people at undue risk. This question can be handled in more specific ways as each enactment situation is planned out. Each enactment sequence should be carefully planned. However, as with any therapy, it must be remembered that some risk is necessary if anything of worth is to be accomplished. It is always a matter of balancing the risk with the potential benefits.

7. Another attractive aspect of the fixed role therapy is that it can be employed as a therapeutic technique by therapists of different orientations. It is a flexible approach that does not require the therapist to be a "pure" practitioner of personal construct therapy.

SOME MODIFICATIONS OF THE TECHNIQUE

At this point our emphasis shifts slightly to address some of the important modifications of the original techniques that have been undertaken by therapists working in this field. Again this is a sampling of the modifications we are familiar with and view as particularly important and promising.

1. One modification to the usual procedure is to have the client write the self-characterization in the form of a letter to the therapist from the perspective of a close friend, as illustrated with Katherine. This puts it into a more lifelike context.

2. Careful attention should be paid to the selection of the name for the enactment sketch. The therapist and client should agree on one that feels just right for the client. It should be one that the client likes and that may represent, in a symbolic way, some of the main characteristics of the fixed role sketch.

3. In some cases, the enactment sketch is kept around for more than the two-week enactment period and fine-tuned by the client and therapist. This is, again, illustrated in therapy with Katherine. She kept the sketch in her purse and pulled it out and read it from time to time and used it when she needed it. In time, the fixed role lost its usefulness, and she began to like her own way of doing things better than the way the fixed role character would have approached it, so the sketch was then discarded.

4. It is often an advantage if the enactment sketch can be written from an extensive knowledge of the client and his or her construct system. Therefore, it is often very productive for the client to have completed a repertory grid test in addition to writing the self-characterization and for the counselor to know other things about the client that have been gained during the normal course of the counseling.

5. Increasingly, there is an acceptance of having the client participate in the initial writing of the fixed role sketch. There is some advantage to having the therapist put in some work him/herself in drafting the initial enactment sketch. The client, however, can be invited to make major revisions in this initial draft.

6. The use of the "opposites" of the construct poles in the enactment sketch is becoming a common and fruitful practice. It seems that much can be gained by having clients explore, in this fashion, the opposite ends of many of their constructs. This is of course in addition to having constructs in the sketch that are independent or orthogonal to the existing constructs. A good example of this procedure can be found in the work of Viney (1981).

7. While keeping the original sequence of enactments in mind, there is now more flexibility in the sequence of the enactment situations. It is still a good idea to start with a less difficult situation for the enactment and to progress to more difficult ones. As mentioned earlier, it has been our experience that the sequence with the parents is the most difficult of all the situations for most clients. This appears to be true for both younger and older clients. It is far more difficult than with spouse or friends. In addition, there appears to be a reluctance for most therapists to move to the end step in Kelly's sequence and have the client carry the enactment sketch into the

area of ultimate values like having the client pray or meditate in the fixed role. This may be a valuable step that is often omitted.

8. For the therapist in private practice with a number of clients in fixed roles, it appears to be adequate for there to be brief 10 or 15 minute check-ins or follow-ups on a daily or every other day basis between regular length sessions. These sessions usually have a specific focus concerning the particular enactment sequence assigned for that day. Another tactic to use, in the context of a private practice, is to have the client think about the role and to enact it only on the day before the next session so that it is fresh when she or he comes in for the therapy hour.

9. The use of fixed role therapy with a group was originally formulated by Kelly (1955) using only three or four clients. The nature of this procedure was described by Epting (1984) and is related to similar innovations in couples counseling (Kremsdorf, 1985) and family therapy (Procter, 1981, 1985). In all of these procedures, it is necessary for other people to be aware of the nature of the role playing as it is initiated. The knowledge does not seem to diminish the effect of the role playing; in fact, there is some attention given to actually coaching others to become effective supports of the enactment as it proceeds. Even with individual clients, it can be beneficial, in some cases, for the client to reveal the nature of the role he or she is attempting to enact in order to get others to assist in role maintenance. Epting (1984) also reports the use of fixed role therapy in a men's personal growth group in which the group members construct roles for each other before enacting them.

10. The development of *multiple role therapy* by Epting and Suchman as reported by Epting (1984) is a direct extension of fixed role therapy. This therapy was undertaken in multiple therapy (two therapists with one client). When the client would get stuck in a particular dilemma, the therapists and client would invent a character who had a particular way of handling the problem. When other problems were encountered, new characters were invented and the client was invited, along with the therapists, to role play the new character who had a particular way of dealing with the problem. Each character had a different name so that when an old problem was reencountered by the client, the character designed for that problem could again be conjured up. By the end of some sessions the therapy room was almost completely filled by these extra characters. Of course, such therapy also requires that time be spent integrating the lessons learned during these multiple role enactments.

11. In another procedure we developed for groups, each member exchanges a brief self-characterization with an assigned partner. Partners are then instructed to write another paragraph that completes the description they have been given, in effect completing a somewhat elaborated enactment sketch for the partner. The two people then take turns discussing the

nature of the enactment sketches that have been created. If the sketches seem plausible and interesting, group members can then be encouraged to experiment with role playing them between sessions.

CONCLUSION

It is our hope that the comments we have made and issues we have raised will excite the creative therapeutic imagination of those who plan to use this technique. Like all other aspects of construct therapy, the work in fixed role therapy is as much an invitation to make something out of it as it is an established technique to be acquired. We also hope that this exploration of fixed role therapy will stimulate the further investigation of the therapy, which has been initiated by Bonarius (1970), Skene (1973), and Viney (1981) using clinical methods and by Karst and Trexler (1970) and Lira, Nay, McCullough, & Etkin (1975) using experimental methods.

REFERENCES

Adams-Webber, J. R. (1981). Fixed role therapy. In R. Corsini (Ed.), *Handbook of innovative psychotherapies* (pp. 333–343). New York: John Wiley & Sons.

Bonarius, J. C. J. (1970). Fixed role therapy: A double paradox. *British Journal of Medical Psychology, 43*, 213–219.

Epting, F. R. (1984). *Personal construct counseling and psychotherapy* (pp. 159–186). Chichester & New York: John Wiley & Sons.

Karst, T. O., & Trexler, L. D. (1970). Initial study using fixed role and rational-emotive therapy in treating speaking anxiety. *Journal of Consulting and Clinical Psychology, 34*, 360–366.

Kelly, G. A. (1955). *The psychology of personal constructs (Vols. 1 & 2)*. New York: W. W. Norton.

Kelly, G. A. (1973). Fixed role therapy. In R. M. Jerjevich (Ed.), *Direct psychotherapy: 28 American originals* (pp. 394–422). Coral Gables, FL: University of Miami Press.

Kremsdorf, R. (1985). An extension of fixed-role therapy with a couple. In F. Epting & A. W. Landfield (Eds.), *Anticipating personal construct psychology* (pp. 216–224). Lincoln, NE, & London: University of Nebraska Press.

Lira, F. T., Nay, W. R., McCullough, J. P., & Etkin, W. (1975). Relative effects of modeling and role playing in the treatment of avoidance behaviors. *Journal of Consulting and Clinical Psychology, 43*, 608–618.

Procter, H. (1981). Family construct psychology: An approach to understanding and treating families. In S. Walrond-Skinner (Ed.), *Developments in family therapy* (pp. 350–366). London: Routledge & Kegan Paul.

Procter, H. (1985). A construct approach to family therapy and systems intervention. In E. Button (Ed.), *Personal construct theory and mental health* (pp. 327–350). Cambridge, MA: Brookline Books.

Skene, R. A. (1973). Construct shift in the treatment of a case of homosexuality. *British Journal of Medical Psychology, 46,* 287–292.

Viney, L. L. (1981). Experimenting with experience: A psychotherapeutic case study. *Psychotherapy: Theory, Research and Practice, 18,* 271–278.

17
Stuttering to Fluency via Reconstruing

Fay Fransella

FROM BEHAVIOR THERAPIST TO PERSONAL CONSTRUCT THERAPIST

All Behavior is an Experiment

> Let me suggest only that when psychology, that harlequin who turns out to be ourselves, rolls over it may realize that, while intellectualization is the method of man the incipient philosopher, behaviour is the method of man the scientist. The philosopher asks questions by disengaging from facts; the scientist inquires by confronting himself with events of his own creation (Kelly, 1970, p. 269).

One of Kelly's most important contributions to our inquiries into the complexities and mysteries of each other was to disengage us from the millstone of behavior having to be the "thing" to be studied by means of experimentation (the dependent variable). In his model of the person-as-scientist, behavior becomes that very experimentation by means of which we, as individuals, come to get our hooks into that world of events "out there" (the independent variable).

In addition to revolutionizing the way I thought about people, Kelly freed me from the prison I had created for myself by continuing to construe research in the way I had been taught. That was, by conducting "good" experiments, you could stick all your hard-sought findings together until, ultimately, you had a "true" picture of the world—or, in the present case, stuttering. He argued that this accumulating of golden nuggets of truth (or accumulative fragmentalism as he called it) was of no use to psychologists.

Instead, he took his model of science directly from his philosophical statement of constructive alternativism. In this, we accept that there is no "truth" in that reality "out there" that we can lay our hands on (not yet at any rate). Every hypothesis we, as professional or personal scientists, put to the test is nothing more than our best guess at the moment. We are well aware that something better will turn up to explain events more fully (see Kelly, 1969).

I now started looking at problems from a new perspective. If all behavior may be looked at as if it is an experiment, then certain behaviors become not "maladaptive," or "symptoms" but questions put to nature. The personal construct inquirer's question thus becomes "what experiment is that person conducting that makes him or her go on behaving in a way that is clearly undesirable from all points of view?" Asking of this question led me to formulate a theoretical model for understanding someone who stutters. After the theory came an approach to helping individuals change their way of communicating—from stuttering to fluency.

Hinkle's Theory of Implications and Methods of Measurement

One year after I was freed from the delusion of accumulative fragmentalism, I was sent Hinkle's doctoral thesis (1965). His extension of Kelly's theory of personal constructs by looking at their implications was quickly incorporated into the rudimentary theory I was developing, but his methods of measurement were of even greater value—two in particular. One was his grid for looking at the implications of constructs and the other was a method for eliciting the more abstract, value-laden, constructs (a method now called "laddering"). Both of these will be detailed in the next section.

PERSONAL CONSTRUCT THEORY OF STUTTERING

Theory

The theory that eventually evolved to account for why some people continue to communicate by stuttering was based on the choice corollary. For Kelly, this means we choose that pole of construct that we feel is likely to lead to the greater elaboration of our construing system. The principle of elaborative choice both limits the choices available—since it can only be between one or the other pole of the constructs we have erected—and yet gives us freedom to choose which pole will give us the greater possibility for further definition and elaboration of our construing system.

Hinkle (1965) elaborated this by saying "a person always chooses in that direction which he anticipates will increase the total meaning and significance of his life. Stated in the defensive form, a person chooses so as to avoid the anxiety of chaos and the despair of absolute certainty" (p. 21).

Following on from this I hypothesized that a person stutters because it is in this way that he can anticipate the greatest number of events; it is by behaving in this way that life is most meaningful to him. By stuttering he is able to anticipate the reactions of others and his own reactions to them. In other words, he can play a role in relation to others by communicating in that way. Most people who stutter have a few communication situations in which they can talk fluently—often with those they know well, children, animals, and various other groups according to individual idiosyncracies. But, to the rest of the world, the person who stutters communicates by stuttering. That other, so desirable world of fluency is unavailable. It has so little meaning as to be worse than useless. It is worse than useless because the person who stutters knows it is there and that however hard he struggles, he cannot attain it. Many, when asked to really imagine what it would be like if they were fluent tomorrow, become overwhelmed with anxiety—it is virtually unconstruable.

Being "a stutterer" is obviously more complex than one single construct. But, as Hinkle says, the meaning of a construct is defined in terms of what it implies and what is implied by it. It was therefore hypothesized that the network of implications centred around being "a stutterer" would be considerably more complex and elaborate compared with that relating to being "a fluent person." It was also hypothesized that being "a stutterer" was, itself, a core role construct.

I would argue that it is impossible for any of us to change certain ways of behaving without a great struggle if we have incorporated them into our core role construing. This applies particularly to the behavior of stuttering if the person has communicated in this way since the onset of speech. But it has been found to apply to those who want to change from anorexic thinness to "being well-covered" (Button, 1985) and used as a basic concept to help those move from obesity to slimness, alcoholism to sobriety, heavy smoking to nonsmoking.

Research into the Process of Change

In an earlier project (Fransella, 1972), 20 people with life-long stuttering were given psychological treatment along personal construct theory lines—much as described in the discussion of Peter to follow. Meaningfulness of being a stutterer or a fluent speaker was measured by the number of implications in bipolar implications grids. These were administered several times during therapy focusing both on being a stutterer and being a fluent person. It was found that as fluency increased so did the number of implications (meaningfulness) to do with being a fluent person along with a decrease in the number to do with being a stutterer.

THERAPEUTIC STRATEGIES

Taking the view that those who continue to stutter do so because this is the way in which the world is best defined, best predicted, and, therefore, best understood, it was clear that the path forward would be to make the desired world of fluency more defined, more predictable, and thereby better understood. The goal must first be to erect structure about fluency where there was little or none before. The next step is to build a causeway across which the client might wander from time to time to see whether or not he/ she liked what was on the other side. After structure has been erected and a causeway built, the person can choose to move across and remain on the fluent side. This case study focuses on a few aspects of change in the construing of Peter that enabled him to make that crossing and why, over nearly twenty years, he has sometimes made the journey back again to stuttering.

CLIENT

It is now nearly 20 years since Peter and I had our first sessions together. During that time he has done well in his job as a scientist, has had his ups-and-downs with regard to speech—many more ups than downs—and has worked closely with a local speech therapist, becoming an adviser and mentor to many others who stutter.

He was one of the sample of 20 people who stutter included in my 1972 research and the person I tape-recorded throughout all 82 sessions spanning three years. He had many more sessions than anyone else in the sample, and only one other person was assessed on five occasions. The research report contained an account of the therapeutic process as an appendix. That therapeutic process now becomes the focus in this chapter.

Peter is, of course, not his real name, nor is it the name he was called in the research report. Just as then, so now, the verbatim accounts are selected and sometimes distorted to eliminate the possibility of identification. The aim is to give a feel for the personal construct approach adopted at that time and elaborated over the years to help those who stutter.

CONTROLLED ELABORATION

Controlled elaboration is one of the four ways Kelly describes whereby a person may come to reconstrue her world. The others are contrast reconstruction, in which the person successively slots herself first at one end of a construct and then at the other; the formation of new constructs; and the reduction of constructs to impermeability. Kelly (1955) describes controlled elaboration as:

> a way of bringing about reconstruction through clarification. This amounts to a reorganization of the hierarchical system of one's constructs, but not essential revision of the constructs themselves. The client is helped to work through his construct system experimentally by verbal as well as by other behavioral actions. He deals essentially with the subordination–superordination features of his system. He brings his constructs into line with his system as a whole. Essentially he works on the internal consistency of his system rather than attempting to make outright replacements of constructs (p. 938).

In using controlled elaboration as the basic route to change that Peter and I evolved, it would be wrong to assume that I see this as *the* way to work with people who stutter. I do not. Peter, in fact, also slot-rattled, formed new constructs, and reduced some existing ones to impermeability. Controlled elaboration was the main thrust of our endeavors. It proved a useful approach with Peter as with many others who stutter.

DATA COLLECTION

In personal construct therapy, no active steps can be taken to help a client change until the therapist has clearly worked out some hypotheses as to why the client is "stuck." It is vitally important to have an idea of the implications for the client of whatever it is that you are about to ask him to undertake.

One of the main tools I used then and almost without exception use to this day, is Hinkle's technique of "laddering." To do this you first have to elicit personal constructs from the client. This is usually done by asking the client to compare and contrast figures from his or her life. However, in Peter's case I asked him to look at two photographs of strange men together with a card on which was written "as others see me when I am not stuttering." I then asked him to state whether he saw any important way in which two of these three people were alike, and thereby different from the third. When that similarity was named, he was asked to name the opposite of that quality. His responses to a series of these "triads" constituted his nonstuttering or "fluency" grid. The procedure was repeated using the same photographs, but paired with a third card on which was written "as others see me when I am stuttering." Peter's responses to this series constituted his "stuttering" grid (for details, see Fransella & Bannister, 1977).

Some of these elicited constructs are then "laddered." This basically involves the asking of "why" a person says he or she prefers to be described by one pole of a construct rather than the other. The first ladder undertaken with Peter was from the construct suave versus not suave.

FAY (F): Which would you prefer to be?

PETER (P): Suave.

F: Why would you prefer to be a suave person rather than not suave?

P: May I just say that the word suave tends to mean a person who is well dressed and relaxed and gentlemanly.

F: Alright.

P: I don't know if I necessarily prefer it, I think that is just the way I am seen.

F: Alright. Which would you prefer to be seen as, more or less suave?

P: Can't win can you! (laughs). Because a suave person is respected and looked up to.

F: As opposed to?

P: Someone who doesn't matter.

F: Last time we talked about this we decided it wasn't a silly question to ask why do you want to be respected and looked up to?

P: Its the case whenever you meet anybody new, say if you go into a restaurant or shop you are treated courteously, people don't ignore you or are not rude to you.

At the end Peter has become more concrete rather than more abstract. He has given examples of what it means to be respected, just as he did with suave in the first instance. He has done what Landfield (1971) calls "pyramiding." Technically, therefore, there is only one step up this ladder from suave and that is respected and looked up to. The number of constructs elicited and laddered from Peter on the five test occasions over the therapy period are given in Table 17.1. At the start of therapy, Peter was unable to produce any constructs at all to do with himself as a fluent person. It was a meaningless task for him.

Table 17.1 Numbers of constructs elicited and laddered from Peter on five occasions in both "stutterer" and "nonstutterer" contexts

Constructs	Occasion				
	1	2	3	4	5
To do with being a stutterer	12	13	10	7	5
To do with being a nonstutterer	0	13	10	12	15

Hinkle's implications grid was modified so that both poles of each construct could be considered. Since the theory was concerned with moving from one pole of constructs or subsystem of constructs to the other, it was important to know what the opposite poles were about. The task involves writing each construct on a card and laying these cards out in front of the client. He/she is then presented with one pole of a construct at a time and asked: "If all you know about someone is that they are (for instance) suave, what, from all these characteristics on these cards, would you expect to find in a suave person?" Most people become quite adept at reeling off the numbers of the constructs implied by the construct pole. (This procedure is detailed in Fransella & Bannister, 1977.) The numbers of implications Peter had in his grids over the five test occasions are given in Table 17.2. If integration is measured by the numbers of implications within each grid, then not only did Peter increase the differentiation of his construing of being a nonstutterer from start to finish (number of constructs, Table 17.1) but also the integration of that construing subsystem. The converse was true for being a stutterer. The marked change in both at occasion 3 plus the marked increase in disfluencies will be discussed later.

I asked Peter, as I do with most clients, for a self-characterization (Kelly, 1955) at the first session. This character sketch is written in the third person as if by a friend who knows the client probably better than anyone can ever know him and who is very sympathetic towards him. Such self characterizations can be written by the client at various stages in the course of therapy. Sometimes they become the basis of the therapy itself (e.g., Fransella, 1981). For Peter they formed part of the data on which the initial hypotheses about his construing of himself and his speech were based. But they were not central to my work with Peter and so will not be discussed here.

Table 17.2. Numbers of implications and numbers in relation to constructs, in bipolar implications grids for Peter on five occasions in "stutterer" and "nonstutterer" contexts, together with speech disfluencies

Constructs	Occasion				
	1	2	3	4	5
To do with being a stutterer:	173	190	152	59	8
implications/constructs	14	15	15	8	2
To do with being a nonstutterrer:	0	219	127	133	319
implications/constructs	0	17	13	11	21
Speech disfluencies per 100 words	39	28	71	18	11

PROCESS OF CHANGE

The goal is to build a causeway from stuttering to fluency so as to allow the person to exercise choice for the first time. But, as everyone who is involved in helping others change knows, some seem to be frustratingly reluctant to move across that causeway. Some need it to be well above the water even with the highest tides, while others are prepared to run across the gap as the tide goes out, nipping back just as the tide comes in again—they may even tolerate getting their psychological feet wet. Not only do therapists have to help the client build that causeway, they also have to diagnose what is going to prevent the client's movement. Within the context of controlled elaboration, aspects of Peter's construing associated with resistance to change are illustrated, particularly regnancy, implicative dilemmas, and threat. As will be shown, none of these things are mutually exclusive, they are just different ways of looking at certain events. An example is also given of how the therapist can fail to facilitate change in the client due to lack of knowledge and experience.

But the exciting optimism of constructive alternativism in personal construct theory is that we *can* change. The person who stutters *can* come to construe himself as a fluent person along with speaking more fluently. And he comes to speak more fluently by elaborating those occasions in which he does, indeed, speak fluently.

Regnancy

All too often with those who stutter, many choices seem to be set in cement. The cement may take the form of regnant constructs. A regnant construct is a kind of superordinate construct which assigns each of its elements to a category on an all-or-none basis, as in classical logic. It tends to be nonabstractive.

Kelly (1955) talks of the importance of this type of construing as follows:

> Since the psychology of personal constructs lays great stress upon the intepretation of the *regnancy* [my italics] of the constructs under which acts may be performed, rather than upon the mere acts themselves, and since it lays great stress upon *personal* constructs rather than *formalistic* constructs, it does demand of the psychologist that he have an acceptance of other persons. One might even say that the psychology of personal constructs is, among other things, a psychology of acceptance. (p. 373)

As a personal construct therapist I accepted the way Peter construed his world even though it was sometimes quite difficult to believe at first that he was not kidding me.

One such case was the first appearance of the regnant construct that was to stay with us through all our sessions. Peter had been unable to produce any constructs at all to do with himself as a nonstutterer on the first elicitation and laddering occasion. But there were 13 the second time round, one of which was worthy of respect versus common. This was significantly related to several poles of other constructs in the impgrid (occasion 2).

Significantly related to worthy of respect	Significantly related to common
Like me	Ordinary
Gentle	Likely to be refused
Respected	Does not have status
More chance of enjoying life to the full	Doesn't matter
	Not like me
Less likely to be refused	Not respected
Relaxed	Aggressive
Fluent speakers	Stutterers

Most importantly, this regnant construct was tied up with being or not being a stutterer. When Peter (and often other people who stutter) saw himself as a stutterer he was, at that same moment, saying he was not worthy of respect, or, in his terms, common. Only fluent people are worthy of respect. But he could not yet see himself as a fluent person. He was trapped by his own construing. It was a massive implicative dilemma.

We had defined our main goals. In the struggle to develop some structure to do with being a fluent person and building a causeway, we would also have to untie the regnant knot. The following exchange took place soon after these goals were formulated. It is a prime example of what I construe controlled elaboration to be.

F: You were going to do some specific tasks, go into shops.

P: Unfortunately, I have only been able to record one.

F: What happened? What was the situation?

P: I went into a sweet shop and said "I'll have a packet of Rowntree fruit pastilles please" (both laugh) . . . .

F: Describe the scene to me.

P: I went into the shop just outside the front door here, and the girl behind the counter looked at me in a sort of questioning way. So I said "can I have a packet of Rowntree's fruit pastilles please." So she said "yes," reached them from the shelf and said "sixpence please" and so I gave her my sixpence and said "thank you" and came out.

F: Did you predict you'd say it fluently?

P: Yes, I did, yes.

Controlled elaboration of the world of fluency involves focusing on those situations in which the client has been predictably fluent. A prediction means we have, at some level of awareness, construed the situation in a certain way. The verbalization of that construing helps develop the new structure.

F: Can you think what made you able to predict?

P: In the first place, fruit pastilles are quite an easy thing to ask for—um—they are not what I shall call a *status-loaded* object—yes.

F: You'll have to elaborate on that I'm afraid, as I don't quite understand.

P: Yes, I've been thinking about the reason why there are some things I find it difficult to ask for and some things I find easy and I have decided that my mind works in this sort of odd way. It attaches to the objects being asked for a certain status; and this status is to do with the showing of my understanding of the object I'm asking for. So, for example, I went into a shop on Saturday to get some wood screws. Now, wood screws come by sizes to which a number is given. To the size also by length and also by heads; there are different shaped heads. So there are three things which one must know about wood screws to be able to ask for them directly. Um—and so if I go into a shop and ask for number ten wood screws, counter sunk heads, half inch long, then that shows I know what I'm talking about in wood screws. If I say I want wood screws, that shows I don't know what I'm talking about. So—um—odd isn't it really! So, in knowing all about wood screws and showing I know what I want, I'm able to *command some respect*. Do you know what I mean? Does it make some sort of sense to you? . . .

F: I'm a bit foxed at the moment I must confess. Do you want to be respected as a man who knows about wood screws?

P: No (laughs). I think that it is probably the case of anything to be respected for—I want to be respected for *anything*.

Peter appeared to see himself as the instigator of eliciting respect rather than being worthy of respect as an individual in his own right. The snag was it turned out that whenever he set up an experiment geared to eliciting respect from the other, he was most likely to stutter.

P: Um—I like the feeling of saying things which are status-loaded say, but at the same time I feel that I should be *honest* about it. That's interesting isn't it? I feel I like doing it but I feel I shouldn't.

It is only when he feels that he can command "genuine" respect that he can be fluent—unless, of course, the situation/item has no status value.

A few sessions later, Peter and I, as fellow scientists, designed his next behavioral assignment. He was to role play being someone who was ignorant about a product to test his prediction that people who are not experts or knowledgeable on a subject would not be respected. But at the start of the next session he pointed out that that was a useless experiment.

P: What I think is an important aspect of this is that if I went in playing a part I would in fact be acting a role and if you remember, I think we found out some time ago that stammerers could act roles other than themselves and be fluent. So on the basis of this I did not deliberately attempt to do this experiment.

Peter then went on to give an account of an experiment he designed himself, which was so clearly better than the one he had designed with his therapist.

P: I did have one situation last week when I was fluent which is an interesting situation because I had some very strange feelings inside me (laughter).

F: What was the situation?

P: Yes, it sounds odd. I went into this shop and I wanted to buy something. I went in and there was a chap serving behind the counter and I imagine that he was the owner of the shop. Um—I said—um—"Do you mind if I just look round, I want some sweets, let's see what you've got." Which was quite a fair sentence!

F: That was fluent?

P: Yes, quite fluent. So he said, "yes, certainly," or something like and—er—whilst I was looking around he said "Oh, shocking day it's been" and I said "yes, it certainly has, it makes one wonder where the summer has gone" or something like that. The usual sort of thing one says. And I decided on the sweets that I'd like to have and that was that. The strange thing and the strange feelings were this—as soon as he started to talk I felt that he was a chap who *respected* me (laugh), he sort of—and to my mind he showed that he respected me by the manner in which he talked to me and the way in which he smiled and was as pleasant as he could be and my response to this was almost *a feeling of trying to put him at his ease*. Now, this is a thing I thought was very odd . . . . I felt throughout the entire conversation that I had to be more and more pleasant to him so that I could put him more and more at his ease. How about that! This is a rather odd thing really I thought, because surely a normal person's reaction, if its obvious that somebody respects you, is one of "Oh, well, that's OK, I accept your respect"; whereas I felt a little uncomfortable I suppose in a way, about this chap respecting me and I tried hard to put him at his ease and to try and *make us equal*.

Here was a situation in which he felt he *was* respected but had done nothing to elicit it. Peter came back to his feelings of unease at the end of the session:

P: I think the main thing is surprising is my attitude. My feeling that I had to even things out.

This encounter had provided him with evidence with which he was unable to deal. He saw himself as being respected as a person rather than as a result of his efforts. But, he was a stutterer and therefore, by definition, not worthy of respect. Here, at last, was evidence of movement. He had begun to question the validity of his regnant construct. This was by no means the only evidence. For instance, just after completing the "nonstutterer" grid he said:

P: I am rather afraid the "me" is not as nice as I would like to think it was; my wife has complained that I am much more critical now.

Threat

Peter continued to improve steadily in his speech between the first and second impgrid sessions. The "stutterer" grids had remained much the same as far as integration and differentiation were concerned; whereas the "nonstutterer" grids had developed vastly, from nothing. Such psychological development can have its penalties, one of which is threat. Peter saw himself first and foremost as a stutterer and therefore not respect-worthy. Faced with what he construed as genuine respect, he could have become aware of the imminent comprehensive change that was taking place in his core role construing. He was threatened by this first glimpse of becoming a fluent person rather than being a stutterer.

Over the next 4 weeks he "went back very badly indeed" as he put it. But we struggled to deal with the threats and to focus on the positive aspects of relapse. He made steady improvement until just before it was time to repeat the impgrids (occasion 3). The week before we started the eliciting and laddering again he reported "my best week ever."

Preverbal Construing: A Voice from the Past

Peter's regnant construct dictated that stutterers were not worthy of respect, only fluent people were. The source of this implicative dilemma seemed highly likely to be in the realm of preverbal construing. It had, in fact, crept into cognitive awareness quite early on. He had suddenly remembered an incident from his childhood which involved his being in a sweet shop (surprising the themes that occur in the examples clients provide) with the squire's son. The motherly shopkeeper patted the squire's son on the head and asked "What would you like today Master John?" and turned to child Peter saying "And what do you want?" But we somehow did not make a great deal of headway with this at the time.

We had reached our twenty-first meeting together, and he reported that he had been lazy in the past:

P: I've a confession to make—probably accounts for my bad speech now! Off we go. I feel that in the past I probably should have taken a more active interest in trying to get rid of my stammer than I have. I feel that I should have been—no, I feel that I'm capable of thinking about the situation during the week and trying to work out some new ideas—and in general help you along as much as possible—and I've been a bit on the lazy side. So, over Christmas, I thought "enough of this laziness" and my wife got on at me as well . . . . I could easily say to myself driving home from work "Right, tonight I'm going to sit down and sort out my stammer," but when it came to the time then I didn't feel like it and I think that this could well be the fact that probably somewhere subconsciously I didn't want to get rid of it because it was—you know—that there was something in the fluent world that I was afraid of.

The next three sessions were largely devoted to eliciting and laddering constructs for the third impgrids. To our mutual interest we found that the vast majority of the constructs in the "nonstutterer" grid were to do with liking and caring. At one point we discussed his feeling of needing to be liked—a close cousin to needing to be respected. He said: "All people have to handle the situation of being disliked except a stammerer." "I cannot bear the thought of people not liking me." The subsequent analysis of the impgrid spelt out the issue in statistical terms.

After the discussion about being liked, Peter reported having had a nightmare:

P: . . . of unusual intensity reminiscent of those suffered in childhood, so you know, I have not had such a bad nightmare as this for a long long long long long time—and afterwards—that is to say, when I woke—it seemed that if I tried to remember a long line suggested by the nightmare I immediately came across a fear block. So what I mean by that was it seemed as soon as I woke up I felt "this nightmare is symbolic"—and feel that—I felt at the time that if I tried to I could analyze what the symbols meant and probably find what the event was in my childhood that caused me stammer—but I couldn't do this.

F: You tried?

P: I tried—but immediately I started to become extremely frightened. I—my head swam and I felt extremely ill—I felt—I thought "I can't stand this—if I try to find out I'll go mad" . . . . I've written down here "I remember a day when for something I'd done, nobody liked me." I know I was about 4 years old and there were two girl evacuees with us because we lived on a farm. I was extremely fond of one of these girls . . . .

F: Has the dream brought any other memories back to you?

P: Yes, I can see myself standing in our sitting-room screaming and stamping and jumping up and down with rage and my parents and the two evacuees sort of looking at me and sort of laughing.

If I had known then what I know now, I would have viewed this as preverbal construing and explored it in much greater depth. Peter had placed before us an experience, in dream form, that could well have helped him find the bases of his need for respect, status, and, at a more subordinate level, the desperate need to be liked. At face value he was describing a situation in which he had received massive invalidation—instead of returning his "extreme fondness" for her, the evacuee is dreamed of as laughing at him. Now I would have used gestalt methods of analyzing dreams. I would have asked him to recount as much of the dream as he could remember as if it were taking place in the present. He would have told the dream from various perspectives—perhaps first as mother and father and then, in turn, the evacuee whom he did not like, himself, and the evacuee he was extremely fond of. But that is not what happened. I do not think I had heard of gestalt therapy 19 years ago, and, even if I had, I doubt if I would have had the therapeutic confidence to embark on such an emotionally demanding exercise. If we had worked on this I seriously doubt that we would have needed to spend another 56 sessions together.

It is worth noting that the third "nonstutterer" impgrid was being completed during these two to three sessions and that the number of constructs is reduced, the number of implications nearly halved, and his speech was extremely bad. That area of preverbal construing gave rise to threat of overwhelming proportions as Peter started to reconstrue himself.

End in Sight

In actual fact we plodded on elaborating the network of construing the self as a fluent person while also examining the validity of the regnancy construing of being worthy of respect. It was slow work but we did make progress.

By our 76th session, Peter was seeing himself about to become fluent—except for these annoying sporadic stutters—and so as worthy of respect. But how could that be? The implicative dilemma was still there, although weakening against the invalidating evidence that was piling up. He was a person who had a degree in science and was climbing the career ladder in a job worthy of his status. His fluency now far outweighed his stuttering. As he elaborated his construing of his alternate self—a fluent person—he became more and more concerned about speaking. He was now focusing on more subordinate issues such as how he would sound, whether his accent would be correct, whether he would be able to get the words out quickly enough. He kept asking why he still stuttered occasionally. He thought the situations were still to do with "this status-loaded thing," that same old underlying theme of "being worthy of respect" and "being liked." I absolutely agreed with him, that regnant knot had not been wholly untied. But I found it more useful to interpret it in terms of the professional construct hostility. If he did not stutter sporadically, he would have nothing to stop him from construing himself as a fluent person. He finally subsumed it all under the construct articulate. He had begun to wonder "whether I'm going to be happy about people's reaction to me being so clever and so articulate."

P: I'm going to become more and more articulate and therefore more and more respected because my true intelligence—my true ability—is going to become more and more apparent—well now I think—that's interesting—I think that perhaps what's happened . . . is not a complete removal of this respect thing—a complete cure of this respect thing—but just that I have accepted my new position in life—and I wonder if now—with absolute fluency and being able to become quite articulate, my position's going to rise even more. Now, what's happened is that I'm not sure about people's reaction to me in this new position. So I wonder if perhaps there is still something in this respect line that has not been cured but has been side-stepped, because rather than digging it out by its roots and chopping all the roots and throwing it away—we put weed-killer on it and it's shrivelled away or it's been accepted but the roots are still there . . . . I cannot feel that I am anything but—I cannot feel myself as being a superior educated person . . . . What I am worried about is that just in talking naturally but articulately—even to other people—supposing I'm talking to A, talking away, and B happens to be listening. The thing which worries me is I think I'll exaggerate it a bit to make it very nonsensical and very obvious—that I suppose, yes, that B is going to be jealous or in fact envious—or at least B is going to say to himself "Ah, that chap talks very well—he's using jolly good words—the correct words in the correct context—yes—he talks jolly well—*what right has he got to be talking so well—he's only a farmer's son.*"

By the 80th session Peter was reporting that "the thing that surprises me is that in the work situation there is just nothing left of that (stuttering) at all—it's just in this social world situation that I have any trouble." It was becoming more and more focused. It now boiled down to "How do you speak to the squire as an equal?"

We decided to tackle what seemed to be a last hurdle by extending his everyday knowledge of events so that he would have something to talk about. For he thought that idle chatter was beneath him, that one should only talk about things on which one was an expert. It was news to him that most people are quite prepared to indulge in social chit-chat with no other goal. He managed to build up a repertoire of topics by reading newspapers, watching selected television programs, and came to find that it was even possible to become knowledgeable about current affairs—and found that it was quite interesting.

In the end, Peter was now able to hold his own in virtually all situations without having to stutter. The validity of the regnant construct to do with respect had been tested and found wanting. He had worked out that he was, in his own right, someone who people respected for certain things, that he was worthy of respect for certain things, that he was a likeable person, but that there were always people around who did not like one, and that was something that had to be dealt with.

However, that this new world in which he had decided to live was not familiar enough to be taken for granted was summed up in the last tape made. He had presented a paper at a conference—much to his delight:

P: A paper was presented by somebody else which I was very interested in— and I buttonholed him afterwards—and asked a few points and I did it really without thinking. And I afterwards realized that I just hadn't stammered at all. It had come so naturally to go up to a stranger and sort of catch hold of his arm so that he would turn round and say "I enjoyed your paper, there are one or two things I wanted . . . "you know.

F: This must have seemed very important to you.

P: I think it definitely was. I definitely didn't realize I was doing it. I didn't realize the *enormity* of what I was doing when I did it. But I realized it afterwards. And it's interesting really, because there I was talking away fluently—and after being there a couple of days the enormity of it was just too much for me and I went into a restaurant and asked for a cup of coffee—I just had to stammer a little!

Relapse

Much that clinicians construe as relapse can usefully be described in terms of threat. Some clients do so well in the first few sessions that the therapist can easily be seduced into thinking they have really done a wonderful job. But all too often this is not the case. Peter was a good example of how a client suddenly becomes aware of the implications of the great strides toward the desired state that he is taking and finds he has no alternative but to go back to the undesired, but known, position. The goal is not yet clearly enough elaborated; to move there would be to experience a comprehensive reduction in the meaningfulness of being oneself. To relapse in the face of this threat is, as is all behavior from a personal construct perspective, a perfectly reasonable thing to do. One can rest there while defining more clearly what that future self is going to be. Relapse allows time for consolidation.

Peter also showed how relapse can be seen in terms of hostility. Most clients at some time or other extort evidence to prove that they have not changed as much as the therapist thinks they have.

Kelly says that when you see hostility you should look for the guilt. With Peter that was not hard to find. He was, in his terms, a stutterer. Increasingly he became dislodged from that core role by finding himself being fluent. He crosses the causeway he has built to fluency when the tide goes out but has to make sure he gets back again before the tide comes in again in case he is left stranded away from his home, his stuttering.

Six months after our last session, Peter rang to make another appointment. He was stuttering badly again. The context in which the relapse occurred was a realization that he was becoming someone he did not like— someone aggressive. He had been experimenting with his new-found "forceful" self to find out its limits, much as adolescents do. He felt that the only way to be fluent was to be ultraforceful. He found himself being aggressive with subordinates. This relapse was probably sparked off by the threat or awareness of the comprehensive change in his core construing if he were, indeed, to construe himself as aggressive. We resumed therapy for a few more sessions to help him moderate his forcefulness, a strategy that met with some success. Peter soon regained his fluency, which he was able to experience in a nonaggressive way.

Some 7 years after the cessation of his sessions with me, I heard by chance that he had joined a 4-week intensive course for stutterers where the technique of prolonged speech is used. He had relapsed once more. What most struck the therapists was the speed with which Peter learned to apply the speech techniques and his subsequent fluency. In a report on his progress, they noted, "It was as if he had learned all he needed to know about his construing and just wanted a helping hand with his speech." The report went on to say that "he was an excellent group member, helping and encouraging those who were experiencing problems with the technique. When he completed the course, his speech sounded very naturally fluent and not as if he was straining to use the technique." At the end of this course he rang me and invited me to lunch to show off his fluency. He was very pleased with what he had accomplished.

One of the issues discussed in my 1972 research was that the personal construct approach to the treatment of stuttering goes far beyond the actual elimination or reduction in speech disfluencies. For it is only after these have been reduced that the elaboration of being a fluent person can be tested out. It therefore seemed reasonable to predict that those who had been able to reduce their disfluencies and who had been able to reconstrue themselves as fluent people should be less prone to relapse. This relapse hypothesis was put to the test in the context of a speech therapy program (Evesham & Fransella, 1985).

After being randomly assigned to "behavioral" or "personal construct" groups, all were trained in speech techniques that result in virtually total fluency (Evesham & Huddleston, 1983). After fluency was established, all had group work and speech assignments; those for the "behavioral" groups were designed to encourage generalization of the fluency, and those for the "personal construct" groups designed to help them reconstrue themselves as fluent people. Follow-up showed that the "personal construct" clients had significantly less relapse than the "behavioral" clients. What has not yet been examined is whether the extent to which the degree of integration as well as differentiation of the construing of the fluent self is related to relapse. The theory argues, of course, that it should be.

THE FUTURE

Who can say what that holds? For Peter there has been 20 years in which his speech has sometimes been important and sometimes not. Is this cycle at an end for him? Who knows? I do know that he is actively involved in helping others who stutter reconstrue themselves.

I have little doubt that he and I were able to bring about some fairly basic reconstruing in how he viewed himself and believe that reconstruing helped him move toward being the master rather than the slave of his stuttering. I think we both learned from the experience. In Kelly's terms we lived—if, indeed, "life is a way of using the present to link the future with the past in some original fashion" (Kelly, 1980, p. 28).

REFERENCES

Button, E. J. (1985). Eating disorders: A quest for control? In E. J. Button (Ed.), *Personal construct theory and mental health* (pp. 153–168). London: Croom Helm.
Evesham, M., & Fransella, F. (1985). Stuttering relapse: The effects of a combined speech and psychological reconstruction programme. *British Journal of Disorders of Communication, 20*, 237–248.
Evesham, M., & Huddleston, A. (1983). Teaching stutterers the skill of fluent speech as a preliminary to the study of relapse. *British Journal of Disorders of Communication, 18*, 31–38.
Fransella, F. (1972). *Personal change and reconstruction.* New York: Academic.
Fransella, F. (1981). Nature babbling to herself: The self characterisation as a therapeutic tool. In H. Bonarius, R. Holland, & S. Rosenberg (Eds.), *Personal construct psychology: Recent advances in theory and practice* (pp. 219–230). London: Macmillan.
Fransella, F., & Bannister, D. (1977). *A manual for repertory grid technique.* London: Academic.
Hinkle, D. E. (1965). *The change of personal constructs from the viewpoint of a theory of implications.* Unpublished doctoral dissertation, Ohio State University.

Kelly, G. A. (1955). *The psychology of personal constructs.* New York: Norton.

Kelly, G. A. (1969). The strategy of psychological research. In B. Maher (Ed.), *Clinical psychology and personality* (pp. 114–132). New York: Wiley.

Kelly, G. A. (1970). Behaviour is an experiment. In D. Bannister (Ed.), *Perspectives in personal construct theory* (pp. 255–269). London: Academic.

Kelly, G. A. (1980). A psychology of optimal man. In A. W. Landfield & L. M. Leitner (Eds.), *Personal construct psychology: Psychotherapy and personality* (pp. 18–35). New York: Wiley.

Landfield, A. W. (1971). *Personal construct systems in psychotherapy.* Chicago: Rand McNally.

Glossary of Major Treatment Techniques

Acceptance: The therapist's willingness to use or subsume the client's personal construct system though not to be encapsulated by it.

Casual enactment: Informal role plays that can be used in therapy with the client and therapist enacting the parts. They are typically used to promote the articulation, preliminary testing, and revision or elaboration of the client's social construing.

Controlled elaboration: The attempt to make a portion of the client's construct system internally consistent and communicable so that it can be tested for its validity.

CPC cycle: A sequence of construction involving, in succession, circumspection (consideration of alternatives), preemption (selection of one among them), and choice (of a particular course of action implied by this alternative).

Creativity cycle: A process of construing that starts with loosened construction and terminates with tightened and validated construction.

Credulous approach: The general orientation to try to understand a client's situation from his or her own standpoint, rather than to immediately critique the logic or validity of the client's construction.

Fixed role therapy: The development of a specially constructed hypothetical identity that the client rehearses with the therapist and attempts to enact in daily life for a brief period of time. The goal is to promote the client's experimentation with new role constructs, not to prescribe particular changes in the client's system.

Interpersonal Transaction group: A special group therapy format in which clients engage in a regulated series of brief, dyadic encounters in addition to larger group discussions. It is used to promote the development of more accurate social construing in a minimally threatening context.

Laddering: A verbal procedure in which the therapist elicits the superordinate implications of a client's bipolar construction.

Loosening: The promotion of inexact, inconsistent, and often difficult to articulate construing in order to encompass experiences not subsumed by the client's tighter, more logical constructions. It typically represents a preliminary means of construing a new experience or a means of buffering the system from disconfirmation until the client is ready to subject his or her thinking to an empirical test.

Reassurance: Placing a simplified superordinate construction upon a problem so that it temporarily will appear to the client to be consistent, acceptable, and organized.

Role construct repertory grid (repgrid): A paper and pencil technique or structured interview procedure in which the therapist first elicits a client's important constructs and then asks the client to rank or rate a set of elements (usually significant others) on these dimensions. The results can be analyzed to produce several measures of construct system content and structure.

Self-characterization: A homework assignment in which the client is asked to write a "character sketch" of him/herself from the standpoint of an imaginary other who knows the client intimately and sympathetically. It thus serves as a fairly unstructured means of exploring the client's core role structure and is often used to set the stage for fixed role therapy.

Support: A broad response pattern on the part of the therapist that permits the client to experiment widely and successfully with his/her constructions. This ordinarily involves the therapist's behaving in accordance with the client's social hypotheses so as to provide validational evidence for them.

Tightening: The promotion of logical, articulate construing having clear predictive implications. It sets the stage for verbal or behavioral experimentation that leads to validation or invalidation of the client's prediction.

Transference cycle: The client's elaboration, examination, and testing of major role constructs against the behavior of the therapist. Generally, the therapist attempts to gradually invalidate global and preemptive *primary transference* constructions and encourage more discriminating and propositional *secondary transference* constructions.

Author Index

Italic entries reflect page numbers on which complete bibliographic references occur for authors' work.

312

Subject Index

ABC procedure, 113
Acceptance, 22, 255, 309
Aggression, 139, 192, 253
Anger, 52, 83, 91, 93, 96, 101, 135, 141–143, 193, 202, 203
Anorexia, 230–231, 234, 235, 238
Anticipation, 4, 5, 174, 176, 194, 199, 202, 203
Anxiety, 14, 22, 93, 98, 110, 115–116, 140, 147, 239
Assertiveness training, 96, 109–111
Assessment, 23–28 (*See also* Repertory grid)
Autopoiesis, 195

Behavior as experiment, 4, 30, 131, 148, 200
Behavior therapy, 60, 231, 306–307
Biographical Construct Repertory Test (BioRep), 6
Bipolarity, 10
Brief therapy, 80, 92, 215, 246, 248
Bulimia, 230–231, 234, 238

Career grid, 262, 267
Catharsis, 93
Choice, 8, 104
Choice corollary, 8, 83, 163
Circumspection-Preemption-Control Cycle (C-P-C Cycle), 66, 115, 144, 202, 238, 309
Cognitive therapy, 4, 10, 23, 95, 96, 231, 274
Collaborative empiricism, 22, 150

Commonality corollary, 15–16, 216, 235
Computer analysis of repertory grids, 26–28, 62–65, 119, 233
Conjoint marital therapy, 127 (*See also* Couples therapy)
Consensual validation, 15, 235
Constriction, 196, 206
Construct content, 25, 108
Construction corollary, 5–6
Constructive alternativism, 57
Constructivism, 4, 173, 184
Contact functioning, 78
Content analysis, 97–104 (*See also* Construct content)
Contrast, 10
Controlled elaboration, 31, 71–72, 113, 201, 293–294, 309
Core role, 14, 16, 39, 53, 58, 65, 87–88, 138, 139, 141, 195
Couples therapy, 11, 15–16, 127–150, 287 (*See also* Conjoint marital therapy)
Creativity Cycle, 72, 203, 309 (*See also* Loosening; Tightening)
Credulous approach, 22, 121, 309

Death anxiety, 25, 93, 98
Denial, 215
Depression, 40, 53, 90, 91, 99–100, 136, 211, 217, 219, 227, 237, 240
Dichotomy corollary, 10
Differentiation, 30, 79, 199
Dilemmas, 108–109, 255, 297–298

315